ENTERPRISE DATA WAREHOUSE

PLANNING, BUILDING, AND IMPLEMENTATION

VOLUME I

ISBN 0-13-905845-1

90000

9 780139 058455

Hewlett-Packard® Professional Books

Atchison	Object-Oriented Test & Measurement Software Development in C++
Blinn	Portable Shell Programming
Blommers	Architecting Enterprise Solutions with UNIX Networking
Blommers	Practical Planning for Network Growth
Caruso	Power Programming in HP OpenView
Chew	The Java/C++ Cross-Reference Handbook
Cook	Building Enterprise Information Architectures
Costa	Planning and Designing High Speed Networks
Crane	A Simplified Approach to Image Processing
Day	The Color Scanning Handbook
Derickson	Fiber Optic Test and Measurement
Eisenmann and Eisenmann	Machinery Malfunction Diagnosis and Correction
Fernandez	Configuring the Common Desktop Environment
Fristrup	USENET: Netnews for Everyone
Fristrup	The Essential Web Surfer Survival Guide
Gann	Desktop Scanners: Image Quality
Grady	Practical Software Metrics for Project Management and Process Improvement
Greenberg	A Methodology for Developing and Deploying Internet and Intranet Solutions
Grosvenor, Ichiro, O'Brien	Mainframe Downsizing to Upsize Your Business: IT-Preneuring
Gunn	A Guide to NetWare® for UNIX®
Helsel	Graphical Programming: A Tutorial for HP VEE
Helsel	Visual Programming with HP VEE, Third Edition
Holman, Lund	Instant JavaScript
Kane	PA-RISC 2.0 Architecture
Knouse	Practical DCE Programming
Lee	The ISDN Consultant
Lewis	The Art & Science of Smalltalk
Lichtenbelt, Crane, Naqvi	Introduction to Volume Rendering
Loomis	Object Databases in Practice
Lucke	Designing and Implementing Computer Workgroups
Lund	Integrating UNIX® and PC Network Operating Systems
Madell	Disk and File Management Tasks on HP-UX
Mahoney	High-Mix Low-Volume Manufacturing
Malan, Letsinger, Coleman	Object-Oriented Development at Work: Fusion in the Real World
McFarland	X Windows on the World
McMinds/Whitty	Writing Your Own OSF/Motif Widgets
Norton, DiPasquale	Thread Time: The Multithreaded Programming Guide
Orzessek, Sommer	ATM & MPEG-2: A Practical Guide to Computer Security
Phaal	LAN Traffic Management
Pipkin	Halting the Hacker: A Practical Guide to Computer Security
Poniatowski	HP-UX 11.x System Administration "How To" Book, Second Edition
Poniatowski	HP NetServer Guide for Windows NT®
Poniatowski	HP-UX System Administration Handbook and Toolkit
Poniatowski	HP-UX 10.x System Administration "How To" Book
Poniatowski	Learning the HP-UX Operating System
Poniatowski	Windows NT® and HP-UX System Administrator's "How To" Book
Ryan	Distributed Object Technology: Concepts and Applications
Simmons	Software Measurement: A Visualization Toolkit
Sperley	Enterprise Data Warehouse, Volume 1: Planning, Building, and Implementation
Thomas	Cable Television Proof-of-Performance
Thomas, Edgington	Digital Basics for Cable Television Systems
Thornburgh	Fibre Channel for Mass Storage
Weygant	Clusters for High Availability: A Primer of HP-UX Solutions
Witte	Electronic Test Instruments
Yawn, Stachnick, Sellars	The Legacy Continues: Using the HP 3000 with HP-UX and Windows NT

ENTERPRISE DATA WAREHOUSE

PLANNING, BUILDING, AND IMPLEMENTATION

VOLUME I

ERIC SPERLEY

TECHNICAL CONSULTANT
HEWLETT-PACKARD
HTTP://WWW.HP.COM/GO/RETAILBOOKS

Prentice Hall PTR
Upper Saddle River, New Jersey 07458
http://www.phptr.com

Library of Congress Cataloging-in-Publication Data

Sperley, Eric.
Enterprise data warehouse: planning, building, and implementation/Eric Sperley
p. cm. -- (Hewlett-Packard professional books)
Includes bibliographical references and index.
ISBN 0-13-905845-1 (v. 1)
1. Data warehousing. I. Title. II. Series
QA76.9D37S64 1999
658.4'038'0285574--dc21 98-44762
CIP

Acquisitions Editor: *Jill Pisoni*
Editorial/Production Supervision: *Kerry Reardon*
Cover Design Director: *Jerry Votta*
Manufacturing Manager: *Alexis R. Heydt*
Marketing Manager: *Lisa Konzelmann*
Editorial Assistant: *Linda Ramagnano*
Cover Design: *Design Source*
Manager, Hewlett-Packard Retail Publishing: *Patricia Pekary*
Editor, Hewlett-Packard Retail Publishing: *Susan Wright*
Comments? Write to HP Retail Publishing at bookreview@hp.com

Published by Prentice Hall PTR
Prentice-Hall, Inc.
Upper Saddle River, NJ 07458

Printed in the United States of America

10 9 8 7 6 5 4 3 2

ISBN 0-13-905845-1

Prentice-Hall International (UK) Limited, *London*
Prentice-Hall of Australia Pty. Limited, *Sydney*
Prentice-Hall Canada Inc., *Toronto*
Prentice-Hall Hispanoamericana, S.A., *Mexico*
Prentice-Hall of India Private Limited, *New Delhi*
Prentice-Hall of Japan, Inc., *Tokyo*
Prentice-Hall (Singapore) Pte. Ltd., *Singapore*
Editora Prentice-Hall do Brasil, Ltda., *Rio de Janeiro*

This book is dedicated to my daughter, Victoria. She and many other young ladies I know and love, such as Tiffany and Ali, do not spend enought time with Dad or other important male figures in their lives. This is due to the many vicissitudes of modern life, including employment, work-related travel, and divorce.

CONTENTS

Preface

The primary goal of MIS managers and CIOs is bringing their IT organizations into alignment with their businesses. However, most MIS managers and CIOs are technically trained and are not skilled in the art of organizational strategy. This is combined with the fact that legacy systems are not organized in a way that facilitates easy integration of data from different systems to provide new information. Thus it is difficult to align IT with the business by modifying operational systems to provide new information. The IT professional ends up in a situation where the need for change is known, but the person does not know how to select a strategy or implement changes with the current technology. This is analogous to being in the water with a shark—knowing the danger is there but not knowing where it is or how to escape it.

The two volumes of this work have been written to help the reader acquire the knowledge necessary to use data warehousing and open systems to align the IT department with the goals of the business. Although most other data warehousing texts have been high-level explanations of the advantages and goals of data warehousing, this book will lead you through the details of planning, designing, building, and using a data warehouse.

Data warehousing, decision support systems, and executive information systems have been discussed in conference and lunch rooms for many years. Yet many professionals still have no clear understanding of what a data warehouse is. For those who know data warehouse basics, success in building a data warehouse has been elusive. Practitioners of data warehousing who have been successful at a few projects have discovered that the warehouses they have built do not work together. In other cases, the techniques used to build small data warehouses do not work when adapted to building large ones. In the end, they have continued the problem present in legacy systems that do not scale and of data islands that are difficult to integrate.

It is the goal of the author to convey a methodology that will enable the IT professional to escape the shark. This book will provide a descriptive strategy to assist the IT professional in the planning, design, and construction of an enterprise-wide data warehouse. To understand how the IT community got in this situation, the development and history of business information technology are reviewed in Chapter 1. Once the current challenges and opportunities are understood, the oppositional characteristics of a data warehouse and operational systems can be examined and evaluated. An easily understood methodology for building a data warehouse based on sound business principles and RAD techniques is introduced and expanded in the following chapters.

In Chapter 2, several ways of characterizing the present position and marching direction of a business or IT organization are introduced. Although a single book on data warehousing will not transform the reader into an expert in business strategy, we can look at ways the business strategy can be stated and understood and a matching IT strategy selected. The most important techniques that we as IT professionals can learn are the use of business executive interviews and joint application development sessions to reveal the gap between where the business is and where the executives want it to be. Finally, we look at ways to justify the costs associated with building a data warehouse.

If you got on an airplane for a commercial flight and the pilot told you that he knew how to steer the plane but did not know how to navigate the plane or where he would land, you would probably get off the aircraft. Planning is critical to both aviation and data warehousing. In Chapter 3, we discuss some ways to architect the data warehouse so that we know how much it will cost to build what we have planned and what we are going to deliver for the cost. This will prevent us from being like Columbus, who set off not knowing where he was going, when he got there did not know where he was, and did it all on borrowed money. Chapter 3 is actually an overview of the rest of the information contained in both volumes.

Selecting the data warehousing project that will have the greatest organizational impact and success is the focus of Chapter 4. The JAD techniques discussed in Chapter 2 are used to discover the project with the largest benefit to the business and what the scope of this project should be. The primary goal of a data warehouse is to deliver information to the business knowledge workers. Since the data is organized in a meaningful way and presented in a business context, it will be the key to a successful warehouse. Chapter 5 focuses on principles and guidelines for data architecture and data modeling. By the end of this chapter, a novice data modeler should understand the basic components of enterprise and decision support data models, and an experienced data modeler will have a better understanding of how to expand known skills into new areas.

Understanding the data that is in a data warehouse is a cornerstone to the success of a data warehouse. A primary cause of failure of a data warehouse project is misunderstanding about the data in the data warehouse. Data about the data in a data warehouse is called metadata. Successful data warehouse projects are connected with successful metadata repositories. In Chapter 6 we present the value of and reasons and methods for the construction of a metadata repository.

The second primary reason for failure of data warehousing projects is lack of good-quality data in the warehouse. Chapter 7 focuses on a methodology for achieving high-quality data in the warehouse. Without understanding the value of high-quality data, it is difficult for management to invest the resources necessary to achieve such data. Thus the chapter starts with an example calculation of the cost of errors in data in the data warehouse. A method for achieving data quality is then described.

Understanding the principles of a field study enables the student of that field to apply the principles to solve new problems. In Chapter 8, we study the principles of data warehouse architecture. These are applied to construct a conceptual data architecture. The conceptual data architecture model is then applied to build a logical data warehouse.

Chapter 9 is dedicated to an understanding of physical data warehouse. The roles, trade-offs, and compromises of the different components of the physical data warehouse are analyzed.

Software that glues the warehouse tiers together and enables its construction is the subject of Chapter 10. Data extraction, transformation, and cleansing software tools are very important to the construction of a data warehouse. The important characteristics of these tools are examined in this chapter.

Once the data warehouse has been built, the data warehouse customer must be given the appropriate tools to access the data in the warehouse. Chapter 11 introduces the different types of access tools and gives the knowledge needed to enable the reader to confidently select the appropriate tools.

Finally, data mining is explained in Chapter 12. There are several different methods of data mining. All the major methods of data mining are explained in this chapter along with the advantages and disadvantages of each method.

As a general statement, this book is for the IT professional who is interested in building or understanding decision support systems. Specifically, CIOs, IT managers, data analysts, data base administrators, designers, and developers should find this book interesting and useful. CIOs and IT managers will find Chapters 1 through 4 particularly useful. Managers, data analysts, database administrators, designers, and developers should find Chapters 5 through 12 helpful for actual implementation of the warehouse, while Chapters 1 through 4 will aid them in understanding the path of their management.

Another potential audience for this book consists of management information systems, business, and computer science students. I have spent nearly five years teaching and found it exciting and easy to include in the book information that makes it a great textbook on data warehousing. Many chapters have a section of questions at the end for the use of both formal and informal students. Most chapters propose projects that the reader can pursue either as a thought exercise or as a physical project.

ACKNOWLEDGMENTS

Several people and organizations have provided information, ideas, debate, and criticism that have contributed to this book; in many ways, they are all co-authors of the book. First, I would like to thank Stanford University professor John G. Linvill for teaching me that clarity and depth of thought, organization, expression, and presentation are more important than any other cerebral endeavor. I have attempted to live up to his example with this book. Alan Camburn was responsible for connecting me to the HP data warehouse delivery team. Alan is a world-class data architect. The following list credits only a few of those who have contributed to this work directly or indirectly. I apologize to those who I have omitted. While the fine people listed below have made many contributions, I alone assume responsibility for errors and omissions of content. I have organized the contributors by organization, and they are listed in no particular order.

The HP Open Warehouse Advanced Technology Group: Pam Munsch, Bruce Jenks, Jim Meyerson, and Glen Kalina.

The HP World Wide Open Warehouse Group: Fran Ioppolo, Cecilia Bolomo, Cecilia Campbell, Roger Eberline, Hal McMillan, and Mike Overly.

The HP TIMBU Data Warehouse Team: Bob Meyer, Alan Camburn, Randall Etheridge, Maya Milster, and Sharon Swaney.

The Tandy Information Services Group: Dick Silvers, Bill Koenig, John Hilton, and Steve McWhorter.

The HP Retail Team: Ray Kelly, Jim Woods, Larry Kohutek, and Terrance Daily.

A special thanks goes to the guy who helped initially to format the book: Jeff Sperley.

Many thanks to Barbara Zeiders for the hundreds of suggestions that helped the readability of the book.

1

Brief History of Information Technology

1.1 INTRODUCTION

In this chapter we investigate the present state of the information systems organization,[1] how we got here, and start the introduction of a methodology that stresses strategic and tactical business thinking and analysis. Stated in the simplest of terms, one purpose of a data warehouse is to move the information access basis of a company from an unarchitected or evolutionary environment to an architected or planned environment. This new environment will provide critical information to answer business needs. This movement of information to an architected environment that meets the needs of the business is a first step in the transition of the enterprise's data to an open and flexible architecture. A data warehouse is one of many possible first steps in the process of developing an architected environment that can meet the information needs of a business.

So what is *architecture*? By definition, architecture is the study of the structure of something. The architecture under study usually has some distinguishing features. For example, Greek architecture has an arrangement of columns and top

[1] The words *organization* and *business* are used interchangeabley throughout. A large number of government, educational, and nonprofit organizations use *data warehouse technology.* An attempt has been made throughout to encompass all of the endeavors where *data warehouse technology* is used.

Figure 1-1 Easily recognizable example of classical Greek architecture.

caps that is very distinctive. Most people would identify the structure shown in Figure 1-1 as a Greek structure. In the case of data warehousing, the focus will be on how the information technology (IT)[2] department has structured the transaction processing and decision support systems (DSSs). The combination of decision support and transaction processing comprises what is known as *information management.* A person who studies and designs the structure of something and is involved in the design is called an *architect.* The principal aim of this book is to help the reader along the path to becoming an information management and data warehouse architect. A knowledgeable data warehouse architect will design a decision support system that will provide business information in an efficient manner.

The development of the evolutionary or unplanned environment was due primarily to the limitations in the technology within which the first systems were implemented. These early systems were designed to meet business process needs using reel-to-reel tape storage and flat file technology. While it is easy to look through the rose-colored glasses of hindsight and wonder why they were designed the way they were, it is true that most of these legacy systems were designed using the best practices and technologies available. These systems successfully advanced the capabilities of a business to make money. Eventually, it became apparent that they were so crucial to the everyday operation of a business

[2] The terms *information technology* (IT) and *information management* (IM) are also used interchangeably. IM is a newer and more appropriate term for what the department in charge of the computers in an organization really does.

that corporate executives would easily become concerned that any changes or reengineering of these systems could bring the enterprise to a painful stop. This is why many of these systems are still in use today and have not been redeveloped. These legacy systems are continuing to evolve through incremental changes to add features such as year 2000 compliance.

Initially, information technology projects were undertaken because they provided cost savings over totally manual systems. Later, information technology projects were undertaken because they provided strategic value to an organization in addition to reduced operating costs. This new way of thinking about information technology will result in the construction of a data warehouse that will be of strategic and tactical value to a company and not just another technology holy grail. We will see later in this chapter how the characteristics of a decision support system differ from the characteristics of an operational system.

1.2 HISTORY OF IT

The history of the world is a study of investment in things that produced more wealth. During the agricultural age, people and organizations used money to purchase land in addition to buying or hiring people to manage and work the land. The land produced crops and livestock that were sold or bartered to produce more wealth for the owners of the property. The wealth could be used to acquire more land. The ownership and control of this asset were critical to making money. Because land was the key to generating wealth, wealthy persons used their prosperity to invest in land to generate more wealth.

After the industrial revolution, money was invested in factories that produced things. These factories used manufacturing equipment and people to produce goods. The ability to produce things was more important than the money because some people and organizations had money but did not have the ability to manufacture machines that could make something from which they could create more income. As an example, the Spanish used gold they had "found" to buy ships from the United Kingdom. After the Spanish Armada was destroyed, the United Kingdom still had the factories to make money by producing goods, but the Spanish no longer had the equipment available to make money. The relative prosperity of the two nations changed dramatically at that time.

Currently, people and organizations are investing money in hardware, software, and people to create and obtain information. Information is now used to create or save money. As an example, people can use the World Wide Web to find the lowest-priced airline tickets for a trip. In the past, people would use a travel agent who had the information to find the price of a ticket. Travel agents might have incentives to sell other than the lowest-priced tickets. People are now using access to information to save money or find products that meet their needs more precisely. Corporations that do not provide the information that their customers demand risk losing customers. Corporations are using information to attract and retain customers in addition to providing better service. Because money is invested in information technology with the expectation that the investment will be rewarded with a capital return, it is absolutely crucial that IT projects deliver the anticipated return on investment (ROI). A data warehouse becomes a tool to increase profit by reducing costs, avoiding future costs, or increasing revenue by providing information to the business decision makers.

As can be seen in Figure 1-2, the history of information technology is short compared to that of other professions. Other disciplines, such as medicine, astronomy, engineering, and architecture, have had much more time to develop their art. Archeologists believe that brain surgery dates back to 2000 B.C., and the Hippocratic Oath for physicians is a statement of best practices that dates back to 400 B.C. On the other hand, the ENIAC computer was unveiled in 1946. This implies that we have not had much time to develop the best processes and procedures for developing information systems. What we learn is tied to the current technology, and it becomes obsolete as that technology becomes obsolete. As can be seen on the time line, computer technology changes very rapidly. This is why information technology is both exciting and frustrating. The new system that is being built is better than anything anyone has built to date, but it will be possible to build a better system tomorrow.

For much of the early history of information technology departments, the selection and goal of each new project seemed clear. Some manually intensive task would be replaced with an automated system, and the cost savings through labor reduction and increased speed would "obviously" justify the project. The data gathered in the manual process would be gathered in an automated process that would support the operational requirements of the business unit. Unfortunately, many of these projects would proceed with very little interaction between the IT

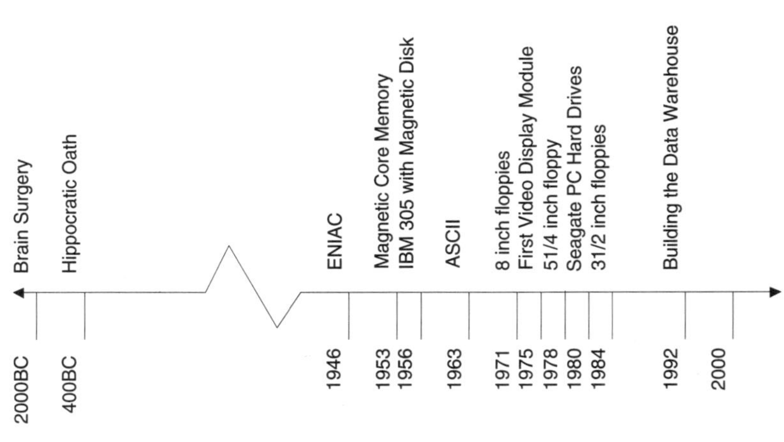

Figure 1-2 Historical time line.

team and the business users. The success or failure of the project depended on the level of business understanding possessed by the IT design team. In many cases, the IT team had experience with the area of the business that was being automated, and the end product delivered to the business was tremendously successful. In other cases, the IT team performed an extensive need analysis and the end product delivered to the business was also tremendously successful. In still other cases, the IT team had only a limited understanding of the business requirements; they expended a tremendous amount of energy, but the end product delivered to the business customers suffered accordingly. Rather than discuss the project with the business professionals who were going to use the systems, the IT professionals would frequently guess as to the processes the system would implement or interview a limited number of business experts. As noted earlier, the goal of the project seemed clear without the help of the business users, so the processes that must be implemented seemed clear also.

A process-driven approach was typically used in the 1960s. Because it was assumed that the processes used by a business were what needed to be automated, the starting point of analysis for the IT design team was the business processes. The data used to support the current business processes was identified and designed into the appropriate segments of the system. While the business processes were designed into the system, the many different ways that data could be used by an organization were not widely recognized at this stage of IT evolution. It also took some time for it to be recognized that while business process would change radically as a business evolved, the data the business needed to operate changed very little over time. As an example, banks have kept track of deposits, withdrawals, balances, and customers for many years. For marketing reasons, the types of banking accounts and the rules for banking accounts have changed, but the data needed to maintain the accounts has not changed. Until this change in thinking was made, the process-driven approach was king.

In the early 1950s, the only widely available mass storage device was magnetic tape. Magnetic tape had a number of limitations that shaped the nature and role of data processing. Because magnetic tape will store only a comparatively small amount of data, the data about a particular subject stored on a magnetic tape must be limited to the data absolutely necessary for a single data processing task. Two different processing tasks that used some similar and some different data elements would generally use two different magnetic tape "master files." Because the same information would be stored in two different locations on two different magnetic tape master files, the "same" piece of information could be different on different magnetic tape master files. As an example, an employee's home address on a human resources master file might be very different from the home address for the same employee in the payroll master file. In all likelihood, the different systems were developed without a plan or architecture for the development of all the information systems necessary for the success of the organization.

Frequently, new systems were developed without regard to the data types and functions already in use in other systems. This led to a situation where different operational systems used different data types, codes, and lengths to represent the same piece of information. Also, what was apparently the same data had different meanings in different systems. For instance, the seemingly simple and benign data field address could have a large number of meanings. There are shipping addresses, billing addresses, and mailing addresses that are all typically different. Clearly, the marketing system will have a mailing address whereas the order fulfillment system has a shipping address and the accounts payable system has a billing address.

Because the physical process of reading the information on a magnetic tape involves moving the tape over a tape head, the information on the magnetic tape must be read sequentially. Because magnetic tape is a sequential access storage device, it is impossible to combine or compare efficiently the information contained in record 5 of tape 2 with the information in record 700 of tape 121. This makes it difficult or time-consuming to compare records at different locations in a tape file or on different tape files. This inability to select data records randomly, combined with the driving need to automate business processes in each of the many different operational departments in a business, led to a situation where each operational department had its own tape master file.

If the master files from the different departments had been merged and the transaction processing of the organization was moved to the new merged master files, the length of tape the record used would increase, and the processing time for each record would also increase. This implies that different business units would pay more to process a given number of records in order to share information with other areas of the business. Batch processing was the norm at this time, and different batches were allotted a time window in which they must complete. The increased processing time that would come with increased record length could push the batch outside the allotted window. These factors, combined with the difficulty of reengineering the computer programs to match the merged tape format, discouraged most IT professionals from selecting this route.

1.2.1 Silos of Business Information

The development of information systems by business operational units led to the development of computer systems that were information *silos* or *wells.* The systems could provide detailed data in a particular area of the business, but the system could not integrate information from other areas of the business. Because there was no single, integrated source of data about the condition of a company, it was difficult, if not impossible, to get a total picture of the company by querying the silos, illustrated in Figure 1-3.

As an example, consider the files that a telecommunications company might maintain. Many telecommunication companies provide local, long-distance, cellular, pager, and data services. Typically, each of these services has an operational system that tracks customers, usage, accounts payable, accounts receivable, and

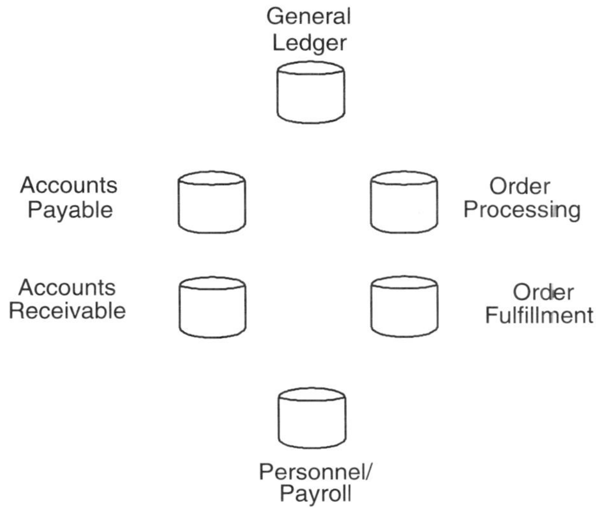

Figure 1-3 Separate but not necessarily distinct silos of data.

service provisioning. Each of the operational systems was constructed without regard to the data stored in the other operational systems. The operational systems cannot provide a single view of a customer and the services that customer purchases.

The construction of information systems and data silos around the operational units was not just a function of the IT department. Most businesses were organized as silos. As an example, consider the structure of a computer manufacturer during this time period. The typical computer company circa 1980 would have units that manufactured microprocessors, entire computers, monitors, and other hardware. The typical computer company would also develop operating systems and applications and would have its own sales and distribution operations. This is depicted in Figure 1-4.

Since the various silos of information contained data that would be very valuable if combined, it became common for IT departments to write extraction programs. These programs, written as requests for reports, came from the different operation units of the company. The extract program would read data from different master data sets, combine or summarize the data in a new way, store the data in an intermediate data store, and make it available as an input to a reporting program. A report program then used the data to generate the desired report.

As more and more requests for reports arrived at the IT department, the IT department was constantly writing new extract programs. There has always been a shortage of IT professionals as compared to the demand, so the backlog in extract and reporting programs grew. As the pace of business increased, the backlog grew as well. The business information consumers had constant requests for

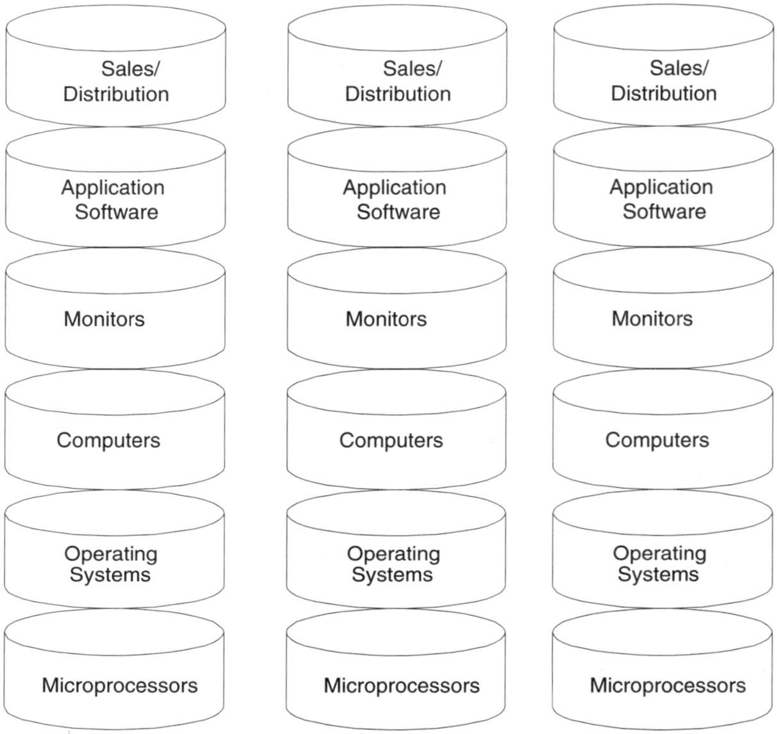

Figure 1-4 Monolithic corporate operating silos.

updates and new functionality in the reports. This caused the extract and report programs to be very unstructured in their flow and the programs became spaghetti code. An unplanned decision support environment is depicted in Figure 1-5. The large number of spaghetti code extract programs, intermediate data stores, and report programs that existed in an unplanned decision support environment became too much for the IT department to handle.

With the introduction of the magnetic disk in the IBM 305 computer in 1956, direct-access storage devices (DASD) became a reality. Records no longer had to be accessed in a sequential manner. Given enough storage space, records in different files on different hard disks could easily be processed at the same time. This technology allowed different records on the same or different file systems to be compared, combined, or used to update one another. The initial small storage capacity and high cost of this storage technology limited its use at first.

Around 1970, several researchers realized that data located in many different master files was identical or related. In some instances, the data was or should have been the same. In other instances, different types of information were stored in different master files. In other instances, information was in different master

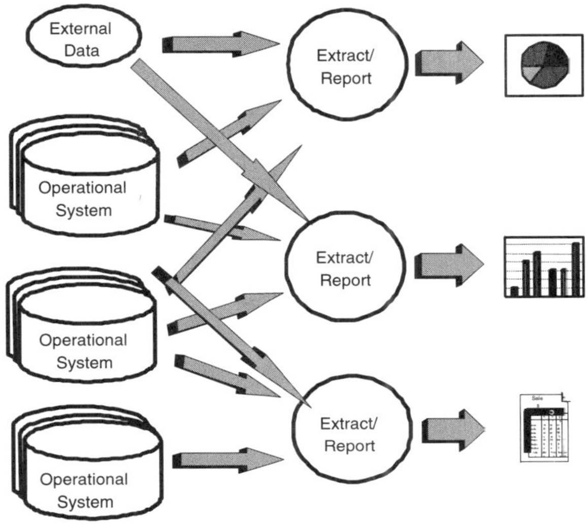

Figure 1-5 Unplanned decision support environment.

files. In other cases, different variations of the same type of data would be in different master records. In the worst cases, what should have been the same information had different values in different files because the files were maintained differently and separately.

Codd did the first rigorous study into the concept that different data elements could be related. This very mathematical treatment of relational database technology preceded actual relational database products by several years. In fact, the original relational database theory by Codd included some strict mathematical ideas, such as that of domains, that still are not implemented in mainstream database software products. To this day, the number of large operational systems using flat files or flat file–like technology is still very large. Simply put, theory has had a large lead on actual practice for a long time. Theory and actual practice both move forward, but theory does not have to contend with the real-world realities of budget constraints and keeping a business operational. Thus, actual practice is not catching up to the theory.

One way that relational database technology promised to improve the lives of IT professionals was by reducing the amount of redundant data. Common data could be placed in a common table or entity, and specialized or repetitive data could be placed in related entities. Many different operational systems could use the same data for different operational needs. The data that is common to different operational systems can be maintained in a single entity and all the operational systems will access this one entity for the necessary information. Relational database technology combined with direct-access storage devices promised to revolutionize the way that IT solutions were architected. While the theory was great, in practice it was difficult to obtain. The systems that ran the business were designed around flat file technology. The task of moving all an organization's operational systems from legacy flat files to relational databases was too large and risky for most companies.

The early 1970s brought the advent of EISs, executive information systems. These systems were typically comprised of dumb terminals connected to mainframe computers. They enabled corporate knowledge workers to view data that had been extracted from the operational systems. The EISs provided ways to organize the data into information, but they clearly did not have the ability to reach out to the operational systems and extract new data for totally new reports. If an executive wanted a new view of the data, he or she would have to wait. According to one survey of IBM mainframe and compatible installations, the average backlog in the IT department was 13.4 months [Hosier].

Around 1975, the first desktop PCs and desktop tools became available. While these early systems were limited in the amount of data they could store and manipulate, they gave early "power users" a taste of the ability to analyze data without the help of the IT department designing the reports. Many business information workers discovered that they could either get access to the data that the IT department had extracted from the operational systems, or they could enter data into a PC database from reports or "green screens." The information workers could also enter data from external sources such as the *Wall Street Journal* or *Business Week.* The data could then be entered into the database with the corporate data for the purpose of adding in the decision-making process.

The business consumers of corporate data were now repeating the path of the IT department and developing their own unplanned decision support environment. People in different departments were creating their own databases with their own structures. The definitions of the data and the way the fields were calculated differed from user to user. These new databases contained data from external sources, and different users selected different external sources. Because some automatic processes did not update users' data that resided on their PCs, the users' data rapidly became out of date. If the users were careful about populating current data, they would spend a large amount of time maintaining their own databases. If the users did not update their local data, incorrect conclusions could be drawn from the wrong data.

The first challenge to business users attempting to work with a nonarchitect legacy environment was understanding the relationships between the data silos. As depicted in Figure 1-6, the data silos did not have a unique way of identifying the records that were common across the silos. These disparate definitions of what appears to be the same data in the different data silos led to huge confusion for both the business user and the IT community. Business professionals thought ill of IT professionals because two different reports that should produce the same numbers for the same quantities would show different numbers. This led to a situation where different decision makers in an organization could arrive at a meeting and report very different numbers for what should have been the same quantity.

While the first conclusion one could arrive at was that either the IT department was incompetent or your business colleague was being less than forthright,

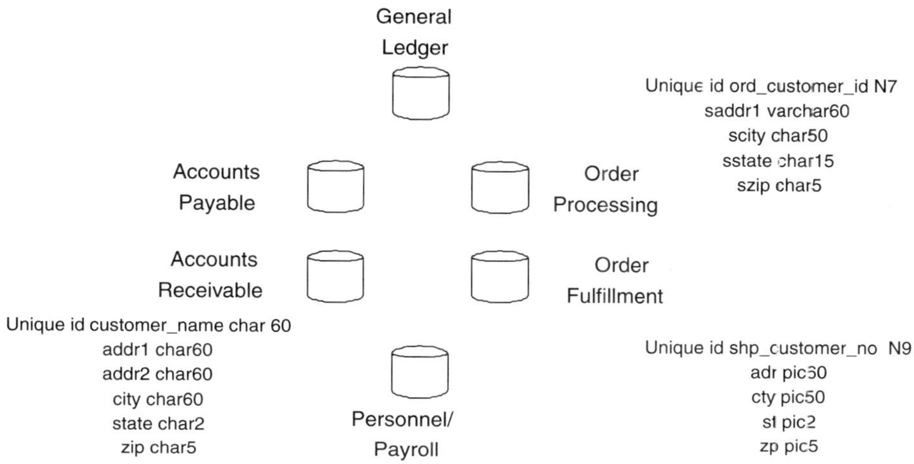

Figure 1-6 Dissimilar fields lead to confusion in the unarchitected environment.

usually neither was the case. The numbers on the reports were computed using different data from different source systems. Often, the data in the different source systems was defined differently. In other cases, two identical reports produced at different times that report on business performance for the same period might disagree. Frequently, this was caused by an update in the data during the period between the generation of the two reports. Another cause for different reports was different sources of external data. One person might have used interest figures from the *Wall Street Journal* while another person used interest figures from Rutgers. Thus, there were many reasons that two different managers could have two different reports with numbers that disagreed. The outcome of this situation was that the organization spent a tremendous amount of time arguing about the data and little time acting on the data.

The basic cause of the confusion was the unplanned or unarchitected nature of the decision support environment. If the organization had thought ahead and planned the reports in advance, a single extract or set of common extracts would obtain all the data needed for all the reports. The data could be stored in a central location. Since most reports were developed independently, it is impossible to plan the central data location.

The astute reader might think the relational database would cure the problem of data discrepancies or data chaos. While relational database technology greatly helped the development of new operational systems, this technology did not solve the issue of data silos and unplanned development of systems. The operational systems were still developed without regard to each other. Systems developed without an overarching design do not have common unique identifiers or coding schemes, and relational database technology does not solve this problem.

In summary, the IT situation was growing steadily worse. The rate at which it became more and more difficult to maintain the spaghetti extraction and reporting programs was slow enough not to alarm anyone. A story is frequently told in high school biology classes about frogs. If a frog is placed in a pan of hot water, the frog will jump to safety, but if the frog is placed in a pan of cold water that is heated slowly, it is possible to boil the poor frog in place. In a similar fashion, the situation in the IT community has been heating up slowly, and the community has suddenly discovered that it is too hot for comfort.

1.3 What A Data Warehouse Is

Many people have contributed to the development of the idea of a data warehouse. Although, early authors and thinkers wrote many seminal works, a 1988 article by Devlin and Murphy was arguably the first data warehouse article. In 1993, William H. Inmon wrote the monumental book *Building the Data Warehouse* [Inmon], in which he defines the a data warehouse as "a subject oriented, integrated, time-variant, non-volatile collection of data in support of management's decision making process."

Subject oriented implies that the data warehouse is designed to provide data that is associated with a single organizational process. As an example that most people can relate to, consider the data that a college or university might store in different legacy systems. A college probably has accounts payable, accounts receivable, payroll, financial aid, and registration systems. The registration system typically keeps a fairly limited amount of historical data and has fairly limited data on the students who are enrolled in classes and teachers who are teaching the classes. The class enrollment subject area would have historical data about student enrollment in classes and the teachers who taught the classes. Whereas the registration operational system will have the final grade the student earned, the class enrollment subject area is probably not concerned with this detail.

As another example of the subject-oriented nature of the data warehouse, we return to the example of a telecommunications company and consider the data that a telecommunications company might keep. As was mentioned before, many telecommunications companies provide local, long-distance, cellular, pager, and data services. Each of these services is operated by a business unit that has its own operational system that tracks customers, accounts payable, accounts receivable, and service provisioning. There is no single database that contains all the information about customers. The construction of a customer subject area would provide a single view into the customer and services purchased. This customer data warehouse would enable the telecommunications company to market new products to current customers based on the customer's demographics and previous buying trends.

The reader has probably deduced from the difficulties of unplanned decision support systems that the fact that a data warehouse is integrated is probably its most important feature. As the various operational systems were developed over the years, different data types, sizes, and coding methods were used. For example, some systems would code month, date, and year as MMDDYY while other systems would use DDMMYYYY. As another example, a gender field in one system may be coded as m and f, whereas the gender field in a second system might be coded as 1 and 0.

When data is moved from the operational systems to the data warehouse, the data is transformed before it is loaded into the warehouse. The inconsistencies in codes, data types, and other "features" of the source systems are removed. This is also an excellent time to review the source system data and reconcile any discrepancies between documented data types and codes and the codes that actually exist. Generally speaking, the construction of a data warehouse will uncover opportunities to remove unwanted "features" from the operational systems.

Another very important feature of a data warehouse that distinguishes it from an operational system is that a data warehouse is nonvolatile. While an operational system performs updates, deletes, and inserts on the stored data, a data warehouse loads large amounts of data and never changes the values contained in the data once it has been loaded. With few exceptions, once the data has been loaded into the data warehouse, it is not altered. Two different business users running the same query at two different times will get the same result. This eliminates situations where unplanned extracts and reports produce different results.

The final distinguishing characteristic of a data warehouse is that it is time variant. While operational systems contain only current data, data warehouse systems contain both historical data and data that was current as of the last warehouse data load. The historical time frame that a data warehouse stores varies greatly depending on the types of systems, but time frames of 15 months to five years are common. The oldest data in the data warehouse is usually archived to magnetic tape or CD-ROM when it is no longer desirable to have it in the data warehouse.

Operational data systems and data warehouse informational systems have a number of oppositional characteristics that are best contrasted side by side. Table 1-1 contains a distillation of important features of each system type.

Data warehouses have been built in subject areas too numerous to mention. The size and usage of these data warehouses vary widely depending upon the type of business and business information they are designed to provide. Some of the most common applications of a data warehouse are:

- Risk analysis
- Financial analysis
- Fraud analysis
- Relationship marketing
- Asset management
- Call behavior analysis

Hewlett-Packard has a program called the Hewlett-Packard OpenWarehouse program to bring the best class hardware, software, and services to the customer.

Table 1-1 Comparison of data warehouse and operational systems.

Data Warehouse Systems	Operational Systems
Used by management	Used by front-line workers
Strategic value	Tactical value
Supports strategic direction	Supports day-to-day operations
Used for transaction processing	Used for on-line analysis
Application oriented	Subject oriented
Stores current data only	Stores historical data
Predictable query pattern	Unpredictable query pattern

Its purpose is to provide one-stop shopping of everything needed to build a data warehouse. Once the decision is made to use the OpenWarehouse program, the relationships are already in place to deliver all the hardware, software, and services necessary to build a successful data warehouse. Conceptually, the data warehouse can be thought of in terms of data flow and storage, as shown in Figure 1-7.

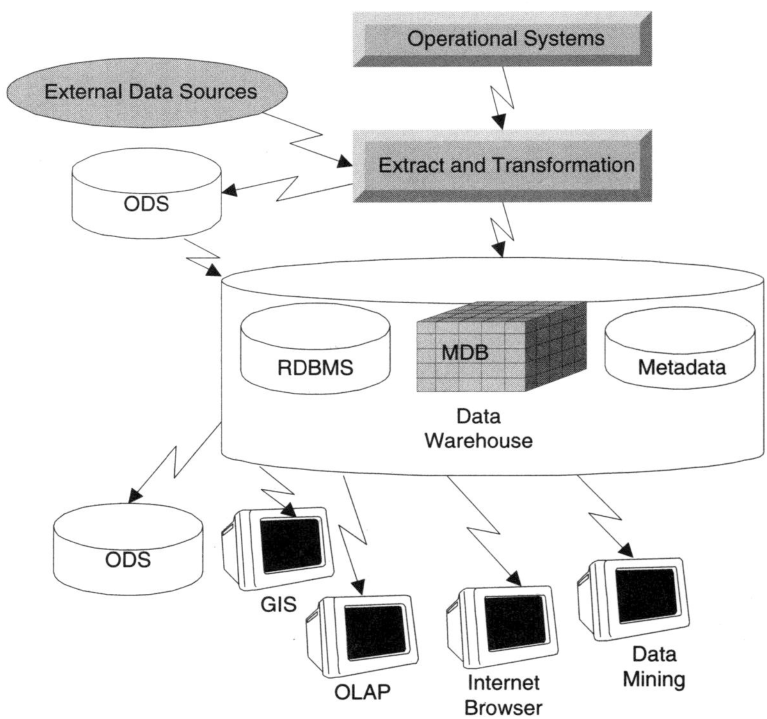

Figure 1-7 OpenWarehouse solution framework.

Another structure, the *data mart,* closely resembles a data warehouse. In much the way that a "food mart" has less selection and availability than those of a supermarket, a data mart is a miniature data warehouse. A data mart typically has a smaller number of data, fewer subject areas, and less history. A data mart can be thought of as a logically or physically partitioned subset of a data warehouse. A data mart is usually constructed to serve the needs of a particular user community. Like a data warehouse, a data mart contains both operational detail data and summarization data.

A second structure that also resembles a data warehouse in some respects is the operational data store. While like a data warehouse, an operational data store or ODS, is organized around subjects, and an ODS contains only current or nearly current data. Because an ODS is typically used by clerical and operational personnel to respond to the daily needs of a business and customers, it does not need to have the historical data that a data warehouse must store for use by strategic decision makers. The data design for an ODS is frequently more normalized than the data design for a data warehouse.

1.4 ANSWERING BUSINESS QUESTIONS

Many IT professionals have approached the construction of a data warehouse like the baseball field in the movie "Field of Dreams": "If we build it, they will come." These projects almost always fail because they do not provide the information needed to solve the burning business problems. In order to answer the business questions, the necessary data must be stored in the data warehouse and organized in a way that is easy to understand by the business user. A data warehouse is not simply a very large database. In addition to being able to provide the information necessary to answer business questions, it must be provided in a manner that is comfortable and intuitive to the user.

In order to supply the needed information to the organization, the organization must know where it is going and what the strategic direction is. The situation where the organization's leaders are unclear as to the future direction of the organization due to rapid change is very common. In this situation, the process of building a data warehouse will actually focus the leaders on critical business issues. In situations where the business planning has already been done, the organizational vision, goals, critical success factors, and hoshins[3] should be available to the team as a starting point for research and discussion. The business plan and strategic vision will provide a road map for the data warehousing team.

Back in 1977, Tony Crawford and Chuck Norris of IBM noticed the difficulty of getting business clients to agree with IT on requirements and design specifications.

---

[3] *Hoshin* is a Japanese word that means breakthrough thinking and objectives.

They thought of an innovative way to accomplish this goal. IBM had a methodology called Business Systems Planning, and they thought of a new approach that was loosely based on that methodology. Their idea was to get all of the interested parties in a meeting at the same time and gain consensus. The first *joint application development* (JAD) sessions were at IBM's offices in Raleigh, North Carolina. When these meetings started to produce orders, IBM decided they had a methodology worth developing—joint application development sessions were born.

The emergence of JAD happened at a time when the organization of corporate America was shifting away from a command and control hierarchy toward functional teams. The other new techniques in system development that appeared at this time were also based on functionally organized teams. For example, *rapid application development* (RAD) is a team-centered method for the development of information systems. These new teams lost the tunnel vision of the hierarchical organization because they were now centered on completing a task and comprised a cross-hierarchy team of diverse individuals. This diversity came from the change in the organization from very structured groups of people organized in a stable architecture working for one type of customer to a diverse mix of professionals from different parts of the business. In the brave new world, companies are buying and merging with other companies all over the world. Many companies are downsizing, rightsizing, and outsourcing. These rapid changes in company organization, strategy, and hierarchy demand teams that are functionally organized and accomplish their goals rapidly. Thus, IT and the business community must work together to be successful, and a natural way to do this is with JAD sessions.

Another factor that has driven the IT community toward the use of joint application development sessions is more sophisticated users. As personal computers have become more prevalent, business consumers have become more proficient with technology. IT professionals are no longer considered to be the gurus that sit high atop the IT mountain. Recent trends in IT budgeting show that most of the money spent on IT will be shifted out of the hands of the IT department and into the hands of the organization. Users have a much stronger sense of ownership of the systems and data because they are funding the projects. The user community is tired of spending more than they budgeted to get a product delivered late that does not do what they want.

What does all this mean? Building a data warehouse is much more than creating a very large database. Building a data warehouse is a process. We as IT professionals must make sure that we are delivering what the customer wants and needs for the cost they agreed to. The JAD process will make sure that we team with the rest of the organization to deliver value by providing the information the business needs. Development methodologies such as RAD help us deliver on time and on budget, but we cannot start a development project until we have a sponsor with funding to solve a business need for information. This business sponsor is a critical input to the whole JAD process. Discovering a strategic business need for information to answer the business questions is done through the JAD process.

1.5 THE ENTERPRISE DATA MODEL

The natural response to unplanned development of both decision support and transaction processing systems is to add planning and analysis to the software life cycle. Software projects failed because of misunderstandings of planning, scope and size, system requirements, or data. Different practitioners developed different methodologies and tools to deal with these different causes of failure.

Some of the early techniques included hierarchical input, processing, and output (HIPO) diagrams or data flow diagrams (DFDs). The purpose of these diagrams was to show how the data flowed in the various processing steps and in the overall computer system. The idea behind these charts was to provide thorough documentation of the data in the system so that necessary data elements would not be left out of the design. The problem with these early techniques is that they did not address the issue of interaction of the pieces of the data model with each other. These techniques also did not help the IT team with the business community.

Entity-relationship (ER) *modeling*, along with normalization, was developed to reduce the amount of redundant data that existed in the organization. In a few words, an entity-relationship model was designed to model the data about the subjects in which the organization was interested, the attributes the subjects had, and the relationships between the subjects. The subjects became the entities in the model, the attributes became the field, and the relationships were relationships between the entities. Entity-relationship modeling is also very much a way to think.

Because the number of times an attribute or field in a data model appeared was precisely once, there was no chance of different values in different fields of what should be the same data. A computer system based on the ER model and a relational database would simply update a single field to update the data for that instance of the subject. As an example, the mailing address for a customer would be stored in a location, and that single location would be the only place the mailing address for the customer would need to be changed. This eliminates the problem of wasting system processing unit (SPU) or central processing unit (CPU) cycles on redundant tasks. The end result is faster processing of updates.

With all of the difficulties with data silos, unplanned operational environments, and unplanned decision support environments, *enterprise data modeling* became popular until this too failed. The general idea behind enterprise data modeling was to start by capturing all of the data in use in computer systems. The data about the data would be placed in a metadata repository. Once all of the data fields were documented, the process of identifying relationships between data in different master records and fields that contained the same information could move forward. The future data needs of the organization could also be planned for and included in the enterprise data model.

Constructing an enterprise data model for a large organization is a monumental task, and most of these efforts failed. The problem was the size of the project, lack of planning, and the moving nature of the target. Very large projects have the difficulty of delivering tangible results before the project sponsor comes to believe the project will fail. A desired feature of a good plan is to have several intermediate deliverables that bring value to the organization. Another desired feature of a good plan and a well-managed project is to have the deliverable ready before the data model has changed too much. Thus, successful enterprise data modeling projects usually end up delivering models for portions of the enterprise early. For large organizations, the models are never enterprise models with any great detail.

Of course, with all we know about IT methodologies, modeling, and tools, organizations are no longer building new systems that are organized around data silos. Wrong! Small organizations, particularly fast-growing ones, are building new systems in a hurry and without planning for the big picture. This is also particularly true of young companies that have not yet developed the corporate culture and discipline of coordination and teamwork between the different operational units.

To be successful at a data warehouse project, it is frequently important to develop a high-level enterprise data model. This high-level model will also help a rapidly growing smaller company. The goal of the model will be to ensure that data warehouse developers do not repeat the history of the IT department by creating a new set of data silos. To avoid the creation of data warehouse silos, the enterprise must be modeled at enough depth to discover the linkages in the transaction systems and the decision support systems.

An example of a very high level conceptual enterprise data model is shown in Figure 1-8. This model was developed by meeting with the executives of the business together with representatives of the IT department. This team worked out what was important for the executives to follow and how they wanted to relate the various areas of the business when doing business analysis. With this

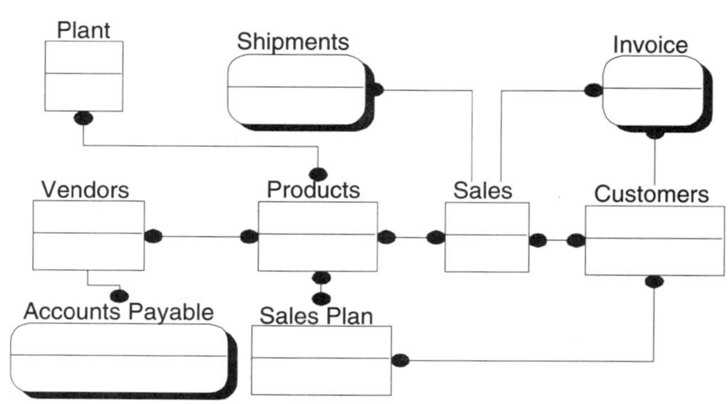

Figure 1-8 Conceptual enterprise data model.

diagram and a little explanation, everyone from the CFO and CIO to the product line managers could understand how the data would relate to the organization.

The techniques used to model transactional system data are different from the techniques used to model decision support system data. While the goal of the normalized entity-relationship model and relational database is to increase update efficiency, the goal of the decision support data model is to increase query efficiency. Query efficiency can be the goal of focus for decision support systems because the data in the systems is loaded in mass rather than being updated. Since the decision support system is designed for fast updates, an organization of the data that is different from that employed by the transactional systems is generally used. Queries asked of decision support systems are usually organized around a set of facts and dimensions that are meaningful to a business. The facts are usually numeric quantities such as sales, and the dimensions typically used are discrete in nature and are things such as salesperson, product, time, or geographic region. This data model that is unique to decision support systems is called a *star schema* or *dimensional data model.*

A best practice to use is to do a high-level analysis of the use of data in both the transactional and decision support systems. A document that maps the data from the operational systems to the decision support systems should be the output of this exercise. If this is done during the early planning phase, it will help ensure that the decision support system is designed based on a database design that can obtain and load data from the operational system.

In order to obtain and load data from the operational systems, the fields must exist and be populated in the operational system. The field types and lengths should also be the same, and it reduces data load processing cycles, complexity, and other headaches if the operational and decision support systems can use the same coding schemes. In short, coordination of fields between the operational and decision support systems will increase stability and supportability of the enterprise's information assets.

1.6 METHODOLOGY OUTLINE: SCOPE, PILOT, PRODUCTION

Although human beings do not usually design large, complex systems correctly the first time, human beings seem to be very good at learning as they go. People are great at doing better the second, third, and fourth times around. People also often misunderstand each other. The author has been told that to make sure that you have understood another person, you should rephrase what was just said and repeat the information back. A good methodology will provide opportunities to iterate to improve the quality of the deliverable, and it will provide review sessions to make sure that what the designers heard the customers say they wanted is what the customers really wanted.

Customers of the data warehouse will frequently think they want to see data organized in a certain way, but upon seeing what they asked for, they will want something different or something additional. This is another human trait that should be accounted for in a good methodology. Iteration should be considered a good thing in human endeavors rather than a sign of failure. Just because the deliverables of a project are not perfect the first time they are viewed by a customer does not mean that the project is a failure. The methodology should encourage continual improvement of the product.

The methodology used by HP OpenWarehouse consultants to build data warehouses is an iterative rapid application development methodology. The three iterative phases along the main track to building a data warehouse are the project, scope, and subject selection phase; the pilot or proof-of-concept phase; and the production phase. At each step of these three phases, we take a "plan, do, check, and act" approach. First we create a plan for that phase. Next, the team executes the development of the deliverables against the plan. At several times during execution of the plan, progress and deliverables are compared against the plan. The team then acts to correct any deficiencies in the plan or execution based on what is discovered. An introduction to this methodology follows.

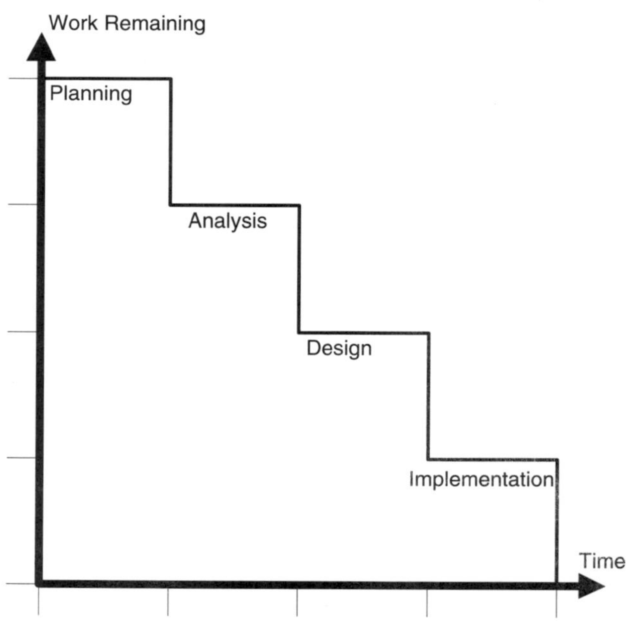

Figure 1-9 Waterfall methodology.

Another approach to building a data warehouse that will fail is to start with tool selection before defining business needs. This is an example of a bottom-up approach to building a data warehouse. These projects fail for two reasons: because tool selection is a technology issue, not a business issue and because there is not enough interaction between the business and the development team. In this approach, there is generally no interaction between the IT team and future users of the technology.

As we mentioned in Section 1.4, many data warehouse projects take a "Field of Dreams" approach and fail. From the author's experience, these projects typically use either the standard "waterfall" methodology or a bottom-up approach to the development of the data warehouse. These approaches fail because there is not enough interaction between the business and the development team. In the waterfall methodology approach depicted in Figure 1-9, tasks are grouped into phases based on the workflow needed to create the system. The typical phases are planning, analysis, design, and implementation. Typically, each phase is performed once and only once during a project that is guided by the waterfall methodology. The project team skill set needed is defined by phase, and it usually changes significantly from phase to phase. Requirements are determined and set in stone early in the project life cycle. Rework of any portion of the project's deliverables after a phase has been completed is considered an indicator of poor-quality deliverables from earlier phases. Rework generally involves changing or removing and throwing away something that was already completed. The cost of fixing something late in the project is high because it is inefficient. It has been pointed out [Wetherbe] that the cost of rework is 50 to 100 times higher than the cost of making the same changes during design.

1.6.1 Spiral Process

An alternative approach to the waterfall type development is a spiral development process. Whereas the team composition changes during the different stages of waterfall development, the spiral approach is a team-centered approach. This approach groups tasks into phases based on a series of products that are given more functionally over time. The phases of the deliverables are usually broken down to smaller but usable units and increasing the functionality of the deliverables over several iterations of the deliverables that occur over time. The point of all this is to deliver something that adds value to the organization and is available for review and feedback as quickly as practicable.

One major difference between the waterfall process and the spiral process is that the cost of rework in the spiral model is low because the rework usually adds functionality to a previous deliverable. Because the phases in the spiral model are defined in terms of increasing functionality of the deliverables and not the process used to create the deliverables, the requirements are not known in advance. The deliverables are incrementally produced and delivered or shown to the customer.

This provides a feedback process that clarifies the customer's needs as the deliverables are created. The spiral model is depicted graphically in Figure 1-10.

1.6.2 Rapid Application Development

The rapid application development (RAD) process is a team-centric process that uses other team-centric processes, such as JAD and the spiral development process. RAD uses other development notions such as time boxing and iteration, to avoid the pitfalls that affect so many development efforts. The most frequently cited success factors for software projects are [Carey]:

- Timely delivery
- Achievement of project objectives
- Building positive communications and relationships with customers

Time boxing guides the way that project money is spent by limiting the scope and linking the customer's needs to the requirements. Fixing a time limit for the iteration does this. Time boxing focuses the team on the priorities of the project. Time boxing also prevents "scope creep" and encourages prioritization of functionality by setting a date by which the deliverable must be complete.

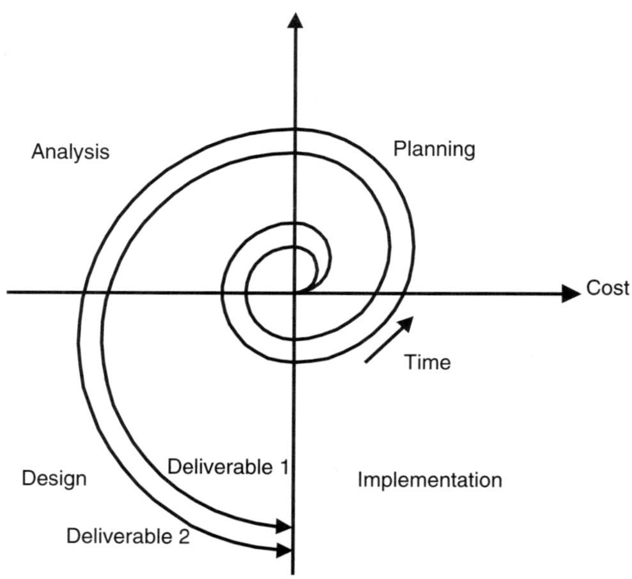

Figure 1-10 Spiral model.

Requirements of a lower priority can be included in the following iteration. *Iteration* implies that the deliverables are enhanced over several phases. Human beings are not very good at completing large, complex tasks the first time. Humans are great at learning as they go, so iteration is a natural process. Time boxing and iteration are used with RAD because they ensure timely delivery, achievement of the project objectives, and positive communications and relationships between IT and the customer.

As noted in Section 1.4, the data warehouse should provide strategic value to a business. The first step in creating a single subject or enterprise data warehouse is to perform executive interviews and at least one JAD session to determine the vision of the executives for the organization and the role of the data warehouse in the organization. This invaluable information will be used by the data warehouse team to prioritize the creation of the different subject areas of the data warehouse. The executive vision will guide the order in which the subject areas are added to the data warehouse and the type of information the data warehouse will provide.

After the vision for the data warehouse has been determined, the state of the corporate data must be determined. A conceptual enterprise data model can by constructed at this point. It is also useful to perform a high-level data quality study during this stage. It is generally the case that the availability, linkages, and quality of data from the operational systems are not understood until the conceptual data model has been constructed and a data quality study has been performed.

To build an enterprise data warehouse, the spiral portion of the RAD process is applied in parallel to as many subject areas as there are resources to perform the work. The different subject areas are developed in a parallel, iterative fashion.

1.7 DATA WAREHOUSE ARCHITECTURE

The architecture of a data warehouse can be broken into three distinct phases or levels of abstraction: the conceptual architecture, the logical architecture, and the physical architecture. The best approach to take is a top-down approach where each architectural layer of the data warehouse is designed starting with the conceptual architecture. If the data warehouse designer thinks about each of these layers in turn, it will help assure that the resulting architecture is the best one possible for the organization.

The *conceptual architecture* specifies the functions and the relationships between the functions that must be performed. The conceptual architecture does not specify how the functions will be accomplished or where the functions will be accomplished. The conceptual architecture conveys the ideas of what the architecture will accomplish. A conceptual architecture shows what inputs are needed,

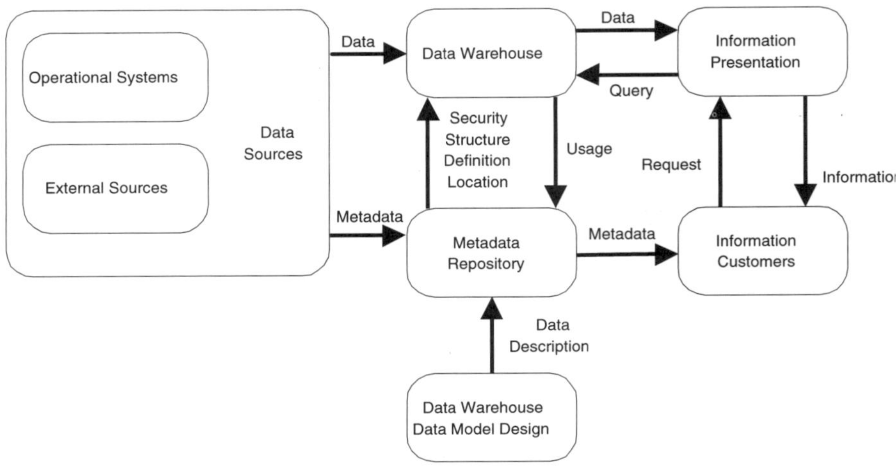

Figure 1-11 Data warehouse conceptual diagram.

what outputs are generated, and a conceptual picture of the functions that happen in the middle. A conceptual warehouse model is shown in Figure 1-11.

The data warehouse conceptual architecture is a kind of caricature of the data warehouse. It shows the major feature without showing the details. Figure 1-11 shows that data is extracted from operational systems and external sources into the data warehouse. The operational and external sources also provide data about the data or metadata to the metadata repository. Metadata from the generation of the data warehouse data model is sent to the metadata repository in addition to usage data from the data warehouse. The business information user or information customer makes a request for data to the information presentation tool. The information presentation tool generates a query that is sent to the data warehouse. If the information customer has the appropriate access as defined in the metadata, the data warehouse will return data to the information presentation tool, and information is relayed to the information customer. The information customer can also browse the data as stored in the metadata repository. Thus, the conceptual architecture explains at a high level the functions and flows of the data warehouse.

Some consultants disagree with this conceptual view of a data warehouse. They would prefer to build *virtual data warehouses.* While it is important to clarify the definition with which you are speaking, the term *virtual data warehouse* usually means a decision support system that sends queries to the actual operation systems. This approach provides a number of problems. Most important, the operational units probably do not want to allow the "mother of all queries" to swamp the operational system and stop the day-to-day operations. Most modern operating systems provide some ability to allocate resources or to virtually partition a computer, so this problem can be worked around. The next difficulty is found in the fact that most legacy systems have different primary key, coding, and data field length standards. This makes it very difficult or impossible to perform joins on data that has very different and inconsistent primary keys.

The entire virtual data warehouse debate points out the purpose of a conceptual data warehouse architecture: to develop a visionary architecture for the organization or enterprise. We noted in our discussion of the history of IT that applications were developed from business requirements. In fact, the entire application architecture, down to the hardware selection, was driven by the business requirements. As we saw before, the results were a numerous redundant, technology-centered implementation of applications. The conceptual architecture is the starting point of a data warehouse architectural framework. The other pieces of the architectural framework are the physical architecture and the actual implementation. The conceptual and physical architectures are principles-based architectures. If the implementation of the architecture is guided by principles, we refer to the architecture as a principles-based architecture. The vision stated by the business executives should be amplified and drive the statement of the principles for the architecture. The principles guide and constrain the use of technology in the data warehouse the way the Bill of Rights guides and constrains the creation of laws in the United States.

The *physical architecture* of the data warehouse starts with the conceptual architecture and arranges the physical components based on organizational principles and standards. Thus, the physical architecture is also a principles-based architecture. The list of principles that guide the physical architecture is usually considerably longer than the list of principles for the conceptual architecture. The physical architecture must account not only for the high-level goals of the organization, but for organizational, sponsorship, and technological boundaries as well. A short list of considerations that guide the development of the principles and hence the physical architecture are:

- Number of subject areas
- Organizational size
- Development directions
- Hardware standards
- Software standards
- Availability requirements
- Business continuity requirements
- Network capacity

Once the physical architecture has been determined, the implementation phase becomes a matter of planning, budgeting, conversion, configuration management, and change management. Books have been written about each of these topics, so we will not delve at any depth into any of these topics. Basically, the organizational goals and priorities will determine the prioritization and funding for each implementation project. Conversion between hardware platforms, database management systems, or programming languages is usually a difficult task that can be aided with tools. Configuration and change management is concerned with both systems and people aspects of keeping the entire operation moving forward while the changes occur.

In summary, the architecture components are designed to ensure that the organizational vision and strategy are brought to realization when the data warehouse is implemented. This is done by identifying principles that are used to guide and constrain the development of the data warehouse. Using these principles will help ensure that the resulting system has broad, visionary, and long-term value rather than being technologically centric.

1.8 INFORMATION WORKER ACCESS

Up to this point in the discussion, we have been focusing on the details of building the data warehouse, but we have not discussed what to do with the data once it has been placed in the data warehouse. Clearly, the business information worker must be able to access the data in a way that is meaningful, efficient, and natural. A tool is used by the information worker to access the data. Most of the tools use some type of workstation to present the information to the information worker. The types of tools available vary widely in functionality. Most organizations discover that no single tool meets the needs of all information workers. The cost of an information access tool is generally small compared to the cost of the data warehouse, and the organization will purchase different types of tools for the different needs that exist in the organization. The major types of tools that exist are:

- Geographic information systems (GISs)
- Data mining tools
- On-line analytic processing (OLAP)
- Relational on-line analytic processing (ROLAP)
- Multidimensional on-line analytic processing (MOLAP)
- Visualization tools
- Executive information systems
- Statistical tools
- Internet browsers
- Metadata browsers
- Fourth-generation languages

- Graphical user interface builders
- Spreadsheets
- Report generators
- Data access tools

While each of these tools has its strengths, weaknesses, functionality, and price/performance point, the data mining, statistical, and on-line analytic processing tools have a huge amount of technical appeal. Because the point of the data warehouse is to answer business questions, we will try not to be seduced by the technical appeal of the tools.

The various flavors of OLAP tools and executive information system tools all help the user form complex queries of the data and generate reports, graphs, and charts. These tools also allow the user to easily "drill down" from summary information such as quarterly computer sales to specific information such as sales of Hewlett-Packard Kayak workstations in Portland, Oregon in March. These tools generally have a standard menu-driven window interface. Drill-down is accomplished by pointing and clicking. The tools are called on-line analytic processing tools because the information worker is performing analysis of the data while being connected to the data as opposed to reading prepared reports.

Data mining and statistic tools search for patterns in the data or data that violates the general pattern. With the exception of neural nets, these tools can plot the points and the formula that follows the data. The human eye and brain are great analytic tools that can be used to gauge the goodness of fit. These tools can indicate which credit card holder demographics are more likely to indicate a problem, or which homeowners are likely to pay off their mortgage early.

Geographic information systems relate data to geography. These tools usually have the ability to determine interesting geographically centered facts, such as the number of customers who live within a certain of a store, or the average travel time between two points. These tools can also be used to determine new store locations by locating areas where there is a large population of a certain demographic group that might be interested in an organization's products.

Tools such as fourth-generation languages, graphical user interface (GUI) builders, and report generators all provide abilities to create special access tools and reports that meet special needs of an organization or operating units. While OLAP tools provide great ad hoc query capabilities, organizations typically have routine reporting needs. Most of the OLAP tools provide the ability to do reporting, but their capabilities are not as strong as the report generators. The fourth-generation language and GUI builder tools provide the facility to build a query program in a limited area with an interface that has a limited number of selections and can guide the user through the process. Although it is possible to build an OLAP tool from fourth-generation language tool, it is not the point of the tool. It would also be a very expensive proposition to build an OLAP tool with a fourth-generation language tool.

In summary, do not get caught in analysis paralysis when trying to decide on an information access tool. They all have an interesting set of features, and many of the tools need to be supplemented with other tools, based on the needs of the organization. Many vendors will supply trial versions, and it is valuable to get a feel for what the tool does other than what the glossy sales brochure says that it does. Most of the tools are not extraordinarily expensive, and more money can be wasted in people time deciding the "right" tool than delivering some value with a different tool.

QUESTIONS

1.1 In 1960, the typical reel-to-reel tape stored 200 bits per inch and had 2400 feet per reel. Today's data warehouses are in the 1.5- to 3-terabyte size ranges. How many reel-to-reel tapes would be required to store a 3-terabyte data warehouse?

1.2 Using the tape parameters specified in Question 1-1, how many reel-to-reel tapes would be required to store a 30-gigabyte operational data store?

1.3 In the late 1980s, the author purchased a 150-megabyte hard drive (DASD) for $1500. Assume that the cost scales linearly and calculate the cost for 1.5 terabytes of DASD given the 150-megabyte cost.

1.4 In the late 1980s, the author purchased 4 megabytes of RAM for $800. Assume that the cost scales linearly and calculate the cost for 512 megabytes of RAM that is typical of a workstation given the cost of 4 megabytes of RAM.

1.5 Why don't different departments of an organization use the same extract to do reports rather than using different extracts?

1.6 Compare and contrast a data warehouse, data mart, and operational data store.

1.7 Why did silo or vertically organized computer companies become horizontal?

PROJECTS

1.8 You have just accepted the position of CIO at a telecommunications company. What subject areas in the company might benefit from a data warehouse? Why? How would a return on the investment be realized?

1.9 You have just accepted the position of CIO at a telecommunications company. This company provides long-distance telephony (voice telephone), pager, cellular, credit card, and data transmission services. The company has a large number of legacy systems with data in many different database structures. How could the company benefit from an architected environment?

1.10 In your new job as CIO of a telecommunications company, you have discovered that the communications network the company has established is a very expensive and valuable asset. How can a data warehouse be used to be more competitive and better enable good network capacity planning for the future?

1.11 Congratulations! You have just been appointed as the CIO of a large supermarket chain. The current legacy systems provide information about what individual items have been purchased for sale, but there are no systems in place to gather data about what items have sold. Since there is no data on what has been sold and at what price, it is impossible to determine what items make money and what items lose money. It is also impossible to determine what items are purchased together. For instance, do people buy beer and chips together? How are you going to fix this?

1.12 You are a consultant working for one of the largest consulting companies in the world. A financial institution has asked you to analyze the use of information technology in general and data warehousing in particular to make the business more profitable. This institution has been receiving poor returns on its credit card and personal loan units. How would you use IT to help the business?

1.13 You are a consultant working for the consulting arm of one of the largest accounting companies in the world. A financial institution has asked you to analyze the use of information technology in general and data warehousing in particular to make the business more profitable. The bank also has not been making much money on its real estate loan division, due to early payments. How would you use IT to help the business?

1.14 You are the CIO of a large financial institution. You have noticed that the CEO is concerned about the amount of money the bank is losing on student loans. How would you use IT to help the business?

1.15 You are a consultant working in the consulting or professional service organization of a large computer manufacturer. One of your clients is a large manufacturing company that would like to use data warehousing to make its manufacturing operation more profitable. How would you approach a solution to this problem?

1.16 You are the CIO of a large manufacturing company. Your company is experiencing severe problems with parts suppliers getting parts to you on time. It appears that some of the suppliers are getting parts to you later than their agreement allows. How could you use a data warehouse to determine which suppliers are complying with their agreements and which are not?

1.17 You are now the CIO of a large health care insurer. While the company insures everyone who can pass the eligibility requirements, certain groups of people are profitable to insure and others are not. How could you use a data warehouse to increase profitability?

1.18 You are the VP of IT for a large hospital. You are constantly negotiating with insurers to increase the reimbursement caps (capitation) on certain procedures and treatments. You are also trying to get the insurance companies to pay for certain procedures and treatments. Could you use a data warehouse? How?

2

BUSINESS AND IT ALIGNMENT FOR THE DATA WAREHOUSE

2.1 INTRODUCTION

For the past several years, the number one goal of CIOs has been to align the IT organization with the business it supports. In this chapter we present an approach to the analysis of the strategic and tactical position of the IT department and compare the IT position with the position of a business as a whole. One of the primary purposes of this book is to help the reader bring the IT department into alignment with the business by constructing an architected decision support environment. A secondary purpose of this book is to give the reader the skills necessary to analyze the position of the IT department and align the IT strategic direction with the overall organizational strategic direction.

The reasons for the misalignment are many. IT has had a difficult time committing to a defined service delivered to a customer at a guaranteed time for a fixed cost and guaranteed level of performance. IT has been suffering a reduction in head count and budget, so it is difficult for IT to respond to all the business requirements. Legacy systems are sensitive and difficult to change. The end result is that the IT department appears unresponsive, unreliable, and inflexible.

There are many times when business management does not understand the technology, and the IT department has not been particularly good at educating and teaming with the business users. This gap in understanding and trust has appeared in many cartoons and contributed to the success of the Dilbert cartoons.

To determine how well the IT department supports the mission of a business, the direction, goals, abilities, strengths, and weaknesses of the business must be analyzed. The direction and goals of the business must be compared with those of the IT department. Once the gaps between the business goals and strategies and the IT goals and strategies have been identified, the IT department must move to fill those gaps.

Over 2500 years ago, the Chinese philosopher Sun Tzu wrote a book on strategy called *The Art of War.* Despite what the title leads one to believe, the book is really a book on the art of strategy. *The Art of War* is required reading in the MBA programs at many schools. Neither this book nor *The Art of War* can train the reader to be a business strategy guru, but we can pass along some ideas that can guide the reader into a more strategic frame of mind. Being able to think like a strategist and understand what business strategists are doing will greatly help data warehouse team members. Team building happens through communication and understanding, and it is difficult to communicate with someone you do not understand.

In the words of Sun Tzu: "The general who wins the battle makes many calculations in his temple before the battle is fought. The general who loses a battle makes but a few calculations beforehand." In other words, a good plan beats a poor plan. In this chapter we learn some techniques for planning the approach that will lead to success for the organization and the IT department. Planning includes thinking about and understanding the qualities of your resources and how they will perform in given situations. Some of the primary qualities that strategists are interested in are range, reach, and maneuverability. The IT strategist is interested in the same quantities. For the IT department, maximum *reach* means that any authorized person in the organization can access information from anywhere at anytime. In the IT sense, great *range* implies that an information asset can be shared across the organization. *Maneuverability* means that the IT department can supply applications that cover the range of IT architecture options. For instance, maneuverability implies great resilience, portability, maintainability, compliance to standards, autonomy, and openness.

The IT department has four main pillars that support everything the department accomplishes: people, process, strategy, and technology, depicted pictorially in Figure 2-1. The successful IT strategist will understand the range, flexibility, speed, and endurance of the four pillars. By understanding the characteristics of these four pillars, we can plan to mitigate their weaknesses and use their strengths to full advantage.

The four key pillars to organizational success are the same as the four components of IT success. The IT department's pillars must align with the pillars of the organization. The IT department must be an enabler to the business. In the book *Reeingineering the Corporation,* Michael Hammer and James Champy labeled information technology an essential enabler because it permits companies to reengineer the organization [Hammer].

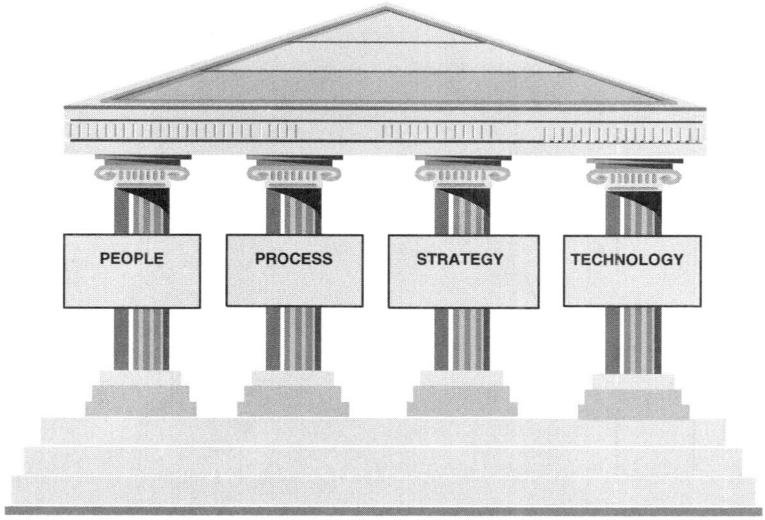

Figure 2-1 Four pillars of business and IT.

Many books have been written about business and IT strategy. There is no possible way that we can present in a single chapter of this book all of the ideas and practices that are available to align the IT department with the organization. The goal of this chapter is to convey some ideas and practices in the area of business and IT alignment and give the reader an appreciation of the topic. For an in-depth study of some of these topics, the reader is referred to one of the books by Bernard Boar.

The basic steps in strategy development are assessment, strategy, and execution. The assessment is imperative because the present situation and the desired situation must be understood in order to plan the path to the desired business situation. It is assumed that a business assessment has been completed before the IT alignment process will begin. The business assessment and strategy formulation will have been done before the data warehouse has begun, and the business assessment, strategy, and execution will be available as an input to the data warehouse team. The data warehouse team will use this information to perform an assessment, strategy, and plan of execution for the data warehouse project.

It is very important to realize that all of the techniques used to assess the position of the business are static representations. They do not explain the changes in the business that will occur if there are major changes in the forces that shape the organization. The reaction of the business to what Andy Grove calls strategic inflection points and the existence of a strategic inflection points will be subject to great debate among business leaders. A data warehouse can provide the information necessary to indicate a need for and guide a change in business processes.

The alignment of the IT department with the business is one of a number of steps in a successful organizational service management strategy. A comprehensive IT service management program will include at a minimum:

- Business and IT alignment
- Capacity management
- Change management
- Help desk operations
- Problem management
- Software control and distribution
- Cost management
- Contingency management
- Service-level management

A very high level introduction to the field of IT service management is provided in Section 2.8.

2.2 DEVELOPMENT TUTORIAL

A brief introduction to JAD was given in Chapter 1. By way of a refresher: Tony Crawford and Chuck Norris of IBM thought of an innovative way to get IT and business users to agree on goals for projects. Their idea was to get all of the interested parties in a meeting at the same time. By having all of the people involved in a project in a room at the some time and having a facilitator to guide the meeting, the kind of healthy information sharing and debate happens that leads to teamwork, consensus building, and the alignment of IT and the business. It is important to understand the basic factors that cause JAD to be used so successfully and widely in business today. These factors, together with a basic explanation of the JAD process, are described in this section.

A number of factors promoted the acceptance, success, and popularity of JAD. These factors included a shift toward cross-functional teams, a shift away from technology toward organizational objectives, and reengineering. It will be beneficial to briefly discuss each of these before investigating the JAD process in more detail.

The development of JAD happened at a time when the importance of teamwork was being recognized in the United States. The other new techniques in system development that appeared at this time were also based on functionally organized teams. As an example, rapid application development (RAD) is another technique centered on teams that is used for the creation of information systems. These new teams lost the hierarchical perspective of the organization because they were not focused on completing a task. The success or failure of the team rather than an organization would reflect on the members of the team. In large part, the success of these teams came from the diverse background, knowledge, and experience of the team members. Thus, the IT and the business community worked together in JAD teams and used JAD sessions to be successful.

The shift in focus from technology to meeting business objectives occurred with the deployment of PCs in place of dumb terminals and window interfaces rather than command-line prompts. With the deployment of technology to the desktop, users became more sophisticated. As users started to understand the technology, the professionals from IT were no longer the revered technology gurus from the glass house. The organizational customer became an informed user of the technology. This more sophisticated computer user started to expect more from the IT department. This sophistication was also reflected in the fact that the IT department's customers lost their patience for receiving a product from the IT department that was not what they asked for.

Many businesses learned during the 1970s that there were ways of doing their business that was more efficient and delivered a better product to the customer. The reengineering of business processes often required an accompanying change in information management. The IT professionals were the only ones who new what could be done with the information, and the business leaders were the only ones who knew where they wanted to go with the business. These changes in both the business process and the IT systems and processes forced careful teamwork.

If the great increase in the number of businesses that are ISO 9000 quality standard certified is any indication, quality has become greatly important. The Baldrige Award is another sought-after quality award. When it comes to software, what is quality? While it has already been stated, it is worth repeating. Carey found that the most often mentioned factors of successful applications were [Carey]:

- Building positive communications and relationships
- Achievement of project objectives
- Timely delivery

The JAD process is worthwhile because it helps the project reach these quality objectives.

A very important side effect of the JAD process is the linking of IT staff and organizational staff at the appropriate levels in an organization. As an example, the CIO will be linked with the CEO and CFO, while system development directors will be linked to line of business directors, and programmer analysts are linked with knowledge workers. These links are vital to the teamwork, cooperation, mutual respect, trust, understanding, and success of both parts of the organization.

Project deliverables that are physical components are frequently classified by logical components, and processes are frequently divided into phases. There are five phases to a joint applications development: project definition, research, preparation, the session or sessions, and the final document preparation. Each of these phases must produce an output before proceeding to the next phase. The final seal of approval is a signed acceptance of the final JAD document.

The JAD project definition is where the entire project starts. During the first phase of the JAD process, you will:

1. Form the JAD team.
2. Interview management.
3. Prepare the project charter.
4. Schedule the JAD session.

An executive has an idea for a project, and the sponsor, together with the project team, will define the project. The JAD process will be led by a JAD leader or facilitator. Imagine for a moment that you are building a house. An architect is in some sense like a JAD leader. The JAD leader will start the project by interviewing the managers of the user departments in much the same way that an architect would begin by interviewing those who will occupy the house. What is the purpose of the house? Will the house be the primary residence or is it a vacation house? What is the scope for the house? How many adults and children will use the house? What are the objectives for the house? A JAD facilitator will ask a similar set of questions of the business sponsors. This JAD tutorial will be written from the perspective of the JAD facilitator.

A successful JAD session will not happen if the right people are not at the session. An important part of the JAD definition phase is to select the right people for the team. The JAD team will have individuals with skill sets from both the business domain and the IT perspective. The team must be assembled during the project definition phase. If the JAD facilitator tries to start the process without the team in place, the process will bog down due to lack of knowledgeable participants. Of course, the composition of the team depends upon the end customer area, but Table 2-1 shows the typical members of a JAD team for a sales system, their roles, and skills.

The point of the JAD process is to bring together a team of people who are empowered to make decisions. It is important to have all of the people necessary to make decisions on the JAD team. If the proper team has been assembled, the progress of the team will never be slowed down with the response "I will check with my boss and get back to you." While forming a data warehouse JAD team, it is possible to discover that the needed skills are not resident in the organization. When a skill gap has been discovered, a decision must be made to hire or outsource the skill set.

Another important part of empowering the team to provide input and make decisions is to make all participants equal. A person's location in the organizational hierarchy should not change the weight of his or her input or give the person an

Table 2-1 JAD team members, roles, and skills.

Title	JAD Role	Skills
Vice president	Sponsor	Business domain expert
Senior systems analyst	Analyst facilitator	JAD facilitation
Sales system programmer analyst	Scribe	Business and IT knowledge
Business and IT knowledge coordinator	Business user	Domain expert
Sales financial analyst	Business user	Domain expert
Sales data entry clerk	Business user	Domain expert
Sales process manager	Business user	Domain expert
Sales force district manager	Business user	Domain expert
Sales force compensation manager	Business user	Domain expert
Salesperson	Business user	
Project manager	IT team	Project management
Data architect	IT team	IT knowledge

advantage at the JAD session. Voting is frequently used to make decisions, and every person on the team gets the same vote.

Clearly, a trade-off must be made between the size of the team and the amount of knowledge and experience that can be assembled. A careful trade-off should be made in the number of IT professionals on the team as well. Large teams have an inclination not to be productive, while small teams might not have all of the knowledge. The optimum number of people is usually 10 to 15 with four or five of the team being IT members. If there are more IT members than users, there is a real chance the project will become an IT-driven project and not a business project.

The JAD project must have a sponsor who has a problem that must be solved and has the money allocated to solve it. The start of the JAD project begins with interviews with the sponsor and other high-level organizational executives. The result of these meetings will be the project charter, which states from a business perspective the purpose, scope, and objectives of the project. These interviews give the JAD project team the necessary focus, and it gives the executives an opportunity to change the approach. The executive interview or interviews will define the initial scope for the project. It is also an important time to identify assumptions and open issues.

The second phase of the JAD process is to do the research necessary to perform a good JAD session. During the research phase, the JAD facilitator must learn enough about the business area to lead the discussion. In this phase, the facilitator will:

1. Familiarize the JAD team with the system and environment.
2. Create initial data models.
3. Prepare JAD session agenda.
4. Obtain initial information.

This phase will produce an understanding of the work breakdown structure, work flow, and computer systems that are in place. The facilitator does not need to know everything about the business area under discussion. The facilitator should maintain the big picture view of the project and depend on the experts on the team to know the details.

Another part of the research required to perform an effective facilitation of a JAD session will be to document the data in the current business system. There are several methods of documenting the data requirements of the business system. One approach is to use entity-relationship modeling to document the relationships among the data in the organization. There is a four-step approach to building an entity-relationship diagram. These four steps should be done by the JAD facilitator with a small subset of the JAD team in order to understand the business area better before the main JAD session. The four steps are:

1. Discover the main groupings of information with which the business works. These are the data model entities.
2. Identify the pieces of data that are kept for each of the entities. These are the fields or attributes of the entities in the data model.
3. Define the relationships between the entities.
4. Normalize the data model.

Data modeling is discussed in depth in Chapter 5. During a JAD session, step 2 is frequently done before step 1. Business users typically identify with pieces of data more than the logical groupings.

Data flow diagrams can also be used to document the data usage in the system that will be designed. In the case of data warehouse and other decision support systems, the main flows of data are from legacy systems to the data warehouse and from the data warehouse to the knowledge worker. Because these data flows are well understood and there are few data flows other than the data load stream, data flow diagrams are not widely used in the decision support system design process.

If the business sponsor has given direction to the type of queries and reports that are desired, the JAD facilitator can develop some sample or canned reports. These reports can illustrate the information that the sponsor is expecting to see as a result of the project. These reports and query results will elicit feedback from the JAD session attendees as to the desired data and format of the data in the reports.

The third phase of the JAD process is to prepare for the actual JAD session. The important things to accomplish in this phase are:

1. Create the JAD working papers or document.
2. Prepare presentation material.
3. Bring the scribe "up to speed."
4. Have a team preparatory meeting.
5. Prepare the JAD meeting room.

At this point in the process, we have done our research work. Now it is time to put all of the information together and get the team ready for the actual JAD session. The JAD team leader or facilitator understands the subject well enough to speak intelligently about the topic. The facilitator has been doing a lot of work, and this foundation needs to be shared with the rest of the JAD process team. The author usually does this by creating the JAD working papers and the presentation and using these to prepare the team for the actual JAD session.

The JAD working papers are the initial point for all discussion and decisions. The author prefers the term *working papers* to *working document* because it sounds less formal and fixed. The working papers will contain the information that was developed during the research and interviews. This will include both the text of the interview results as well as the data models, diagrams, and source system descriptions. In addition to rough formatting and the usual document niceties, such as title page, preface, and introduction, the JAD working document will cover the following areas:

- Agenda
- Overview
- Explanation of a data warehouse
- Participants
- Requirements
- Assumptions
- Parked or open items
- Distribution for final document

The process of bringing the scribe up to speed depends on the scribe. If the JAD leader and scribe have been working together for some time and the scribe has done this before, the amount of preparation will be small. If the person acting as scribe is new to the role, the amount of preparation required is obviously much greater.

The process of preparing the scribe to be effective during the JAD session is very important. Although the name *scribe* implies a menial role, this is far from reality. The scribe is the person who acts as that is the conductor between the energy and information that were developed during the session and the final document. Subtle differences in statements made during the JAD session can have a large impact on the outcome, and the scribe must be knowledgeable enough to understand and document these distinctions. One way to help everyone on the team appreciate the importance of the position is to have the scribe summarize the progress of the meeting periodically. This not only gives the scribe a more active role but also provides good meeting checkpoints.

To get an inexperienced JAD scribe up to speed, it is usually necessary to stress how important it is for the person to do great work. It is important to explain to the scribe that his or her work will make the final document. The five phases of the JAD process should be described to the scribe. The scribe should be given the project charter and the JAD working papers, and these documents should be reviewed with the scribe. The scribe can frequently provide some good feedback at this point, and it is critical to capture this information. The JAD facilitator should then go into great detail regarding the actual JAD session. The scribe should be familiarized with the presentation materials and precisely how they will be used. The scribe should also be told where to write notes about changes in the working papers and presentation materials. Finally, the scribe should be asked to be at the session meetingroom an hour before the session is to begin, to help the facilitator prepare for the session.

About one or two weeks before the actual JAD session, it is important to have a JAD presession meeting. Although it is frequently difficult to get the entire team to dedicate time for another meeting, it is imperative to get the best outcome from the JAD session. The best way to get a presession meeting and the JAD session scheduled on the teams calendar is to do the scheduling well in advance. The presession meeting will start to establish goodwill in the team, so be sure to make it comfortable and pleasurable for everyone. The presession meeting is also a great time for the project sponsor to make a statement of commitment to the project and reliance on the JAD team to develop the proper business processes. Because most of the participants will be participating in a JAD session for the first time, it is important to explain the process to the group. The JAD working papers should be distributed to the team with the disclaimer that everything in the document is just a starting point for discussion. The author usually has the team refer to the table of contents while summarizing the content of the working papers.

The final step before the JAD session is to prepare the meeting room. The room must have tables and chairs arranged in a manner that is conducive to interaction. The JAD standard seems to be to have the tables arranged in a large U with the opening at the front of the room. White boards and flipcharts are placed at the front of the room. The name tags should be distributed on tables near each sitting position. Everything that can go wrong usually does, so it is a good idea to have an overhead projector with spare light bulbs. It is easy to run out of flipchart paper and have all pens dry out, so it is a good idea to have plenty of both available. To avoid writing on a white board with a permanent flipchart pen, the author uses erasable white board pens for everything.

The actual JAD session is here. It is usually a good idea to have the session at a location away from the normal work location. This will minimize the opportunity for people to leave the meeting to work at their desks for "a minute or two." The JAD facilitator will start off by introducing himself or herself. The next item of business is usually the administrative details, such as the location of rest rooms, the schedule, where phone calls can be made, and introduction of the participants. The following item of business will be to state the objectives of the session and relate them back to the project charter. These steps will get the session off to a good start.

Next, the session agenda is reviewed. It is generally a good idea to have it on a piece of flipchart paper that is displayed in the room. This will give everyone the ability to check progress against the agenda. It is usually necessary to establish the ground rules for the session, which generally run as follows:

- Be on time.
- One person speaks at a time. No JAD minimeetings are allowed during the JAD meeting.
- Silence means agreement.
- All participants are equal.
- Certain difficult, unrelated, or multifaceted problems will be placed in the "parking lot" or open-issue list.

Now it is time to dive into the details of the project charter and the JAD working papers. As the JAD session progresses, there are three things that can happen with the material in the documents. The material can:

- Remain in the document unchanged if the team can agree to a resolution or wording
- Become revised
- Be moved to the open-issue list if the team cannot agree to a resolution or wording

The JAD scribe documents will make the changes in the document as the session progresses. Although it is handy to have a computer connected to an overhead projector screen so that the team can see the changes happen as the session progresses, it is not imperative. The scribe can just make notes in the document.

The JAD session then proceeds from the big picture down to the little details. A good place to start is with a definition of a data warehouse. Next, it is important to do a high-level review of the business area. The business overview will indicate at a high level what impact the proposed decision support system will have on which organizational units and functions. It will also indicate the general types of problems that a data warehouse could assist in solving.

Now that everyone is up to speed on the business area, it is a good idea to review the project charter. The present author usually reads the portions of the project charter document aloud that cover the purpose, scope, and objective of the project. This is usually a good time to review a diagram from the document that shows the scope of the system under design and the other systems that will be interacting with the system being designed.

A good way to start a discussion of the assumptions is to remind the session participants that the assumptions are up for review. One way to approach the assumption discussion is to review the assumptions in the project charter, then review the assumptions in the working papers. Because discussion of the assumptions generally covers a lot of topics, it is not unusual for the discussion to move rather slowly. It is generally a good idea to warn the session participants of this in advance by telling them that the session usually moves much faster after the assumptions are out of the way.

The author develops the data requirements through a series of brainstorming questions with the JAD participants. The first question open for brainstorming session is: "If you had a data warehouse of the kind we described today, what questions could you answer that you can't today?" The session participants volunteer questions, and all the questions are written down. Next, a good question to ask is: "If you had a data warehouse of the kind we described today, what decisions could you make or make better that you cannot make today?" We have developed a series of questions and decisions would improve the position of the business.

At this point in the meeting, a list of 20 to 30 questions and decisions will have been documented. What do we do about this wish list? We must develop a plan to maintain focus by reducing the number of questions and decisions. Thus, the next great question to ask is: "What are the criteria that should be used to decide the most important business questions that must be answered by the data warehouse?"

The present author usually tries to guide this discussion by reminding the group that the business expects the investment in technology to lead to a better bottom line. The question will generally lead to a suggestion of 10 to 20 things that should be the top priorities of the business. The group is asked to vote on the three or four items that should be the most important. Every person at the meeting gets three or four votes. The top candidates of the voting are used to reduce the selection of questions and decisions by having the participants use the selected priorities to vote for their favorite questions and decisions.

Now that we know the questions and decisions the organization would like to make, it is time to develop the data models that support the questions. The questions that the JAD participants proposed usually point to the facts and dimensions of analysis that are important to the user community. These are imperative to the data modeling discussed in Chapter 5. To lead into the data modeling portion of the JAD session, the question "What data do you need from the data warehouse to answer these questions and support these decisions?" works nicely. This question can be used to work through the facts, dimensions, and attributes of the data warehouse.

Another useful tool for the JAD session is to have the attendees bring their favorite reports to the meeting. The reports that are in support of the selected questions and decisions are used to develop the canned reports for the data warehouse. All of the data on the reports should have been identified in the preceding JAD question. This is an opportunity to discover missing elements in the data design.

The last question the author typically asks in a data warehouse design JAD session is: "If the data warehouse that has been designed is available, what business processes can be done differently?" This will generally lead to a very interesting discussion of business process reengineering. It is also another opportunity to examine what data is needed and the format of needed data to support the business process reengineering effort. This is another opportunity to discover missing elements in the data design.

At this point there exists a good description of the data warehouse. It is important to gather some information that will help in the design of the data warehouse technology and infrastructure. While there is no substitute for skill and experience with data warehouse construction to guide the questions, some of the questions that are typically asked are:

- How many people will use the pilot system?
- What is the expected usage pattern for the pilot system?
- How many people will use the production system?
- What is the expected usage pattern for the production system?
- At what locations are the users?
- How often must the data be loaded?
- What length of history must be maintained?
- How much data history do we need in the pilot system?
- How much data history do we need in the production system?
- What query response is expected?
- What disaster recovery need is there for the production system?
- What training requirement is there?
- What end-user support requirement is there?

At all times during the session, it is important to avoid *scope creep*. The JAD facilitator must focus on the original scope for the project as defined by management and stick to that scope. It is easy to lose control of the meeting. This results in participants' having an expectation for a system that may be much more expensive and take longer to develop than the sponsor is willing to endure. The JAD facilitator must not let the scope creep without the explicit consent of the business sponsor.

The last step in the JAD process is to produce the final document. All of the information that was revealed during the JAD session must be captured in a manner that is usable by the data warehouse team. Although it is easy to relax after the JAD session is completed, you should resist the urge. Unless a document is produced that captures all the information and consensus that was developed, the entire effort will be negated. All of the agreements, understandings, and trade-offs that were made during the JAD session will be quickly forgotten unless they are captured in writing. Remember, we promised the JAD session attendees that a draft would be in their hands in a few days.

The present author prefers to use flipcharts or a white board that copies to paper during JAD sessions. This guarantees that what was written down during the meeting can return to the office with me for preparation of the report. Using a scribe who is a fast typist or good with a CASE tool also ensures that information is captured at the JAD session and available for use to prepare the final document.

The final document is a distillation and organization of everything that went into the JAD session. This is THE deliverable that shows the JAD session's role in and impact on the business—IT alignment and data warehouse process. The business sponsor will generally be required to justify the project at some future time, and the JAD session document will be one of the tools available to show the progress of the project. The original business goals and requirements together with the proposed solution developed during the JAD session must be captured in this document.

The working document prepared during the preparation phase was established using the form and content that is desired in the final document. Thus, we have a good head start on the final document. The additions, deletions, and changes that were recommended during the JAD session will be incorporated in the working document as a draft of the final. This draft is then delivered to the JAD participants for their review, comments, and approval. Once the comments have been reviewed and incorporated into the final document, the document is delivered to management for their approval. After the final approval has been received, it is possible to proceed with the rest of the data warehouse project.

2.3 BUSINESS PROCESS REENGINEERING

In 1776, in his book *Inquiry into the Nature and Causes of the Wealth of Nations,* Adam Smith described an idea that he called the *division of labor.* Smith observed that the manufacturing of pins was more efficient if different individuals were responsible for performing the various steps in the manufacturing process. For example, one person would straighten the wire, another would sharpen the point, another would

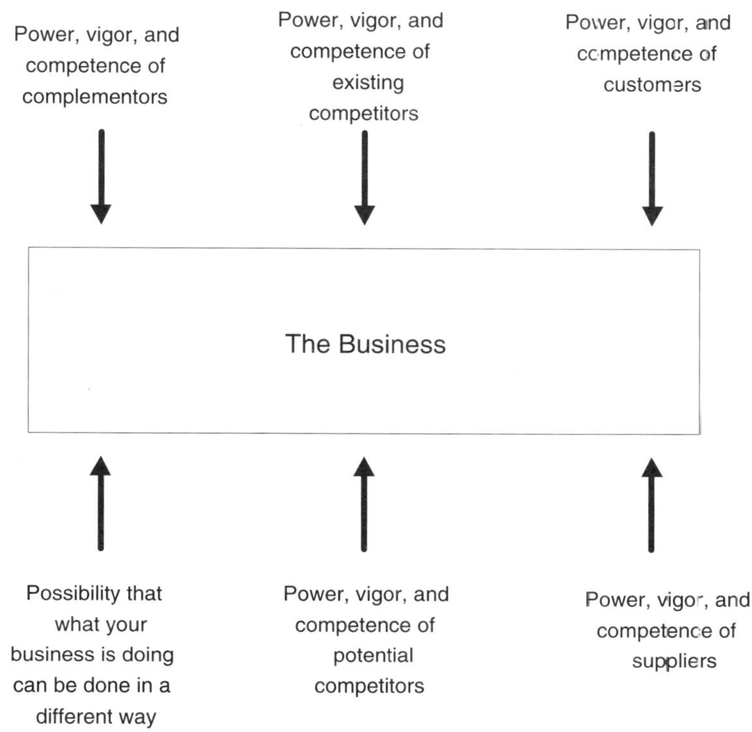

Figure 2-2 Six-forces diagram.

manufacture the head, and another would fasten the head to the pin. This approach to manufacturing pins was many times more efficient than that of one person performing the entire process. This was a clear example of improving a process over the usual method of having a person make a pin from start to finish. Americans especially put this assembly-line approach to manufacturing to excellent use.

Michael Porter of Harvard University has identified the major forces that act on a business to determine how successful and competitive a company is. Understanding Porter's model will provide a tool to the reader for the successful analysis of a business. It will also provide a tool for discussion with business colleagues. Porter originally identified five forces: recent theory has added the force of complementors. Using an example from the PC world, personal computer manufacturers benefit greatly from complementors that manufacture peripherals and software. The six-forces model is shown diagrammatically in Figure 2-2. The forces are:

- *The power, energy, and competence of the company's existing competition:* Are they concentrating effort on your business? Do the have lots of capital? Are there many of them?

- *The power, energy, and competence of the company's suppliers:* Are the suppliers good long-term partners, or are they interested primarily in short-term gain? Are there many suppliers to partner with, or are there only a few on whom you must depend?
- *The power, energy, and competence of complementors:* Are there a large number of other companies that manufacture products that make your product work better? Is your product totally self-sufficient?
- *The power, energy, and competence of potential competitors:* Other businesses may decide to offer the same or similar products or services that your business offers. These potential competitors may be better organized and funded than your company.
- *The power, energy, and competence of your customers:* How many customers and potential customers are there? Are they easy or difficult to partner with?
- *The possibility that what your business is doing can be done in a different way:* Either through business reengineering or substitution, is it possible for your business's products or services to be offered in a more competitive fashion?

The force in which we are most interested is the possibility that what the business is doing can be done in a different way. A decision support system is an enabler in monitoring all of these factors, and a decision support system can provide very valuable data to help business leaders decide if a strategic inflection point is in place.

Of these six forces, the one we are interested in is the possibility that what the business is doing can be done in a different way. This is the *business reengineering* focus. The way the business was doing things can be changed to make the business more competitive. The compelling reason for the change may be internal or external. In his book *Only the Paranoid Survive,* Andy Grove points out that a very large change in the balance of six forces in the market causes a strategic inflection point. Grove terms these very large changes in the balance of forces a "10X" change. This strategic inflection point can be caused by your business, or your business can be reacting to a strategic inflection point in the market. A business process reengineering effort either caused the strategic inflection, or a business process reengineering effort will be caused by the strategic inflection. In the first case, business and IT alignment will be used to cause the strategic inflection in the market. In the second case, business and IT will work together to react to the strategic inflection point. In either case, IT is an essential enabler to the business reengineering process and the possibility that the business can function differently. While Henry Ford caused a 10X change through business process reengineering, most reengineering will happen with changes in IT. This change in the way business is done is illustrated in Figure 2-3.

An example of using a data warehouse to reengineer business processes is to market customized products to consumers. By gathering data on the demographics and buying habits of consumers and storing it in a data warehouse, business-

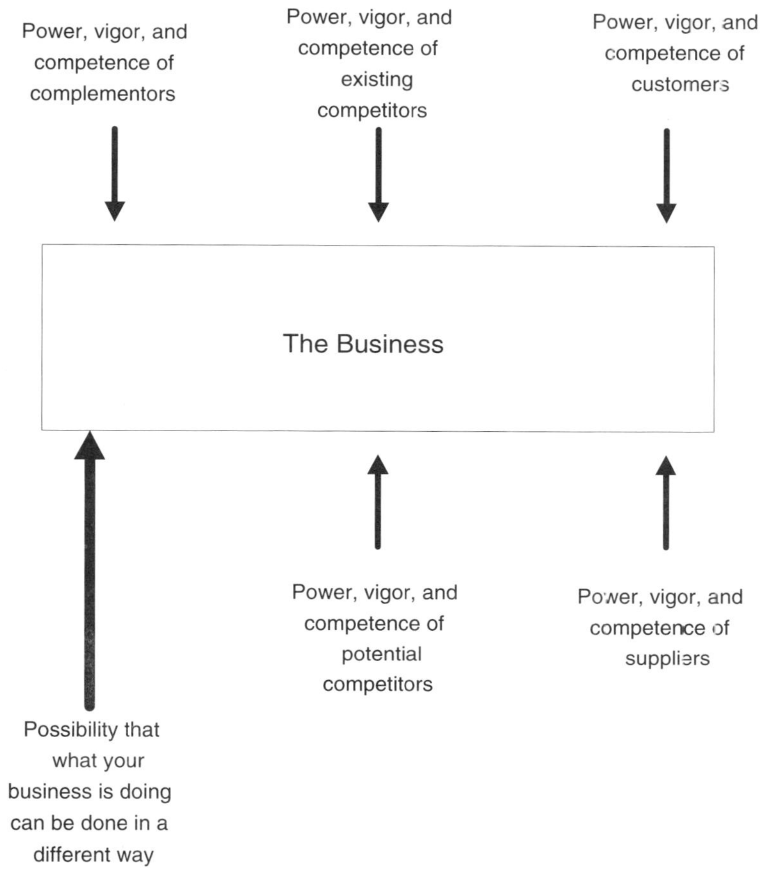

Figure 2-3 A 10X change in the possibility that what your business is doing can be done in a different way.

es are able to develop products that are tailored to specific buying habits of segments of the market. This is usually called *mass customization* [Kelly] or one-to-one marketing [Peppers]. The usual figure that is stated is that it costs 30 times more to get a customer than to keep a customer. The lifetime value of a customer can be very high, so this points to a desired solution to keep your customer where your business can offer a better and possibly more customized product than that of your competitor. If products are not profitable, a decision support system can be used to determine if the product is typically sold in a way that adds overall value to customers or if the product should be dropped.

Credit card companies have access to information about types of products that a consumer buys on credit. This information can be combined with demographic

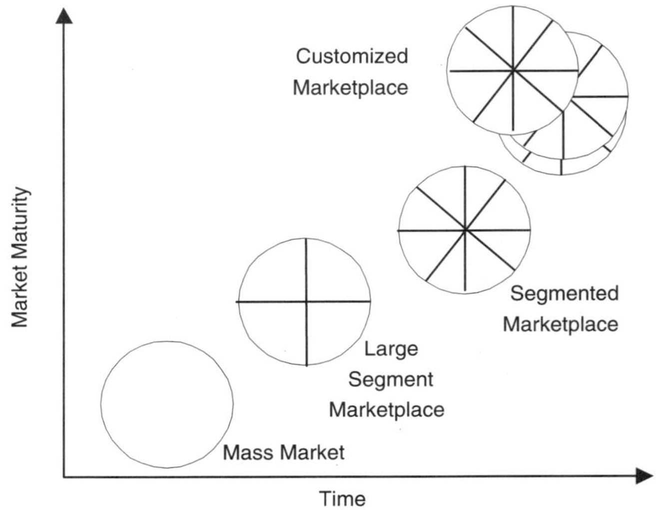

Figure 2-4 Marketplace segmentation and customization.

data about the customer to determine the purchasing habits of various consumers. While consumers with different incomes, number of children, and lifestyles naturally select different products, the organization should seek to develop the information necessary to understand these market segments. The concept of market customization over time is illustrated in Figure 2-4.

2.4 BUSINESS AND IT ALIGNMENT

In Section 2.1 it was noted that the purpose of data warehouse is to align the IT department with the business. Alignment with business strategy and goals, no matter the form in which they are stated, must be started by analyzing the position of the IT department and comparing it with the position of the business. An existing business assessment and strategy is the key to this process. The gap between the IT department's position and the position of the business can then be identified. Once the gaps have been identified, a plan can be developed to remedy these gaps.

There are a very large number of ways to assess the state of the business. The position of the organization is an analysis of the organization's location in one or more areas of strategic importance. These areas of strategic importance are often called *strategic dimensions.* A strategic dimension is a quantity that is critical to the success of a business. The position of the business is usually stated as the sum of the positions in each strategic dimension. Situational analysis is the analysis of information about the business for the purpose of developing a picture of the state of the business. Positional analysis is strategic, while situational analysis is more tactical. An annual report contains both a positional and a situational assessment. Both positional and situational assessment methods are explained in this section.

The business assessment usually states the *scope* of the, usually stated as the areas of operation of the business in addition to a statement of the vision, value, and mission of the organization. A simple way to depict the scope of the business is pictorially, with the operational units of the business inside a scope circle and everything else outside the scope circle. This is illustrated in Figure 2-5. While the business scope development is clearly not "rocket science," it does provide a good starting point to the discussion. Generally speaking, the IT department will be in good alignment with some of the areas of the organization but not others. The business scope can be used to identify and prioritize the areas of the business that will be addressed in the alignment study.

The vision of the organization is typically a one-page statement of the kind of business it is and its plan for the future. The vision statement should give everyone in the organization a sense of personnel and business empowerment. The mission states in a clear and concise form the purpose of the business. The value statement describes what the business believes in. The value statement should help people align their work behavior and direction with that of the organization. The value statement makes it possible for empowered employees to make decisions in accordance with the value statement without consulting management.

Once the business scope, mission, values, and vision are stated, we can evaluate how the business is doing compared with the goals. The ability of the IT department to support the various areas of the organization in the implementation and execution of the business mission, values, and vision can also be evaluated.

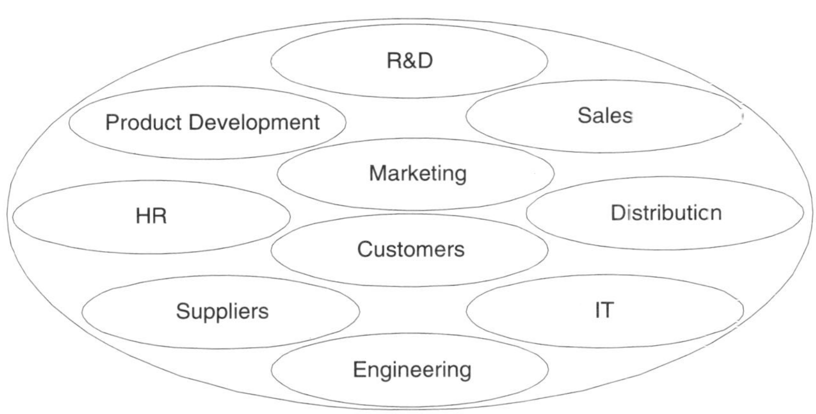

Figure 2-5 Business scope.

This can be done at a high level for the entire organization or in a detailed manner for each of the organizational units.

2.4.1 Positional Assessment

A positional assessment of an organization is a strategic assessment of the organization's general health and position in the market. It is important for the IT department to understand the position of the organization and develop methods for the department to align with the total organization to improve the situation of the organization. There are many ways to analyze the position of the business and the IT organization. Six of these methods are introduced in this section. Many books on business analysis are available. It is usually simple to extend the general business analysis to the IT department and develop some ways of using information assets to advance the position of the organization.

Financial Position. A positional assessment of an organization generally starts with an assessment of the financial position. A balance sheet is a standard method of stating the financial position. Other statements of the financial health of the organization include net margin and per unit revenue and expense. The key feature of interest to the IT department is how it is measured in comparison to the business. There are several ways that an IT department can be funded, and the usual business funding models will be applied to IT.

It is vitally important that the IT department have a funding model based on metrics that will align the department with the parts of the organization it serves. One of the author's favorite methods of IT department funding involves the creation of a service-level agreement "contract" between customers and the IT department. The IT department is reimbursed for services provided to the customer and the level of service. Superior service is rewarded with superior billing or measurement against metric, and inferior service results in reduced billing for services or reduced measurement against metric. Other ways to measure the IT department are return on investment (ROI), budget as a percent of revenue, and cost reduction.

Six-Forces Position. Another key indicator of the position of an organization is its position with respect to the six forces. The six-forces model can be used to understand the competitive position of the organization in relationship to its external environment. Organizations are constantly working to improve the competitive situation of the organization. The six-forces concept models how the organization is being affected by external forces. The six-forces model will indicate one of four types of states. One possible state is that there are no changes in the six forces. Another type of state is that an act by another organization, such as a competitor or supplier, caused a change in the six forces. Furthermore, your organization may have initiated an action to change the six forces. Finally, an external event or act such as a general business downturn may have caused a change in the balance of the six forces.

The IT department can help the business react to changes in the six-forces model by providing information about competitive factors in different market segments. The IT department can also help the business react to changes in the six-forces model by providing information that will help the business achieve a more favorable market position. Another way that the IT key department can help the business is to provide information that will enable business to develop blocking strategies to prevent competitors from entering the field.

Suppliers. Good partnerships between customers and suppliers are frequently key to success in highly competitive environments. Consumers and suppliers work together to ensure that goods are available to the customer in a timely fashion and in the quantity required. The IT department acts as the glue that brings these two entities together. The IT department can provide information about the quantities of goods and services that the organization uses in a given period of time. The organization's IT department can also act as an integrator between the organization's information systems and the supplier's information systems. For instance, a data warehouse can be used to provide seasonal trends in the demand for products. Information about the exact amount of goods needed can be extracted from the organization's operational systems and sent to the supplier. This allows the supplier to plan accordingly and provide the correct amount of product at the correct time. The sharing of appropriate supply chain information between suppliers and consumers allows the supplier to produce goods at reduced costs.

Market Position. Every product or service that the organization provides has a position in the market. This market position can be characterized by the market share the organization enjoys, the market shares of the other major competitors in the market, and the compounded annual growth rate of the goods or services in the market. It is important for the business to understand these factors in addition to the various market segments that exist. It is important for the organization to understand the various market segments because it helps the organization understand what it is selling to whom, and what needs your organization is trying to meet.

The IT department can align with the business by providing information that is crucial to the understanding of the market segments that exist and the products and goods that are sold into the market segments. This can be done by analyzing both the organization's point-of-sale data and data purchased from other suppliers. Because much of this data can readily be available from public sources, the data itself is not as valuable as insightful ways of processing the data into information. The processing of data into information will enable the organization to understand the marketplace better and create a competitive advantage.

Core Competency Position. Core competencies are the sum total of the collective understanding of an organization. As an example, Hewlett-Packard is particularly good at developing diverse technologies and turning them into products. Core competencies are the foundation for competitive advantage in the marketplace because they can be leveraged in multiple products in different market segments. A core competency has four key attributes:

1. It is difficult to reproduce.
2. It provides access to a variety of markets.
3. It increases the customers' perceived value of the product.
4. It often involves a complex coordination of different technologies.

Typically, one or more core competencies are used to produce a core product. One or more core products are used to produce end products that are purchased by the consumer in a given market segment. The core competencies and core products are used repeatedly to develop new products and services for new market segments.

To align with the business, the IT department should analyze its own core competencies. Areas of core competency of the organization that are not supported by IT core competencies should be investigated by the key department for possible support for newly developed IT core competencies. In this way an IT core competency is used together with the organization's core competencies to produce a core product.

2.4.2 Capabilities Position

Capabilities are the answer to the question "How do we compete?" Strengthening capabilities is a process that strengthens the primary business processes that deliver a valuable service or product to the customer. A capability has six key attributes: speed, process, agility, cross-functionality, customer focus, and complementary core competency.

The IT department will align the business by creating and developing its own list of capabilities. Typical capabilities for an IT department include:

1. Project management
2. Network operations
3. Client-server development
4. Contingency planning
5. Availability management
6. Capacity management
7. Configuration management
8. Infrastructure development

In areas where there is a gap between what the business needs and what a key department can provide, the IT department can develop new capabilities, improve existing capabilities, or reengineer existing capabilities. In areas where the capability access to capabilities is not sufficient form a task required by the organization, the IT department will improve the capability. This would be a quality improvement program. In areas where the IT department's processes did not match the organization's processes, the IT department would reengineer its processes. In either case, the process-oriented framework of the capabilities strategy drives change.

2.4.3 Situational Assessment

A situational assessment is a more tactical evaluation of the organization's capabilities and place in the market. A situational assessment requires the gathering of a large amount of information about business processes and data about the performance of the business. Because a situational assessment requires the gathering of large amounts of data, it tends to be a very demanding endeavor.

The IT department should perform a situational assessment and compare the strengths and weaknesses of the department with the needs of the organization and external suppliers. This enables the IT group to develop strategy and tactics to best serve the entire business.

2.4.4 Value Chain Assessment

Michael Porter of the Harvard University Business School has developed a concept called the *value chain,* a combination of infrastructure and a sequence of processes and events that an organization uses to add or develop value in the goods or services it offers to the world. A value chain has both a sequence of steps that the organization uses to add value to goods and services and an underlying infrastructure. Figure 2-6 shows a value chain in which IT and personnel are examples of infrastructure portions of the value chain. The R&D, technology, design, product, marketing, sales, and support portions are the information and goods flow part of the value chain. Manufacturing organizations have a repetitive

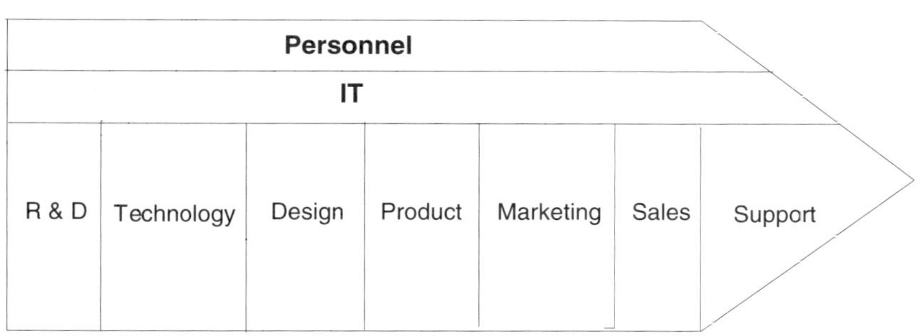

Figure 2-6 Value chain.

input, process, and storage cycle in the value chain. These parts of the value chain would be included in the product portion of the value chain.

The discussion of the value chain with executives during the executive interview part of the JAD process can lead to understanding of critical locations in the value chain. Places in the value chain where information technology can be used to greatly improve the ability of the organization to add value at that stage in the chain can then be identified. The requirement of information technology systems can then be developed to match the needs of the organization at that place in the value chain. In the case of data warehousing, locations in the value chain that need large amounts of integrated historical information will be investigated as potential recipients of a data warehouse.

Critical success factors, or CSFs, are a way to state what a business must do correctly to be successful. Critical success factors, usually tactical in nature, can be thought of as the list of fundamental tasks the business must be focused on to be successful. An example will help to make the discussion more concrete. For a data warehouse, the critical success factors typically are:

1. Answers business questions
2. Provides high-quality information
3. Delivers on time
4. Uses modern technology
5. Provides large return on investment
6. Has a business partnering orientation
7. Has a proper selection of technology to support the business
8. Is easy to use

If the data warehouse does not succeed in one of these areas, the data warehouse effort will not be as effective as it could be or may even fail.

2.5 THE FLEXIBLE IT DEPARTMENT

The keys to success for both the business and the IT department are maneuverability, range, and reach. The organization must be able to respond rapidly to take advantage of current conditions or changes in the marketplace. As the organization changes, the IT department must be able to change with the organization. To have a truly flexible IT department, all four of the pillars of people, process, technology, and strategy must be flexible.

Flexibility of people in this case is clearly not a gymnastics accomplishment but the ability of the IT personnel to learn new skills rapidly and adapt existing skills to new situations. The ability of IT professionals to use their skill to solve new problems depends upon the types of skills these people posses and their ability to use these skills and new situations. The IT department must be committed to a program of constant training for their professionals. This is particularly true because of the rapid change in technology and the introduction of new technology.

Most IT departments have well-developed policies and procedures that are the result of many years of development. These reflect a combined learning and knowledge of the organization. We'll show different levels of success by different organizations using this technology to solve problems that develop. The ability of IT departments to use existing policies and procedures in new situations is a function of both the core adaptability of these policies and procedures, and the ability of the organization to use the procedures in new situations. In other words, some policies and procedures can be adapted to new situations by their very nature. Other policies and procedures may be difficult to adapt to new situations, but clever professionals understand the subtle differences between the old and new situations and adapt the procedures accordingly.

Flexible strategy is more difficult to develop. A flexible strategy implies that a wide variety of changes do not destroy the strategy. While there are many approaches to developing a flexible strategy, a flexible strategy frequently has a multipronged approach. This enables different parts of the strategy to move forward even though a single part of the strategy has been blocked. As an example from the IT world, the strategy to move to open systems might involve the deployment of both UNIX and NT servers. When the strategy moves to tactics, it is possible to discover that one of these platforms does not have the applications desired. In this case it is really possible to move forward with the strategy with only one of the two servers. Thus, the overall strategy of moving to open systems is accomplished while a single element of the strategy has been blocked.

The need for flexible technology is driven by a need for the IT department to align with the business and deploy new applications rapidly to support business goals. As global marketplaces change rapidly and competitors develop new products and services, it is a business imperative to develop new products and services rapidly. In many cases, time to market is everything. Information technology is frequently a key part of developing new products and services. If the IT department cannot keep up with the rest of the business, it certainly cannot assist in the development of new products and services.

Flexible technology includes both hardware and software that have the key features of range, reach, and maneuverability. These are accomplished in technology by selecting standard components that are capable of deploying a wide range of applications. These applications could be common off-the-shelf technology or custom developed. In either case, the infrastructure must be able to support the applications. This implies that the best of class applications, development, support, and maintenance tools are available for the hardware selected. This need for decreased development times comes at the same time as reduced budgets and increased backlogs.

At one time, the monolithic mainframe environment was the prevalent computing environment. This environment is illustrated in Figure 2-7. Applications in this environment were designed for a single mainframe computer to which terminals and algorithm roles such as disk drives and printers were attached. The major problem in this environment was that applications would run on only one type of computer. This greatly limited the ability of the IT department to maintain flexibility.

The reader may have been to a conference where a large meeting hall can be rearranged into smaller meeting rooms of various shapes by arranging movable partitions. This gives the conference planners great flexibility in accommodating the widely varying number of people who might sign up for different conference sections. If it were not possible to move partitions around the large meeting room to divide it into smaller rooms, it would be very difficult to have an effective and efficient conference. It would be necessary either to have smaller groups use the large meeting hall at the same time or to have several small meetings going on at the same time.

Client–server computing and other multitier architectures (Figure 2-8) are much like a large conference hall that can be divided into smaller sections. Much in the way the movable partitions allow the conference organizers to adapt the meeting room to meet the needs of the smaller meetings, client–server computing

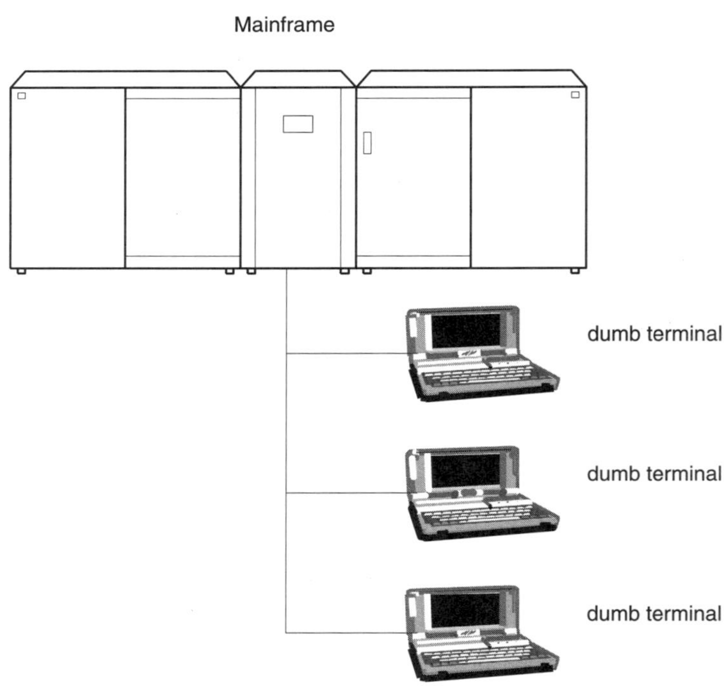

Figure 2-7 Mainframe "closed" architecture.

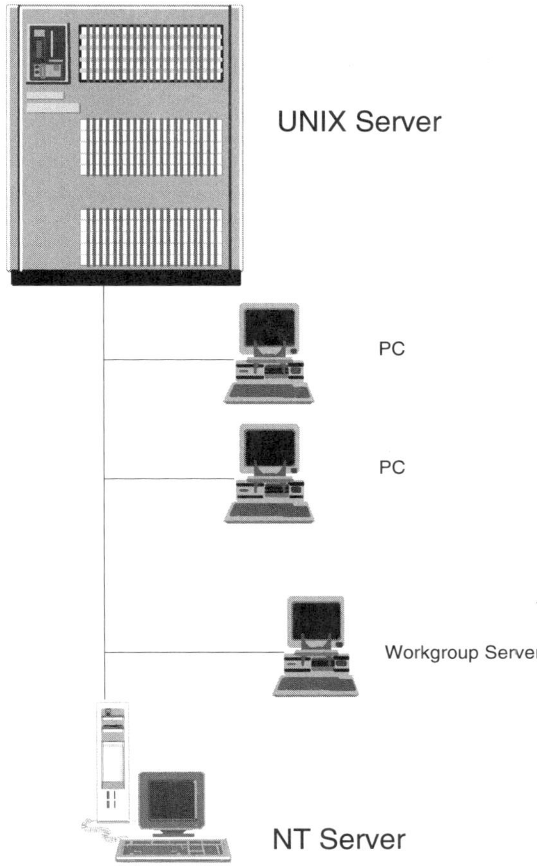

Figure 2-8 Open-system computing.

allows computer resources of different sizes to be selected for different business needs. This enables the IT department to provide maximum flexibility through the selection of appropriate resources. Client–server computing does have the additional overhead cost of managing a more complex environment. This price is usually small compared to the great value gained through client–server cooperative computing. The monolithic mainframe environment has evolved into an environment where both computers and people work cooperatively in a number of different locations. In this environment, a number of network computers function transparently as if a single large computer performed all the functions. Cross-functional teams must work together across dispersed geographic regions to make a relatively complex arrangement of networks and computers appear as one monolithic mainframe. This complexity is why IT service management is so important.

A flexible data architecture is also a key to a flexible IT environment. Flexible data architecture implies that any piece of data to which the user has security access should be available from any platform at any location in the organization. In other words, there are no barriers between users and their information. This is achieved through the use of hardware, networks, and software that will interoperate to deliver the necessary data to the user. While it may be physically possible for the user to access the data, it may be impossible for the user to access the data in any meaningful fashion. Without an appropriate corporate data model, it can still be impossible for the end user to integrate and make sense of available data. Data models and structures that enable the end user to access data easily and convert it into information is also important to the development of flexible data architecture.

Flexible methodologies are also vital to a flexible IT department. Warehouse methodologies are inclined to follow blindly the methodology adopted by the corporation. In any set of methodologies, there are built-in assumptions about the types of projects and the need for these projects. Frequently, projects are encountered that don't meet the assumptions of the methodology. In these cases, the IT professionals involved must be willing to be adaptable and select the portions of the methodology that suit the current project. Failure to do this frequently causes failures in entire projects.

2.6 OPEN SYSTEM

What are open systems? A simple definition is that *open systems* are systems that can be supplied by numerous companies and usually follow standards that are in the public domain. If a single company has architectural control, it is not an open system. Open systems have a number of characteristics:

- They are vendor independent and widely available.
- They are based on products and technologies that are implemented and designed in accordance with de facto and established standards.
- They can interoperate in a heterogeneous environment.
- The interface, software, or specification must be available from several vendors.
- There must be no royalty or only a small royalty for implementing the interface.

As an example, the relational database vendors follow the SQL standard and add extensions. If your system uses standard SQL and relational architecture, switching between the various database vendors is a minor endeavor. Similarly, providers of enterprise software usually have the software available for all of the major UNIX system hardware vendors. Moving the software from one system to another involves some teething pain, but it is not insurmountable. The ability of the purchaser to select between vendors increases the supply of the product in comparison to the demand. This forces the vendors to provide competitive products at competitive prices.

In addition to advantageous pricing, the majority of new system sales are for open systems. New entrants into a field generally pick the market with the largest share. This implies that new entrants into the market will select the open-system world for the creation of new products. Existing software companies with products in markets other than open systems see the opportunity to obtain sales in a new market. The creation of new products and porting of existing products to open systems mean that there is usually a much larger selection of products covering the price–feature–performance space in the open system world. Generally speaking, the best-of-breed products are available on open systems.

Returning to the ideas of range, reach, and maneuverability for strategic alignment of IT and the business, open systems generally have the best range, reach, and maneuverability. Usually, best-in-class application software products are available on open systems but might not be available on other systems. This enables the IT department to select from the best possible solutions to meet business needs that will also operate with existing corporate hardware standards.

De facto standards are standards that were originally specified by a single vendor or developer but became so widely used in the industry that they became unofficial standards. Examples of de facto standards are the C programming language, the IBM PC, ARPA networking services, and Berkeley networking services. *Industry standards* described the structure and functions of hardware or software based on an agreement among vendors within a control standards organization. Examples of industry standards are ANSI C, IEEE POSIX 1003.1, and ANSI SQL. The only way to ensure cooperative computing and that software will run on the largest possible number of hardware and operating systems is to use standards.

It was implied in the last paragraph that there are a number of standards bodies. This is certainly true. The International Standards Organization is the coordinating body for all worldwide standards. Most standards-related open systems are approved through the ISO's Joint Technical Committee 1 (JTC-1) or its subordinate working groups. ISO committee members are countries, not companies or individuals. As an example, the open-system interconnection reference model is the ISO's effort to develop open standards for multivendor networking. The American National Standards Institute, or ANSI, is the primary organization in the United States for coordinating standards. It has set standards for most popular programming languages, including C. The CCITT, or Comité Consultatif International Télégraphique et Téléphonique, is the international communications body responsible for wide area network and modems standards. These organizations and standards work through ISO working groups for approval. This process is shown in Figure 2-9.

Standards for operating system and application interfaces are necessary and desirable because they guarantee that operating systems and application are

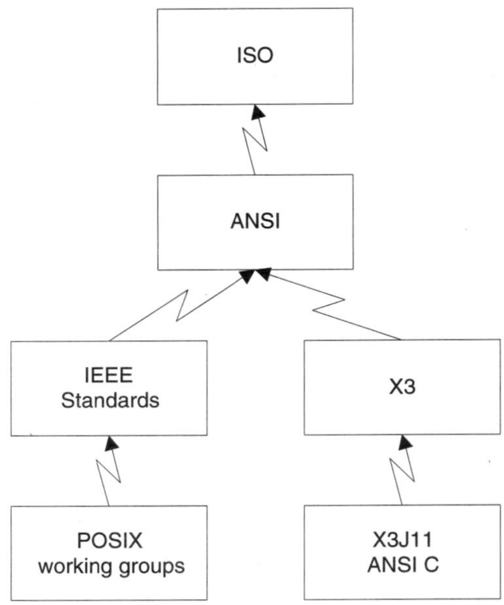

Figure 2-9 Development of ISO standards.

available on the widest ranges of platforms. This helps guarantee economies of scale and that the application you want will be available on the platform that you have or need.

For an organization that is currently operating on monolithic mainframe computers, it is often necessary to justify the move to open systems. This can be done using the ROI process defined in Section 2.7. Both data warehouses and open systems provide a competitive advantage because they enable the IT department to solve business problems faster and take advantage of business opportunities. Open systems also offer better productivity. This is particular crucial during times of declining budgets and personnel in IT departments. This better productivity is due to:

- Transparent information interchange
- Less expensive computer power
- Better customer service
- Fewer system management bottlenecks
- Faster access to new technology
- Scalable growth
- Wide-ranging available products

There are also cost savings and investment protection for open-system hardware and software. This is due to:

- Lower development costs
- Lower support costs
- Reduced incremental upgrade costs
- Reduced database design and maintenance costs

Open-system standards and technology is what enables the flexible IT department. Without the standards that make it possible for the various components of Figure 2-5 to communicate, share data, and share the processing load, the only possible solution would be the monolithic approach shown in Figure 2-7. In the open-system solution, network standards make it possible for computers to communicate. Application programming interfaces and distributed computing environment standards make it possible for the computing workload to be distributed and moved around the architecture. Database access standards such as Open Database Connectivity (ODBC) make it possible for an application on one computer to interact with the database on another computer.

The approach to moving from a monolithic mainframe environment to open systems is similar to the approach for building a data warehouse. The first part of this approach is a small pilot to demonstrate the ability and cost savings of open systems. The pilot is then moved into production. Over time, larger numbers of users are allowed access to the systems as techniques are developed to deploy open systems across an organization. This approach minimizes the risks of moving open systems while providing immediate value to an organization.

2.7 ROI AND JUSTIFICATION

By presenting needed business information, data warehousing technology can enable informed decisions. An informed decision will generally yield a much higher ROI than a decision based on instinct and no data. A recent International Data Corporation (IDC) study analyzed 62 successful data warehouse projects and found that organizations are showing a fantastic average three-year ROI of 401 percent.

An approach to estimating data warehouse ROI (return on investment) is to look at the returns that a company gains over time. The incorporation of data warehouse technology and information into an enterprise takes time. As a data warehouse is implemented and becomes part of the corporate culture, a business will find that gains are realized at different stages of the data warehouse implementation, and at different levels of the organization, over a long period of time. In the areas of timeliness, data quality, access, and report sharing, knowledge workers' efficiency gains are realized most quickly. Although important and easily quantifiable, these returns are insignificant compared to the returns, due to the competitive advantage that is generated through timely decisions.

To perform the calculations given below, we have made some assumptions. One of the assumptions is that workers' time spent is valuable and should be used wisely. Using this assumption as a starting point, calculations based on the amount of time saved can be converted to an approximate dollar figure. While the sustainable competitive advantage that can be created with a data warehouse is very valuable, it is difficult to convert it to equivalent worker time. The organization's executives must make an estimate of the value of a data warehouse that creates a sustainable competitive advantage. This value can be stated as a dollar amount. The time value of the total return expected from savings in workers' time must exceed the cost of the warehouse for the project to go forward.

For many organizations, the mainframe environment is something that grew with the organization. The monolithic architecture of the mainframe and the IT infrastructure that grew up around it became reliable and familiar as the organization grew. While this infrastructure is known and very stable, it is frequently very expensive compared with open-system platforms. Many organizations that the author has worked with have experienced 30 to 70 percent reductions in operating cost by moving from the mainframe to open systems. This alone can justify the cost of data warehouse development.

There are occasions when a growing company will be near the limit of what the present mainframe environment will provide. An upgrade to the environment is an option, but it can be more expensive than moving the decision support activities to an open-system environment. Avoidance of an expensive mainframe upgrade is another way that the construction of a data warehouse on open systems can be justified.

The increase in knowledge worker efficiency is usually the first return to be gained by organizations. This return is very small compared to the returns that organizations can realize over time by having more timely information with which to make better decisions. The longer-term gain of more timely information begins to be effective as knowledge users across an organization access information more easily. The knowledge workers will be able to spend more time asking what-if questions of the data and in analyzing the data before giving management results. Thus, knowledge workers should be able to provide better information quickly to management. Many companies have shown a reduction in operating costs of 30 to 70 percent due to the availability of timely information.

Most companies that implement a data warehouse have legacy systems that collect copious amounts of good data but do not let users access it in a timely fashion. A pulp and paper plant the present author worked with depended on reports on process quality and efficiency that could take up to three days to produce. This means that the plant operated blindly for three days at a time. The construction of a data warehouse enabled the creation of nearly instant reporting. A Hewlett-

Packard customer in the consumer products goods business reported a savings of $3 million to $5 million per year by using their data warehouse to operate more efficiently.

As the data warehouse is enlarged from a few subject areas to eight, the ROI should increase rapidly. Corporations with distributed operations should be able to use the information to better understand the performance of the entire organization. These corporations will be able to use information to optimize the supply chain, manufacturing, and distribution. One of the present author's clients reported increases in supply chain efficiency that saved his organization $5 million. A retail customer reported an increase in revenue of the $6 million due to target marketing enabled by a data warehouse.

When a data warehouse is first deployed, the first savings will be in the ability of knowledge workers to produce reports much faster than they had before. In the days before the data warehouse, knowledge workers were writing SQL queries to generate reports. Once knowledge workers had a data warehouse available to them, a query tool with a graphical user interface could be used to produce the same reports rapidly. Some knowledge workers were spending up to a quarter of their time writing SQL queries. With a more advanced report writing tool, these knowledge workers could produce the same reports using only 5 to 10 percent of their total time.

One of the difficulties of an unplanned reporting environment is the disagreementamong various reports. Many organization managers are spending weeks of time every year understanding and correcting these discrepancies. Using a data warehouse to generate reports that agree will help the managers make decisions faster and not waste time validating reports. This can save managers anywhere from two to five days per month. Given that the fully loaded cost of functional managers is anywhere from $300,000 to $1 million per year, this can result in substantial savings.

Once the reports are in agreement, a second benefit of the data warehouse will become obvious. Different users will no longer need to spend time generating the same reports. In many cases, the more advanced users could port a report from the legacy environment to the data warehouse in a very short of time. Once the legacy report has been ported to the data warehouse, all knowledge workers who require this information can share the same report. This results in substantial savings over the same reports being produced by many different knowledge workers.

Many organizations have noted that the more capable users provide unofficial help in support and training of new or less capable users. Both the IT department and most capable end users may be overwhelmed with questions from other users. In a legacy environment, it is not uncommon for a new user to take up to six months to be productive. After creation of a data warehouse, new users can frequently be productive in less than a day. Because experienced users might be spending up to one quarter of their time helping less experienced users, substantial savings can be generated by making a data warehouse available that is easy to use.

As mentioned earlier, the migration to open systems frequently saves the IT department large amounts of money. While this savings alone frequently justifies the creation of a data warehouse, there are a number of other reasons associated with IT operating efficiency that should be considered in the return-on-investment equation.

One area where the efficiency of the IT department can be increased is through a reduction in redundant data stores. A telecommunications company the author worked with had approximately 4 terabytes of redundant information. This redundant information was in numerous data stores in the organization. About 30 information technology professionals were involved in the maintenance of these numerous data stores. By creating a single data source for all of the corporation's needs, the number of IT professionals could be reduced to five or ten. In addition to reduced operating costs, DBAs and programmers moving from one part of the business to another need three to six months of training on how the information was organized in the new operating unit. By using a data warehouse with a common data structure, the business could have many months of training time every year.

The point of the ROI calculation is to help the organization commit limited resources by justifying the commitment of those resources. When developing the first few data warehouses in an organization, a marketing and sales effort will be needed, much like a commercial product enterprise. The approach various people in the organization about the adoption of a data warehouse must be fine tuned to meet the needs and goals of each person. Geoffrey Moore has been a pioneer in the field of marketing high-technology items. In his book *Crossing the Chasm,* he identifies different types of adopters of technology that will be of interest to the data warehouse implementer: technologists, visionaries, and early adoption pragmatists.

Technologists are interested in sponsoring a project just for the sake of being able to play with the new technology. Technologists are not focused on producing a return on investment to the business. Generally speaking, technologists want an opportunity to see the latest and greatest products in action and have an opportunity to play with the products. A business sponsor who is a technologist is generally easy to get along with from the perspective of the IT department, as they generally are not focused on adding value to the business. While many good warehouse projects have been sponsored by technologists, the lack of business focus usually means that the data warehouse that is created will not answer burning business questions. This means that this data warehouse will not be a good reference source for the rest of business. The first data warehouse constructed for the business should not only provide value to that area of the business but should also be a learning experience that can stimulate opportunities for the rest of the business. This makes a technologist a risky sponsor for the first data warehouse.

Visionaries have a very conceptual picture of technology. Visionaries understand what the data warehouse can do for a business and are not interested in the details of the technology. Visionaries have a conceptual understanding of what the technology should be able to do. A visionary's tolerance for the inevitable difficulties of technology can range from good to poor. A visionary with good tolerance for the inevitable difficulties with technology can be a great data warehouse sponsor. These people understand what a data warehouse can do for the business and are generally very eager to help the warehouse team achieve the data warehouse dream.

Early adoption pragmatists have a more practical view and understanding of the technology and what can be done with it. Early adoption pragmatists have a specific business goal in mind and understand that the early adoption of technology will not be without difficulty. Early adoption pragmatists understand that some of the technology is not well developed but that the rewards to the business outweigh the implementation difficulties. For the first data warehouse subject area to be deployed in the business, the early adoption pragmatist is often the best sponsor.

Data warehouse technology is so well developed at this point that many middle to late adopters of the technology are now eager to sponsor a data warehouse. The difficulty with this type of sponsor is that they frequently assume that data warehouse technology is as easy to deploy as simpler technology such as a canned report or spreadsheet. While the integrated data warehouses that are becoming common with packaged enterprise software can be relatively simple to deploy, a custom enterprise data warehouse is still a very large task. Assuming that a fully custom enterprise data warehouse is as easy to deploy as a packaged data warehouse is a mistake that is frequently made.

In summary, the decision to build a data warehouse and selection of the subject area must be based on sound business fundamentals. There are many ways to evaluate the decision to build a data warehouse, and one of the best is to evaluate the ROI. It is important to include intangible factors such as inflection points, strategic advantage, and business reengineering. These are very difficult to include in an ROI study, but the visionary business leader may be willing to make a decision based on the intangible factors alone, due to business experience. A visionary leader can probably place a price tag on these intangible factors that others with less experience or vision would find it difficult to understand.

2.8 IT SERVICE MANAGEMENT

When monolithic mainframe applications were used to run a business, the process of delivering service to users was simpler and easier. When paper reports delivered by interoffice mail were the norm, it was possible for the IT department to "paint the front of the barn" and have everything look great to users passing on the street. With the deployment of DSS, EIS, OLTP, and other client-server applications, users could "see" parts of the IT farm that they didn't have access to in the past. The process aspects of IT service management became more important.

In Section 2.1, it was pointed out that business and IT alignment was a small but very important part of the overall goal of a successful IT service management (ITSM). Other areas of IT service management include capacity management, change management, help desk operations, problem management, software control and distribution, cost management, contingency management, and service-level management. The successful IT service management program will leverage the four pillars of people, process, strategy, and technology in all service management areas.

As an example of the four pillars in action, it is usually a strategy of Internet service providers to have as little unavailability as possible. On the network side of this problem, people are trained to monitor the network. Technology components such as software and hardware are used to monitor the network. If a problem is detected, a process to resolve the problem is invoked. The people who use the process have been trained in the process and technology of the situation. The strategic goal of the company is to have the people and processes in place to use technology to develop a service, deliver a service, monitor a service, and help end users with the service. These correspond to the major parts of ITSM.

The major components of ITSM are business–IT alignment, service planning, service development, operations, change management, and configuration management. These components and their subcomponents are shown in Figure 2-10.

An excellent place to start an ITSM project is with a business and IT alignment, or BITA project. This will provide a clear picture of the goals and value of the project to the high-level business sponsors. It also provides a very valuable output by starting movement toward the alignment of IT and the business. In the business and IT alignment process the current goals and objectives of the business are evaluated compared with the abilities in the IT department. To plan needed scalability into the process, it is important to ask at every stage of the IT service management and the data warehouse process what the future goals and direction of the business might be. This will enable the designers of the IT architecture and IT service management processes to build in the necessary features for further growth. It will also enable the IT department to develop a plan for the evolution of legacy applications or the development of new applications.

Once the IT services that are needed to support the strategic vision of the organization have been identified, it is the role of service development to develop a blueprint of the service from the rough description given by organizational leaders. This is the point of the service development phase. In this phase, the operational requirements developed through the BITA process are developed into a definition of new services. Part of the new service definition process is to identify the financial impact of the new service, develop the data model, and identify the gap, if any, between IT abilities and new service demands. Another part of developing a new IT service is to plan for service levels, growth of service levels, performance, capacity, and continuity management. While most customers would like 24-hour availability seven days a week, most customers are not willing to pay for this service. Managing the costs of services delivered is also a function of this stage.

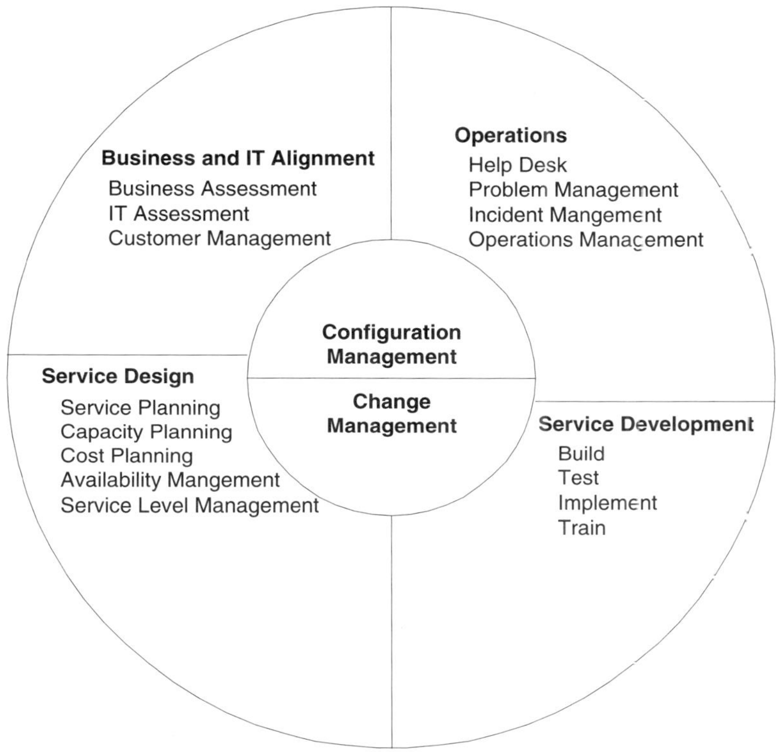

Figure 2-10 Components of IT service management.

It is the job of service development to develop, test, and deploy IT services according to specifications developed during the BITA and service design processes. In this group of processes the services IT infrastructure required to deploy the services are developed. This stage in the process involves not only the software tools required to develop new applications, but also the training plans, hardware preparation plans, and other tools needed to deploy successful applications. Once the new IT service has been developed and tested, the change management process will be used to move the new service into production. Once the new service has been moved into production, it will undergo another round of rigorous testing before being released.

Successful IT organizations typically have carefully designed interfaces between the customer and the IT department. The purpose of operations management is to ensure that the IT department runs so smoothly that it almost appears to be magic to the customer. Operations management will be focused on the delivery of service to the customer. The operations management department provides command and control of the IT environment to reach this end.

Operations management also provides a help desk, problem tracking, problem escalation, problem analysis, and root-cause analysis. All of these areas help reduce the number of difficulties experienced by the end user.

It is impossible to provide seamless operation of the IT data machinery without strict control of the IT production environment. The business and IT alignment process, service planning process, service development process, and operations management process cannot accomplish their goals without journal control of the IT environment. To this end, there are two other IT processes that are are required to stabilize the IT production environment: the change management process and the configuration management process. The change management process is the process that coordinates and allows all change-related work to happen to the production environment. The configuration management process tracks and controls changes in the hardware, software network, people, documentation, and the relationships between these objects. This information about the current configuration of the environment is absolutely necessary to understanding and developing new services.

Every data warehouse developed should go through all the steps in the ITSM model. These steps help ensure that users are getting what they want to the level of service they want, for the price to be paid. It also helps ensure that the end users can obtain help when needed to resolve issues. While all of the processes in the ITSM framework need to be considered at the appropriate level of detail, they do not all need to be developed in depth.

It is also very important to measure the responses of the IT environment. It is impossible to correct what hasn't been measured. There are many ways to measure the performance of the IT environment. Tools such as HP's OpenView and MeasureWare products measure the performances of specific pieces of the architecture. Other tools, such as Prolin, help the IT department measure the overall performance of services.

In summary, the development of new IT service such as a data warehouse must align with the rest of the needs of the business. A plan must be developed that will deliver the type of service the business wants for a cost that is predictable and controlled. The new service must include a method for introducing changes in the existing production environment in a way that does not interrupt existing service. The plan is then converted into a design and implemented according to the plan. Progress must be compared with the plan and future direction modified as necessary to ensure that the product delivered meets the design within the constraints of time and financial resources allotted.

QUESTIONS

2.1 In your own words, explain why JAD helps met the three software quality factors defined by Carey.

2.2 Explain the five phases of the JAD process.

2.3 In your own words, explain the business–IT alignment.

2.4 In your own words, define and explain the six-forces model.

2.5 In your own words, define and explain core competencies. What are the core competencies of a great college or university?

2.6 In your own words, define and explain the concept of critical success factors.

2.7 Explain the process and subprocesses of service design.

2.8 Explain the process and subprocesses of service development.

2.9 Explain the process and subprocesses of operations management.

2.10 Explain the process and subprocesses of configuration management.

2.11 Explain the process and subprocesses of change management.

2.12 In your own words, define and explain a value chain.

2.13 Create a value chain for an educational institution.

2.14 Create a value chain for a bank.

2.15 Create a value chain for a telecommunications company.

2.16 Create a value chain for a retail store.

2.17 Create a value chain for a hospital.

2.18 Create a value chain for a hotel chain.

2.19 Create a value chain for a manufacturing company such as an auto manufacturer.

PROJECTS

2.20 At various points in your life, you must have used a class registration system. How would you improve on this system? Would there be improvements in process, data collection, reporting, or all of these? Please present the design of your system by forming a JAD team with you colleagues and following the JAD process. You should document all the steps in your JAD process.

2.21 Your bank statement is printed on paper and arrives in the mail. How would you improve on this system? Would there be improvements in process, data collection, reporting, or all of these? Present the design of your system by forming a JAD team with you colleagues and following the JAD process. Members of your team can role play as the bank executives. You should document all the steps in your process.

2.22 Call behavior analysis is the analysis of the phone calls that a traditional phone or long-distance customer might make. The information is gathered by the switch that routes the call. This information will include the number of the phone originating the call, the phone number of the receiver of the call, and how long the call lasted. The newer switches, called SS7 switches, can capture other information, such as calls that are not completed because of a busy signal. How can this technology be used to better align the IT department with the business? What would the critical success factors be? How would this change the six-forces diagram? Why would these changes occur?

2.23 The network that connects a telephone call and carries the voice data is a very expensive and valuable resource. Planning for network expansion is a very important task due to lost revenue if telephone calls don't go through or to increased cost if the network is too large in the wrong location.

2.24 Buying trend analysis is performed by car manufacturers and dealers to best determine the car and options that certain demographic groups are likely to purchase. Suppose that you are a regional sales manager for an automobile manufacturer. What information would you want to better prepare you to sell cars? How would you measure the success of this program? How would this change the six-forces diagram? Why would these changes occur?

2.25 Stores can use a data warehouse to do buying trend analysis to best determine the products that certain demographic groups are likely to purchase. For example, an electronics store could determine which demographic groups are likely to purchase which products. A premium clothing store could track demographic groups that are likely to purchase certain products. Suppose that a data warehouse was implemented in this area. What would the critical success factors be? How would this change the six-forces diagram? Why would these changes occur? What different user communities would there be at the store? What information would the various user communities want to see?

2.26 Manufacturing organizations can use a data warehouse to track the compliance of their suppliers to their agreements. The agreements normally cover at a minimum the delivery timing of products and product quality. A manufacturing organization does this to increase the quality of goods and reduce the cost of having too much inventory. Other technologies, such as an electronic data interchange (EDI), enable the manufacturing company and its suppliers to exchange information orders for parts and deliveries of parts electronically. How would a data warehouse in the vendor compliance area be used? What information should it provide? What decisions could be done differently? How could this information be used in negotiations with vendors?

2.27 Recall that financial organizations can use a data warehouse to analyze the risk of consumer and certain other scenarios. This data warehouse can use data such as demographic data or payment history data to determine the risk of the loan. This enables the financial institution to estimate and manage the risk.

2.28 Create a list of data that should be in this data warehouse. How would this data be used? What other opportunities would this create?

2.29 Airlines can analyze the travel trends of their frequent fliers in different demographic groups. This information can be used to target market frequent fliers in the correct market groups. The demographic data is usually obtained from external sources.

2.30 Airlines can use a data warehouse to track the seasonal variations and growth expected in travel between locations. This data could also show how much food and beverages are consumed in different flights. This will help the airline select aircraft and catering to match needs. What information would the airline need from this data warehouse? What advantage would there be to having "atomic" data such as the passengers on a particular flight as opposed to summary information such as the total number of passengers flying from one town to another on a given day?

2.31 Educational institutions can use a data warehouse to analyze trends in class enrollment, grade history, and student evaluation of professors. The data for the data warehouse will be loaded at the end of every academic period. Information about class enrollment will come from the registration system, and student evaluation data can be loaded from the academic dean's computer system. What information should be in this warehouse? What decisions could the institution make with this new information? What are the critical success factors for the warehouse? How would this change the six-forces model for the institution?

2.32 Health care providers can use a data warehouse to track diagnosis codes (called ICD9 codes), the procedures and treatments for that diagnosis (called CPT codes), and the cost of those procedures and treatments. This can be used to analyze the success rates of procedures for a diagnosis or the cost versus the insurance reimbursement. How could the management of a health care organization such as a physicians group or hospital use this information? Precisely what information would be needed? What information would a medical director or researcher need to analyze patterns of outcome? Could these data warehouses be combined?

2.33 Hotels can analyze the staying trends of their frequent guests in different demographic groups. This information can be used to target frequent guests for vacation packages. The demographic data is usually obtained from external sources. What information would the person in charge of marketing need in order to target select demographic groups? How could this information change the six-forces model? Why would these changes occur?

2.34 Hotels can use a data warehouse to track the total value of a frequent guest's stay. The value of the stay is the total amount the guest spends during the stay, including room, restaurant, room service, gift shop, and other incidental charges. What information would the person in charge of marketing need to target select demographic groups? How could this information change the six-forces model? Why would these changes occur?

2.35 Assume that you are asked to build a data warehouse to analyze the sale of products at your local grocery store. You are to construct a system to analyze the sale of all items in a shopping cart or basket. This is frequently called market basket analysis. The point of this analysis is to obtain an understanding of product sales and products sold together.

3

How to Plan and Build a Data Warehouse

3.1 INTRODUCTION

One characteristic of creative human beings is a tendency toward a lack of methodology and planning. The human spirit seems to fill many of us with hope, optimism, and excitement about new projects. We start such projects with much enthusiasm and without the necessary planning. Once we have been either a part of a project that didn't succeed or have heard horror stories from those involved, we start project planning as part of our ad hoc project management methodology. In other cases, the company for which we work will have a formal methodology that covers the appropriate planning steps. Most formal methodologies are designed to handle projects that range in size from a homemade ice cream business to the construction of an aircraft carrier. Thus, the problem with most general methodologies is that they are not tuned to the specific problem. They will frequently contain steps that are not needed or not have steps that cut quickly to the heart of the solution.

My own horror story of lack of planning involves a software project that I was assigned to work on as my first project after graduate school. I was assigned the task of merging two different 150,000-line FORTRAN programs. The two programs had a common origin in a program that had been written at Stanford University five or six years before the merge was to take place. Two different organizations had each invested many programmer years modifying the code to represent their particular needs. In some cases, the modifications were in mutually exclusive directions. Managers from the two organizations got together, wet their fingers, placed them in the air, and decided that two or three weeks of a programmer's time should be sufficient to merge the two versions of the program. Needless to say, what was really required was two to three weeks of work and study in producing a plan to solve the problem. While the project produced a usable end result, the result was a limited merge with limited usefulness. The overall difficulties of the merge were so great that the project was abandoned.

Too much planning and analyzing can also be a danger. The scene is the fortieth floor of an office building the client owned. The Hewlett-Packard team started to explain to a crowded room of business executives the methodology that H-P would use in building data warehouses. We started the meeting by explaining that H-P takes an iterative approach to building a data warehouse by starting with a warehouse in one subject area that expands to include more subject areas. The CFO interrupted to express his concerns that this would lead to a number of data warehouse silos that could not be connected to provide a total picture of the business. The preferred method is to produce an enterprise-wide data model in just enough detail to discover the linkages that will occur between the different data warehouse subject areas. This approach has the advantage of producing results quickly that have an understandable business benefit and return on investment without tackling the entire enterprise data modeling project and waiting several years before starting a data warehouse. We explained this process in great detail to the assembled team of executives to no benefit. The client decided not to do the project. Several years have passed. We have constructed many other very large warehouse and decision support systems since this meeting, but this client is still in a state of analysis paralysis. The plan will never be perfect, and an attempt would be made to plan for something that is not even known. The moral of the story is to plan to the appropriate level of detail, then stop planning and start building.

In the words of Sun Tzu, "Only one who knows the disastrous effects of a long war can realize the supreme importance of rapidly bringing it to a close." In other words, plan to bring the data warehouse to a rapid and successful finish. A good methodology will have a certain level of detail of planning built into the methodology that will help this occur. This general level of planning indicates what skills are needed at what time periods in the development and what deliverables should be created in what time frames.

The difficulty with a long warehouse development project is that the business strategy can change during the data warehouse development. People near the level of the CIO frequently fund these projects, and the average tenure of a CIO is approximately two years. It is clearly important to the future of the CIO to demonstrate successful completion of important projects. Because data warehouses are projects that are highly visible and can show future returns to the organization, successful completion of a major data warehouse project can help the success of the entire IT organization. It will also improve the perception of the technology organization in the business.

The problem with most projects is that they are started with a large number of unknowns and risks. It is important to select a methodology that reduces these early in the process. This makes the entire process more reliable and comfortable by identifying possible risks and show-stoppers early in the project, before a lot of money and time have been invested. Because project errors have a tendency to snowball and become larger over time, the cost of fixing an error early in a project is much smaller than that of fixing an error late in the project. Occasionally, a data warehouse project needs to be delayed or canceled. As an example, some data warehouse projects require data elements that are not available in the current operational systems in order to supply meaningful information to the business decision maker. It is much better to stop or delay a project that has just started than to spend large amounts of time and money to develop a system that does not deliver the needed information.

Another interesting thing that people do is to create things that may not be profitable. Painters must paint, writers must write, and IT professionals create IT systems. While the world would be a very bland place without the works of William Shakespeare, Claude Monet, and Norman Maclean, business is focused on the creation of profit. Many data warehouse projects have been undertaken as fun projects to create something without consideration of the financial impact on the organization. While some of these projects are valuable learning experiences and create an information store for the business, most of them failed do lack of involvement of business leaders.

The purpose of information systems is to provide information that is valuable to a business. It seems obvious that the place to start a data warehouse is with the business. The H-P process is to use the joint application development (JAD) sessions to discover what the business needs. These JAD sessions are part of a need analysis workshop that is conducted with the top executives. The outcome of the need analysis is the identification and prioritization of different data warehouse subject areas. This may also be by everyone attending the JAD sessions with an understanding of the decisions made and the prioritization selected. This helps everyone feel involved in the project and empowered in the process of changing the organization's information infrastructure. Without this involvement, people will not feel committed to the process of change and contribute the energy and thought needed to build a successful data warehouse.

Continuous verification and validation with management of a project's goals is a very important part of most methodologies. The reason for the validation process is to ensure that the project is meeting the needs of the business for the price that the project sponsor expects to pay. A key strength of the methodology discussed in this book is the continuing opportunity for executive validation of the project. The verification happens at team meetings and JAD sessions where the progress and decisions of the team are presented. The verification process also happens through written documents that are delivered to the project stakeholders. Written documents, team meetings, and JAD sessions all work together to guarantee continuous revalidation of project goals and progress against expectations and schedules. This is illustrated in Figure 3-1.

It is the goal of this chapter to help the reader gain an appreciation and understanding for the importance of initial project selection. Because the first data warehouse will prove the value of the concept to an organization while it causes some major changes in the IT configuration, it is important to select a project that meets a business need and introduces new technology to the organization while providing valuable information that justifies the cost of the project. Selecting the first project is a careful trade-off between business and technology, IT preparedness and business needs, and present technology infrastructure and future infrastructure. If a project is selected that requires too much new technology, it may fail due to the inability of the IT department to deploy a large amount of new technology. If a project with too little need technology is selected, it is possible that the IT organizations may be seen as being unresponsive to user needs. If a project is selected that will deliver huge amounts of new information to the business, it may collapse under its own weight. If a project is selected that delivers too little new information to the business, the IT department can once again be seen as being unresponsive to user needs.

This chapter is an introduction to and overview of the rest of the book. With the exception of project selection, every topic in this chapter will be expanded in more detail in future chapters. The proper design of a data warehouse requires a top-down approach. Each level of detail in the warehouse design includes more details. In the same way, this book starts by describing topics at a high level before describing them in detail. Readers only interested in an overview of the data warehouse arena should have their interest met by reading Chapters 1 through 3.

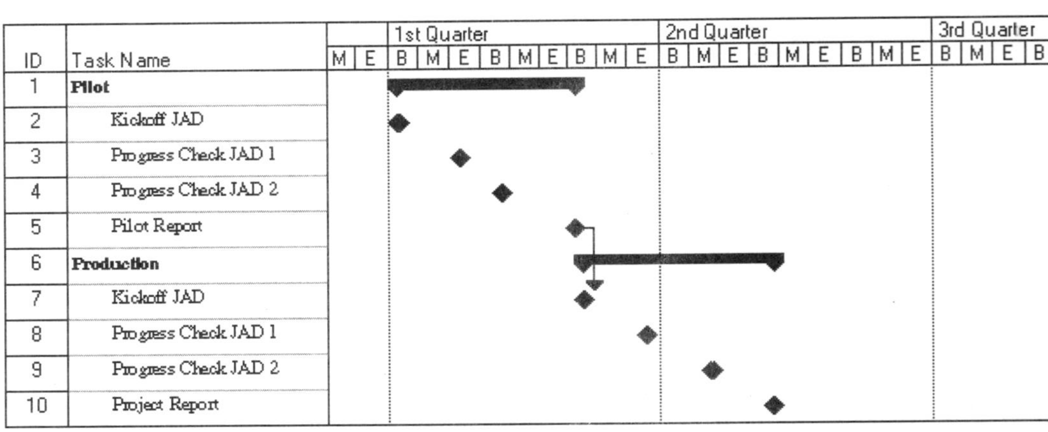

Figure 3-1 Showing verification of the progress of a plan across project phases.

The book can then be a reference as other topics become of interest. For readers who are interested in the details of data warehouse construction, this chapter establishes a road map of the remainder of the book. Once the road map has been drawn, the various locations along the route are more easily understood. Without the high-level view presented in the following sections, it is easy to get lost in the details and not see the big picture. The following sections should paint the big picture of the construction of a data warehouse.

The present author is a private pilot who very much enjoys the experience of flying small aircraft. The two instructors who trained me both emphasized the fundamentals. In the case of flying, the fundamentals are rather simple: airspeed, attitude, navigation, fuel management, weather, and flight planning. The construction of a successful data warehouse is all about attention to the fundamentals. A plan must be developed to bring the IT department into closer alignment with the business by construction of a data warehouse. This data warehouse must provide information to answer critical business questions. This is done through a series of JAD meetings to identify the key areas of the business that have information needs and then understanding those areas further through JAD sessions that are specific to each area. A plan is then developed to construct the warehouse with an agreed-upon set of features by a particular date. To fulfill this requirement, it is important to practice good software engineering practices and to avoid the usual software project mistakes. This book stresses the fundamentals.

3.2 BUSINESS NEEDS ANALYSIS

There are many ways to discover the information needs of an organization. While JAD techniques routinely deliver the most consistent results, there are other methods of discovering business needs for information. These other methods range from financial analysis to simply walking around the organization and talking with those doing the day-to-day operations. Some of the other methods of discovering the information needs of a business are discussed in this section. Astute readers will also be able to develop ideas for their own approach to business information needs discovery. The JAD technique of executive interviews is introduced here and discussed in depth in Chapter 4. The necessary sequence and the reason for the sequence of JAD sessions is introduced in this section. In general, any technique that improves the confidence of business leaders in the IT department and helps the IT department understand the organization's need for information is fair game. Still, a series of executive interviews and JAD sessions starting with the executives and continuing with organizational unit teams is a great way to design the decision support system from the top down.

One of the first steps in the JAD process it is to do the homework necessary to understand the organization. Due to the difficulty of getting time with executives given their busy schedules, it is particularly important to do the research necessary before meeting with these people. In the introduction to JAD techniques in Chapter 2, several methods for researching the current state of the business information systems were suggested. In addition to these methods, general business analysis techniques can be used to analyze the health of the business and determine where help might be needed. Without obtaining an MBA, there are several techniques a computer analyst can learn to analyze business health. For example, the last 10 or 12 quarterly financial statements can provide very interesting information about the state of the business. Front-line and functional managers should also have insight into the state of the business that can provide crucial knowledge that will enable a better executive interview and JAD session. The front-line people who are actually performing the business processes on a daily basis also have key knowledge as to what is working and not working. Interviewing both managers and performers will help the warehouse designer understand the business better and conduct better interviews and JAD sessions. An example of team composition for the first high-level JAD session is shown in Table 3-1.

We have mentioned several times the need to bring information technology systems and infrastructure into alignment with the business. In the world of data warehousing, this is done by building a data warehouse that answers the needs of the business user and provides a high return on investment (ROI). Another way to state the answer is that data warehouses should be built in subject areas that provide the best ROI to the business. The way to discover the different subject areas and those with the best ROI is to perform executive interviews and joint application development sessions with upper management. Because the goal of the sessions is an understanding of and agreement to the locations of the business pain and opportunities that must be seized, upper management and senior executives

Table 3-1 Example of team composition of first enterprise warehouse JAD session to identify subject areas to match business direction, strategy, and profitability

Title	JAD Role	Skills
Vice president–Sales	Potential sponsor	Business domain expert
Vice president–human resources	Potential sponsor	Business domain expert
Vice president–manufacturing	Potential sponsor	Business domain expert
Vice president–finance	Potential sponsor	Business domain expert
Vice president–R&D	Potential sponsor	Business domain expert
Line of business functional manager(s)	Business user(s)	Domain expert
JAD facilitator	Business user	Domain expert
JAD scribe		
Project manager	IT team	Project management
Corporate data architect	IT team	IT knowledge

must be in attendance. Because a single executive can have a very important perspective that no other person has, it is critically important that all members of management who are stakeholders in the project be present. It is possible and frequently the case that the input from a single executive will change the course of a project. If all the stakeholders will not be present at the business analysis JAD session, the JAD session should be rescheduled to a time when management stakeholders can be present. The users in the trenches typically do not have this strategic view, but they do have a very important view of the everyday operation of the organization. The initial JAD session is to identify the possible subject areas and interactions between subject areas.

During the need analysis, the various subject areas will be identified. As defined previously, a subject area is a distinct information area associated with a thing or process of interest to the business. Different business users will propose how information can enable them to move the business to do new things. In some cases, the users will be in agreement that a certain subject area is the most important, and in other cases the users will be in disagreement about the subject area that is most important. In the cases where it is difficult to gain consensus and no clear business motivation is apparent, it is important to stress that construction of the other subject areas will follow the initial one in a brief period of time.

If the goal of the data warehouse is to create the giant database in the sky that will answer all questions, why is it necessary to select the order in which it is constructed? While the goal of the data warehouse is to create a unified database for reporting and decision making, it takes a long time to get there. While moving toward that goal, it is important to provide incremental value to the business. No business will pour money into a data warehouse construction project and wait 10 years for the result. By constructing the data warehouse subject area by subject area and then linking the subject areas together, it is possible to provide incremental value to the business while moving toward the concept and reality of a giant unified database. Thus, the reason to carefully prioritize the subject areas of the data warehouse is to provide the best information value to the business while making sure that the project will be successful.

Once the initial subject areas have been identified, more JAD sessions will be conducted with the stakeholders of these areas. These JAD sessions will amplify and clarify the ideas set forth in the original, executive-level JAD session. When the details are added to the original outline of the subject area, it is necessary to have people at the JAD session who understand not only the strategic purpose of the warehouse but who understand the day-to-day impact and implications of the decision support system proposed. For this reason, it is important to have end users present at subject area JAD sessions. The initial need analysis steps of building an enterprise data warehouse from the top down are:

1. Conduct executive interviews.
2. Hold an executive JAD session to identify needs, subject areas, interdependencies, and ROI.

3. Hold JAD sessions to develop subject areas.
4. Develop a high-level enterprise data model.

During the JAD sessions, it is frequently difficult to get users to think in new and novel ways to the solutions of problems they have already faced and solved without the aid of a decision support system. Many users will be used to making their decisions based on predetermined or canned reports. In many cases, users will have gotten into a rut of thinking about the business in terms of the dimensions of analysis on the existing reports. For users who are accustomed to this type of information, it is really difficult to imagine new ways of making decisions. In this case, it is very helpful to have a consultant involved in the JAD session who is very familiar with the industry and can propose new ways of solving problems. An outside consultant can bring a set of experiences to the JAD session that executives in the company do not have. These new ways of solving problems can be related to the topics that are most important to the business executives at the meeting.

It is possible to construct the warehouse from the bottom up, but the information needed to correctly follow this path is similar to that needed to construct the warehouse from the top down. It is necessary to identify the needs, subject areas, interdependencies, and ROI. In the case of construction from the bottom up, relatively small departmental data stores and multidimensional data stores can be constructed first. The project is "back filled" with an actual data warehouse. Other physical architectures for the data warehouse system are possible. These various approaches to the physical construction of the data warehouse are be examined in detail in Chapter 9.

As an example of the selection process to which it is easy to relate, let's look at a chemical product manufacturing company. The major organizational areas of this company are:

- Research and development
- Manufacturing
- Sales
- Marketing
- Finance
- Human resources

Sales were divided into two parts: industrial and retail. The sales process for each area was very different. Also, while some manufacturing companies' R&D departments use a data warehouse to investigate yields as a function of process parameters, this company had no such interest. Other organizations' marketing departments track sales by purchaser demographics, but this organization sold the product through traditional retail channels and did not have this information. The effect of advertising on sales was interesting to the company management. The financial operations of the organization were straightforward and driven by sales success. The interesting human resources issue was compensation of the sales force as a function of actual sales. Finally, the manufacturing part of the organization was very interested in sales because it helped the scheduling of the manufacturing process. In summary, all parts of the organization were interested in and driven by the sale of product. Industrial sales were smaller than retail sales and more predictable. Thus, a retail sales data warehouse was the first subject area of interest. All other areas would connect and leverage from the sales data warehouse.

At this stage in the process, the link between the different data warehouse subject areas will start to become apparent. Using the example above, sale of product is key to the entire organization. Sales drive the scheduling of the manufacturing process and the purchase of raw material. Careful quantification of sales also helps the marketing department analyze its effort. The human resources problem of correct compensation of the sales force is aided by careful measurement of sales. Thus, information about sales drives much of the information need in the organization. These linkages between different subject areas of the data warehouse for the example company mentioned above are illustrated in Figure 3-2.

It is also very important that users of the warehouse in the business area being considered have routinely used computers to analyze data and are relatively computer literate. Although it is possible to train the end users to be computer literate while deploying a data warehouse, it is really a lot to ask of both the business user community and the IT training group. The much more successful approach would be to deploy a pilot data warehouse with a group of business users who are more computer literate and have skills in the computer analysis of data. These experienced business unit users will become the champions and trainers for future deployment of subject areas of the data warehouse.

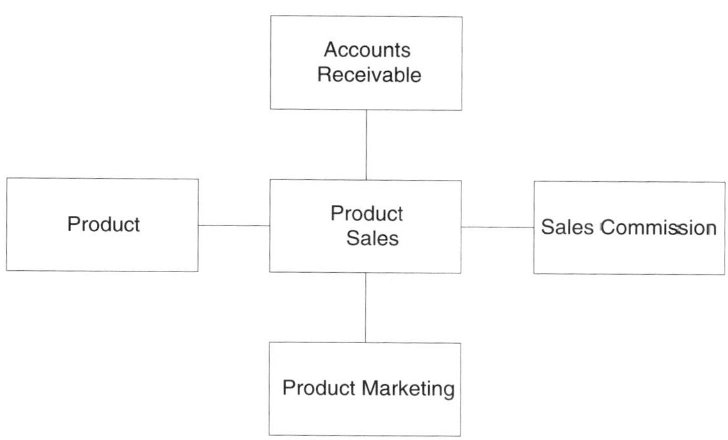

Figure 3-2 Linkages of entities in the data warehouse.

Return-on-investment analysis is certainly not the only method of selecting the subject area where the first or next data warehouse should be constructed. There are times when a competitor is using information in a way that must be countered with information. In this case, building a data warehouse will simply be the ante to stay in the game. In other cases, building a data warehouse will totally change the nature of how the business is operated. The data warehouse provides the information to surprise the competition by moving the competitive battle to a new location. Business leaders would rather define a method of attracting and keeping customers than let the competition do it for them. The organization can thus be responsible for projecting its own future rather than responding to the actions of the competition. It is a lot more fun to be a business leader than a business follower.

A way to help the analysis process for the selection of a data warehouse is to create a gap assessment. This gap assessment analyzes current business conditions, desired future business conditions, and the gap between the two. The gaps in the business must be addressed before successful deployment of the production data warehouse. Very large gaps might be another indicator of projects that are impossible or unlikely to be successful as initial data warehouse projects. The business gaps will be corrected by changes in organizational processes. Other gaps will be changed by the use of warehouse information.

Another key piece of information that must be determined is how committed the organization is to a particular subject area. For a data warehouse to be successful, it must be constructed for a stable part of the organization that has a long-term commitment to the warehouse. At times, the organization will appear to have a critical need for information, but the need is only transitory. Once the current firefighting exercise has passed, the organization will no longer have this desperate need for information. In these cases of temporary information need, the need for information may be solved through more traditional report generation. This will avoid the costly construction of a warehouse in an area of the business that does not have a long-term commitment.

For a data warehouse to be successful, it must be able to provide information that will lead to quantifiable results. These results must be part of a solution to a present business problem. The most desirable situation is when a warehouse can provide information to solve a critically important business problem. In this case, the warehouse will have visibility in the organization and be positioned to solve a problem. This will help justify the cost of the data warehouse by connecting the measurable results to the business problem.

One way to measure the commitment of the organization is by examining the commitment of the business executive who is sponsoring the data warehouse. If the warehouse does not have a business sponsor, it has a very small chance of success. The successful data warehouse project must not only have the commitment of financial resources from a business sponsor, but the sponsor is also the organizational champion for the warehouse. The sponsor will help steer the project through the maze of political difficulties that always come with projects that promise change. The sponsor has the organizational knowledge necessary to make sure a warehouse is constructed that will provide the right information and avoid major political problems.

In summary, a data warehouse project must have a total, long-term commitment from the business unit and business leaders to be successful. If this commitment is not available, the data warehouse will probably not be successful. This will happen due not only to a shortage of fiscal support but also to a lack of thought support. The data warehouse must also provide a solution to a critical business need that justifies its costs. This implies that the ROI must be calculated carefully and realistically. The business and technological gaps that must be diminished while creating the data warehouse must not be too large, or the data warehouse might not make it off the launching pad. Of all these factors, a total long-term commitment from the organizational leaders is the most important.

3.3 IT READINESS EVALUATION

Continuing our discussion of the factors that affect the selection of the first data warehouse subject area or areas to be constructed, it is important to consider the ability of the IT department to support the subject areas under consideration by the business. The selection of a project to be constructed may seem obvious given the output from the business needs analysis. The reader might think that the first project that should be constructed is the project with the highest ROI. Unfortunately, the selection of the first project must be a careful trade-off between the IS department's ability to implement the project and the benefit to the enterprise. In other words, the enterprise's business leaders may want a data warehouse around, but the information systems department may not have the operational system readiness that is necessary to implement the project. The key questions for the IT department are:

- Does the data exist?
- Is the data "clean"?
- Is the data understood?
- Will the IT architecture support the data warehouse?
- How many data sources are needed?
- How many users will there be?
- How much data will be moved into the warehouse?
- How good are the local and wide area networks?
- Does the IT department have previous DSS experience?
- Does the IT department have previous open-system experience?

There are times when a business that wants a data warehouse must have data that does not exist. For example, the business executives may want to construct a data warehouse in the subject area of point of sales, but the point-of-sales operational system might not have the necessary information. Some point-of-sales systems maintain only summary-level information. The existence of only summary data would be why IT preparedness would not score well for this subject area. In this case, the operational system would have to be updated to provide the data needed for the data warehouse.

In many cases, legacy systems have certain features that make it difficult to use the data in a warehouse. In many cases, early systems did not have extensive edit checks, and incorrect data was frequently entered into the system. In other cases, the system, and thus the coding values, changed over time. In still other cases, the values changed over time and weren't well documented. People who understood the codes have moved on, leaving no one in the IT organization who understands the data. The presence of several data sources with different unique record identifiers can be particularly challenging. The problem of data and information quality is addressed in depth in Chapter 7.

A large number of users will stress almost every part of the IT environment. A large number of users will tax both the CPU and the network. A large number of users increases the chances finding of bugs and odd cases in the software. A large number of new users to the data warehouse will cause a large increase in the call volume to the help desk. This increased number of calls generally indicates an increase in all aspects of end-user support. One way to help mitigate these factors is through comprehensive training of the user community.

It is critically important to understand that the selection of the first subject area and the user requirements of the subject area can have a huge architectural impact. Some projects require a frequent warehouse data load, the load of a very large amount of information, a multidimensional database, data mining tools, or an operational data store. Frequent data warehouse data loads will tax both the source and receiving systems. Cleansing, loading, and indexing large amounts of data provide an opportunity for the discovery of features in the data, hardware, or software that no one else has discovered. A multidimensional database, data mining tools, or an operational data store can stymie the technical staff if they have not worked with these technologies before. If the IT department does not have experience with these architectural structures, it will be very challenging to learn them while building a data warehouse. Loading large amounts of data can be a challenge not only in the amount of CPU resource that is required, but the process can also be challenging to the network.

In summary, true data warehouse projects are very large projects that should be approached with caution. Previous decision support experiences in the IT organization that can be brought to a data warehouse project will greatly increase the chance of success. Data warehouse construction and operation will stress all parts of the IT infrastructure as few other projects can. It is very important that every component of hardware, software, data, and process be well understood before wandering into a data warehouse project.

3.4 PROJECT SELECTION

The selection of a project to be constructed may seem obvious given the output from a business needs analysis. The reader might think that the first project that should be constructed is the project that has the highest ROI. Actually, selection of the first project must be a careful trade-off between the IS departments ability to implement the project and the benefit to the enterprise. In other words, the enterprise's business leaders may want a data warehouse around, but the information systems department may not have the operational system readiness that is necessary to implement the project.

The first executive JAD session identified all of the subject areas for the business, and the executives probably developed some consensus as to the first warehouse subject area that should be constructed based on ROI. Why don't we just pick that subject area and proceed with detailed analysis, subject area JAD sessions, pilot, and production?

At times, the ROI may be exaggerated. An executive eager to have a data warehouse supply information for his or her area may do this so as to be the first to have a data warehouse. A corporate financial analyst who is not tied to a particular business area can be beneficial at this time. The financial analyst can provide an unbiased view of the return on investment the enterprise will receive from a data warehouse. The financial analyst will act as an auditor to make sure that all factors have been properly taken into account in calculation of the ROI. They will help the business make correct decisions about the proper subject area and help keep the IT department out of trouble by not trying to deliver a warehouse subject area with unreasonable expectations.

Project selection is also a political process. Subject area A might be the most profitable, but subject area B is under the control of a person who has greater political influence or has not received the support of the organization that he or she should have received. In these cases it is not uncommon for a data warehouse subject area to be selected and a data warehouse to be constructed for a part of the business that does not make the most financial sense at first glance. In these cases, the selection of a data warehouse subject area is made on the basis of important organizational considerations. Although it is more difficult to quantify these types of decisions, they can be every bit as important as the ones based on financial reasoning alone. The JAD sessions with the business leaders don't always sort out this, or business sponsorship correctly.

As mentioned Section 3.3, the level of preparedness of the IT department can also influence the selection of subject areas for the initial or follow-on data warehouse subject areas. In many cases, a data warehouse will be an organization's first venture in the world of open systems. This new platform requires a considerable amount of training. While in the middle of learning a new operating environment is not the best time to take on a very large data warehouse project, it has been done and done well. An easier option that usually leads to better success is to start with a smaller data warehouse and tackle the larger ones later, once the initial learning curve has been climbed and success established.

One way to help the analysis process for the selection of a data warehouse is to create a gap assessment. The gap assessment analyzes current conditions, desired future conditions, the gap between the two, and a plan to close the gaps. The gaps must be addressed before successful deployment of the production data warehouse. Very large gaps might be another indicator of projects that are impossible or unlikely to be successful as initial data warehouse projects. A gap assessment may cause important factors to be expressed in words that would otherwise be missed.

The most analytical approach to the selection of the subject area is to enter the appropriate factors into a table and compute the overall score for the different subject areas. The score for each factor is weighted by some amount that gives credit to the importance of that factor to the selection process. As an example, business sponsorship should have greater weight than user attitude. A scheme for determining the scores and weights for the various factors should be agreed to before the subject selection process begins. This will prevent the score card from being altered to change the outcome after a favorite subject area loses the competition. An example scoring table with weights is shown in Figure 3-3. The subject area with the highest score is typically selected for implementation. Other subject areas generally follow in order of score. Because the business environment and competitive factors change over time, it is a good idea to recalculate the scores before starting the next project. If this matrix can be developed during the JAD session, it will help develop consensus and a feeling of ownership with the participants.

CATEGORY	WEIGHT	A1 POINTS	A1 TOTAL	A2 POINTS	A2 TOTAL
Business Sponsorship					
Data Source Knowledge					
Solves Business Problem					
Measurable Results					
Dat Extract Experience					
Number of Users					
Commitment					
Data Size					
User Ability					
Politics					
DSS Experience					
Network					

Figure 3-3 Matrix for the selection of subject area A1 or A2.

3.5 WAREHOUSE CONCEPTUAL ARCHITECTURE

In much the same way that the architecture of a building starts with high-level site drawings and works its way down to greater and greater detail, the architecture of the data warehouse starts with the high-level architecture and works its way-down to levels of greater detail. The starting point for warehouse architecture is the conceptual architecture. The conceptual architecture is expanded and clarified through the logical physical architectures. Each layer of the warehouse architecture provides an increasing level of detail. This increasing level of detail with the various layers of the architecture is illustrated in Figure 3-4. Although the various layers of the architecture actually form a continuum, lines are drawn between the layers in the figure. Although we examine these concepts in depth in Chapter 8, this section will serve as an introduction to these concepts.

Traditionally, IT application architectures have been developed from the bottom up. IT application architectures were developed by starting with a set of low-level technology recommendations and business requirements. Without an overarching architectural framework, application architectures were siloed and not able to leverage the data and technology between each other. The architecture of each application was very closely aligned with the function of the application and was not generally applicable. Applications did not share common underlying technology. The resulting applications were narrowly defined and technologically centric. This resulted in applications that were inflexible, costly, and difficult to maintain.

A better way to develop IT application architectures is a top-down, principle-based approach with layers of abstraction or tiers in the architectural description. The principle-centered, top-down approach will lead to architecture that is more flexible, less costly, easier to maintain, and can be leveraged between applications.

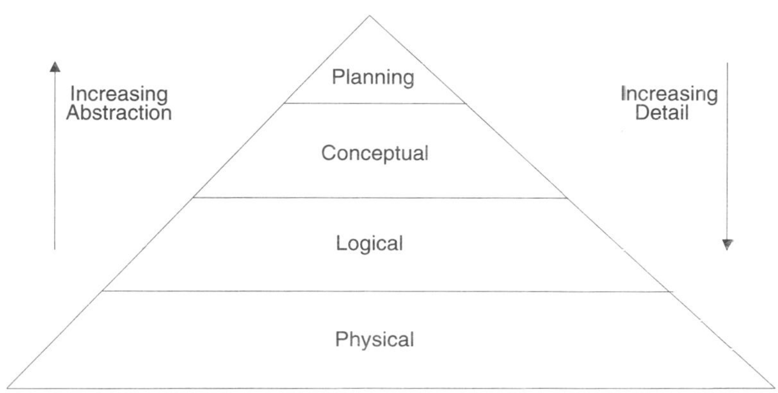

Figure 3-4 Layers of abstraction of the IT architecture.

The overall IT architecture must include both a technology architecture and data architecture. This definition of an IT application architecture is one of the pieces of the complete ITSM strategy. This definition of the organization's desired IT architecture, best practices, standards, and preferred vendors greatly increases the ability to leverage technology and data between applications. It also reduces the total cost to the organization for maintenance of the solution. This notion of the leveraged reuse of architectural complements is illustrated in Figure 3-5.

The best place to start the construction of the architecture for a data warehouse project is to examine any previous documents that exist that specify the information system architecture (ISA) or IT master plan for the organization. These documents will contain specifications of architectural standards for the entire organization. For a data warehouse to fit into the overarching IT structure, it must integrate into the IT structure of the rest of the organization. To do this, the data warehouse should follow the information system architecture or IT master plan. Significant deviations of the data warehouse architecture from the information system architecture or IT master plan should be selected carefully and the impact of these deviations well understood.

In situations where an information system architecture IT master plan does not exist or these plans do not cover the data warehouse, the data warehouse architecture must be developed from scratch. The purpose of the warehouse conceptual architecture is to understand the functions and processes that must occur to build, maintain, and use the data warehouse. The H-P approach to the design of the data warehouse conceptual architecture is a principle-based one. This means that the design of a conceptual architecture starts with the selection and agreement to a set of principles that should guide the design of the data warehouse conceptual architecture. To select a set of architectural principles, it is best for the IT team to start by agreeing to the set of principles that will guide the

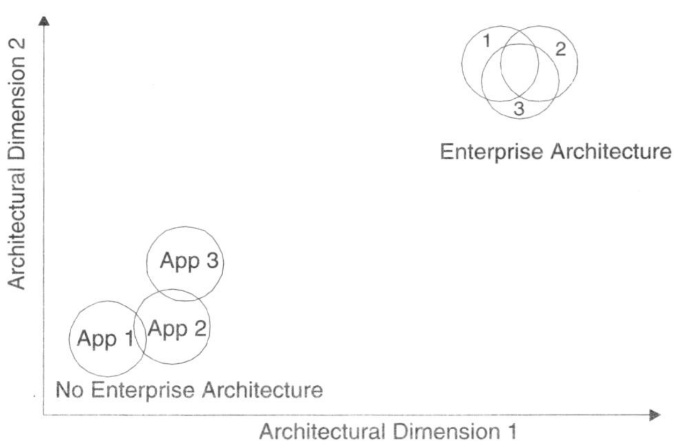

Figure 3-5 An enterprise architecture helps the reuse of architectural components in different applications.

development of the architectural principles. These principles about principles are called *metaprinciples*. These will help the team understand the purpose of principles for the principle-based architecture. The data warehouse metaprinciples and principle-based architecture must be globally applicable to all business units and geographys. Because the notion of principle-based architecture is new to many people, it is important for the IT team to understand and carefully derive the principles and hence the architecture.

The conceptual principles of the data warehouse are divided into groups. These groups cover particular aspects of the data warehouse. There is also a set of architectural principles that are generally applicable. These data warehouse general principles are derived from Inmon's definition of the data warehouse, JAD principles, RAD principles, and data architecture best practices. Because the data warehouse loads data operational sources, there should be a set of principles that specify how data is obtained. One such principle is that the data warehouse is not updated, only refreshed. Once data has been loaded into the data warehouse, there must be a set of principles to guide the query and presentation process. Some users will create a subset of the data warehouse for their own use or the use of their working group. There must be a principle that guides the creation maintenance of these working stores. Because of the importance of understanding and describing the data in the warehouse, there must be a set of principles that describe the creation, use, and management of metadata. There must be principles that guide scalability. Finally, there must be a set of principles that specify how the warehouse is managed.

While different warehouse practitioners will have different groupings of architectural principles, the principles listed above are at least a minimal set. This basic set of principles can be expanded upon, depending on the situation. In the summary, the major groupings of principles are:

- General principles
- Data principles
- Query principles
- Working store principles
- Metadata principles
- Scalability principles
- Warehouse management principles

The architecture itself is usually divided into three parts. These parts are the access architecture, the data architecture, and technology architecture. The access architecture is centered on how data from to the warehouse is made available to the end user. The data architecture is a description of the structure and life cycle of warehouse data. The technology architecture is a description of the technology details of the warehouse and how the data warehouse interacts with legacy systems and existing technologies.

Once the definition and purpose of the data warehouse as given in Chapter 1 and the principles given above are accepted, there is not much room for variability at the highest level of the architecture. This high-level conceptual architecture is shown in Figure 3-6. When the architecture is expanded in greater detail and the goals and needs of the organization are included, the architectures of different organizations will become distinct. While the high-level conceptual architecture remains fixed over time, the warehouse logical and physical architecture will change as the warehouse and enterprise evolve. Part of the solution will be planned for the growth of the data warehouse, part of the evolution will be due to changes in technology, and the rest of the evolution will be caused by changes and growth in the enterprise.

A very high level conceptual architecture was shown initially in Chapter 1. It is illustrative to compare the brief description of the principles given above with the conceptual architecture. This high-level architecture is repeated in Figure 3-6. The left side of the figure illustrates the loading of raw and metadata from the operational data sources. The general and data principles cover this part of the high-level architecture. For instance, the warehouse is traditionally updated by the source systems, and user queries actually stop at the warehouse. The right side of the drawing illustrates a query coming from the information customer, through the presentation application, to the information customer. The center portion of the drawing illustrates the metadata principles through the interactions of the source, design, user, and warehouse systems. Working store, metadata, and management principles are not easily seen in this high-level architecture.

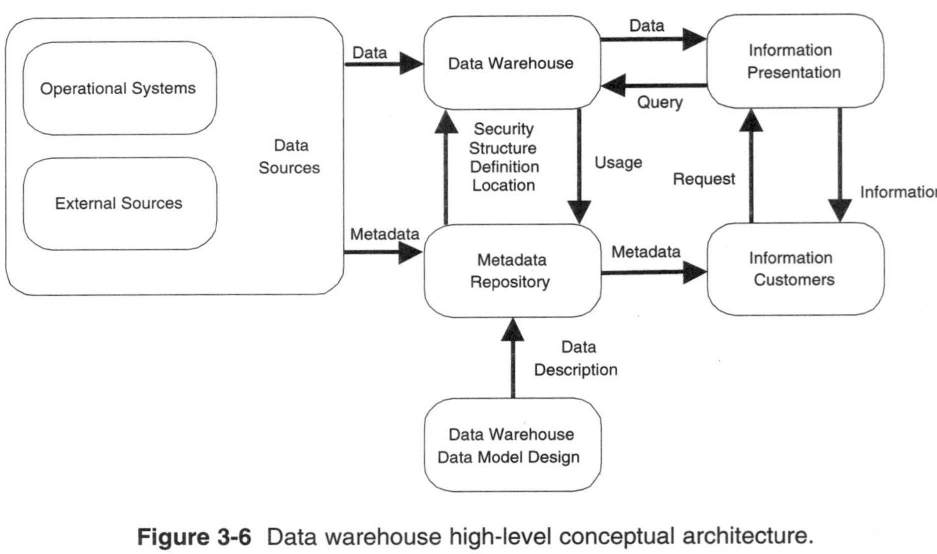

Figure 3-6 Data warehouse high-level conceptual architecture.

There are a number of ways to design and deploy the conceptual, logical, and physical architecture of the data warehouse. If five different data warehouse experts were asked to give a detailed operational definition of the data warehouse, five different definitions would probably be given. This implies that there are significant differences of opinion as to the design of the data warehouse. There are also a number of different physical structures that have different operational characteristics but can all be considered to be a data warehouse under the definition of the data warehouse given by Inmon and repeated in Chapter 1.

As an example, data marts and data warehouse have very similar conceptual, logical, and physical architecture. Data marts are different than data warehouses in that they contain fewer subject areas, have less time history, and have fewer users. The term *semantic complexity* is frequently used to indicate the number of subject areas in the data warehouse. In other words, the data warehouse with the numerous subject areas has a high semantic complexity. Using the distinction just given between data marts and data warehouses, the data warehouse has a higher semantic complexity than a data mart. Because a data warehouse has more history, finer granularity, and more subject areas to do analysis, it is also more analytically complex than a data mart. In other words, there is nothing sacred about the architecture of the data warehouse. The important part is to meet the needs of the organization, minimize cost, and provide the information needed by the organizations.

Why are we discussing semantic and analytic complexity? Doesn't the warehouse conceptual architecture and data warehouse definition keep us well constrained to a solution? While this may seem true at first glance, hardware and software costs combined with physical limitations will guide us to a solution for the logical and physical architecture. As an example, the data warehouse depicted in the conceptual architecture may be very difficult to implement in real life. For very large data warehouses with a large number of users, it is difficult to give end users direct access to the data warehouse and still maintain query performance. Users typically only need access to a single subject area, and the introduction of a data mart will give the users access to the data they need without saturating the source of the cleansed and rationalized data. Designing the data warehouse architecture will be an iterative process that will include changes in the logical and physical layers as the architecture is refined.

The interesting question is: What is in the data warehouse box that stores the operational system extracts and responds to requests for information? This could be the giant database, it could be single or multiple subject areas stored in one or multiple databases, it could be multiple subject area databases logically integrated through the query process, or it could be an intermediate data store that populates subject area databases. All of these structures would provide a subject-oriented, integrated, time-variant, and nonvolatile data source for management decision making.

The four data warehouse architectures that consultants at Hewlett-Packard recommend are the monolithic warehouse, the standard data archive, virtually integrated data marts, and the extract coordinated or semantically integrated data marts. Each of these four data warehouse architectures requires further explanation, and this will be done in the following paragraphs.

The *monolithic warehouse* includes what is sometimes called the *business data warehouse* or *intermediate data store* by consultants. The purpose of this warehouse is to store the set of all the operational data that is available. The data in this warehouse has undergone some cleansing and transformation, but it is still a normalized and atomic data store and thus is not designed for decision support queries. From the business data warehouse, further extracts are made to populate the business information warehouse, which are then used to populate data marts that users access. This type of data warehouse is a very large undertaking with a lot of redundancy and data, hardware, and software, and thus is only recommended to very large organizations with large IT staff and specific needs for this type of structure. It can be recommended to other slightly smaller organizations in modified form. Because the structure can satisfy the needs of all users in an organization, it can be classified as enterprise data warehouse architecture.

The intermediate data store architecture of the data warehouse creates a standard data archive or intermediate data that represents semantic integration of the legacy operational systems. This persistent data store is then used to populate the data marts that are the sources of information for end-user queries. The data architecture of the intermediate data store is optimized for further data extracts; it is not optimized for data warehouse queries. In some cases, a central data warehouse could be placed between the intermediate data store and the data marts. This would be used to process queries that cannot be answered by the data marts. This type of structure can certainly be classified as enterprise warehouse architecture.

At the other end of the architecture spectrum from the monolithic warehouse is what some data warehouse consultants call a *semantically integrated* collection of data marts. This architecture is an improvement over unplanned decision support systems in that the numerous redundant extracts have been replaced by a carefully designed group of data extract programs. These data extract programs are developed through the use of a high-level operational and decision support data model. This high-level data model of the enterprise decision support and operational system needs to make it possible to design a single-set data extract program to populate the data marts. The data marts used to satisfy user queries. While this architecture will satisfy the needs of most decentralized organizations, it is difficult to move this type of data warehouse architecture to an enterprise structure.

An improvement on semantically integrated data marts is to use the query management tool to virtually integrate the data marts. This tool makes it appear to the end user that the queries are running against a single large data store. The query management tool hides the complexity and location of the data to the end user. Once again this architecture will satisfy the needs of most decentralized organizations, but it is somewhat difficult to move this data warehouse architecture to an enterprise structure.

The type of data warehouse architecture that will be recommended to an organization depends upon the goals of the data warehouse for that organization, the size of the organization, and the size of the organization's IT department. As an example, a relatively small business with limited IT resources will find that semantically integrated data marts satisfy most of the organization's decision support needs. On the other hand, a very large organization that depends upon data almost is much as its products or services might select a monolithic data warehouse to support its needs.

3.6 WAREHOUSE LOGICAL ARCHITECTURE

The warehouse logical architecture uses architectural principles to map the structures that were defined in the conceptual architecture to the real world of available software, processes, and architectures. While the high-level, conceptual architecture shown in Figure 3-6 will hold true for data warehouse architectures in general, the logical architecture starts to reflect principles, values, and decisions that the organization has made. In very simple cases, this is a selection or design of software, business processes, and IT processes that becomes an instantiation of the warehouse architecture. For example, Platinum Technologies might be a strategic supplier of information technologies to the organization. In this case, Platinum InfoPump would be an excellent choice for a data extraction and cleansing tool. Similarly, Platinum Repository might be the metadata repository selection that would meet organizational standards. For the first iteration of the warehouse, the users will be learning a lot about ad hoc queries, so an easy-to-use tool is important. It may also be an organizational requirement to have a Web interface. Brio Tools provides both a powerful and easy-to-use tool that has a Web component. This proposed architecture is shown in Figure 3-7. A logical architecture as simple as the one shown in Figure 3-7 would typically be either for a single subject area or for a very large monolithic warehouse.

Once an architecture has been proposed, it can be compared against the principles of the architecture that have been developed. Deficiencies in a proposed architecture must be rectified before the architecture is implemented. Some deficiencies will be caused by the fact that the state of the art in information technologies is frequently not as developed as the theory. Although usually not the case, some deficiencies in logical architecture will be caused by an "overprincipled" conceptual architecture. At times, the author has been involved in the review of principle-based architectures in which one or more of the principles were not attainable in real life. It is most often the case that the logical architecture needs to be corrected to meet the principles of the architecture. In any case, JAD techniques can be used to develop and modify the logical architecture. Once the logical architecture is complete, the logical architecture can be mapped to a physical architecture.

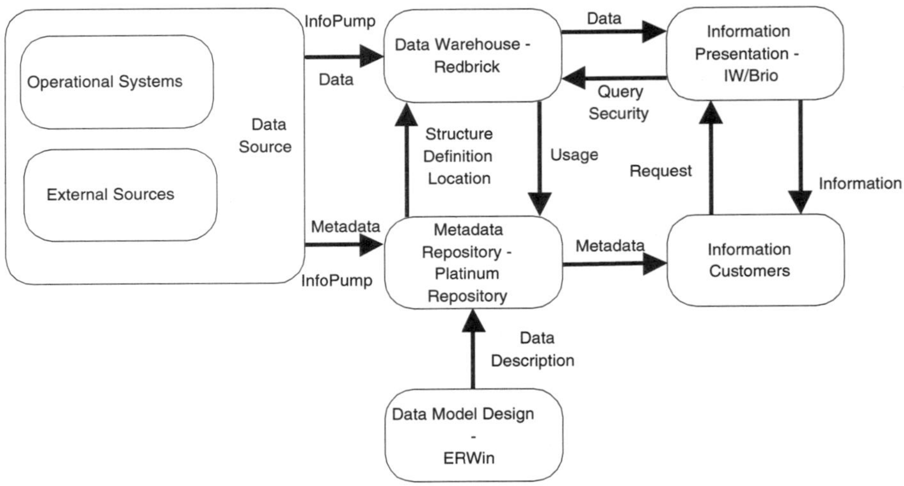

Figure 3-7 Simple logical data warehouse architecture.

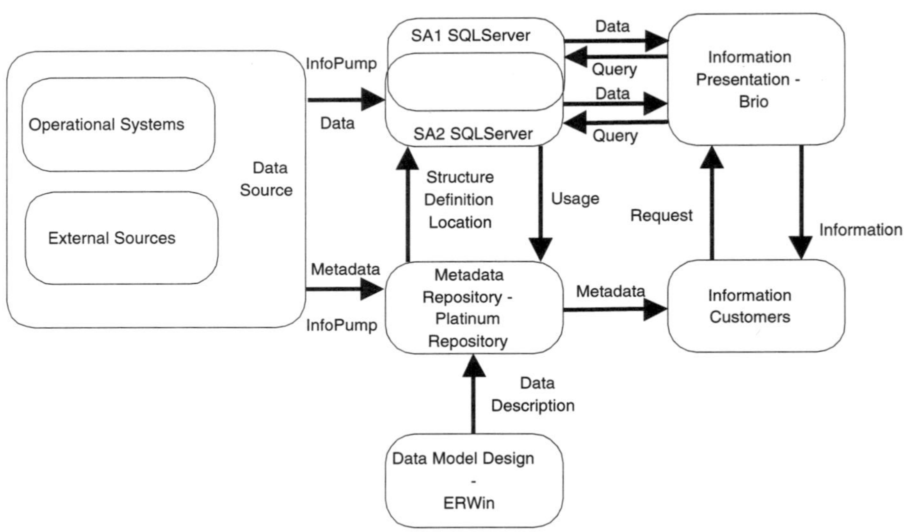

Figure 3-8 Logical architecture for semantically integrated data marts.

It is important to remember that the logical architecture is something that will evolve over time with the data warehouse and the organization. In some cases, the organization will impose new requirements on the data warehouse. While the business requirements generally do not change the warehouse conceptual architecture, these changes frequently affect the warehouse conceptual architecture. In other cases, the IT department will make changes based on warehouse requirements, performance, or manageability. As the feature sets of available data warehouse products change, it is only natural that the warehouse logical architectural also change. It is best to plan for these changes in the architecture and accept rather than resist them.

The four data warehouse architectures that were discussed in Section 3.5 have logical architecture implications. These implications affect primarily the data extract, data warehouse storage, and query portion of the data warehouse architecture. As an example, the semantically integrated group of data marts will have an extract program that feeds each data mart. Each data mart will have a separate physical data store, and the data marts will be queried by the user as individual data stores. In this case, Microsoft SQL server might be selected as the data mart database for the individual data marts. Figure 3-7 has been revised to reflect the changes to semantically integrated data marts, and these changes are shown in Figure 3-8.

3.7 WAREHOUSE PHYSICAL ARCHITECTURE

The physical architecture uses architectural principles to map the logical architecture to hardware. At this level of the architecture, the processes are mapped to hardware, networks designed, processing loads balanced, and physical storage designed. It is possible from the physical architecture to simulate the behavior of the system to user loads. The physical architecture is to a data warehouse what construction drawings are to the construction of a house. The physical architecture defines in great detail the construction and interrelationships of hardware, software, and users. The physical architecture should include a build diagram that actually shows details including how the equipment is racked and the cabling between the equipment. Other parts of the build documentation will include data layout on the hard disk to optimize performance and expected bandwidth usage and allocation on the network.

The warehouse physical architecture will evolve over time as the data warehouse grows and as the conceptual and logical architectures evolve. Much of this evolution will be planned. For example, as an enterprise data warehouse grows into the multiterabyte range, it is usually necessary to use multiple database servers and parallel database features. This is a natural evolution of the data warehouse. As the data warehouse grows and the organization develops some history as to data warehouse usage, it is common to build a departmental or personal data store for certain users. This will move the warehouse data closer to those using the data to make decisions.

The four data warehouse architectures that were described in Section 3.4 all have different physical architectures. Each architecture must have a physical architecture designed to optimize performance, maintainability, and implementation costs. These physical architecture design decisions have implications on everything from network and user workstations to database design and hard disk usage. These physical design decisions are the focus of Chapter 9.

As an example of one of the items in a physical architecture, the server hardware configuration for a medium-sized data warehouse is shown in Figure 3-9.

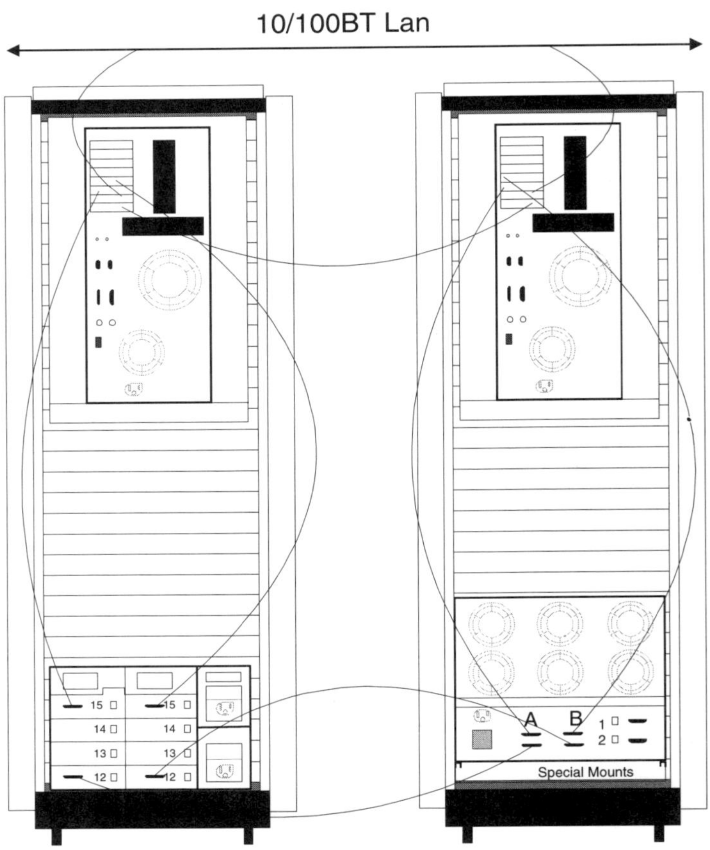

Figure 3-9 Server configuration for a small but highly available data warehouse.

This figure illustrates a design decision. The decision was made to have redundant compute servers with one server acting as the query engine and the other acting as a database server under normal operations. During a hardware failure of one of the servers, all operations would be transferred to the remaining server, and the warehouse would remain available at reduced capacity. This creates a highly available data warehouse server configuration.

3.8 DATA ARCHITECTURE

The point of executive interviews is to determine what the executives want from a data warehouse. The data warehouse data architecture will be designed to supply this information. This is a piece in the puzzle of aligning the IT organization with the business. Just like the hardware architecture, there are several layers of detail or abstraction to the data architecture. Starting with the planning of the decision support data architecture, each lower layer in the data architecture provides more technical detail and specificity. While the technology foundation of the data warehouse is clearly not as important as providing the business information, it is obviously important to provide the information in a timely and relevant way. A proper data architecture is key to meeting this objective.

We have noted many times in the book thus far that the data architecture of an operational system is considerably different from the data architecture of a decision support system. The various warehouse architectures discussed in Section 3.5 of this chapter all had different ways of migrating data from the operational system to the warehouse. Planning and controlling the migration of data from legacy systems to the decision support structure become more difficult as the number of legacy sources and DSS subject areas grow. The various architectures are best suited to meet this challenge under different organizational and IT situations.

A good place to start to understand the data architecture challenge is to understand the relationships between the different pieces of the total IT architecture, shown in Figure 3-10. The four pieces illustrated are the operational system hardware architecture, decision support hardware architecture, operational system data architecture, and decision support data architecture. This illustration can be thought of as the view looking down on a pyramid from directly above. The various layers of the pyramid represent the different levels of design abstraction in the IT information architecture. The different layers of the pyramid represent the planning, conceptual, logical, and physical layers of the architecture.

The sides of the pyramid are arranged to show the parts of the IT architecture that are most closely associated. As an example, the hardware for the operational and decision support systems is probably more similar and shares more items in common than the hardware shares with the data architecture. The decision support data architecture will have elements that were originally defined in the operational data architecture. Thus, the operational and decision support architectures have much in common and share an edge of the pyramid. The operational data is hosted on the operational hardware, and the decision support data is hosted on the DSS hardware. This is the reason for their adjacent locations on the pyramid.

What does this architectural pyramid have to do with anything? The starting point for the design of the data warehouse hardware will usually be the existing hardware standards for the operational systems. Similarly, the starting point in the design of the data architecture for the decision support systems will be the data architecture of the operational system. This is illustrated in Figure 3-10.

While the starting point for the DSS data architecture will be the operational data architecture, the decision support or data warehouse architecture will be tuned for query performance, not update performance. This conversion of data from operational to decision support is the purpose of the warehouse system. The data warehouse system must be carefully designed to transform data from the

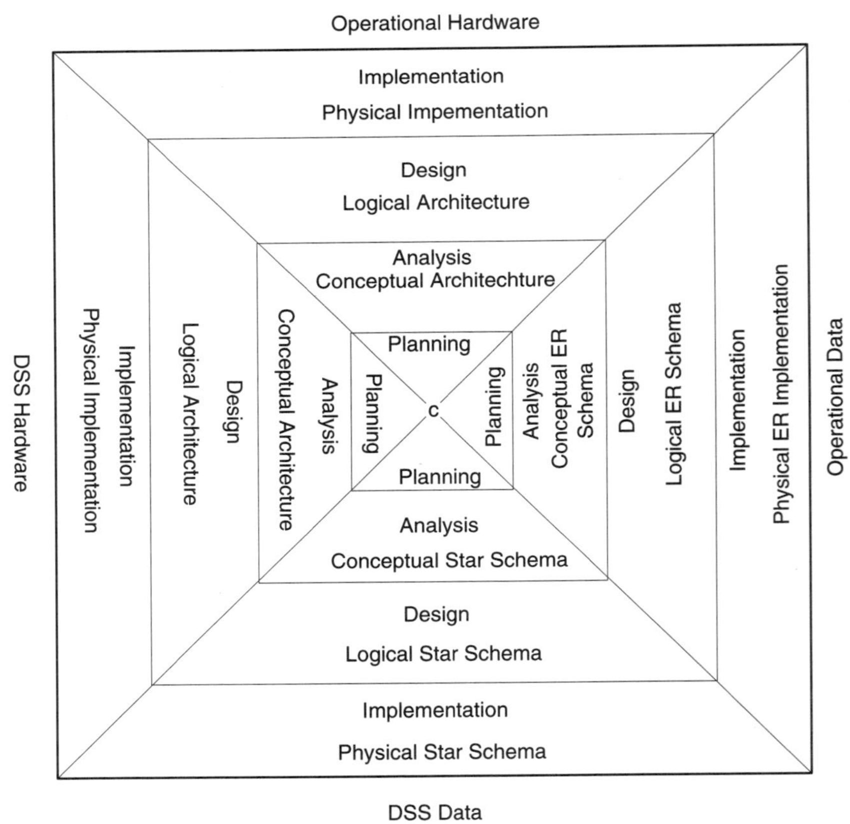

Figure 3-10 The various faces of information system architecture.

operational systems to the decision support systems in a reliable and accountable way. Stated in the simplest of terms, the data warehouse converts operation data from normalized entity-relationship or flat file data silos of unmatched or conflicting data into a star schema format of rationalized and cleansed data that is easy for a person to query. The operational systems are tuned to put data into the system rapidly and assure that it is not redundant, and the decision support system is designed to find data in the system rapidly and to report it.

To this end of being able to find data rapidly, the decision support data is structured in a different manner. While the data in the operational system is designed to minimize the size of the data that is stored, the DSS system actually denormalizes the data and increases the size of the stored data to provide better query response. In this structure, usually referred to as a *star schema structure*, the data details of the business subject area are placed in a central table called a *fact table*, which contains the facts that will be queried to answer business questions. Other tables, called *reference tables*, are connected to the central fact table to provide details about the items on the fact table. This structure is called a star schema because it consists of a central fact table with reference tables connected to it like arms of a star.

At this point the reader is probably wondering: "What is so difficult about taking data from the operational systems and loading it into the data warehouse? It should be a piece of cake. All you have to do is get the data and load it." Many data warehouse projects have failed by taking this approach. The first difficulty in this approach underestimates the problems of data quality: the lack of a unique identifier, and the nonuniform use of field codes. The next problem is that in order to design the star schema model to answer the business questions, you must interview the business executives to discover what questions the data warehouse is to answer. This layer of the data architecture, which is the design to provide the answers to the business, is the conceptual layer of the data warehouse. This layer typically is used to communicate with the business leaders and IT community.

If the data in the data warehouse is not architected properly, the physical size of the warehouse could easily be 20 to 50 percent larger than it needs to be. The next layer in the data architecture is the logical architecture, whose purpose is to define in detail the structure of the star schema. This layer of the data architecture will include any changes that are necessary to the conceptual architecture to structure the data better. As an example, it is possible for the conceptual architecture to have several subject areas that are connected and look more like a snowflake than a star. Any many-to-many relationships that were in the conceptual model should be resolved in the logical model. Data types should be specified at this layer. This layer of the data architecture should also contain a mapping of fields from the operational systems to the decision support system.

The physical layer of the architecture includes all the details necessary to locate the data on storage. This will include things like physical partitioning and key identification. Restructuring of the database to improve performance or maintainability will occur at the physical layer.

Once again, the design of the decision support data architecture does not seem like rocket science. Indeed, anyone familiar with the design of an OLTP system has performed technical tasks like the ones necessary to construct a data warehouse data architecture. Experience is a good teacher for many things in life, and many of the skills needed to build an enterprise data warehouse are enough different from OLTP design that the inexperienced data warehouse designer or implementer will probably make several mistakes on the first few projects. It is important to add extra time and money in the project schedule to account for this.

Another key component to the enterprise data architecture is a high-level data model that shows the operational systems, decision support systems, the links within each data model, and the links between the two. Development of this type of data model starts with an analysis of the operational systems. The model only needs to be developed in enough depth to design the DSS data architecture. Part of the development of the high-level enterprise data model should be a data and information quality improvement project like the one outlined in Chapter 7. This will help identify the definitions of the data fields that will be loaded into the data warehouse. It is impossible to develop the high-level enterprise data model that will guide the data extraction process without a firm understanding of the definitions of the data fields and their interrelationships.

3.9 IMPLEMENTATION

The implementation approach that we introduced as the method of choice in Chapter 1 is the rapid application development approach. In Chapter 1, rapid application development was closely tied to spiral development. While spiral development is frequently associated with a rapid application development approach, it is certainly not the only way to use RAD techniques to develop and deploy a data warehouse. Rapid development is actually a statement of best practices for software development. True rapid development is the appropriate use of all the correct factors that speed software development. This includes everything from project scope selection and control through project management to proper testing and deployment. What is generally recommended is not all-out rapid development, but what the author would call best schedule-biased efficient development. Unless some other distinction is made, the author will use the term *rapid application development* to mean best schedule-biased efficient development.

For running most businesses, including software organizations, the four key components, pillars, or dimensions to success are people, process, technology, and strategy. Rapid development of applications has the pillars of people, process, product, and technology. This is illustrated in the now familiar four-pillar diagram shown in Figure 3-11. Numerous studies have shown that people are the most important component of a software development project. Process refers to both project management and methodology. Product is what we are trying to develop.

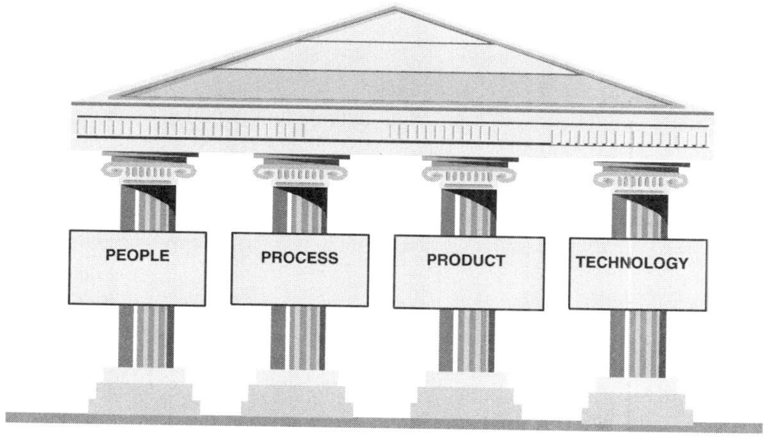

Figure 3-11 Four pillars of software development.

The product is the most quantifiable of the four pillars. Technology is a description of the tools and products that we use to create the data warehouse.

One important aspect of the successful development of the data warehouse is avoiding making the same mistakes that caused other software and data warehousing projects to fail. These failures can be categorized into the four areas that also cause success: people, process, technology, and product. Factors with people who contribute to failure in data warehouse projects are such things as destroyed morale, unskilled personnel, office hygiene, or no stakeholder support. Examples of problems with process that lead to failure are optimistic schedules, poor project risk management, bad design, and bad planning. Examples of product problems that cause difficulty or failure are poor feature selection and scope creep. Examples of technology failures are a hardware platform that doesn't scale well or a network that doesn't support the bandwidth demanded of knowledge workers using a data warehouse.

Another key feature to a successful data warehouse or software development is risk identification and control. Every data warehouse project is different and has its own unique set of challenges and risks. Identifying the risks in each project is the first step in managing the risk. The next step is prioritizing the risk. Once the list has been prioritized, risk control can be done and effort assigned based on the prioritization. Because the risks change at different stages of the development life cycle, it is important to reprioritize the risk on a regular basis. Risk factors are discussed in detail later in the book.

The major point of the data warehouse pilot project will be to demonstrate the benefits of a data warehouse and prove to doubters that this type of decision support system will help align IT with the business and provide useful business information. As mentioned in Section 3.1, it is important to stick with the basics. During a pilot project is not the time to become a technology evangelist. The critical success factors for the project should be business oriented and well defined. These factors will help the data warehouse team stay focused on the objectives. Most data warehouse pilot projects have at least two critical success factors. The first critical success factor is to ensure that the IT group and the business group are mutually successful. For different business groups to be successful, they must be willing to share their ideas and data with the rest of the organization. They must also be willing to place value on the interpretation of information and not on the control of data. Data must be shared across an organization to provide a unified view of the organization. This means better information access for all warehouse users. This leads to better alignment of the business with its IT department.

A second critical success factor it is to strike a balance between business and technology issues. The pilot data warehouse will usually be challenged by a set of problems that are both technical and business oriented. The sponsor of the data warehouse is usually a senior line of business managers. These managers will be interested in the demonstration of easy access to information. At the same time, the information technology group will be interested in seeing a very large database perform well. These requirements must be included in the pilot for it to be a success.

It will be the job of the data warehouse project manager to identify all major issues that might affect the pilot project negatively and minimize the risks appropriately. Many of these risks are not unique to data warehouse projects. Experienced project managers should have seen similar risks and challenges with OLTP application development. The data warehouse pilot project is a learning experience for everyone, and even experienced project managers who are new to data warehousing will experience an opportunity to learn new things.

During the development of the data warehouse, there are many occasions when consultants can be very efficient and cost competitive. If it is the organization's first attempt at a data warehouse, it can greatly increase the efficiency of the total team to hire an external project manager or data warehouse lead architect. An external consultant can be an unbiased arbitrator involved in everything from subject area selection to end-user tool selection. An ideal consulting team will have experience with data warehousing in the subject area being discussed and will provide business consulting expertise where the organization does not have the necessary experience. In addition to general business and project consulting, consultants can provide specific skills or recommendations on tools or techniques that are new to the organization. For example, it might be important to use a consultant to give specific recommendations on the RAD technique best suited to the organization and project.

Once the pilot has demonstrated the feasibility and usefulness of the data warehouse, it is important to start the process of JAD sessions to identify the feature that should be in the production warehouse. The purpose of this new round of JAD sessions is to identify any changes that need to be made to the pilot before moving to production in addition to identifying the charter, scope, and critical success factors for the production system. In other words, the output of the pilot is the start of the production system, but some midcourse corrections are made between the pilot and production systems. The pilot is not a disposable system but is part of the evolutionary development of the data warehouse. An iteration of the project will add functionality, reduce risk, increase the number of users, and increase the size of the warehouse. This different view of the spiral development life cycle is shown in Figure 3-12. The enterprise warehouse is developed through the development of many such projects.

The life cycle for the development of the data warehouse does need to match the life cycle for deployment. A data warehouse can be deployed in a fashion that looks closer to a waterfall life cycle. This is done by waiting for an iteration or two of the development cycle to complete successfully before deploying the data warehouse to any users. At that point, the functionality of the warehouse will be well developed. The difficulty of this approach is that there is a lot of talk in the form of JAD sessions without much delivered. The user community has a tendency to get frustrated with the lack of progress, and a worthwhile product was produced and is available in the meantime. One way to keep at least some of users happy while not spending time deploying the product to a large number of users is to allow a select group of users access to the warehouse on a limited basis. This not only provides valuable feedback but also provides additional quality testing.

There are many alternative life cycles that can be used to develop a data warehouse. The traditional spiral model that is proposed as the standard in this book can be modified in many ways. After the first few spiral iterations, the requirements and risks are better understood. The development can switch to a waterfall at that point. For example, evolutionary prototyping can be used to develop the warehouse if the customer has a difficult time stating the objectives at the start. The difficulty with this project and approach is that a clear business justification is probably missing and it is difficult to determine when the project will be over. The life cycle that is the most effective for any particular organization will depend on the organization and the project.

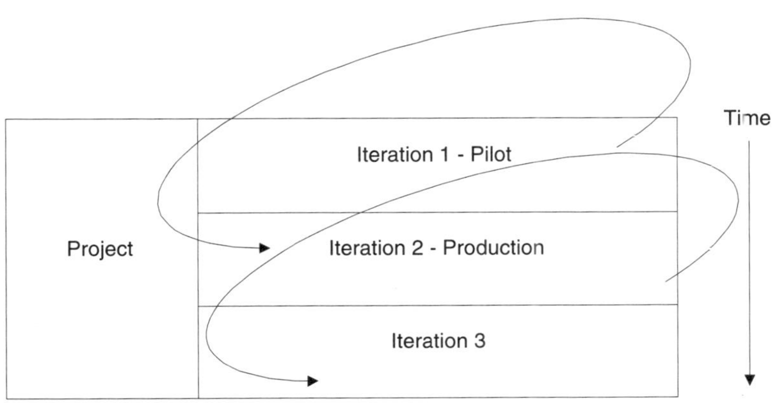

Figure 3-12 Iterative development of the data warehouse project.

In summary, the development techniques must match the warehouse project and the organization. Also, the needs of the organization and project will change over time. It is important to modify the approach as needs change.

QUESTIONS

3.1 Suppose that the CFO is the sponsor of a data warehouse project. You are leading the IS team that will deliver the data warehouse solution. You have a JAD session scheduled with the CFO and the senior business VPs of the company. The purpose of the JAD is to discover the information that the data warehouse must deliver to the business. A week before the scheduled time for the JAD session, the CFO telephones you with the news that he will be unable to attend and suggests that you proceed without him. Should you continue with the JAD session or reschedule? Why? Why not?

3.2 Information from the warehouse can be fed back to the operational systems. This "closes the loop" in the flow of information. How does this closed loop change the conceptual architecture? This question can best be answered through both a word explanation and drawing a new architecture diagram.

3.3 Information from the warehouse can be fed back to the operational systems. This "closes the loop" in the flow of information. How does this closed loop change the logical architecture?

3.4 Information from the warehouse can be fed back to the operational systems. This "closes the loop" in the flow of information. How does this closed loop change the physical architecture?

3.5 In this chapter, we introduced the terms *semantically integrated* and *analytically complex*. Define these terms in your own words.

3.6 Assume that you are asked to build a data warehouse to analyze the sale of products at you local grocery store. You are to construct a system to analyze the sale of all items in a shopping cart or basket. This is frequently called *market basket analysis*. The point of this analysis is to obtain an understanding of product sales and products sell together. How semantically and analytically complex would this system be?

3.7 You are asked to build a data warehouse to analyze the demographics (income, home size, home location, hobbies, etc.) of customers for your products. This warehouse should be able to supply information about the stores that sold particular products to particular people in defined demographic groups. How semantically and analytically complex is this data warehouse?

3.8 Suppose that you are asked to build a data mart for the analysis of sales of goods that have a week-long marketing campaign. To do this, you must have information about the total quantity of selected items sold the week before, during, and after the marketing campaign. How semantically and analytically complex is this data mart?

3.9 Explain in as much detail as you can the different ways that a data warehouse can challenge an IT infrastructure.

PROJECTS

3.10 We all get calls from a number of long-distance telephone companies trying to get us to sign up for their service. We could design a data warehouse that would help a telemarketer target specific services to specific customers. This is frequently called *relationship marketing*. A business would study the habits of its customers and try to offer goods or services that match what the customer might need. What type of data would we need to gather to do relationship marketing to purchasers of long-distance services? What type of information would we provide? Use whatever you know about data organization to design a database at the conceptual level that will track the necessary information.

3.11 You are now the administrator of a hospital or clinic. What information would you need to track diagnosis codes, the procedures and treatments for that diagnosis, and the cost of those procedures and treatments? This can be used to analyze the success rates of procedures for a diagnosis or the cost versus the insurance reimbursement.

3.12 You are now the manager of a large supermarket. What type of data would you need to match promotions to items that an individual consumer is likely to purchase? How would you connect the person purchasing the items to the cash register transaction?

3.13 This project is an extension of Project 3-12. You are still the manager of a large supermarket. In addition to tracking products sold, you suspect that you have sales on items at the same time that would naturally sell together anyway. Use whatever you know about data organization to design a database at the conceptual level that will track the necessary information.

3.14 Recall that call behavior analysis is the analysis of the phone calls that a traditional phone or long-distance customer might make. The switch that routes the call gathers the information. This information will include the number of the phone originating the call, the phone number of the receiver of the call, and how long the call lasted. The newer switches, called SS7 switches, can capture other information, such as calls that are not completed because of a busy signal. Create a conceptual architecture IT architecture to capture this information at a central location for analysis by the marketing department.

3.15 Use whatever you know about data organization to design a database at the conceptual level that will track the necessary information for the call behavior analysis data warehouse.

3.16 The network that actually connects a telephone call is a very expensive and valuable resource. Planning for network expansion is a very important task due to lost revenue if telephone calls don't go through or the increased cost if the network is too large in the wrong location.

3.17 Manufacturing organizations can use a data warehouse to track the compliance of their suppliers to their agreements. The agreements normally cover at a minimum the delivery timing of products and product quality. The manufacturing organization does this to increase quality and reduce the cost of having too much inventory. Other technologies, such as electronic data interchange (EDI), allow the manufacturing company and its suppliers to exchange information orders for parts and deliveries of parts electronically. Your task is to design a conceptual IT architecture to support this endeavor.

3.18 Design a data warehouse conceptual data architecture to track vendor compliance of component delivery times and quality for the last project (Project 3-17).

3.19 Recall that financial organizations can use a data warehouse to analyze the risk of consumer and certain other scenarios. This data warehouse can use data such as demographic data or payment history data to determine the risk of the loan. This enables the financial institution to estimate and manage the risk.

3.20 Most college and university IT needs can be broken into academic and administrative. Design a logical architecture for a college or university that takes both of these needs into account. Most of the administrative needs are for OLTP applications, e-mail, and Web access. The academic needs range from e-mail and Web access to compilers. Given this high-level description, please create a high-level conceptual IT architecture.

3.21 Airlines can analyze the travel trends of their frequent fliers in different demographic groups. This information can be used to target-market frequent fliers in the correct market groups. The demographic data is usually obtained from external sources. Your task is to design a conceptual IT architecture to support this endeavor.

3.22 Airlines can use a data warehouse to track the season variations and growth expected in travel between locations. This warehouse could also track how much food and beverages are consumed on different flights. This will help the airline select aircraft and catering to match needs. Your task is to design a conceptual IT architecture to support this endeavor.

3.23 Assume that you are asked to build a data warehouse to analyze the sale of products at your local grocery store. You are to construct a system to analyze the sale of all items in a shopping cart or basket. This is frequently called *market basket analysis*. The point of this analysis is to obtain an understanding of product sales and products sold together. Design the IT architecture for this system from point-of-sale system to data warehouse.

3.24 Assume that you are asked to build a data warehouse to analyze the sale of products at your local grocery store, as described in Project 3.23. What data would you need to do this?

4

Project Selection and Scope

4.1 INTRODUCTION

Until this point in our development of a methodology for data warehouse construction, the focus has been on understanding the big picture of the data warehouse. The development thus far has been designed to draw a picture of the data warehouse landscape in similar detail to what a landscape artist might be able to draw of the landscape from an airplane flying at 10,000 meters. From this altitude it is easy to see the location of the mountains and the rivers, but it is hard to see the leaves on the tress. Now that we have drawn a map with the location of the large features, it is time to start examining the data warehouse landscape in detail.

The data warehouse is to help bring alignment between the business and the business's IT department. To this end, the technique of joint applications development, or JAD, is used foster dialogue between those who need the information and those who are developing the systems that will provide the information. The JAD process begins with doing research to understand the situation of the business and the business's IT resources. The next step is to interview the business executives to determine their needs, vision for the business, and direction of the business. This executive interview process is the focus of Section 4.2.

After the executive interviews have gathered data about the general needs of the business, it is time to get very specific. This is done through the JAD session. General techniques of the conduct of JAD sessions were discussed in Chapter 2, but in Section 4.3 we go into detail and give some specific examples. These examples should serve to illustrate the selection of a subject area and gathering of requirements for the data warehouse.

Once a subject area has been selected and the requirements are gathered, it is necessary to determine:

- Scope of the project
- Scope of the pilot
- Schedule
- Risks
- Development life cycle
- Deployment life cycle
- Required skills
- Staffing

Once these factors have been determined, it is possible to estimate the size of the project and plan accordingly.

4.2 BUSINESS REQUIREMENTS DISCOVERY: EXECUTIVE INTERVIEWS

The first phase of the joint application development process is the executive interview. The purpose of the management interviews is to obtain the perspective of what management wants from the project. This must be done not only for the initial JAD session that will identify the individual subject areas, but also at the start of the JAD process for the individual subject areas. These management interviews should be done before the rest of the research for the project is done. In other words, it is impossible to analyze the system that is to be designed if the system remains undefined. The requirements for the new system will be gathered through management interviews. The management interview will establish the scope and purpose for the project. The management interview also aids the JAD facilitator in understanding the project and enough detail to select the JAD team. While speaking with the management team, it is important to get dates when the managers will be free to participate in the JAD session. This will enable the JAD facilitator to better schedule the session.

The management interviews will not only assist the JAD facilitator in the correct selection of project scope and objectives, but will also give the management team an opportunity to modify the entire approach. It is important to change the direction of the project as early is possible. Late changes of project direction or scope kill morale and are very costly in terms of project rework. Thus, it is imperative that the JAD facilitator understand management's objectives and goals for the project before the JAD session.

Some JAD facilitators find it useful to use forms. Although usually simple in nature, forms do help the JAD facilitator organize their thoughts. At a minimum, the forms should cover the basic information that must be gathered from management. This would be:

- Project charter
- Purpose of the project
- Scope of the project
- Management objectives
- Constraints
- Assumptions
- Business processes affected
- Resource requirements

The first thing to do in preparation for any management interview is to decide the objective of the interview. Some management interviews will be targeted at obtaining in-depth business goals and alignment, process, and constraints details. This is particularly true of interviews conducted near the start of a data warehouse project. Later in the project, the purpose of a management interview may be to give information such as a status update to management. The fundamental point is to define the objectives for the meeting and have a meeting plan in mind. If the facilitator gets confused or stymied during the meeting because of any number of unusual things that can happen, the best thing to do is try to obtain a second meeting at a later date. This will give the interviewer time to regroup and continue the interview later. Given the difficulty in obtaining management time, this should only be done as a last resort.

After the list of people who will be interviewed has been developed, it is time to start preparing for the interviews. We now know whom we are interviewing and what we want to learn from each of them, so it is possible to start planning each interview. Although it is not possible to write a script that will cover the interview, it is a good idea to create an outline of the anticipated interview. This can be called the *interview plan.* Once the outline has been created, it should the reviewed to see if there is anything that the interviewees should bring to the meeting. User documents, reports, or screen captures might help the interview. The interviewees should be sent an e-mail or voice mail message asking them to bring these with them to the interview. For example, the author usually asks the interviewees to bring their five favorite reports.

It is very important to meet with the proper people. Only the proper levels of management will have the necessary insight into the business to set the project charter, scope, and direction. The first set of management interviews are designed together with the requirements for the enterprise data warehouse. Subsequent interviews, if needed, will identify the requirements for each warehouse subject area. As the enterprise warehouse project progresses, it will be necessary to interview people who have detailed working knowledge of the business. In this case, it is important to interview the workers in the trenches. As the interviews progress, other people will probably be named during the interview process as those who understand certain aspects of the organizations operations. These people can be interviewed later.

Sometimes it is possible to meet with, and interview, small groups of people. The group should be small, no larger than four or five people, and its members should have similar organizational interests, performance, and position in the organization. Everyone in the group should have the same perspective on the organization. Never combine managers with those they manage. The people in the trenches might not be willing to discuss how unproductive they are within the current system, and the managers might not be willing to discuss planned reorganization that will affect the knowledge workers' jobs.

The best place to interview people is in their own work environments. Because we are trying to gather information from these people, the information we're trying to gather might be in their office or cubicle. In addition, most people become slightly on edge while being interviewed. People generally are more creative and share better information when they are relaxed. Holding the interview on their own turf will help them to be more relaxed and share information more freely. In some cases, questions will arise that require people to look something up that is in their office. In this case, already being in their office will greatly increase the speed at which the person being interviewed can find the answer. For interviews of groups of people, the interview should take place near where the people work. This will help make the people in the group feel at home and allow them easy access to their office for necessary information. The fundamental point is to keep the people being interviewed comfortable and give them access to their information.

Another reason to interview people in their offices is to see their work environment firsthand. If the people you are interviewing are looking through stacks of printed reports to enter data into a spreadsheet, you will probably want to find out what information they are trying to create in the spreadsheet. If there are stacks of paper reports around that do not look used, you will probably want to find out why this is. It is also important to note the type of computer equipment that is available to knowledge workers. Although this information should be available from IT asset management and configuration management reports, there is nothing like seeing the configuration and environment firsthand. In any case, it is as important for the JAD facilitator or warehouse project manager to see the physical and technical environment the knowledge workers are in as it is for a detective to visit a crime scene.

The way to start the interview will be different, depending on the interviewer's relationship with the people being interviewed. To many people not in the IT part of the organization, the IT personnel are viewed as agents of change who can either automate and eliminate jobs or create IT systems that make work harder for everyone. If the interviewer does not have a personal relationship with the person being interviewed, he or she must start from the beginning. If the interview is starting from the beginning, it is important to explain to the interviewee the JAD process and the interviewer's role with the project. A good starting point for a data warehouse project is to explain that we are attempting to build a very large database that can be used to create reports that span the organization. It is important to emphasize that this will result in better information being delivered to them at their request.

Once the ice has been broken, the interviewer can delve into the specific questions. The exact questions to ask will come with experience and an understanding of what pieces of information must be gleaned from which users. Remember, this should have been developed in outline form during development of the interview plan. Although the list of potential questions is endless, here are some sample questions:

- What significant problems are there in the business?
- What significant problems are there in this business area?
- What activities does your business area carry out?
- How did the data warehouse project start?
- What would happen if the data warehouse were not built?
- Who will use the information from the data warehouse?
- What other areas of your organization will be directly affected by the data warehouse?
- What other areas of your organization will be indirectly affected by the data warehouse?

In Chapter 2 it was pointed out that the progression of the interview or JAD session was from problem to solution to information that aided dissolution. There are questions that the interviewer really does not want to ask during the interviews. For instance, it is generally not a good idea to start out with the questions such as "What information do you want?" Managers are generally very clear about problems and possible solutions. It is important to focus the question on problems, possible solutions, and then information that will help the solution. While the distinction between the two approaches may seem inconsequential, there really is a very large change in mind set between the two.

As an example of how not to work from information into a design, the author once took the approach of showing a small group being interviewed each of their reports in succession. As the report was shown, the author would ask the group if they needed that report. The answer was always "Yes." The difficulty with this approach is that the problems and solutions have not been defined. The group did not know what was needed to implement a solution to a problem.

Given this lack of knowledge, every report might be useful, so it was appropriate to ask for all of them. Even if the problems and solutions have been identified, it is probably important to ask the group to place some value on the reports. A type of bidding process helps sort the important reports from the more trivial ones. If we start by telling the group they each have an imaginary $1000 to spend buying reports they need, and the minimum bid forces them not to select all the reports, the most important reports can be selected by noting those that receive the highest sum of bids.

Although it may seem obvious, it is important to take notes. After the interviews are complete, the management team will expect an accurate and thorough account of the interviews. Frequently, some subtleties will come out in the interview, and it is imperative to document these subtleties. While you will probably remember exactly what was stated five minutes after the interview, the situation becomes a lot less clear a month later. The notes will give the interviewer the necessary record of the interview. Taking notes during the interview not only provides a thorough documentation of what was said for use later, it also provides the interviewer with information to look back on during the interview.

Another valuable technique is something called active listing. The good interviewer will repeat what they have heard stated slightly differently. This provides an opportunity for the interviewer to make sure that what they thought they heard is what the person intended to say. This will eliminate many of the common errors of understanding. The experienced interviewer will restate things with phrases like: "What you are saying is..." or "In other words...." When you restate what you have heard, you give the person being interviewed the opportunity to correct any errors or misunderstandings.

The notes from the interview are used to create a management definition guide. If the management definition guide can be delivered within a week or so of the interviews, it is a good idea to call those who have been interviewed once they should have received their copy of the management definition guide. This provides a great opportunity to thank the managers for their time and see if there are any errors or omissions in the management definition guide. If it will take longer than this to produce the management definition guide, it is important to call those who have been interviewed and thank them for their time. You will also usually have a few additional questions that the management team might be willing to answer while you are talking with them on the telephone.

Once the management definition guide has been approved by management and distributed, we are ready to move ahead with the JAD sessions. The management definition guide will be the starting point for the JAD sessions. It will state what management wants from the project and the data warehouse. It is the written statement of management perspective, purpose, scope, and objectives for the project. It will state both strategic and tactical direction and management's commitment to the project. The process that creates this document and the document itself are important to the alignment of IT with the organization.

4.3 BUSINESS REQUIREMENTS DEFINITION: JAD SESSIONS

The overview of the JAD technique that was given in Chapter 2 was very general. The general techniques given there could be used to conduct a JAD session about anything from donut making to launching the space shuttle. Given that we are building a data warehouse, there are some specific questions that should be asked of the JAD participants. As was introduced in Chapter 2, the general flow of the questioning is:

- What problems are there in your business or business area today?
- If you had a data warehouse of the kind we described, what questions could you answer that you can't today?
- If you had a data warehouse of the kind we described today, what decisions could you make or make better that you cannot make today?
- What products or services could you offer that you can not offer today?

At this point in the meeting, a list of 20 to 30 problems, questions, and decisions will have been documented. What do we do about this wish list? We must develop a plan to maintain focus by reducing the number of questions and decisions. Thus, the next great question to ask is: "What are the criteria that should be used to decide the most important business problems and questions that must be answered by the data warehouse?" The question will generally lead to a suggestion of 10 to 20 things that should be the top priorities of the business. The group is asked to vote on the three or four items that should be the most important, starting with the problems. Once the problems have been voted on and a winner selected, we move on to questions. Every person at the meeting gets three or four votes. The top candidates of the voting are used to reduce the selection of questions and decisions by having the participants use the selected priorities to vote for their favorite questions and decisions.

Now that we know the questions and decisions the organization would like to make, it is time to develop the data models that support the questions. "What data do you need from the data warehouse to answer these questions and support these decisions?" is an excellent way to move into the data modeling part of the JAD session. The questions that the JAD participants proposed usually point to the facts and dimensions of analysis that are important to the user community. The facts, dimensions, and attributes of the data warehouse will be identified in this process. In Chapter 5 we develop the concepts of data modeling further.

Another useful thing to do is have the JAD session attendees bring their favorite reports to the meeting. The reports that are in support of the selected questions and decisions are used to develop the canned reports for the data warehouse. This is an opportunity to discover missing elements in the data design because all of the data on the reports should have been identified in the previous

JAD question. As an example, the VP of sales might bring her favorite set of reports that show sales by store, region, product, and salesperson.

The last question the author typically asks in a data warehouse design JAD session is: "If the data warehouse that has been designed is available, what business processes can be done differently?" This will generally lead to a very interesting discussion of business process reengineering. It is also another opportunity to examine what data is needed and the format of needed data to support the business process reengineering effort. This is another opportunity to discover missing elements in the data design.

At this point, there exists a good description of the data warehouse. It is important to gather some information that will help in the design of the data warehouse technology and infrastructure. Some of these questions will be answered by the IT staff, and other questions will be answered by the business users. While there is no substitute for skill and experience with data warehouse construction to guide the questions, some of the questions that are typically asked are:

- How many users will there be in six months?
- How many users will there be in three years?
- Is the business likely to change in ways that would affect the data warehouse?
- At a minimum, how many weeks or months of data must be available to answer the question?
- How valuable is more data history? Why?
- What type of summary information do you use weekly? monthly? quarterly?
- What should we expect the size of the data warehouse database to be two and four years from now?

The questions about the changing nature of the business over time extract valuable information about the need for scalability and adaptability in the warehouse. Few things hurt the credibility of the IT group as much as creating a system that is not flexible enough to change as the business changes. The appropriate questioning about the similar changes the business will go through over the next few years helps build a system that will grow with the organization.

Before you close the JAD session, there are a number of expectations that must be set and administrative details to settle. For instance, the distribution list for the final JAD document must be developed. This is usually done by having a rough draft of the distribution list prepared before the JAD session. A transparency of this list can be placed on the screen near the end of the JAD session. The list should contain the names of the people to receive the document, the number of copies to be sent, and any other administrator information, such as address or mail stop for the recipient. The people who will receive the document must also know the process for reviewing, final editing, and accepting the final document.

The best way to accept changes to the document is for all of the JAD session participants to meet to recommend and agree upon the changes. The final document is usually accompanied by an approval form. There should be consensus developed as to the people who must sign the approval form. The project sponsor is always someone who must sign the approval form. It is also customary to have two or three essential business managers as signatures on the approval form in addition to an IT project manager.

The final thing the JAD facilitator should say is something in thanks to the JAD session attendants. The author typically thanks them for their enthusiasm, dedication, and productivity. It is also a great idea to remind the attendees that they should expect the document in a couple of weeks. This sets their enthusiasm and places the JAD team on a delivery deadline.

There are several very popular ways to really mess up the JAD process. The best way to mess up at JAD is not to have great business sponsorship and management commitment. While management is frequently enthusiastic at the start of the process, the real test of management commitment comes when the JAD facilitator requests management to commit 10 to 12 essential people to the process. If management is not willing to commit the necessary people for the required length of time, there is a much greater risk that the project will fail.

Another good way to mess up a JAD session is not to have all the necessary participants present at the session. There are many causes for this. One cause is failure to identify a person as necessary for the meeting. In this case, probably not enough research was done, and the person's contribution to the organization was missed. Another reason for missing a necessary participant is the failure of one of the management team to identify this important person during the interviews. Another reason for not having all of the right people there is either lack of management commitment or because these people believe that they are too busy to attend the JAD session. The stated commitment to management to the team should stress the importance of the project and the JAD sessions. If all the right people are not in the session, either the system designed will not meet the needs of everyone or the JAD facilitator will spend huge amounts of time after the session collecting the necessary information from the missing participants.

Another common problem in a JAD session is the notion that all attendees are equal. At times, it is very difficult for a senior executive to admit that the supervisor of an area might know more about that area of the business than he or she does. The job of the JAD facilitator will be to help the team clearly analyze the views, facts, and issues of the problem. The skilled JAD facilitator should be able to blunt the personality differences and expose the issues. The fact that the supervisor in the trenches with the workers may know a tremendous amount about the details of operating that part of the business is frequently difficult for a VP or director of a $100 million business to understand.

It is easy for the JAD facilitator to abdicate his or her authority to run the session. This is another fine way to have the JAD session go awry. The JAD facilitator usually sits at the level of a senior programmer analyst in the organization. It is a difficult thing to have a person at that level of the organization try to maintain authority over someone one or two levels from the CEO. The authority of the JAD session facilitator is granted by the sponsor of the project. Besides the delegated authority from the sponsor, authority is a perceived thing. The JAD facilitator who runs the session with authority will keep the authority.

There is nothing like a concrete example to help illustrate the abstract idea. The author worked with a company that manufactured products for retail sale through a variety of retail channels. Because the manufacturing company never knew who the person was who bought the product, the retail store that purchased the product for resale was considered the customer. This manufacturer not only offered products to its customer for resale but was starting to offer a set of services such as optimum store shelf arrangement, optimum stock level, and category management.

When asked to brainstorm what were the problems of the business, a long list was developed. After further development, some of the items on the list were different views of the same thing. Other items on the list were deemed transitory or already in the process of being fixed. These items were removed from the list. This resulted in a much smaller list. The smaller list was put to a vote and all participants from VP to supervisors had three votes to cast. The top five problems were:

1. We don't know how profitable we are on what we ship to customers.
2. We don't know if promotions affect sales.
3. We don't know how to optimize our manufacturing and operating efficiency.
4. We don't know how our market share has changed over time.
5. We don't know how specific products are selling.

Next, the JAD session participants were asked to list the questions to which they wanted to have answers. This started with a brainstorming session where a large number of questions were put forth. After considerable discussion, the list of questions was reduced to about 20 to 30. Some of the questions were very similar to others, and these were combined into one more general question. For example, "What is the effect of pricing on sales?" and "What is the effect of promotions on sales?" were combined into one question. Other questions were felt not to be that interesting. The list of questions was reduced to the top five through voting. The top five questions were:

1. How profitable are we on a shipment-by-shipment basis?
2. How has market share by product and category changed over time?
3. How do we improve operational efficiency?
4. What is the impact of pricing and promotions on sales?
5. What are the product sales trends?

Next, we ask the question "What decisions could you make with the data warehouse that you couldn't make without it?" Again, the session is started with brainstorming; then the ideas are condensed to four or five essential points through discussion and voting. The winners were:

1. How to curtail or extend products, promotions, and programs
2. How to improve sales and production forecast
3. How to use the sales force more productively
4. How to identify new market opportunities

Once the key points have been selected, significant support for them is usually developed. Most of the JAD participants will agree that the ideas selected will help their favorite one if their favorite one was not selected.

Finally, the question was asked, "If you had a data warehouse of the kind we described today, what products or services could you offer that you cannot offer today?" The group was very focused by this point, and the discussion quickly led to two ideas. The company could help customers select the best mix of product and amount of product to maximize profit. The company could do this not only for the products they supplied, but if they were given the data, they could do this for similar products supplied by other manufacturers. In other words, they could manage the entire category of products for the customer. Thus, two new services could be offered:

1. Management of inventory for the customer
2. Category management for the customer

The JAD session was typical in approach and results to other JAD sessions with which the author has been involved. The sessions usually start out with a lot of brainstorming and ideas. This appears to be a little chaotic at times. As the group starts building consensus and focus, the apparent orderliness and cohesiveness build. By the end of the team meeting, the majority of the team is focused and feels good about the results, but frequently a portion of the team wanted something slightly different.

4.4 SCOPING AND ESTIMATION

Before a data warehouse project is started, there must be agreement between the business sponsor and the data warehouse team as to the scope of the project. There are many ways to specify the project scope. One way is to create a project charter if this was not done during the initial executive or business requirement definition JAD sessions. If the project charter has already been created, this is a good time to review the charter and modify it as necessary to bring it into agreement with the results of the JAD sessions. The project charter document must contain specific information about what the project should accomplish and how we will know if it is successful. This should be stated in terms not of only strategic vision and goals but also measurable results. One example of the definition of success would be enabling the business user to create a specified list of reports. Another example of a measurable definition of success would be the creation of five predefined reports.

The selection of the scope of the project is by mutual agreement of the IT team and the business customers. It is important for everyone to understand that the 80-20 rule affects software projects. Eighty percent of the entire project will take 20 percent of the time to complete. If the business is willing to live with the 80 percent, it can be delivered in 20 percent of the time and budget required to complete the entire project. If the warehouse team keeps this in mind while determining the scope, the entire project will proceed much more smoothly than projects that try to create the complete, gold-plated warehouse.

There are many methods to communicate and gain agreement as to the scope of the warehouse. One method is to take the conceptual-level enterprise data model or multiple-subject-area data model and draw a circle around those entities that will be included in the first release of the warehouse. Using this circle as the starting point, it is then possible to define the types of reports and dimensional analysis that can and cannot be done if that warehouse is constructed. A related illustration is an organization chart with the part of the organization circled that is expected to be the main benefactors of the warehouse project. Again, it is important to stress that other warehouse areas will be added in rapid succession.

To perform proper planning, we must first determine the level of effort required and difficulty of the various components of the project. There are many components that go into the estimation of time and resources required to complete a project. The essential components that will go into the estimation are the factors that were discovered during the JAD session and certain IT factors, such as the staff knowledge, availability, and experience to perform the development work. The factors that should have been determined during the JAD sessions are:

- Number and type of users
- Location and number of locations of users
- Number and type of sources
- Number and type of databases source
- Number and type of data warehouse databases
- Load frequency
- Length of time available to prepare and load data
- Length of time required to prepare and load data

- Complexity of typical ad hoc queries
- Complexity of canned reports

These factors should have been discovered either during the research for the JAD session or during the JAD session itself. Most of these points were identified in the subject area selection criteria.

It is probably obvious to say that a large number of users make it much harder to develop a data warehouse than a smaller number of users. The type of users is also very important. Business analyst, marketing, or actuarial users are much more demanding than more casual information consumers in the type of data they want and the end-user tool they use. This usually increases the difficulty of the warehouse project. Another information consumer detail that increases the level of difficulty of the project is the location of the information customer. It is much easier to work with an information consumer who is down the hall than with several different groups of users in different states who have no relationship to each other on the organizational chart.

It is probably obvious to state that a single legacy system that is the source of the warehouse data is easier to manage than multiple warehouse systems. Similarly, it is easier to load one warehouse data store than to coordinate the loading of data into a data warehouse data store and multiple subject area or multidimensional database data stores. In addition, it is generally easier to extract and load on the same computer platform and database than it is to move data across platforms and databases. It is also usually easier to load 50 gigabytes of data once a month than 50 gigabytes of data everyday. If the time needed to clean, load, and index the data is expected to be long compared to the time allotted, the warehouse team must evaluate the design carefully. The author was asked to help with a data warehouse project where the initial data design caused the monthly data to load and index in three weeks. This meant that the warehouse was only available for one week a month. A change in design brought this down to 26 hours to load and index the data.

The complexity of both the typical ad hoc query and canned reports will affect the size and difficulty of construction of the data warehouse. If most of the queries use a field or two in the fact table joined to a reference table or two, life in the realm of data warehouse construction should be good. If the decision support data model has multiple fact tables joined through reference tables, the design of the data model and canned reports must be done with care and careful testing.

The warehouse development methodology that this book espouses is spiral development with time boxing to control the risk, size, and scope of the project. One important point that the data warehouse construction team should seek advice about is the idea of time boxing. This returns to the idea that it is better to receive 80 percent of what I want sooner than never receiving 100 percent of what I want. Part of the JAD session results should be a prioritized list of canned reports and amounts of data to be loaded. The information customers should understand and agree to the notion that they might not receive everything they wanted, but they will receive something of value when they were told they would receive it. Thus, scope, resources, and time required for completion are clearly interrelated quantities.

4.5 PLANNING

While data warehouse projects may not be large in the number of business processes they affect directly, they are very large in the effect on the business, in the size of the database, in the visibility of the project to the organization, and in the number of IT systems that are affected. This implies that it is very important that these projects progress smoothly and are well managed. This implies that the project must be well managed. All of the skills of the project manager will be used in the construction of the data warehouse, and every good project management practice that is deemed appropriate can be used to help the project progress smoothly.

The major components in project management are to define the project, plan the project, and manage the project. The project management methodology has a life cycle in the same manner that the development methodology has a life cycle. Most project management models are waterfall life cycles. The project management methodology will go through each step in the methodology in succession and not go back to earlier steps.

4.5.1 Define the Project

To define the project, we must define the project organization, define the project parameters, and establish the project working methods. Most of the steps to define the project were accomplished as part of the JAD process. For instance, the project sponsor who will support the project and provide a budget has been identified. The project sponsor should be the one who appoints the JAD facilitator and the project manager. The project sponsor will either identify or help identify the project core team. The core team will frequently be assigned tasks to accomplish during the development cycle. The core team will also identify other people who will contribute to the project. These people will become part of the extended team. For a very large or multinational organization, other people will be involved with the project on an advisory or review basis but will rarely attend the project meetings. These team members are virtual team members. The entire team will be organized by the project manager. This structure is shown in Figure 4-1.

The project parameters are another part of the project definition. The project parameters are also defined as part of the JAD process. The project parameters will state the objective for the project, the major deliverables, and assumptions. The project parameters should all be well developed and documented in

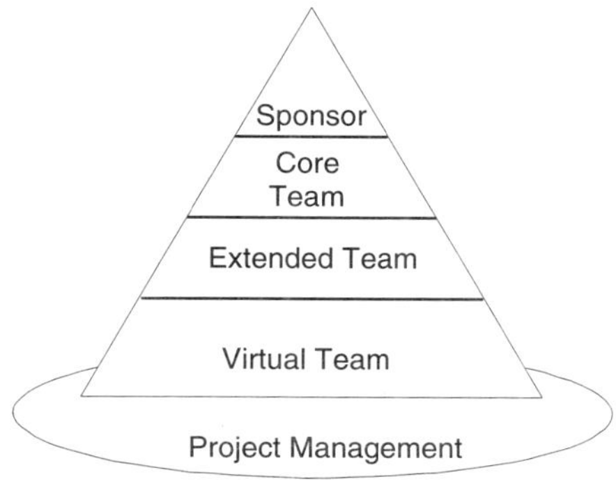

Figure 4-1 Warehouse team structure.

the management guide that was produced as part of the JAD process. The project framework will define who is responsible for developing the project plan, what the project plan includes, those involved in decision making, and so forth. This should been developed during the JAD process.

4.5.2 Plan the Project

There are many advantages to planning a project properly, most of which were espoused in Section 2.2. Some of these advantages are improved communication within the project team, reduced schedule slippage, increased quality, increased risk management, and reduced rework. Because people are the most important part of the project, the author believes that the moral boast that comes from working on a well-done project is worth the effort if no other benefits were realized.

The JAD session is finished, and the business problems have been identified. We must now generate a conceptual solution to solve the business problems. From the conceptual solution, a technical solution is developed. Frequently, several different technical solutions are possible. Each solution must be evaluated to determine which solution best solves the business need. Once a technical solution has been selected, it must be checked against the problem to make sure that it provides the correct solution. This process is illustrated in Figure 4-2.

Once the technical solution has been developed, the first step in planning the project is creating the work breakdown structure a comprehensive methodology for identifying all of the work in the project. It is a hierarchical logical structure for organizing the project work. Creating a work breakdown structure starts with the scope of work, where all major complements of the work are identified. Each of the major components is then broken down to the constituent tasks that must be done to complete that component. This process is repeated until each task in the work breakdown structure has one owner, a clear deliverable, a duration less than

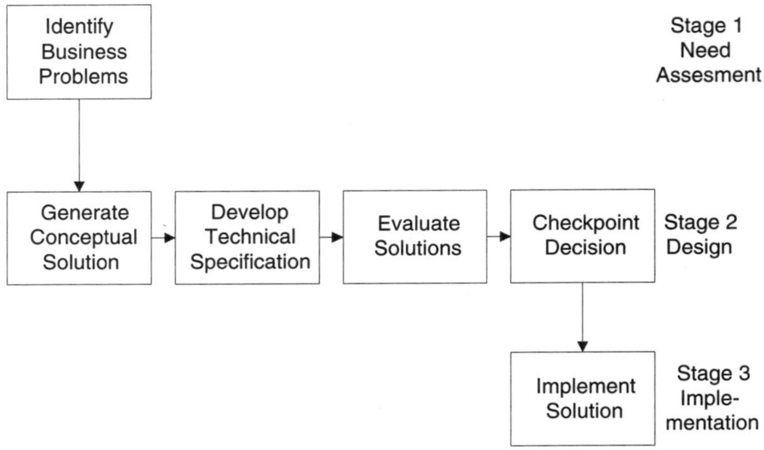

Figure 4-2 Steps in the spiral leading to development.

a month, and the ability to be tracked. Fortunately, the work breakdown structures for most data warehouses are usually similar to those for the first few levels. This means that once you have created a work breakdown structure for a data warehouse project, it can be used as the starting point of the discussion of the work breakdown structure for the next project.

Once the work breakdown structure has been developed, the project can be scheduled. This involves estimating the time to complete each task in the work breakdown structure and the logical relationships between the tasks. Once the relationships between the tasks have been established, it is possible to determine the critical path for the project. The critical path is the sequence of tasks in the work breakdown structure that due to their logical relationship determine the duration of the project. The only way to reduce the time of the entire project is to reduce the time to complete tasks in the critical path.

Another important feature of proper planning is the creation of a responsibility matrix (Figure 4-3). This matrix shows the members of the team on one axis and the tasks in the work breakdown structure on the other. Checks are placed at the intersection of a team member and any task of the work breakdown structure for which he or she is responsible. When creating the project schedule, it is important to remember that members of the team cannot be scheduled to be working on two tasks at the same time. The responsibility matrix can be compared with the project schedule to determine if a resource or team member is double-booked.

Another important detail to resolve at this time is the team structure for the project. The most important consideration is to match the team structure with the project. The most common team structure is the business team. This is the typical structure of a peer group reporting to a manager. Another team structure is the master craftsman and journeyman structure. Many researchers have noticed that some

	Extract Data	Design DB	Define UI	Load DB	Define Req.
Jane Doe–Project Supervisor					X
Bill Jones–JAD Facilitator					X
D. Ata Base–DBA		X			X
Ana List–System Analyst			X		X
Janet Smith–Systems Programmer	X			X	
Phil Expectations			X		X

Figure 4-3 Simple example of a responsibility matrix.

software developers are 10 times more productive than others. The person who is 10 times more productive will be placed in the role of master craftsman. In the data warehouse world, this role is usually filled by the data warehouse architect. The other people on the team will perform tasks in support of the master craftsman. Although many other team structures are in use, those listed are the ones the author has most often seen used to achieve success in data warehousing.

Part of the planning of the data warehouse should be to plan for the total IT service management. The IT service management model is repeated in Figure 4-4. The JAD process was part of what was required for the business and IT alignment process. Now that the data warehouse is being planned and designed, we are in the lower left quadrant of the ITSM model. To maximize the chances of success, the data warehouse project should go through all of the service planning, capacity planning, cost planning, availability management, and service-level planning.

The data warehouse will affect the configuration of the IT environment and the way work is performed in the rest of the organization. These are configuration management and change management issues. It is imperative that an organization that is implementing a data warehouse considers not only the technical issues, but the human issues must also be recognized and planned. People can get very possessive of their data. Telling people they are going to share data, reports, or information with the rest of the organization can cause emotional havoc. It is much better to plan to minimize this than to react to problems once they arise.

4.5.3 Manage the Project

Once the plan has been put into place to create and deploy the data warehouse, we must manage the project as it progresses. An important component of the management phase of the project is the cycle plan, do, check, and act. The plan is created for the construction of the warehouse. The team then works against the plan. At some point, progress of the team is checked against the plan. Corrective action is then taken and the cycle repeats. This process is illustrated in Figure 4-5.

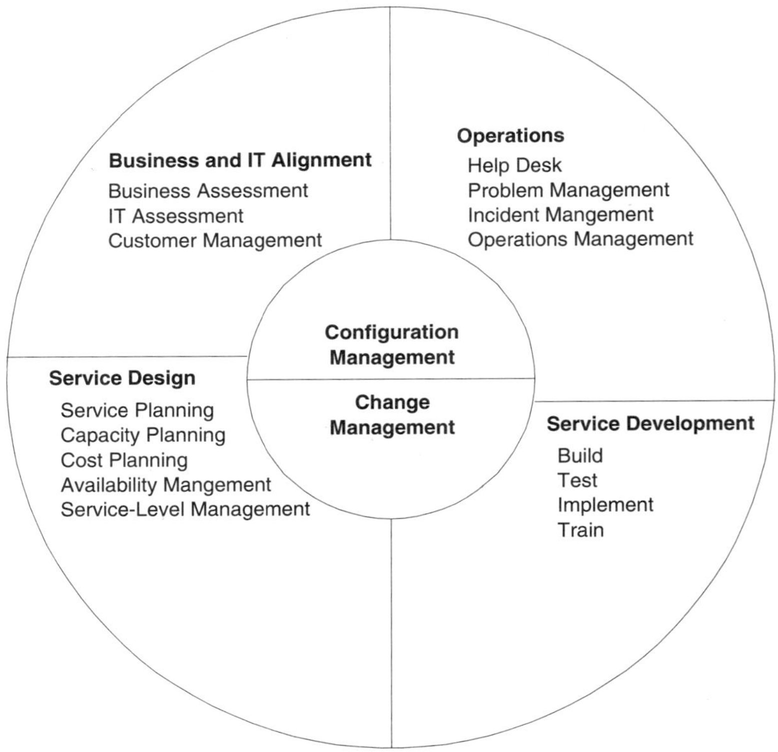

Figure 4-4 IT service model.

To track the project against the plan, data must be gathered. There are hard data and soft data that will help determine the progress of the project against plan. Hard data is measured by such things as task start dates, completion dates, and expected completion dates for tasks in progress. Soft data is information about such things as difficulties encountered, resolved, or expected in addition to individual productivity, productivity inhibitors, and persistent problems. This data should be gathered at least every week or two. For fast-paced projects, data gathering should happen twice a week.

Once the data has been gathered, the variance of the project to plan must be analyzed. The best way to do this is through trend analysis. Trend analysis seeks to differentiate between actual trends in the progress of the project from one-time occurrences. As an example, the data load might take longer because the database needed a patch. Once the patch has been applied, future loads occur as planned. On the other hand, the database loads might go more slowly than anticipated because the estimate is optimistic. In this case, the plan will need to be modified.

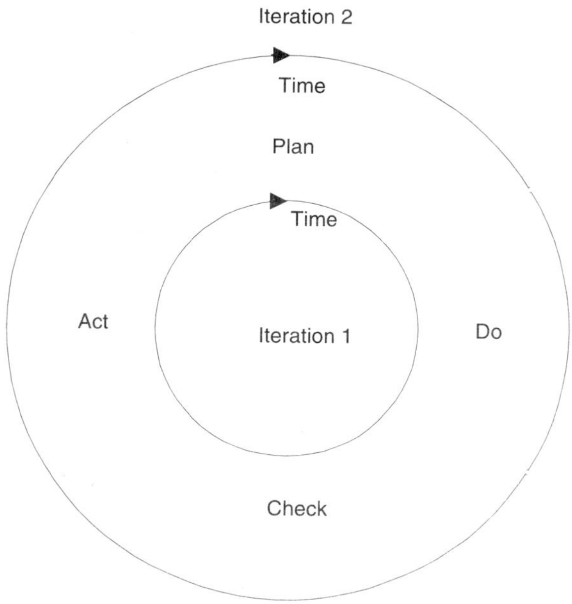

Figure 4-5 Cycle of plan, do, check, and act.

The key here is communication. The team must know what is expected of them, and the team must feel free to communicate problems to the project manager. The project manager must communicate project progress, including the impact on future tasks and problems to the entire team, including the sponsor. This will provide an opportunity to modify scope, resources, or schedule.

4.6 TEAM MEMBERS AND SKILL SETS

The richness and complexity of data warehouse projects imply that data warehouse teams typically have a large number of participants with a variety of skills. Small organizations might meet their needs with a small team and data warehouse organization such as one shown in Figure 4-6. In fact, one or two individuals may fill all the positions shown on this organizational chart. The important point is that the organization of the data warehouse team and skill sets matches the needs of the project and the organization. The desired data warehouse team structure and skill set requirements are a function of not only the entire organizational structure and the data warehouse project but of the IT architecture. As an example, the required data warehouse project organizations, skill set, and team

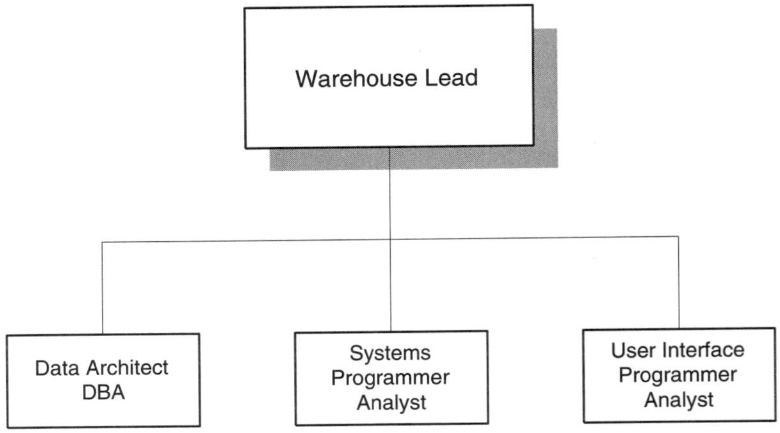

Figure 4-6 Data warehouse team structure for a small organization.

size are much different for a 20-gigabyte data warehouse deployed on NT than for a terabyte data warehouse deployed on UNIX using EMC storage and multiple tiers in the architecture. The data warehouse team organization for a larger team is shown in Figure 4-7. It is important to understand the data roles that are involved in the construction of the data warehouse. These roles are explained in the following paragraphs.

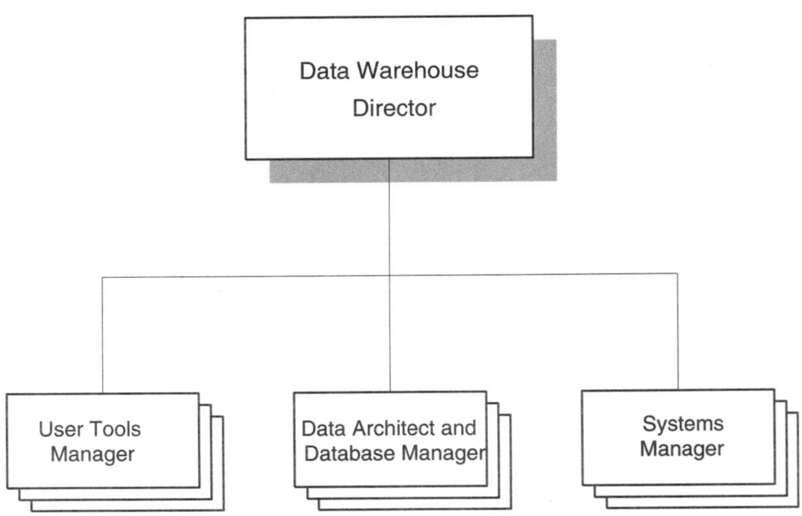

Figure 4-7 Data warehouse team structure for a large organization.

The main role of the data warehouse manager is to promote the development of data warehousing in the organization. To this end, the data warehouse manager will build relationships with top management and educate them as to the benefits of data warehousing. Once top management is convinced of the value of the construction of the data warehouse, the data warehouse manager will find the potential sponsors with business needs and funds to solve them. The warehouse manager will also be responsible for assisting in the allocation of limited resources to construct data warehouse subject areas. The data warehouse manager also performs other more typical managerial functions, such as setting budgets, schedules, and writing performance evaluations for the data warehouse team. In addition to this, the warehouse manager must keep abreast of emerging technologies and participate in data warehouse and industry associations.

The data warehouse architect has responsibility for setting standards and overall architecture for data warehouses for the entire organization. The warehouse architect will select or lead a team to select all of the necessary data warehouse components. These include:

- Hardware
- Networks
- Database management software
- Middleware
- Data extraction, transformation, a cleansing software
- End-user tools

The data warehouse architect must also have some skills similar to those of the data warehouse team manager. These include the education of end users and monitoring data warehouse industry trends for the selection of emerging technologies.

Database administrators in the data warehouse projects come in two flavors. Database administrators for the data warehouse source systems automate the data extraction process. They must also develop and maintain monitoring processes that ensure that the data has been extracted properly. Source system DBAs must also develop or acquire the necessary metadata to document the source data properly. The data warehouse database administrator is responsible for automating the loading of data, and maintaining and updating this process. The data warehouse database administrator must also develop or acquire the metadata for the data warehouse.

The data warehouse data architect is responsible for the development of data models and metadata for the data warehouse. The warehouse data architect is also responsible for identifying data sources and monitoring data quality. The warehouse data architect assists source system DBAs in analyzing the causes for updating compatibility between the warehouse and stores systems. The warehouse data architect will also perform database administration tasks on the data warehouse database.

The data warehouse auditor is responsible for auditing the procedures and processes that are used to acquire and transform the data warehouse data. The editor should also ensure that data warehouse reports agree with published financial reports and other enterprise information. In general, the data warehouse auditor is responsible for the information quality of the data warehouse.

The warehouse system administrator will be responsible for typical system administration tasks. These tasks include:

- User management resource allocation
- User security administration
- User account information collection
- System management software management
- Software patch application

The data warehouse business analyst or user liaison is the end users' chief human source of information about the data warehouse. The user liaison will be responsible for educating and training users about data warehouse capabilities. The user liaison also assists users in trading reports in finding the right information. At times, the user liaison will help the end users create or test reports that have already been developed. The user liaison is usually in charge of documenting reports and applications created by the IT group.

A warehouse programmer-analyst is responsible for converting reports existing today into warehouse reports and testing these applications to ensure correctness. The warehouse programmer analyst will also assist an OLTP programmer-analyst in creating closed-loop applications. These tasks are very similar to typical OLTP tasks programmer analysts perform.

In summary, many tasks must be performed by the data warehouse team. Some of the skill sets required to perform these tasks are very similar to those required to construct an OLTP application. As an example, the warehouse system administrator, user liaison, and programmer analyst roles and skill sets are similar to what they would be on an OLTP team. Other skills, such as those of the data warehouse architect and data warehouse auditor, are somewhat different.

QUESTIONS

4.1 During the executive interviews, the VP of sales and marketing who is sponsoring the project states that she is not interested in doing the JAD approach. She knows the problems with the organization, what the information need is, what questions need to be answered, and she is sponsoring the project. What do you do, and why?

4.2 You are getting ready to start the JAD sessions when you note that two of your scheduled attendees are not present. Ten minutes after the scheduled start time, these people are still not there. These two people are a sales district manager and an IT analyst. Their managers are present. All the other people are there. What do you do?

4.3 In your own words, define *work breakdown structure.*

4.4 Create a work breakdown structure for changing a tire on a car.

4.5 Create a work breakdown structure for getting ready to go to a job interview after having been jogging.

4.6 In your own words, define *critical path.*

4.7 Explain the PDCA cycle.

4.8 Create an organizational structure for your educational institution's IT department, including academic computing. Explain your structure in as much detail as you can. If you have the organization chart for the IT department at your educational institution, explain the diagram and comment on any features, including political implications.

4.9 Write a report on various project team organizations, including the strengths and weaknesses of each. Explain what type of projects might be best suited for each organization.

PROJECTS

4.10 Recall that call behavior analysis (CBA) is the analysis of the telephone calls that a traditional telephone or long-distance customer might make. The information is gathered by the switch that routes the call. This information will include the number of the telephone originating the call, the telephone number of the receiver of the call, and how long the call lasted. The newer switches, called SS7 switches, can capture other information, such as calls that are not completed because of a busy signal. Write the management guide for the CBA system.

4.11 How large is the scope of a CBA pilot project that gathers information from one switch, and loads the information onto a UNIX server? The number of calls going through the switch is 100,000 per day and we extract 128 bytes per call. We wish to store 90 days of information. The pilot group of users will use terminals connected to a hub that is connected to the server. Commercial off-the-shelf query tools will be used to perform the call behavior analysis. State your analysis in as much depth as you can, using whatever information you know or have developed to this point. State your assumptions.

4.12 Repeat Project 4.11 with the following changes. We wish to move into production with 1000 switches that are in a specific area code.

4.13 The network that actually connects a telephone call is a very expensive and valuable resource. Planning for network expansion is a very important task, due to lost revenue if telephone calls don't go through or the increased cost if the network is too large in the wrong location. Suppose that we are to construct a data warehouse for network traffic management. Write the management guide for this data warehouse.

4.14 What is the scope of a telephony network data warehouse that gathers data for a single switching office that handles 250,000 calls per day? The traffic on the network is gathered every second, and there are seven network segments leaving the switching office. We wish to keep three years of data.

4.15 Repeat Project 4.14 for all 750 offices in an area. There are 8000 network segments of which to keep track.

4.16 Buying trend analysis is performed by car manufacturers and dealers to best determine the car and options certain demographic groups are likely to purchase. What is the scope of this project for a single car dealership? The user group will be the dealership management.

4.17 Repeat the analysis of Project 4.16 for all the dealers selling a certain brand of car in Florida. The user group is now the dealership management and 20 users at the manufacturer, including the VP of manufacturing.

4.18 Stores can use buying trend analysis to best determine the products that certain demographic groups are likely to purchase. For example, an electronics store could determine which demographic groups are likely to purchase which products. A premium clothing store could track demographic groups that are likely to purchase certain products. Each store has 900 transactions per day. A transaction is stored in roughly 500 bytes and includes all items on a single cash register receipt. The user group will be the store management. What is the scope of this problem for a single store?

4.19 Repeat the analysis of Project 4.18 for the entire chain of 1400 stores and assuming that the user group is all of the store management, including corporate.

4.20 Manufacturing organizations can use a data warehouse to track the compliance of their suppliers to their agreements. The agreements normally cover at a minimum the delivery timing of products and product quality. The manufacturing organizations do this to increase part quality and reduce the cost of having too much inventory. Other technologies, such as electronic data interchange (EDI), allow the manufacturing company and its suppliers to exchange orders for parts and deliveries of parts electronically. What is the scope of this project for an organization that receives 300 parts per day in 20 categories? There will be four users. We want to keep five years of data.

4.21 Repeat Project 4.20 for an organization that receives 1,000,000 parts per day in 90,000 categories and has a user base of 350 people distributed around the world.

4.22 Financial organizations can use a data warehouse to analyze the risk of consumer, commercial, and governmental transactions. This data warehouse can use data such as demographic data or payment history data to determine the risk of the loan. This enables the financial institution to estimate and manage the risk. What is the size of this project for a small credit union with 10,000 members that have credit cards? There will be 15 users of the system.

4.23 Repeat Project 4.22 for a very large bank with 25 million total customers and 10 million credit card customers. There will be 100 users of this system, ranging from the senior VP of credit card services to customer service representatives.

4.24 Airlines can analyze the travel trends of their frequent fliers in different demographic groups. This information can be used to target-market frequent fliers in the correct market groups. The demographic data is usually obtained from external sources. What is the scope of this project for a regional carrier that operates 150 flights a day with 4500 passengers and wishes to keep five years of data? The user group is four people at the airlines headquarters.

4.25 Repeat Project 4.24 for an airline that operates 900 flights every day with 90,000 passengers. There will be an international group of 40 users in five countries.

4.26 Recall that airlines can use a data warehouse to track the seasonal variations and growth expected in travel between locations. This data could also show how much food and beverages are consumed in different flights. This will help the airline select aircraft and catering to match needs. What is the scope of this project for a regional carrier that operates 150 flights a day with 4500 passengers plus cargo and wishes to keep five years of data? The user group is four people at the airlines headquarters.

4.27 Repeat Project 4.26 for an airline that operates 900 flights every day with 90,000 passengers plus cargo. There will be an international group of 40 users in five countries.

4.28 Educational institutions can use a data warehouse to analyze trends in class enrollment, grade history, and student evaluation of professors. The data for the data warehouse will be loaded at the end of every academic period. Information about class enrollment will come from the registration system, and student evaluation data can be loaded from the academic dean's system. They wish to keep 10 years of data. How large is the scope of this problem for a school with 2000 students and 15 users of the system?

4.29 How large is the scope of Project 4.28 for a school with 40,000 students at three campuses with 200 users of the system?

4.30 Health care providers can use a data warehouse to track diagnosis codes, the procedures and treatments for a diagnosis, and the cost of those procedures and treatments. This can be used to analyze the success rates of procedures for a diagnosis or the cost versus the insurance reimbursement. What is the scope of this problem for a clinic with 15 doctors and 18 users of the system? Each doctor sees 20 patients a day and has 5000 patients in his or her care.

4.31 Recall that hotels can analyze the staying trends of their frequent guests in different demographic groups. This information can be used to target-market frequent guests for vacation packages. The demographic data is usually obtained from external sources. How large is the scope of this project for a single hotel with 300 beds and an 80 percent average occupancy? They wish to track 18 months of data and there will be seven users of the system.

4.32 Repeat Project 4.31 for a hotel chain with 500 properties in 23 countries around the world. There will be 115 users of the system in four countries.

4.33 Recall that hotels can use a data warehouse to track the total value of a frequent guest's stay. The value of the stay is the total amount the guest spends during the stay, including room, restaurant, room service, gift shop, and other incidental charges. How large is the scope of this project for a single hotel with 300 beds and an 80 percent average occupancy? They wish to track 18 months of data and there will be seven users of the system.

4.34 Repeat Project 4.33 for a hotel chain with 500 properties in 23 countries around the world. There will be 115 users of the system in four countries.

5

DATA MODELING

5.1 INTRODUCTION

The common intellectual thread in Chapter 1 was that a data warehouse is a new architecture. The new architecture is important because it enables the users and builders of the data warehouse to access information. The data from the operational systems becomes information because this new architecture makes it possible for the business knowledge worker to find the data, understand how to access the data, and believe in the data. A correct data model is an important part to turning data into information. A data model is a way to provide different levels of abstraction to the business knowledge worker's and IT professional's mental picture of the data. Data modeling is a process that is used to conceptualize, analyze, identify, and organize the business's data. For more information about data modeling for the data warehouse than can be provided in this chapter, the author recommends Ralph Kimball's book *The Data Warehouse Toolkit*.

Data modeling is both an art and science that became popular when Chen created entity-relationship (ER) or entity-relationship-attribute (ERA) modeling [Chen]. ER modeling formalized operational system or on-line transactional processing (OLTP) data modeling techniques that had been used in the industry for a decade. The basic idea of ERA modeling was that the business kept track of data about things or entities in which it was interested. These entities were frequently related through business rules. By properly structuring an organization's data, the data architect can eliminate the data redundancies that were the demons of unarchitected systems.

Like all forms of modeling, data modeling is important because it provides a tool for the human mind to understand and organize information. One way data modeling does this is through graphical presentation. Another way that data modeling helps the human mind understand the data is through levels of abstraction. A simple entity-relationship graphical model is shown in Figure 5-1. This graphical model will be explained in a following paragraph.

The concept of relational data modeling and the relational database products that supported these ideas in a physical design brought improvements in design philosophy and implementation that could potentially be passed on to the user. Earlier database systems, like hierarchical databases such as IMS, forced the user to structure queries starting at the top or root and query down the structure. With the relational model and database implementation, no entity is more important than another entity. All of the entities are created equally, and a query could start anywhere.

Recently, data warehouse and other decision support system database designers have used an old concept in dimensional modeling and called it *dimensional, star schema,* or *star join schema modeling*. Power users, IT professionals, and merchant data suppliers such as IMS America and A.C. Nielsen have organized and supplied data in an easily understood "data cube" structure. This structure has many features of operational systems data modeling, with some important differences. While entity-relationship models are generally symmetric with no single entity appearing to be greatly more important than another, star schema modeling places one large table in the center of the graphical model, with smaller "subordinate" tables located in a radial pattern around the center table. The center table has the facts of interest, such as amount or number of items sold. The subordinate tables have information that is static or nearly static over time, such as the description of a product or sales region. The graphical representation of the

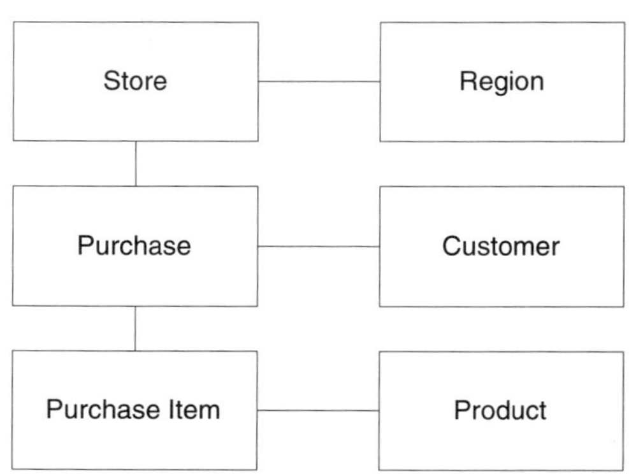

Figure 5-1 Simple entity-relationship model.

model has the appearance of a star. The graphical representation of a star-join model is shown in Figure 5-2.

What information do these models contain? Both the E-R and star join models use boxes connected with lines to represent the data and the relationships in the data. The boxes in the model represent entities, and the lines between the boxes represent the relationship between the data entities. The attributes of the entities are not shown on the model, but the attributes can be shown.

5.1.1 Entities

Entities are commonly defined as objects, things, or events that an organization wants to keep information about. Examples of entities are accident, employee, or sale. We are usually interested in being able to make a distinction between the concept of a collection of data about something and the actual data. The collection of data about an accident or employee in the database is called an instance of the entity. Entities are usually mapped to an entity or entities in the physical database.

Because the goal of an operational system is to capture data that enables the business to perform daily processes, the data is designed to represent the current condition of the business. The goal of the OLTP data design will be the proper structure and organization of data to eliminate data redundancy and remove the chance that conflicting data values are stored in different locations. As an example, there is only one correct mailing address for the customer entity shown in Figure 5-1. Redundant data is eliminated through proper design and normalization. OLTP data architects are focused on designing complex data dependencies that eliminate redundancy and optimize database update performance.

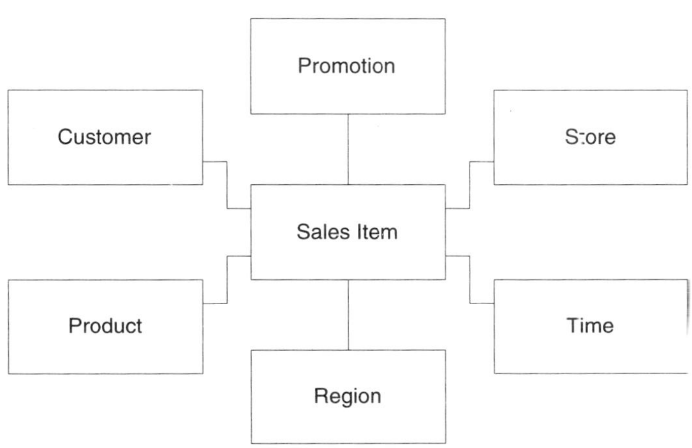

Figure 5-2 Simple star-join model.

Data warehouse database architects are interested in designing entities that will make it easy for business analysts to perform queries and generate reports that provide information about the business dimensions of interest. As an example using the data model of Figure 5-2, a business analyst could find out the amount of a product sold in a store in a period. The decision support data architect is interested in capturing the history of changes in the business that will allow rapid access of data along the dimensions of analysis. Staying with the previous example for a minute, the business analyst would be able to obtain detailed facts about sales and analyze them in light of the areas or dimensions of analysis. These dimensions are time, stores, products, and customers. Thus, the decision support data architect is interested primarily in supporting users' queries about the dimensions of analysis.

The starting point for the modeling exercise is the business process that was selected as part of the JAD exercise and the subject area weighting exercise. Without the selection of the subject area and business process, the data warehouse architect is without direction as to what to model. With the prioritization of business processes and subject areas that was the output of the executive JAD session, we have the business process selected and a first pass at the order in which they will be modeled.

Process modeling and data modeling are activities that are linked in the world of OLTP systems, and these activities must be coordinated. Because a data warehouse is generally constructed to support query and reporting applications but not operational activities, it would appear that the warehouse architect would be uninterested in business process modeling. To construct fact and summary tables, it is necessary to understand the business processes. Also, warehouses are frequently deployed into closed-loop applications where the warehouse updates the operational systems, and the business process that the closed-loop application is designed for must be understood and modeled.

It is recommended that readers interested in an in-depth treatment of data warehouse data modeling consult Ralph Kimball's book *The Data Warehouse Toolkit.*

5.2 ENTERPRISE DATA MODELING

The design of the data warehouse database does not start in a vacuum. The data for the warehouse will come from an existing system or a system that must be in place before the warehouse can be implemented. In either case, a data model will be available to start the process of creating the data warehouse.

The reader can recall from the first chapters of this book that the IT community got into the predicament of an unplanned decision support environment by creating these systems without planning. Now, organizations are creating separate data warehouse subject areas without regard to possible connections between these areas. This will repeat the problem of creating islands of data that do not integrate.

The creation of a truly enterprise data warehouse will require the creation of separate subject areas that can be linked. The various areas are created separately according to the needs of the organization, then are integrated as they become operational. Just as Rome was not built in a day, an enterprise data warehouse will not be built quickly either. It is important to build the different subject areas as quickly as possible but in a fashion that enables the subject areas to be linked when appropriate. The ability to both link data warehouse subject areas and create operational systems that can interoperate depends on an enterprise data model or some other organizational standard.

Enterprise data modeling drew much excitement in the 1980s when it was seen as a way to save the IT department from the evils of unplanned development. The problem with enterprise data modeling was that it is an enormous undertaking and the target is moving. While the model is being developed, new projects are being developed and old projects modified that change the nature of data usage in the organization. Most of these projects failed to produce the lofty goals to which they started out, but they did produce a valuable product of one type or another. A high-level enterprise data model is depicted in Figure 5-3.

The author is going to make the problem slightly worse before making the problem better. What the IT department really needs is a data model for the entire organization that covers both OLTP ER data models and decision support dimensional or star schema models. This type of enterprise data model would guide the development of both OLTP and DSS systems. The metadata or description of the purpose and use of the data created with this type of model would guide the users and developers of both OLTP and DSS systems. This is depicted in Figure 5-4.

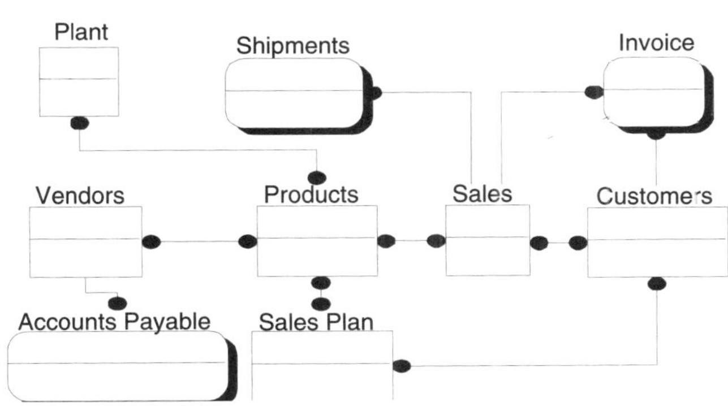

Figure 5-3 High-level enterprise data model.

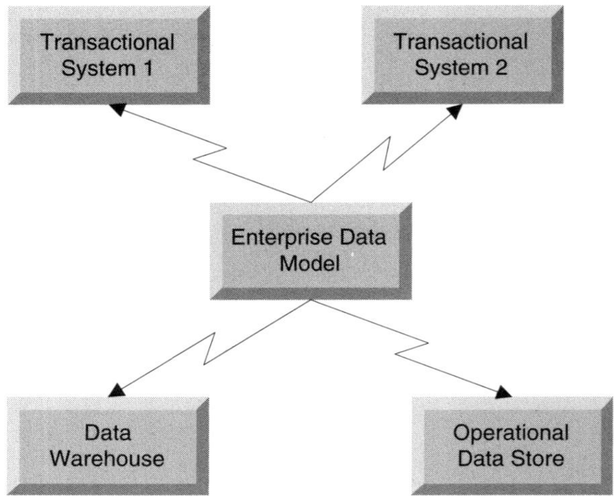

Figure 5-4 The enterprise data model should guide both data warehouse and decision support systems.

5.2.1 Just-Enough Enterprise Data Model

Previous approaches to enterprise data modeling have usually taken a waterfall life-cycle approach to construction of the data model. The data model was not released until it was complete or was at least complete for a particular area. Since the model usually never reached completion due to the moving nature of the target, the enterprise model never saw the light of day or an overworked developer's eyes. Some groups took an approach to being successful through limiting the scope of the project, but this did not seem to be the norm.

A different approach to the construction of the enterprise data model is to model just enough of the subject area to provide needed information as the information is needed. Think of this as just-in-time data modeling. As an example, if we are to build the data warehouse to analyze sales for a grocery store, the point-of-sales system probably has hundreds of fields that are used for a variety of purposes in the point-of-sale OLTP system. Only a few of these will be of interest to the data warehouse. The just-enough enterprise data model construction will start with these few fields. The data model for both the OLTP and the decision support systems will be developed. As the data warehouse development effort or OLTP redevelopment process proceeds, the enterprise model will grow both in the number of subject areas that are covered and their depth.

As an example, suppose that a retail store wishes to construct a data warehouse for analysis of point-of-sale information. Many point-of-sale terminals use the store membership or frequent shopper card to identify the person purchasing the items. In addition, the point-of-sale device connected to a UPC scanner certainly

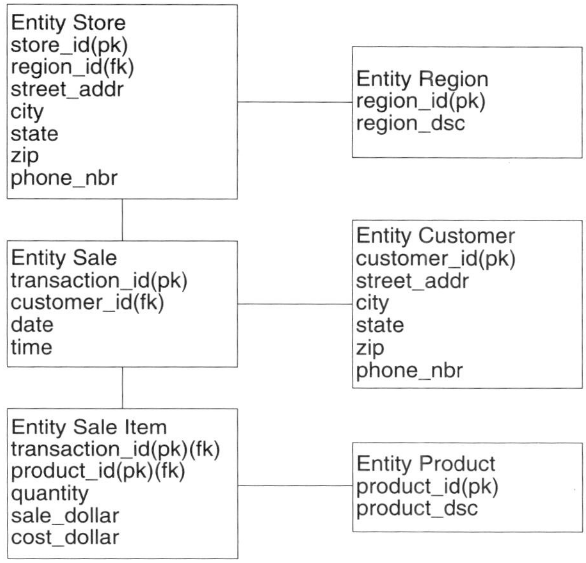

Figure 5-5 Simplified point-of-sale normalized data model.

captures a record of all the items purchased. Other information is also typically captured, such as the employee identification number of the clerk who is helping the customer. Only a limited number of the total fields in the point-of-sale system will be of interest to the sales data warehouse. The OLTP and decision support data models can start with these fields. Other fields that are primary keys and provide vital links to other systems can be added as soon as they are identified. As other data warehouse subject areas are constructed, normalized entity-relationship and star schema models will be added in these other areas and connected to the models already developed. The initial normalized ER diagram for the sales system is shown in Figure 5-5. This will be the starting point for the decision support system.

5.3 STAR SCHEMA ANALYSIS: CREATING THE DIMENSIONAL MODEL

Data in a database can be separated into major categories: descriptive values and quantitative values. *Descriptive values* define unique quantities that are associated with transactional events. Examples of this are customer name, flight number, product number, product name, product supplier, and location. This type of data is usually referred to as reference or business dimensions data, and it is stored in entities called *reference entities*. *Quantitative values* such as numbers that are continuously valued and that may be summed arithmetically, such as amount sold, cost of unit, and sales amount, are frequently referred to as business facts and stored in entities called *fact entities*. A single fact entity generally has many business dimensions associated with it. This implies a data model where the fact table is central to a large number of subordinate or dimension tables, as was shown in Section 5.1.

The example of the retail point-of-sale system is valuable for the development of a simple and illustrative decision support data model. If we are told that we are to develop a data model where the quantitative values about product sales should be in one table and all descriptive quantities should be in subordinate tables, the data model shown in Figure 5-6 is easily developed from the normalized ER data model. All of the additive values are placed in a single entity called *sale item*. All of the descriptive information about the sale of products is placed in dimension tables around the fact table. Most data models are more involved than this, and we will investigate the process of developing a data model further in the next section.

At first examination, the reader may think that it is obvious that quantities such as dollars, number of units, or travel expenses must be additive. To be even more general, we would expect that we should be able to add these units along

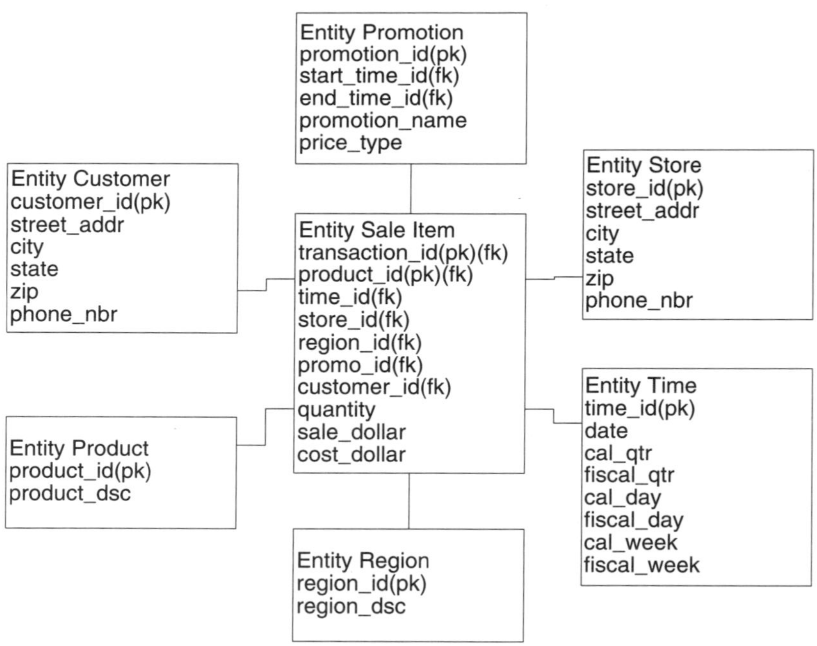

Figure 5-6 Dimensional or star schema model for the analysis of customer buying habits.

any of the dimensions of business analysis. Actually, the ability to add quantities is something that the database designer must work hard to create. As an example, if the author has $500 in the checking account in April, May, and June, it does not mean that the author has $1500 total. Some business facts are called *semiadditive* because they can only be added along a specific dimension or two, and other facts are nonadditive.

5.3.1 Model Development Methods

Using the normalized ER model as the starting point to construct the dimensional model is one of three common approaches. This is called the *modification* or *leverage approach*. Another way to approach the problem is to start with a template or generic data model and customize it to fit the needs of the particular organization. The final approach is to develop the dimensional model from the beginning. These three approaches to dimensional modeling are a little like the three approaches to getting a custom home. A person can buy a home that is already constructed and knock some walls out to add new walls, baywindows, and some skylights. A second option is to buy some existing home plans and have a house built to the plans or a modified version of the plans. The final option is to contact an architect and start from scratch. Each of these methods of construction has a set of trade-offs that are much like the data warehouse construction trade-offs.

Development by Modification. The modification strategy for a house works best with a new house. If an old house is modified, there is a high likelihood that the old design principles and building codes that were followed will cause major problems to the new construction. A similar principle is true for data model design. The modification strategy will work best when the following factors are in place for the the data models for the source systems that are the starting point:

- The models are new, well designed, and normalized.
- The IT staff is very familiar with the source system OLTP models.
- The IT staff understands the data that is already in the database.
- Many warehouse reference and fact tables are already in the OLTP model in a different form.

This approach has the benefit of using both IT and end-user professionals to examine the OLTP model and develop the decision support model. This increases the feeling of involvement and ownership of the end user for both the OLTP and decision support systems. The development happens rapidly since the work starts with existing OLTP data models. The development is very efficient since the work that was done to develop the OLTP model is being reused in the decision support model.

This approach also has some problems. The data architect leading the design effort must have a tremendous knowledge of both OLTP and data warehouse data modeling. Depending upon the level of abstraction of the OLTP data model, there will be relationships in the model that are not business rules but performance-enhancing relationships. Finally, the OLTP model might be inaccurate or incomplete. Using the famous garbage-in/garbage-out axiom, the dimensional data model will be no better than the model that is modified to create it.

Development from Template. While there are many different ice cream manufacturers in the country, the ice cream business is much the same from one manufacturer to another. Although this seems like a trivial example, it leads us to the point that most businesses within the same industry will have the same primary subject areas. Why should they all invent the same data warehouse subject area models? Industry experts have developed subject area models for the main subject areas of many common industries. These frequently provide 80 percent of the information that the business users would develop during a JAD session, and they frequently provide some information that the business users would not have foreseen.

This approach compares with the house building analogy of starting with existing house plans and modifying them. By starting with existing plans, it is easy to see what is liked and not liked about the initial design. From the initial design and an understanding of the goals of the new house, a few changes can be made to accommodate the particular customer.

Since these models are industry specific, their starting point is knowledge about the industry. Since no two organizations in the industry typically have the same legacy systems, the industry models do not consider source system. Since there is no mapping to the source systems, these template solutions work particularly well in those situations where the legacy systems are about to be replaced because they are no longer fulfilling the business needs. This approach also works well if the organization is small and cannot dedicate a warehouse data modeler, or the initial information requirements are difficult to define but the subject area is clear.

The best way to select a template is to have the supplier of the template explain the template. They should be able to tell you not only what information the model supplies but also what information the model cannot supply that might be expected. If the vendor cannot discuss both the strengths and limitations of the model, it is time to be careful.

The best way to execute this approach is to buy the standard industry data model and hire a data model consultant from the company that supplied the data model. The consultant will provide expert advice for the interpretation and implementation of the model. The consultant should become part of the data model development team, which will be composed of select members of both the IT and end-user community.

Full Custom Development. Building a house from an idea is a tremendous amount of work. The structure must be specified, colors selected, and finishes chosen. The client must meet with the architect and builder and state clearly what is desired. As the process proceeds and the home is taking shape, the owner must frequently meet with the builder and architect to examine the materials, review decisions, and clarify wishes. This process produces the house that the owner specifies to the ability of the owner to specify it, but it is a very time consuming and costly process.

The custom development approach requires that the DSS data model be developed from the beginning. This approach ignores the existing data model during the initial model development, and it places a lot of trust in the ability of the business customer to define their data requirements. A typical RAD methodology that uses JAD to formulate the specifications is a good approach. This approach to developing the specification of the data model is illustrated in the next section.

This approach works well under a variety of conditions. If the subject area is relatively small or a full implementation of the subject area is not needed, a custom data model development can be effective. In some cases, a template for the subject area does not exist and the source systems data models are not trusted, so the custom development approach is the only option.

The custom development approach has the advantage of tightly coupling the business's needs with the data model for the decision support system. The features of the source systems that might cause difficulties with the data warehouse data load can also be discovered at this time. This approach can be very expensive in terms of project dollars, human resources, and time. It is important for the team not to get distracted by features they discover in the existing systems. Time boxing the development of the model for the first iteration or two of the data warehouse is a good way to keep the team focused.

5.3.2 Granularity

The proper selection of data granularity is very important to proper construction of a data warehouse. The initial data model that is constructed is frequently at a lower level of detail or granularity than what is really needed. Returning to the retail sales example, the level of granularity in the model is every item that is sold. If the purpose of the data warehouse is to investigate the buying habits of individual consumers, this is the appropriate level of granularity. If the purpose of the data warehouse is to analyze general sales trends, this level of granularity is too small. Sales trends could be done with summaries that show the total of the items sold on a given day rather than each individual item sale. There are a number of methods for reducing the amount of information that the data warehouse must maintain.

One way to reduce the size of the data warehouse is to keep the finest level of granularity but keep the detail for only the minimum amount of time. This approach works well if the usefulness of the data to the organization is within a short period of time. As an example, most sales analysis systems compare this quarter with the same quarter last year to look for trends with various products. The system only needs to maintain information about the last fiscal or calendar quarter and the same quarter a year ago. Thus, 15 months of data are all that is needed.

An alternative approach is to model only summary data. In this case, all detail data is summed and only aggregate-level information is stored as fact tables. Although this is a very effective way to reduce the size of the data warehouse database, it is imperative that the much-reduced amount of information be adequate to meet the need of the warehouse users.

A third approach is to provide both detail and summary data in a balance. As an example, the most recent fiscal quarter will be kept in the data warehouse at the lowest level of granularity along with aggregates for the quarter. Previous quarters will have only aggregate information available.

Each of these three options may be applied differently to different fact tables in the data warehouse. There may be nothing that can be done about reducing the amount of history on the sales item entity, but there may be a vendor payments table that can be kept only in aggregate form while the vendor compliance table is kept with a mix of detail and aggregates.

The selection of the right level of detail or granularity is a complex decision that involves business, hardware, software, and usage trade-offs. The RAD approach is to make the best design decision rapidly and fix any problems on a future iteration of the data warehouse database.

5.3.3 Time

Time changes everything, including the dimension tables that we thought were constant descriptors of other things. As an example, we can consider the sales region from our retail store example. The sales item table is connected to the region table to indicate the region in which the sale took place. Now, suppose that the definition of the region changes. Region 1, which was Missouri and Illinois, is now just Missouri. If we just change the reference table to reflect the new definition, comparisons of this year's to last years region 1 sales will be all wrong. If we tackle the very large task of changing all the detail information to reflect the new definition of region 1, a user can run the same report they ran before the change and get a new answer.

If this all sounds confusing, it is because it is confusing. There are several ways to tackle the problem. The first way is to change the definition of region 1 in the dimension table and ignore the fact that all the reporting will now be wrong until all of the facts in the table are cleared out by new data that matches with the new definition of the region. This is not a very appealing option in this example, but there are situations where it works. As an example, if we track the income bracket of a customer, we will probably just change the income level of the customer when we receive new information. Thus, the historical data in the fact table is associated with a different level of income from what is now reflected, but the result is probably not important to the business.

Another option is go back and restate the fact table data to reflect the new partitions. Depending on the size of the database, the partitioning, and the amount of time you have, you might not get this done before the database is archived. This also has the unusual side effect of changing large amounts of history.

The third and probably best version of a solution is to have version numbers associated with dimension tables and refer to the dimension table version in the fact table. This allows us to keep track of which region a sale was in and in changes in the region over time. Reports on region 1 version 3 should remain the same through this process, although version 4 is now current.

5.3.4 Events

Events usually appear in the dimensional model as fact tables without fact attributes. As an example, a school will keep a record that a student is enrolled in a certain course, the instructor, the academic quarter, and other pertinent information. Usually, there is nothing additive or continuously valued in this record. This would be an example of what some people call a "factless fact table." Such a table would be very important to an academic data warehouse, but it doesn't have additive facts. Other such event fact tables are common to the insurance, travel, hotel, and medical industries.

5.4 DEVELOPING THE DIMENSIONAL MODEL

The best way to create a dimensional data model in the full custom approach is to interview the appropriate people and conduct a JAD session. Continuing the JAD example from Chapter 4, the author asked the group what the critical success factors would be for operation of the business with a data warehouse of the type that we described. This question is really asking, "What do you want to know and do in order to solve the business problems?" The brainstorming session elicited the following factors:

1. Ability to judge the performance of the sales plan
2. Ability to analyze our prices of products compared to costs of products
3. Rapid delivery of information

4. Sales and profits, by product, customer, and region
5. Ability to ask "What if?"
6. Ability to analyze the effect of promotions

Although this is not a long list of CSFs, the JAD group was asked to vote on their favorite CSF. As the reader might expect, sales and profits by product, customer, and region was the runaway winner. The rapid delivery of information and the ability to ask "what if" are both technology and database organization questions that can be answered later.

Next, we asked the JAD group to answer the question, "What information do you need to answer the winning factor from above?" We organized the results by sales and costs or expenses. The results were as follows:

For sales, we want to keep track of what the customer is doing:

- What do they buy?
- How often?
- When?
- Where are they located?

We also want to keep track of how products are selling:

- By size/unit
- Discount by product
- By product group
- By product class
- By promotion

Expenses affect our bottom line, so we want to see our expenses by customer:

- Discounts
- Advertising
- Literature
- Merchandising

and by product:

- Promotions/discount
- Distribution costs
- Unit cost
- New development

From this JAD exercise, we gathered the dimensions of analysis for the business. The team was not interested in the impact of promotions on other product sales. The difficulty that developed was that much of the information about costs was not in the current information systems. The team agreed that rather than assign costs based on product or shipping and handling, we could come up with some fairly accurate cost estimates based on standardized costs by customer and location. For instance, development cost can be rolled into unit cost until we can determine development costs and have them in the transactional systems. When the transactional system is upgraded to capture this information, the decision support system could be upgraded as well. Also, the costs by customer are not gathered at this time. Because the JAD participants requested the lowest level of detail and it was easy to support with current hardware, the design used the lowest level of product sale detail. The resulting star schema is shown in Figure 5-7. This model is not very different from the one developed for a generic sales analysis system.

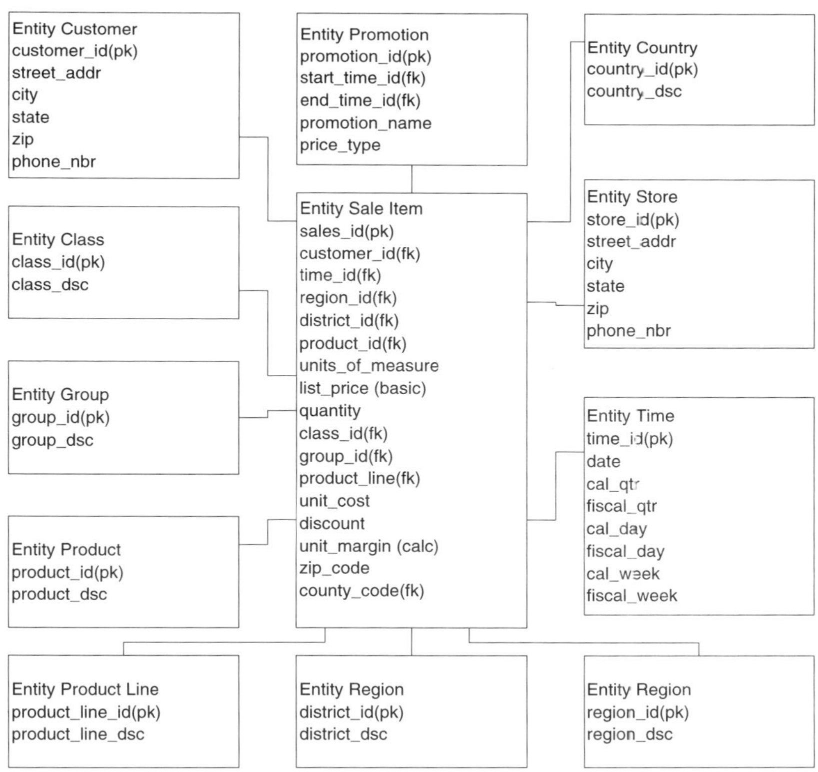

Figure 5-7 Dimensional data model from the example JAD session.

5.5 SNOWFLAKES

Those of us who have done large amounts of OLTP design find it hard not to normalize or resort to old design habits. The most tempting place to do this is with the lager dimension tables or with dimension tables that the designer has normalized in a previous design life. This snowflake pattern is illustrated in Figure 5-8. It is important to resist these urges.

While some normalization techniques may save some disk space, disk space is still much cheaper than CPU or human time, so it is important to resist the urge to normalize. Disk space is cheaper to start with, and the cost of disk is dropping at 15 to 25 percent per year. By the time the organization has grown into its disk, the price of new disks is drastically reduced. It is common for an organization to decide during the scoping phase that 15 months is all the history they need and then ask for three or five years after they see all of the great information. For a very large dimension such as a large product table of 250 megabytes, it is possible to save a few megabytes through the careful use of normalization. Because the entire

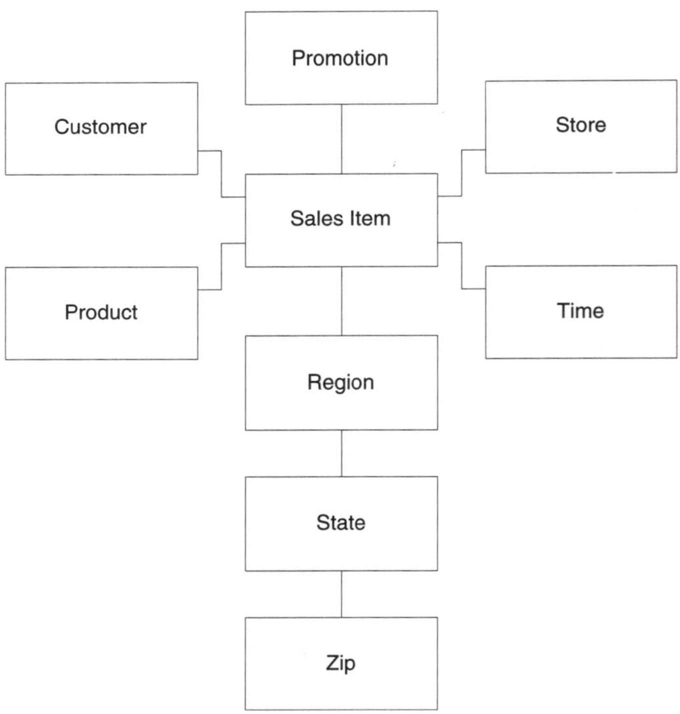

Figure 5-8 Snowflake data model.

database for a warehouse is at least in the multigigabyte (if not terabyte) range, it is meaningless to save a few megabytes on the dimension table.

The ability to browse the data will be destroyed by the snowflake. A one-way join between the fact table and the dimension table is easily accomplished by the database. The join of a billion-row fact table with two other tables along the normalized dimension is a much different story. It is important for users to be able to browse the decision support database, and the multiway join will prove too much for the database to allow real-time browsing.

The one place where creating a snowflake is acceptable is when two warehouse subject areas are being joined. As an example, we may have customer demographics available. The customer demographics combined with the sales information will enable us to do target marketing at those demographic groups that have the highest demonstrated likelihood of buying a certain product. The difficulty is that most demographic databases are extremely large. Billion-row tables are the norm in demographic databases. The demographic database is connected to the customer database, and the customer database is connected to the sales item database. This is a snowflake effect, but we have done this because we are connecting the customer demographic subject area with the sales subject area to provide better functionality and the creation of something closer to an enterprise warehouse. There is no other way to accomplish this realistically.

5.6 PHYSICAL MODELING

Many of the difficulties of creating and managing a data warehouse are centered on the size of the warehouse database. A single subject area data warehouse can be over a terabyte in size. Doing anything with a terabyte of data takes a long time. The secret to being able to work with something of this size is using a variety of techniques to reduce the amount of data that we are working with at a given time.

Physically partitioning the database is one way to reduce the size of individual database tables. With physical partitioning, a single conceptual and logical database table is divided into multiple physical tables. As an example of physical partitioning, consider the sales star schema shown in Figure 5-9. There are many ways to partition the database, and data ranges or primary key ranges are generally used. If the data warehouse stores 36 months of data, the sales item fact table could easily be divided into 36 physical partitions. When a new month is available to load into the warehouse, the oldest month is archived and the new month is loaded into the database. Other than the one physical partition that is under construction, the warehouse is available to users during this transformation.

Another advantage to physical partitioning is that it enables symmetric multiprocessor computers to parallelize the query and run it on multiple processors. Each of the partitions can be processed independently and the results placed into

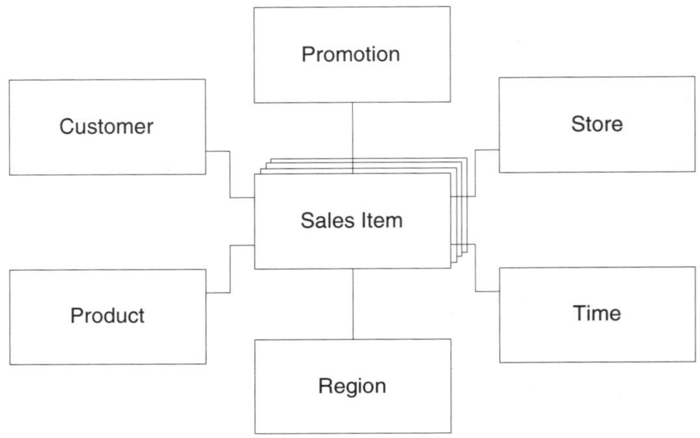

Figure 5-9 Physical partitioning of a table with many rows.

a temple table. The results are joined to give the result or the input to the next step in the query processing.

Assume for a moment that you are analyzing the sales information for a large grocery chain. You are convinced that facial tissue should be sold in a two-pack because that is what people buy. We could use one of the months of the physically partitioned data, but this might lead to misleading results. We don't sell as much facial tissue in July as we do in December. If the sales item entity had a random number in the range zero to one, we could select 10 percent of the data by selecting the sales items with random numbers between 0.1 and 0.2. If the result of this investigation proved promising, the entire database could be used for a more exhaustive study. This technique can be applied to any table in the database where selecting a random sample may be useful. This is shown in Figure 5-10.

The proper creation of indexes is another challenge to the data warehouse designer. For the reader unfamiliar with database design, an index is like a card catalog at the library. It is much simpler and faster to search the card catalog than to search the entire library. In a similar fashion, it is much faster to search the index for the location of values in the database than to search the entire database. The place to start creating indexes in the database is on fields that are known to be a parameter in a report. As an example, if the VP of sales said she would be doing reporting on sales by region, the region field in the sales item should be indexed. The way to discover the other indexes that are used is to have a database system management tool that monitors the queries. For routine queries for which no index is found to be available, an index should be created.

Summary or aggregate tables are another feature of database modeling that is a matter of trade-offs. A summary table provides instant access to the sum of an attribute of another table. As an example, a summary table could be constructed that sums the sales item information by item by day, by item by month, by item

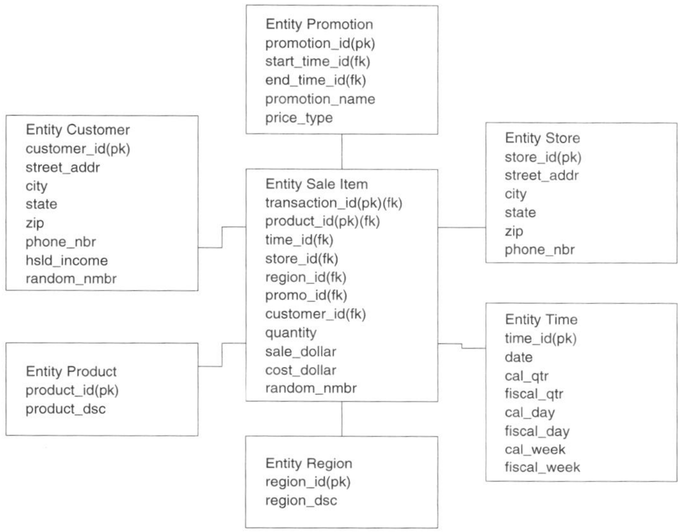

Figure 5-10 Introduction of random numbers to allow the selection of random sample sets.

by region by day, and so on. Just like indexes, the creation of unused summary tables wastes disk space, and the creation of two few summary tables means that the database will need to perform the summaries every time a query is executed that requires them. This is another instance where a database system management tool that monitors the queries is useful. Routine queries that don't have a summary available indicate that a summary should be created. Summary tables cannot be created for everything, but the appropriate creation of summary tables greatly enhances performance. In the chapter on aggregates in his book, Ralph Kimball points out that summary tables are the best way to control performance. Warehouse management tools such as Intelligent Warehouse will automatically direct a query to the appropriate summary table.

In Section 5.5 we pointed out that this will cause degradation in performance of the data warehouse. Although a true flat file design would have good performance but waste large amounts of physical storage, if the data warehouse database design is close to flat, the performance of the data warehouse to browsing queries will greatly increase. Some tools, such as neural net tools, need a database that appears to be flat. Although database views can be used to create structures that appear to be flat, there is still a performance penalty and maintenance overhead to this approach.

Other aspects of physical data modeling will depend on the type of database that is being used. Physical modeling best practices can be found in the specific database vendor's documentation or in other books on the art of database performance tuning.

5.7 TEN COMMANDMENTS OF DIMENSIONAL DATA MODELING

1. Thou shall answer the burning questions. If the data warehouse will not be able to answer the questions that were identified during the JAD session, it will have been a waste of time, money, and loss of potential competitive advantage for the organization.
2. Thou shall get the fact tables right. In order to answer the critical business issues, we must have the fact tables right. By "right" we mean that the tables must have the necessary values and the values must be correct. In other words, the tables must be structured correctly to answer the query, and the information quality of the table must be very high.
3. Thou shall have correct dimension tables. All of the necessary descriptions must be present in the design and in the instances of the table. The descriptions must be in the business terms of the end user.
4. To get the design right, thou shall understand the business process affected by or that affects the data warehouse.
5. Thou shall have the correct "grain" for the fact tables.
6. Thou shall have the correct length of business history stored in the data warehouse and partition as necessary.
7. Thou shall be able to incorporate all of the necessary data in a way that makes sense to the business.
8. Thou shall create the needed summary tables.
9. Thou shall create the necessary indexes.
10. Thou shall be able to load the data warehouse database and make it available in a timely fashion.

5.8 TWO FACES OF THE PYRAMID: TRANSACTIONAL ER AND ANALYTICAL STAR

The concept of the interconnections between the transactional and decision support systems was introduced in Chapter 1 and reiterated in Chapter 3. While the DSS system receives data from the transactional systems and organizational information system standards guide the construction of both systems, the two systems are fundamentally very different. It has been noted several times before in this book that operational systems are designed for rapid update performance, and decision support systems are designed for rapid query response. These two diametrically opposed goals lead to two different types of systems. These different design requirements not only necessitate different data models, but also usually imply either different hardware systems, logically partitioned systems, or resource managed systems to run the various applications. If a decision support system is operated on the same hardware as the transactional system without some type of resource management, the large queries that are typical of the DSS environment will destroy OLTP performance.

At the risk of belaboring the point, it is important to realize that neither the operational ER models nor instances of the data nor the decision support systems stand alone. All of the systems affect each other, and the architecture of each system has an impact on the others. Although there are no cases were this is truer than for a closed-loop decision support system, it is true in all cases. The modification approach of constructing the data warehouse data model acknowledges this fact by starting data model development with the existing OLTP model. The template approach admitted that the data needed to make the model work might not be in existence in current systems. The custom development approach develops the DSS data model from scratch, but at some point the new model must be connected with the old for both data descriptions and data loading. The similar, yet distinct nature of the data warehouse and operation systems is illustrated in Figure 5-11. The distinction between the data models will blur when we discuss operational data stores in Volume 2.

The reason the author keeps stressing this integration is simple. He has been asked to consult on many projects that were having difficulty either because the

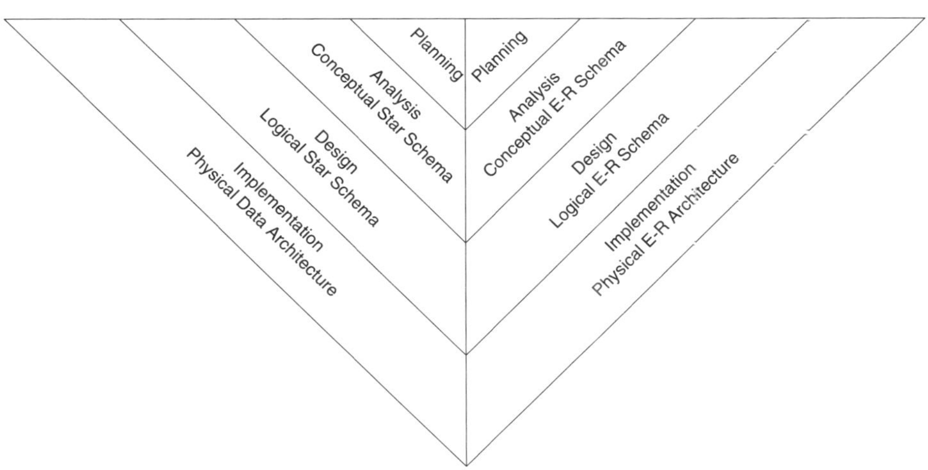

Figure 5-11 Distinct yet similar data architecture: entity relationship and star schema.

data model was not correct for the business and data source or because the data and information quality of the source system was poor. The information quality should be determined during an information quality exercise that is conducted in parallel with the model development. The entire IT information factory must be well designed and integrated in order to work smoothly.

As an example of a tightly integrated OLTP and DSS data model, the models shown in Figure 5-12 illustrate the point. Although these models are only examples, the point is that there is clear and seamless integration of the two models. Data from the operational sources can easily be loaded into the data warehouse. If an examination of the two data models does not show at least some clear similarity of data, it is important to discover the reason. In some cases, the data names and types change drastically between source data and warehouse systems. There are usually clear reasons for this. In other cases, a poor design may be the culprit.

The next best thing to a tightly integrated and designed set of data models for the organization and something that is important in any environment is metadata creation and management across the enterprise. This is illustrated in Figure

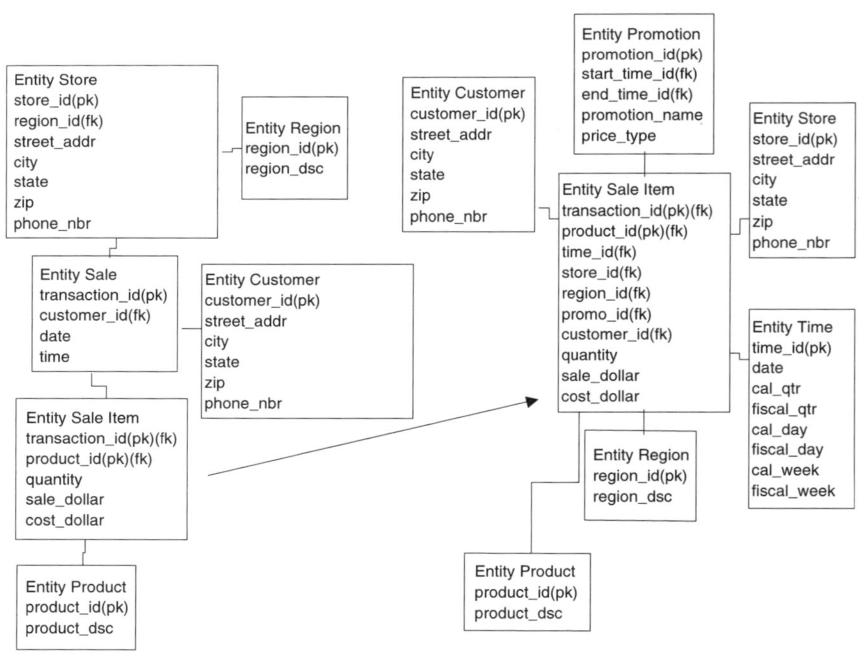

Figure 5-12 Tightly integrated OLTP and data warehouse system.

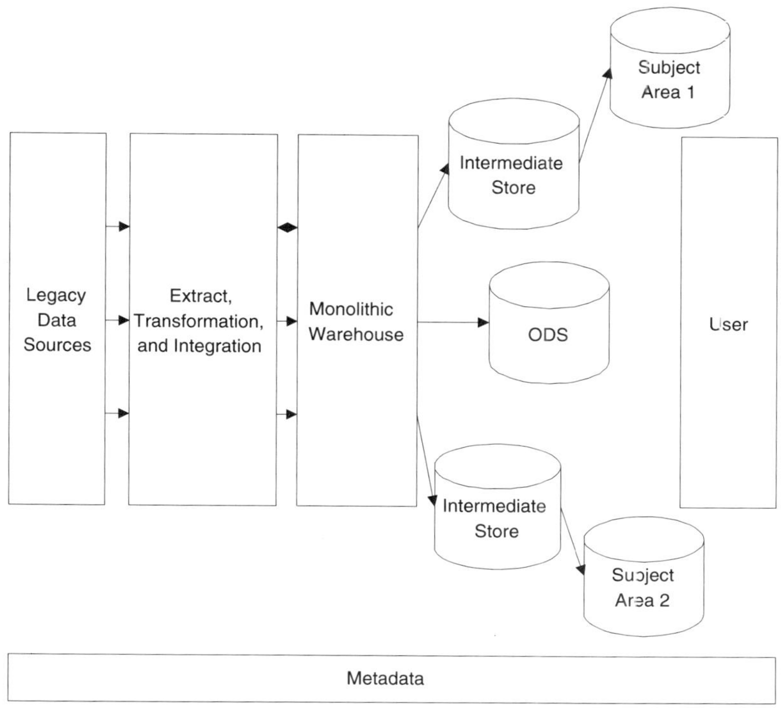

Figure 5-13 Uniform layer of metadata from source to user.

5-13. While this problem is being addressed by new product offerings, it is usually the case that legacy systems have a different set of metadata than the newer operational systems. The newer operational systems use a different metadata tool than the decision support tools, and each decision support tool has its own set of metadata. Simply put, there is way too much metadata available, and much of it is redundant or conflicting.

There are new breeds of tools from several vendors that will integrate the metadata. This will enable the end user of the data warehouse or the team creating the data warehouse to have access to metadata from across the organization. If the models and field definitions in the source records conflict, the nature of the conflict and the transformations that occurred between the source systems and the data warehouse can be documented. The documentation not only provides the IT team with better information with which to construct the data warehouse and user tools, it also provides the basis for automated generation of reports.

QUESTIONS

5.1 Define the term *entity*.

5.2 Define the term *attribute*.

5.3 Define the term *relationship*.

5.4 Define the term *fact table*.

5.5 Define the term *semiadditive*.

5.6 Define the term *nonadditive*.

5.7 Define the term *dimension* or *reference table*.

5.8 Explain what a factless fact table is and give some examples that were not given in the text.

5.9 Using the sales star schema that we developed in this chapter as a hint, develop a star schema model to track shipments of items sold.

PROJECTS

5.10 Recall that call behavior analysis is the analysis of the phone calls that a traditional phone or long-distance customer might make. The information is gathered by the switch that routes the call. This information will include the number of the phone originating the call, the phone number of the receiver of the call, and how long the call lasted. Design a conceptual data architecture for this data warehouse.

5.11 Design a logical data model for a CBA data warehouse.

5.12 Design a physical data model for a CBA data warehouse.

5.13 The network that actually connects a telephone call is a very expensive and valuable resource. Planning for network expansion is a very important task due to lost revenue if telephone calls don't go through or the increased cost if the network is too large in the wrong location. Design a data warehouse conceptual data architecture to track the network traffic.

5.14 Design a logical data model for a network data warehouse.

5.15 Design a physical data model for a network data warehouse.

5.16 Recall that buying trend analysis is performed by car manufacturers and dealers to best determine the car and options that certain demographic groups are likely to purchase. The demographic information is purchased from an outside source. Design a data warehouse conceptual data architecture to track the network traffic.

5.17 Design a logical data model for an automobile purchasing data warehouse.

5.18 Design a physical data model for an automobile purchasing data warehouse.

5.19 Recall that stores can use buying trend analysis to best determine the products that certain demographic groups are likely to purchase. For example, an electronics store could determine which demographic groups are likely to purchase which products. A premium clothing store could track demographic groups that are likely to purchase certain products. Design a data warehouse conceptual data architecture to track purchases by demographic group.

5.20 Design a logical data model for a demographic purchasing data warehouse.

5.21 Design a physical data model for a demographic purchasing data warehouse.

5.22 Recall that manufacturing organizations can use a data warehouse to track the compliance of their suppliers to their agreements. The agreements normally cover at a minimum the delivery timing of products and product quality. The manufacturing organization will do this to increase part quality and reduce the cost of having too much inventory. Design a data warehouse conceptual data architecture to track vendor compliance.

5.23 Design a logical data model for a vendor compliance data warehouse.

5.24 Design a physical data model for a vendor compliance data warehouse.

5.25 Recall that financial organizations can use a data warehouse to analyze the risk of consumer and certain other scenarios. This data warehouse can use data such as demographic data or payment history data to determine the risk of the loan. This enables the financial institution to estimate and manage the risk. Design a data warehouse conceptual data architecture to analyze risk.

5.26 Design a logical data model for a risk analysis data warehouse.

5.27 Design a physical data model for a risk analysis data warehouse.

5.28 Recall that airlines can analyze the travel trends of their frequent fliers in different demographic groups. This information can be used to target-market frequent fliers in the correct market groups. The demographic data is usually obtained from external sources. Design the data warehouse conceptual data architecture for a frequent flier analysis.

5.29 Design a logical data model for a frequent flier data warehouse.

5.30 Design a physical data model for a frequent flier data warehouse.

5.31 Recall that airlines can use a data warehouse to track the seasonal variations and growth expected in travel between locations. This data could also show how much food and beverages are consumed in different flights. This will help the airline select aircraft and catering to match needs. Design the data warehouse conceptual data architecture for an airline travel data warehouse.

5.32 Design a logical data model for an airline travel data warehouse.

5.33 Design a physical data model for an airline travel data warehouse.

5.34 Recall that educational institutions can use a data warehouse to analyze trends in class enrollment, grade history, and student evaluation of professors. The data for the data warehouse will be loaded at the end of every academic period. Information about class enrollment will come from the registration system, and student evaluation data can be loaded from the academic dean's operational system.

5.35 Design a logical data model for an academic data warehouse.

5.36 Design a physical data model for an academic data warehouse.

5.37 Health care providers can use a data warehouse to track diagnosis codes (ICD9 codes), the procedures and treatments for that diagnosis (called CPT codes), and the cost of those procedures and treatments. This can be used to analyze the success rates of procedures for a diagnosis or the cost versus the insurance reimbursement.

5.38 Design a logical data model for a medical data warehouse.

5.39 Design a physical data model for a medical data warehouse.

5.40 Recall that hotels can analyze the staying trends of their frequent guests in different demographic groups. This information can be used to target frequent guests for vacation packages. The demographic data is usually obtained from external sources.

5.41 Design a logical data model for a hotel stay data warehouse.

5.42 Design a physical data model for a hotel stay data warehouse.

5.43 Recall that hotels can use a data warehouse to track the total value of a frequent guest's stay. The value of the stay is the total amount the guest spends during the stay, including room, restaurant, room service, gift shop, and other incidental charges.

5.44 Design a logical data model for a hotel spending data warehouse.

5.45 Design a physical data model for a hotel spending data warehouse.

6

The Metadata Repository

6.1 INTRODUCTION: WHAT IS METADATA?

A rather literal definition of metadata is that *metadata* is "data about data." Metadata has been around for as long as computer programs. The first instances of metadata were in-line comments in the code and paper documentation. The point of this metadata was to make it easier for programmers doing code maintenance. Metadata is much more important in the decision support system world than the definition "data about data" would imply. In the world of data warehousing, metadata is a map to the data in the data warehouse.

A definition of *business information* is "data in a business context." Because the purpose of a data warehouse is to provide information to the business knowledge worker, a context must be provided for the business consumer of the warehouse data. This context is provided by the metadata. If metadata were not available, the business user probably would not have a chance of figuring out what the data means or where to start querying. In the data warehouse world, the user must be able to find out how a particular piece of data was calculated, what the source system was, and when it is valid. Because metadata provides an explanation of the data, where it came from, and user access, metadata is the big bolt that holds the data warehouse together. Metadata can be thought of as the lifeguard of the data warehouse. Nothing is allowed into or out of the data warehouse without an entry being made in the metadata. As an example, the data in the metadata database or repository tracks:

- Data transformations
- Valid dates and ranges for the data fields
- Source system or system of record
- Source system file and field mappings
- History of extracts
- Security

Most users access the data warehouse through the use of a tool with a graphical user interface. The nice thing about a graphical user interface is the ability to see all of the options that are available to you. The difficulty with a data warehouse is that so many options are provided to the user. There is a tremendous amount of data available, and most user access tools provide a wide range of options of ways to analyze the data. In operational systems, the user will be guided through the process with menus and prompts. Reports from operational systems will be selected from the list of canned reports. Without this structure, it is easy for the warehouse user to get lost. The metadata is the guide that helps the information worker navigate through the oceans of data.

A good name for the metadata repository from the information consumer's point of view would be the *information users' guide.* The guide would be comprised of the metadata database and a browser to view the data. In Section 6.4, we will see an example of an information users' guide. The guide will provide all the pertinent data to the user in an easy-to-browse format.

Metadata is stored in a metadata database or repository. When the value of metadata first became recognized, many vendors developed commercially available metadata repositories based on a wide variety of database management systems. Organizations also developed their own metadata management system. Some of the metadata systems were advanced documentation systems. Other metadata management systems were a piece of a large computer-aided software engineering tool. Still others were specialized metadata repositories. Regardless of the type of metadata repository, it must meet the needs of the organization.

We could joke at this point that there are two types of people: those who classify metadata and those who do not. The author is an avid classifier. At the planning phase, a three-part classification scheme is useful. The three types of metadata under this scheme are operational system metadata, usage metadata, and warehouse control metadata. This classification scheme is very valuable during the scoping and planning phase of a project because it provides focus on the details that are required at this stage. When the project moves from the planning phase to the pilot or production phase, a more elaborate scheme that classifies metadata into six dimensions is helpful.

The two different classification schemes are also useful for different size projects or types of organizations. For small projects with a small team and a small number of users, the number of details that need to be tracked is smaller, and the classification of metadata based on usage is probably sufficient. For large projects with a large team and a large number of users, the six-dimensional model provides an additional framework of rigor to help keep the project structured.

Why are we so interested in the classification of metadata? Organizations are not building metadata repositories anymore. A number of vendors have metadata repositories that can be purchased. Given that a metadata repository can generally be purchased for less it would cost to build, most organizations buy their metadata repositories. If you are going to buy a metadata repository, for what should you look? The type, amount, depth, and breadth of data in the repository are good starting points. The type, amount, depth, and breadth of browsing and reporting capabilities are another. The ability to scan existing databases and programs and populate the repository is another feature. Other systems must interface with the repository, so an API or other method, such as published metadata about the metadata repository, must be available. Of all of the desired features of a metadata repository, the hardest one to analyze is the breadth and depth of the data in the repository. This is one reason why a classification scheme is useful.

It is interesting to note that metadata typically exists in silos around the organization. The operational units have different metadata databases from each other and from the decision support organization. It is easy to imagine a metadata data warehouse where historical data about the organizations data is kept. Using a large metadata repository, an organization could get a handle on the amount of duplicate data that exists in the organization. A metadata data warehouse is the only way to maintain a history of the different versions of the data models that exist in the organization. Fields that appeared to be the same and have the same coding schemes could be compared to each other and with the definition of the data in the repository to get an estimate of the quality of the data in the organization. This metadata warehouse could then be used to identify potential data-quality troublespots in the organization.

Because metadata exists in silos throughout the organization and the different areas of the IT department, there is usually too much metadata in existence. As we work our way from transactional source system to the decision support data warehouse, we will note that every layer of software along the way has metadata. The OLTP application that captured the data has metadata. The database management system that stored the data has metadata. The middleware software that extracted the operational data has metadata. The data warehouse database has metadata. The data warehouse design system has metadata, and the user tools usually have metadata. The Metadata Council was born to develop a standard so that all of this metadata could reside in one location. To date, this council has not made great progress toward this goal.

Metadata is used throughout the process of implementation and operation of business systems. The metadata is used in very different ways during construction than during operation. Implementation-time metadata is used to aid in consistent use and reuse by database and application designers. Run-time metadata is constructed to help the information user understand the data in a business context and control access to the data warehouse. Implementation-time metadata is very different from run-time metadata.

Metadata can be classified as to whether it is active or passive. The term *active* or *passive* applies to the run-time behavior of the metadata. Active metadata will control the functions or behavior of some other application. Passive metadata is used by people in an informational sense. For instance, a data warehouse analyst looking up the definition of a field is using passive metadata. As another example, Hewlett-Packard's CASE tool SoftBench maintains metadata. When the metadata is used to specify the type of variable and control compiler options, it is operating in an active role. When a software engineer is browsing the metadata for a variable name, the metadata is operating in a passive role.

In review, the three different roles of use of metadata in the data warehouse are active, passive, and implementation-time metadata. These are explained in detail in Section 6.2. A six-part classification is introduced in the following paragraph and explained in detail in Section 6.3.

The six-part classification scheme divides the data into the six dimensions that a good writer covers in a story: who, what, when, where, why, and how. The dimensions reflect what data the metadata must be able to contain. These dimensions, together with the perspectives of the different users, form the basis of the Zachman framework. The Zachman framework is well described in several publications [Zachman][Inmon97]. Staying with the dimensions for just a moment, the dimensions of data that a good metadata repository must contain are:

1. The activities that occur with the data—how
2. The locations important to the data warehouse—where
3. The entities or contents of the data warehouse—what
4. The people who use the data warehouse—who
5. The motivation for the data—why
6. The times that things like data loads and summary table calculation occur—when

These dimensions deserve a further brief introduction. The metadata about activities contains data about business processes and functions in addition to data warehouse activities. The configuration information about the data warehouse components explains what physical equipment is located where. The entities dimension contains data about the source and content of the data warehouse. The data about people will define individuals' access and responsibility to the organization and the data warehouse. The business goals and objectives describe why the data is important. The time dimension describes the schedule of important processes that occur to provide the data warehouse and the relationships between process. This is the six-dimensional view of the data warehouse.

Thus, we have identified three types of metadata based on use. The types of metadata that have been identified are implementation-time metadata, active run-time metadata, and passive run-time metadata. The reader of this book interested in data use classification would find the book by Barry Devlin worth the time to read [Devlin]. We have also identified six dimensions that can be used to classify metadata. We will investigate each of these two classification methods in turn.

6.2 THE METADATA USAGE MODEL

Now that we have identified three types of metadata based on how the metadata is used, we can delve into the details of each of these three types. Recall that the three types of metadata are implementation-time metadata, active run-time metadata, and passive run-time metadata. Each of these is discussed below.

6.2.1 Implementation-Time Metadata

The first location for information about data in the operational system that will be loaded into the data warehouse is of course found in the operational system and the tools used to implement the operational system. The implementation metadata from existing database and file designs will be the first source of record for data warehouse metadata. Newer applications are usually designed with the help of CASE tools. These tools capture metadata through the process of designing the application and the application's data model. The metadata in these tools will be an additional source of metadata for the data warehouse. If the applications are maintained with CASE tools, the CASE tools will also provide information about changes in the source systems.

Other than for some reference table metadata changes, implementation-time metadata changes rather slowly over time. Whereas operational systems usually move to new versions only once or twice a year, decision support systems may have monthly upgrades. This means that the task of keeping current metadata from the operational source systems in the data warehouse is not as daunting a task as it might seem at first. Even when the source applications are updated, usually only a limited portion of the software is updated. This leaves most of the source system and metadata unchanged.

Once information from the operational source systems has been loaded into the data warehouse, the remaining metadata in the data warehouse is generated by the warehouse or the construction of the warehouse. This data warehouse–generated metadata is the active and passive run-time metadata, discussed next.

In the six-dimensional model of metadata, the implementation-time metadata corresponds to the dimensions of entities, locations, and motivations.

6.2.2 Active Run-Time Metadata

There are two sources for active run-time metadata. These sources are the implementation-time metadata and elements of the data warehouse environment itself. This type of metadata is actively used in the data warehouse environment to command and control the run-time data warehouse environment. Thus, this metadata is clearly run-time metadata. Unfortunately, this metadata is usually distributed in the user access tools, the data warehouse design CASE tools, and the database management software. The passive metadata discussed in the next section is also frequently distributed in several locations in the data warehouse. The distributed nature of the metadata in the data warehouse environment is illustrated in Figure 6-1.

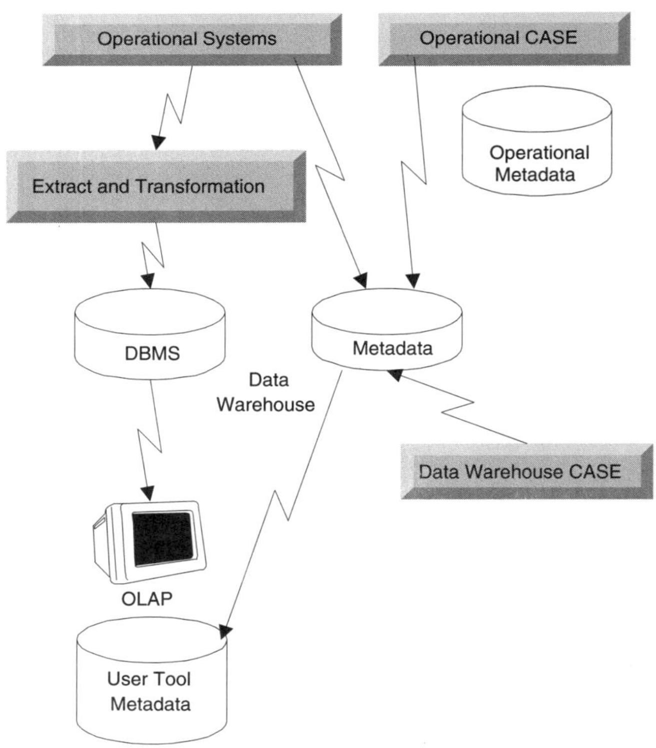

Figure 6-1 Metadata in the data warehouse environment.

Active run-time metadata is used to manage security and access to data in the data warehouse. This information also helps the data warehouse administrator gather data about how the data in the warehouse is being used. This usage data can enable the warehouse administrator to tune the data warehouse for better performance. It also enables the ability to charge for the information the data warehouse provides to the end user.

Because active run-time metadata captures access information for the data warehouse, it can capture large volumes of data. The typical approach to reducing the amount of stored data in the run-time database is to purge data older than a few months. This data should only be used for database tuning, charge back, and other generally positive purposes. Using this data in a police or big brother fashion will discourage users from accessing the data warehouse.

Data warehouse users need to know the last time a table was updated or the last time a new summary was created. This information usually comes from the extract and transformation tool, the user access tool, or manual entry. Like most time-sensitive information, this time-sensitive information exists as time stamps in the individual records in addition to summary information that is placed in information user guides. Because every individual record can contain time information, the volume of time-sensitive information can become very large.

This data about the currency of data in the data warehouse is very dynamic. Any time a table in the data warehouse is refreshed, the time stamps must be updated. Typical events that cause data in the data warehouse to be updated are scheduled data loads and business events such as end of a quarter. Information about the date range of data captured in the data warehouse and the date of last update enables the business user to place the data in a business context.

In the dimensions model of metadata, the utilization part of active run-time metadata matches the dimensions of people and activities. The time-sensitive part of active metadata obviously corresponds to the time dimension.

6.2.3 Passive Run-time Metadata

Passive run-time metadata might be the most important type of metadata in the data warehouse. We defined information as data in context, and passive run-time metadata creates the context for the business data. Thus, this data is imperative to utilization of the data warehouse. The business information customer is able to use the data intelligently with the help of passive run-time metadata, and the IT department achieves higher productivity through the documentation of existing systems.

Passive run-time metadata is originally loaded from the operational systems. The business users who are the chief consumers of the passive metadata in the data warehouse environment need different information than that needed by the database and application designers who were the original consumers of the information. When the metadata is loaded into the data warehouse, it must be reorganized for the business customers. The business customers will be browsing the metadata to understand the fields and usage for query purposes. Undoubtedly, the most important aspect of this metadata is the leverage it provides to consumers of the data warehouse information in understanding the meaning of the data in the business. The metadata must be organized and presented in a way that helps the business consumer understand the data elements and relate to their meaning. For instance, example values, ranges of values, and queries with an explanation of the results will all help the business consumer internalize the meaning of a data element in the data warehouse.

In many data warehouse environments, the information consumer must be able to view the technical organization of the data. The passive metadata would help provide this view. As an example, the business information worker must be able to understand the link between a product sold, product description, and sales region. Most access tools and middleware tools such as Hewlett-Packard's Intelligent Warehouse provide a means of presenting a virtual or logical view of the data. This removes the burden from the user of understanding the technical organization of the data.

It is sometimes important that the business consumer of the data warehouse information know the original source of the data. In addition, the information consumer may want to know the person or department that is responsible for the accuracy and maintenance of the source data. Similarly, it is important to be able to determine which person or organization is responsible for cleansing the data and loading the data into the data warehouse. At times the business users of the data will want to know more about the technical aspects of the data in the data warehouse than data warehouse builders thought, and the passive metadata should provide the answers.

Some portions of the data warehouse application details will need to be visible to the business information workers. For instance, the update schedule can be critically important to the knowledge worker. If the knowledge worker is developing information on the first fiscal quarter, he or she must know when all the data will be available in the data warehouse to generate the report. At times it is necessary to restructure the data in the data warehouse in stages. This information and the plan for completion of the restructuring must be presented in the metadata. This metadata can be used both by the business information workers and the maintenance programs that schedule and load data into the data warehouse.

Other application details will be stored in the data warehouse metadata for use by the data warehouse development and maintenance team. As an example, the programming language and author of an extraction program or report should be stored in the metadata. The date of the last maintenance revision of a program is typically very useful as well. The impact of particular data models on the decision support system is important to know, and this linkage of programs to data models must be stored somewhere. CASE tools that are used to design the decision support environment are nearly priceless for storing and maintaining this type of application detail.

6.3 THE METADATA DIMENSIONS MODEL

By way of refresher, the reader will recall that the data warehouse metadata can be divided into the same categories or dimensions that a good writer will cover when creating a story. A writer will cover the important dimensions of how, where, what, who, why, and when. The corresponding dimensions are activities, locations, entities, people, motivations, and times. These are discussed in detail in this section.

6.3.1 Activities Metadata

Activities metadata covers the how of the metadata. The most important activities information to be captured is metadata about the data source systems and the transformations that must occur in order to load data into the data warehouse. It has been pointed out several times that one of the difficulties with decision support in the unarchitected environment is the different unique identifiers and field codes that exist in the source systems. The various unique identifiers and coding schemes must be converted to a single coding scheme for the data warehouse, and all data moving to the data warehouse must be converted to this single coding scheme. The scheme used to convert the data before it is loaded into the data warehouse must be documented and readily accessible to the data warehouse support team. Some sophisticated data warehouse users will have an understanding of the source systems, and some of these users will also want to be able to view the data transformation rules part of the activities metadata.

The databases in the source systems are the original source of the data for the data warehouse. Although generally it is not a great idea to re-create the source system data models and maintain these data models, it is important to have enough information in the entities part of the metadata to enable a proper description of the transformations. It is also very important to document common activities that occur in the data warehouse. Users and data warehouse maintenance staff will want to see information on scheduled load times, scheduled report run times, and scheduled maintenance times that will affect the availability of the data warehouse. These details correspond closely to the availability, capacity planning, and service-level agreement portions of the IT service management model.

6.3.2 Locations Metadata

The locations of servers, workstations, software, and network components that form the parts of the data warehouse are the most important types of information to be stored in the locations metadata. This information is the basic part of a configuration management database. The information in the locations metadata can be used to determine the impact of changes in the configuration on the data warehouse system. It can also be used to determine the maintenance requirements of the system components.

The locations or configuration data can be created by loading a copy of the configuration from the operational system for the pieces that are shared. Another method that is used to populate the data is to perform an inventory of the technical environment. The quality of data in a metadata database should be checked from time to time, and one way to verify the quality of data on servers, workstations, software, and network components that form the parts of the data warehouse is to perform an audit of the existing data.

Building a data warehouse is a monumental undertaking in and of itself. The middle of a data warehouse project is not the place to start an entire configuration management project. A complete configuration management project is also a monumental task. Both Hitler and Napoleon discovered the difficulties of undertaking two major endeavors on two fronts at once. Undertaking a full configuration management project while working on another large project like a data warehouse project is not a good choice to make. A simple but effective approach is to keep just the smallest amount of information needed on the system configuration for the data warehouse. The data warehouse project may reveal the need for a larger configuration management project that will occur as a separate project.

6.3.3 Entities Metadata

The entities dimension corresponds to the contents of the data warehouse. While one tenant of the Zachman framework is that all dimensions are of equal importance, this dimension is arguably the most fundamental dimension in the metadata. If the contents of the data warehouse are incorrect, the rest of the project can be perfect and the entire project will still fail.

In the initial JAD sessions for the data warehouse project, the subject area or areas that are of interest to the business were identified. These subject areas will be documented in the entities metadata. For data warehouses that have established or are establishing multiple subject areas, the business rules that describe the relationships between the subject areas are also documented in the entities metadata. The entities are defined in the data modeling stage as to the type of information that is kept in the entities and the subject areas to which the entity will belong.

The attributes are the fields of data in instances of the entities. These fields provide the data that the warehouse user will have available to perform analysis. The metadata must have the business name, definition, and examples of the data in the data warehouse. The name of the field or fields and file or files in addition to the source system must be stored in the metadata as well. Some fields will exist only in the operational system, some elements exist only in the data warehouse system, and other elements exist in both.

The relationships in the data model correspond to business rules that define how the business operates and how the business uses data. These relationships are documented in the entities metadata and help the users of the data warehouse understand the connections between the entities. The cardinality and optionality of the relationships are also documented in the metadata. Some products, such as H-P's Intelligent Warehouse, provide virtual groupings of the entities into table sets. These virtual groupings eliminate the burden on the warehouse user to understand the relationships between the entities.

Different members of the team will view the data model differently. The business sponsor is interested primarily in a high-level view of the subject area and how the entities will provide the data that answers business questions. Power users will be interested in the description of fields and the types and number of codes that will be used in the entities. The physical database designer will be interested in creating a view of the database that can be implemented in a merchant database. The fact that the different members of the technical team can view the metadata differently is a sign that the metadata is doing its job and providing lots of data to the end user.

6.3.4 People Metadata

People are a very important part of any computer system. The roles and responsibilities that individuals assume in the data warehouse are documented in the people metadata. There is a wide variety of roles that individuals serve in the construction of a data warehouse. Although the precise name and responsibility of the role changes from project to project and organization to organization, some roles are common in all data warehouse projects. For example, every data warehouse project must have a sponsor. Other roles that are typical are data architect, IT architect, project manager, database administrator, business analyst, and line-of-business manager. These roles and the people who perform these roles must be documented in the data warehouse. The organizational structure is also documented in the data warehouse, but the data is typically copied from some operational source to the data warehouse. Like most data warehouse data, this data is maintained in the operational system and copied to the data warehouse on a regular basis.

User access and other user security features are based on the people metadata. People who access the data warehouse will be granted certain security privileges based on their logon and the security groups to which they belong. A security group allows the data warehouse administrator to assign a large number of security parameters to a group. Users will inherit the privileges of the access group by being assigned to the group. This enables the warehouse administrator to change the access rights of a large number of users by changing one group.

We have mentioned several times that the data warehouse team must stay focused on deploying a successful data warehouse. The data warehouse project may uncover the need for better security policy or systems in the operational source systems. In the midst of a data warehouse project is not the time to adopt an enterprise IT security project. Implement the prudent security measures that will protect the organization's data and finish the data warehouse project.

6.3.5 Motivation Metadata

In Chapter 2 we investigated a number of reasons why a data warehouse project would be undertaken. The reasons or business goals and objectives for the data warehouse project are the motivations. These motivations must be understood by all members of the data warehouse team. Thus, it is important to have the data warehouse motivations well documented in the motivation metadata.

The "what must get done" or motivation for the data warehouse is taken together with the activities that must happen with the data warehouse to indicate the time frames in which the activities must occur. These time frames will be used to set either formal or informal service-level contracts with customers of the data warehouse. An example of an item in a service-level contract would be that all end-of-quarter sales reports will be completed before 8 A.M. one week after the close of the quarter. These service-level expectations also drive the capacity planning and continuity planning aspects of the IT department.

There are many ways to capture the actual performance of a data warehouse system. Query-time or run-time data is easy to capture. This data clearly corresponds to the run-time metadata that was discussed previously. Although it is easy to capture this data, generally it is important to plan ahead to gather the information or design a method of capturing the information. Even if formal service-level agreements do not exist, users will frequently complain that the system is slow. The only way to respond adequately to the user is to have the facilities in place to capture the data that is needed to respond to the question.

There are many software tools that will assist the data warehouse administrator in diagnosing problems in the data warehouse. Some tools, such as H-P's Intelligent Warehouse, will provide information on the length of time a given request for data took to complete. Other tools, such as H-P's OpenView or Computer Associates' Unicenter, will gather information on network and server performance. All of these tools are invaluable to taking a proactive approach to maintaining good data warehouse performance.

6.3.6 Time Metadata

The data warehouse must track the date ranges for events and time periods that are important to the business user. As an example, the business knowledge worker might ask for a report showing all sales of a certain model of PC in the third quarter of 1998. To form the query properly, the system must be able to map from

Q3 1998 to all the days that correspond to Q3 1998. The time dimension must be able to keep data about these times of interest.

The time dimension also provides the information about the times and time periods that are important to the data warehouse infrastructure. Much of the time dimension information is actually stored as data stamps in the entities for other data warehouse metadata. Entities such as job schedule time and job time actual could be added to the time metadata to provide data about scheduled processes and actually track these processes in the actual entity. This gives both the business end user and the data warehouse team information about the scheduling of processes so that they can attempt to use the machine at a different time.

In summary, two different approaches to metadata classification have been introduced. The three-category classification scheme is not as comprehensive as the six-dimensional model, but it is easier to understand and provides plenty of detail. The six-dimensional model provides much more rigor and detail, along with plenty of opportunities for thought linkages to the ITSM process introduced in Chapter 2. A cross-reference between the two models is shown in Table 6-1.

6.3.7 Metadata Capture and Maintenance

When describing the process of creating a data warehouse metadata store, it is tempting to describe it as metadata creation and maintenance. However, much data about the data warehouse data existed in source systems before the data warehouse was created. Thus, the data warehouse environment just captures the existing metadata and adds to it. The difficulty is that this data must exist in the first place for it to be captured by the data warehouse. In many cases, all of the desired information was not placed in the sources systems when they were created. Documentation of systems is something that is usually left to the end of the project. Given that most programmers prefer dental root canals to documentation, and the work is left until the end of the project when the time and money run out, it should not be a surprise that most source systems are not well documented.

Table 6-1 Comparison of the usage and dimensional metadata classification schemes

	Implementation Time	Active	Passive
Activities		✓	
Location	✓		✓
Entities	✓	✓	✓
People		✓	
Motivation	✓		✓
Time		✓	✓

It was mentioned in Section 6.1 that metadata is dispersed throughout the organization. The metadata exists in silos around the different parts of the organization IT infrastructure. The metadata is usually not kept consistent throughout the organization. The task of maintaining the metadata requires discipline and dedication. The only thing worse than no metadata is out-of-date metadata. If an item of metadata is not maintained, the users of the information should not be allowed access to the out-of-date information. If it is impossible to maintain an item of metadata, it should not be included in the metadata database model.

It was mentioned earlier that it is both possible and desirable to build a metadata data warehouse. The metadata data warehouse would contain date information and possibly version information for all the entries that are made in the data warehouse metadata. Through careful use of the date information, it is possible to track the history and changes of the metadata. Depending on the granularity of date-stamped metadata, a version tracking system is also needed to provide information about the history of changes in the metadata.

6.3.8 Initial Metadata Creation

Many decisions about the creation of a data warehouse are made based on the size of the data warehouse and the number of people involved in the project. The decision to create a metadata repository is no different. For a small data warehouse that is the first such endeavor of an organization, the cost of the metadata repository might be large compared to the data warehouse if there are no metadata facilities. Thus, for initial data warehouses with fewer than 100 to 200 elements, it is probably a wise decision to forgo the use of a full-feature metadata repository. The purpose of the initial data warehouse will be to demonstrate the value of a data warehouse. Simultaneous construction of a metadata facility will distract the data warehouse team and discourage them from focusing on the task at hand.

A combination of commonly available desktop products can be used to create a simple metadata facility. For example, Microsoft Access could be used to create a database of extract and transformation rules. Access could also be used to provide an information users' guide. Mail facilities such as Microsoft Exchange, Lotus cc:Mail, or Hewlett-Packard OpenDesk can be used to notify users of process schedules and data load completions. Application and data access security can be provided by the user access application or the database.

6.3.9 Large Warehouse or Multiple-Subject-Area Metadata

If an organization is dedicated to creating a data warehouse with a large number of elements or a large number of users, it should consider purchasing tools to ease the task of metadata capture and maintenance. As mentioned earlier, it is important first to determine what an organization needs in a metadata repository. Once the list of needs has been created, the features of commercially available tools can be compared with the list of needs. It is usually important to assign weights to the desired features and to assign scores to the products that are being compared. This will enable the creation of a weighted score for each of the products being assessed.

Commercially available metadata repositories have a breadth of features for initial population of the repository. Most of the tools have the ability to scan COBOL code for data type description. CASE tools have facilities for the creation and storage of metadata about conceptual, logical, and physical data models. Most metadata repositories have a variety of abilities to load metadata from CASE tools. Metadata repositories also have the ability to scan merchant database management systems for metadata as well. It is important to match the abilities of a metadata repository tool to load data with the environment from which it will load the data.

Controlling the consistency of the metadata throughout the enterprise is a constant challenge. If a new valid code is added to a field in an operational system, this new code must propagate from the legacy systems, through the metadata repository, to the extract and transformation and end-user tools. To maintain consistency, change management policies, procedures, and tools are usually used to move this addition through the enterprise. Depending on the metadata architecture of the organization, tools such as database replication products or a publish–subscribe mechanism can be used to guarantee metadata consistency. In other cases, a part of the architecture might have a proprietary interface, and the update will be done procedurally. In addition to the metadata changes, the reference tables will need to have fields updated as well. This adds to the difficulty of maintaining synchronization of data in the operational and decision support systems.

6.4 THE INFORMATION USERS' GUIDE

The business user must have a map that will be a guide to the data that is stored in the data warehouse. This guide must provide a description of the tables and columns in the data warehouse. A simple but very effective form for the description is free-form text. The descriptions should include:

- Calculation method
- Valid dates
- Sample values
- Department or person responsible for the data
- Relationships to other data fields
- Source system
- Time of last load

There are several software packages on the market that provide the facility to do what was just described. Some of the programs available to do this are:

- Hewlett-Packard Intelligent Warehouse
- Prism Directory Manager
- Platinum Repository

The Hewlett-Packard product Intelligent Warehouse (IW) is a tool to help in the usability and manageability of a data warehouse. It was recently sold to Platinum. Intelligent Warehouse adds usability to the data warehouse by hiding the data warehouse complexity. A warehouse administrator creates virtual tables by identifying physical tables and defining join paths with the IW administrator tool. The administrator tool can then be used to create virtual tables by identifing the columns in the physical tables that will be mapped to the virtual tables. Many different groupings or sets of virtual tables can be created for different business users. Once these virtual tables have been created, they can be used by the organization's knowledge workers in place of the complex physical tables. The users'

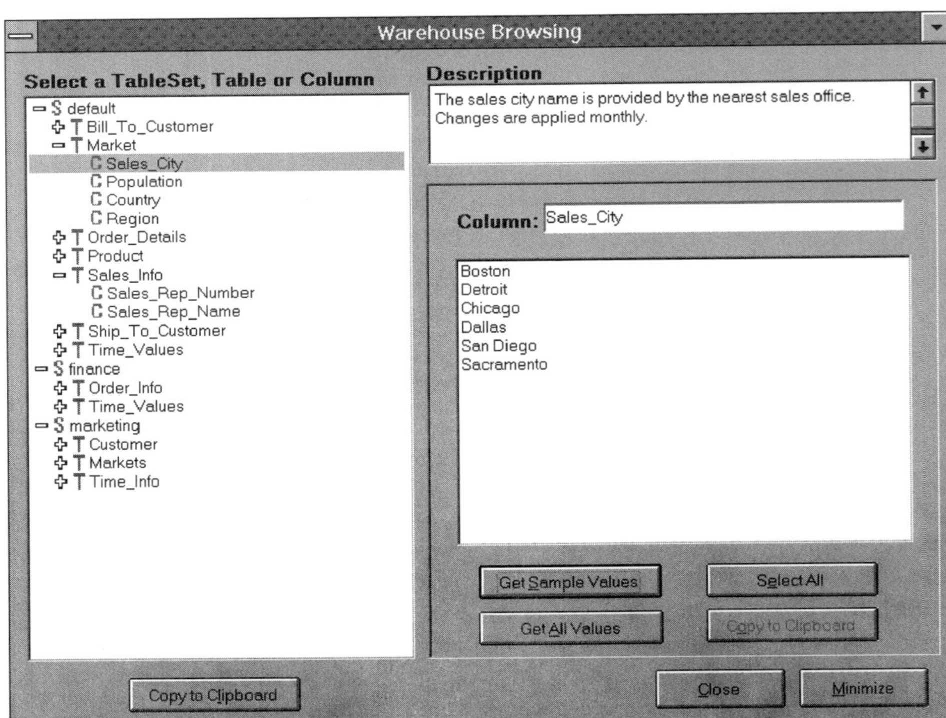

Figure 6-2 Browsing the data warehouse with the IW guide.

access tools, such as Microsoft Access, will see the same virtual files by connecting to IW through an ODBC connector.

The work of a single data warehouse administrator with the IW administrator tool makes it much easier for all who access the data warehouse. Because the data warehouse administrator defines the join paths, the user does not need to learn or be bothered with that detail. This greatly increases the productivity and reduces the training for people who use the data warehouse. With a middleware tool such as IW, it is easier to maintain than the large number of SQL views that could be used instead of IW. IW also keeps track of run-time use information such as query time and number of rows returned. Finally, the metadata information about the meaning and use of the virtual columns, tables, and table sets can be presented with a metadata browsing tool called IW guide.

With the IW guide, the virtual columns, tables, and table sets are presented on the left, and the definition of the data along with sample data values are shown on the right. The IW guide not only presents the metadata definitions but also has the ability to select a limited number of samples from a predefined sample set or retrieve all of the unique data values in the warehouse. This facility also enables the user to learn about the data in the warehouse by exploring its meaning, context, source system, values, and use of the data in the warehouse.

QUESTIONS

6.1 Create your own meaningful definition of metadata.

6.2 In your own words, explain the usage model for metadata.

6.3 In your own words, explain the dimensions model for metadata.

6.4 In your own words, explain the use of and need for a metadata data warehouse.

6.5 Explain the need for date stamping the entries in a metadata repository.

6.6 What features would you add to the information users' guide example shown in Figure 6-2?

6.7 How useful would it be to have a single metadata repository that integrates all the systems, including the legacy batch systems, OLTP systems, and warehouse systems?

PROJECTS

6.8 Create a conceptual data model for the activities dimension of a metadata database.

6.9 Create a conceptual data model for the location dimension of a metadata database.

6.10 Create a conceptual data model for the people dimension of a metadata database.

6.11 Create a conceptual data model for the entity dimension of a metadata database.

6.12 Create a conceptual data model for the time dimension of a metadata database.

6.13 Create a conceptual data model for the motivation dimension of a metadata database. (Conceptually difficult)

6.14 Create a single, conceptual data model for Problems 6.1 through 6.6. (Very difficult)

6.15 Create a conceptual data model.

7

Achieving Quality Information in the Data Warehouse

7.1 INTRODUCTION

As you will recall from Chapter 1, the main reasons for the construction of the data warehouse is the ability to integrate data from many different legacy systems. Before the introduction of decision support and data warehouse systems, different managers could produce reports showing different numbers or indicators of business health. These reports are produced by different systems or two different report routines in the same system. In some cases, the different values of different reports were due to different reporting techniques. It other cases, the different numbers were due to different data values or incorrect data values in different legacy systems. Although the data warehouse can remedy the problem of nonintegrated data sources, it cannot solve the problem of incorrect or bad data in the operational systems. This will be done by a program of data quality improvement. The improvement of data quality is the subject of this chapter.

The problem of poor data quality is one of the most difficult problems to solve while constructing a data warehouse. Although most failures of data warehouse projects can be attributed to process problems, source system data quality is one of the issues that must be part of the process of constructing a data warehouse. Even when data quality initiatives are included in the data warehouse methodology and project plan, the problems with source system data quality are generally worse and consume more time than anyone estimates initially. In the author's experience, problems relating to general data quality are the most frequent cause of extensions to the project schedule.

There are many different ways to improve the quality of information in the data warehouse. The first step in the program is to discover where data quality problems exist in the source systems. Where sources for improvement have been recognized, methods must be developed to improve data quality. One way to improve the quality of data in the data warehouse is to improve the quality of data in the source systems. Another way to improve the quality of data in the data warehouse is to correct the data during the movement of data from legacy systems to the data warehouse. Although this all sounds easy in theory, a commitment to the improvement of data quality in the data warehouse requires commitment to a continuous process of information quality improvement in the enterprise.

Why do we use the term *information quality improvement?* The goal of a data warehouse is to provide good answers to questions. To do this, we must not only have the right bits in the right fields but must also have rigorous definitions of the values of data in these fields. Only by having thorough definitions of the data fields can we also determine whether the data in the fields is correct. After the quality of the data in the fields has been determined, a process to clean up the data loaded into the data warehouse can be implemented. Similarly, other processes can be undertaken to improve the quality of the data definitions and quality of the data in the source systems. When improved data sources and definitions are integrated in the data warehouse, improved information in the form of accurate integrated data and definitions in the warehouse is the result.

The process of information quality improvement in the enterprise has several interconnected steps. This process is shown in Figure 7-1. The starting point of this process is to determine the value of quality information in the enterprise. Incorrect information has a cost to the enterprise, and this can be determined as well. Next, the quality of data definitions in the enterprise can be determined. After the quality of the data definitions has been determined, the quality of the captured data can be determined. Once the quality and difficulty of the data definitions and stored data have been determined, a process can be developed to improve the quality or information in the enterprise.

This process will be aimed not only at the cleansing of data to be loaded into the data warehouse, but also at the quality of the definitions and data stored in the legacy systems. The high-level conceptual diagram of the flow of information in the data warehouse was introduced in Chapter 1 and is repeated in Figure 7-2. It is important to remember that the legacy systems are sources of both data and information about the data or metadata.

Enterprise information quality improvement programs are projects that can be very large and very daunting. It is very important to approach them with the same principles as those used for a rapid application development project. The best place to start is with the identification of a data quality improvement sponsor. This sponsor must have the ability to fund the project and an understanding

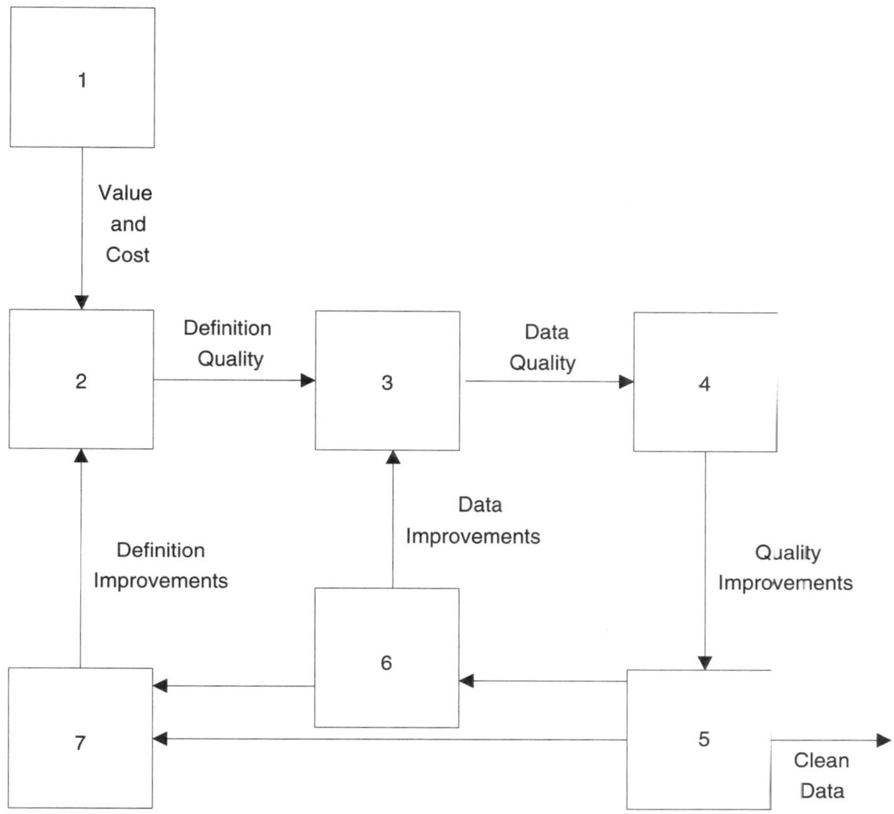

1. Determine Information Value and Cost
2. Determine Quality of Data Definitions
3. Determine Quality of Data Content
4. Implement Information Quality Program
5. Implement Data Cleanup
6. Implement Data Quality Program
7. Implement Definition Quality Program

Figure 7-1 Process flow for a data quality improvement program.

of the return on the investment in information quality. The sponsor should also identify and empower an information quality czar or project manager.

Once the sponsor and quality czar have been identified, the next step is to identify the data that is the most critical to the success of the data warehouse. This can be done during one of the data warehouse JAD sessions. A list of data that is critical to the success of the warehouse will be developed. Rough estimates of the

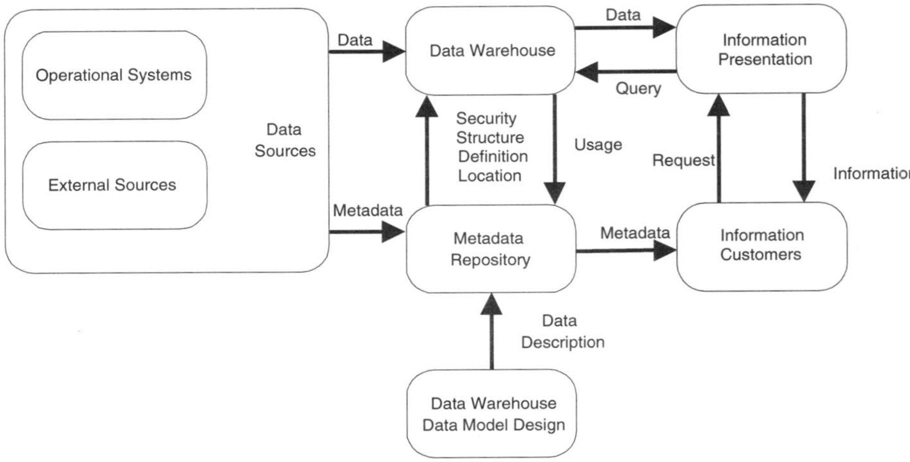

Figure 7-2 Legacy systems must be the source of quality data and metadata for the warehouse.

level of quality desired and the costs associated with poor data quality can be developed during the JAD session. The information quality improvement program can run in parallel with the data warehouse data modeling effort. Once the data modeling effort has started, the data elements in the data warehouse and the source of record will be identified. A gap assessment can be done to identify the gap between the quality of the data in the operational system and the quality of data desired in the data warehouse. A plan can then be developed to increase the quality of the data to the level required and the cost of implementing the plan identified. The information quality sponsor must then support the program to improve the data quality and develop the support of the other parts of the organization that might be affected.

An information quality program is similar to any total quality management program. Lessons and tools that are taught and used in total quality programs can be helpful in the data quality program. Examples of other useful tools are Pareto diagrams, impact analysis, and the Shewhart cycle of plan, do, check, and act.

7.2 VALUE OF QUALITY INFORMATION

There are many ways to state and understand the value of quality information. The benefits of quality data are both tangible and intangible. Clearly, the decisions by the organizational leadership will only be as good as the information on which they are based. While good decisions are a clear potential benefit of quality information, it is difficult to calculate the return on the benefit of better decision making. In other cases, the benefit of quality information can be calculated. As an example, we all receive advertisements in the mail. Errors in the data used to generate these mailings will cause the mail either to be returned or delivered incorrectly. As an example, many of us receive mail that has an obvious error in the name, and we place this mail in the recycle bin unopened. This information quality problem has a cost associated not only with the piece of mail that was ignored, but a cost associated with the lost opportunity to contact a potential customer.

We discuss data mining later in this book. The goal of data mining is to find trends in the data. The ability of an automated process to find trends in the data can be drastically altered by the quality of the data. As an example, fraud detection is based on the idea that fraud will have some characteristics that are different from normal events. A record of an event with incorrect data will have characteristics that are different from normal events. Thus, incorrect data might be indistinguishable from data representing fraud and make it impossible to automate the detection of potential fraud. This could be a very high cost of poor data quality.

Data gains value as it is processed into information in the organization's information factory. As an example, data about an order from a customer is very important because it enables the organization to fulfill the order, but the order data has limited value. Once the order data is integrated with shipment data, customer data, customer demographic data, and payment data, it becomes very valuable information. This information value chain is shown in Figure 7-3.

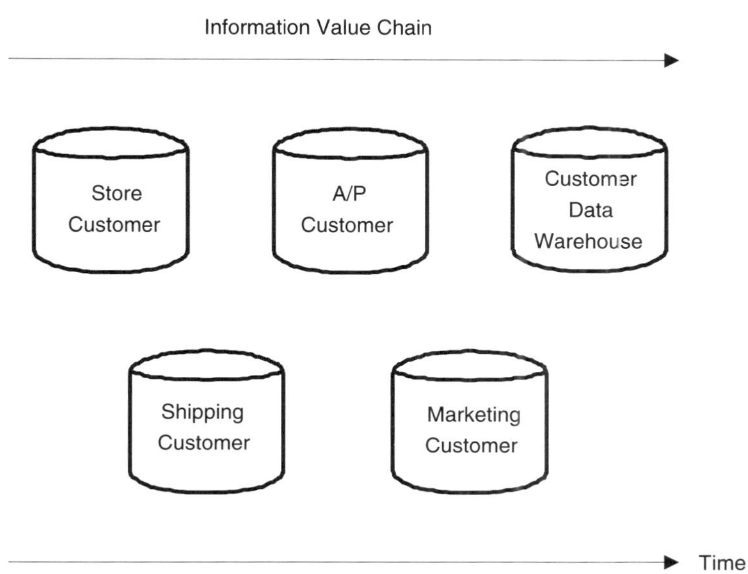

Figure 7-3 Information value chain.

As data moves through the organization's information value chain, errors can propagate and grow as data is integrated into information. As an example, if a store's point-of-sale terminal captures an incorrect customer identifier, that transaction will be associated with the wrong customer. As that data is integrated in the data warehouse, it will incorrectly match other information with that transaction based on the incorrect customer identifier. This illustrates the importance of identifying and correcting errors as early as possible in the data life cycle.

7.3 DIFFICULTY OF OBTAINING QUALITY DATA

There are many reasons why it is difficult to capture and maintain quality data. Some of the difficulties are process problems, some are people problems, and other difficulties are technology problems. Regardless of the cause for the data quality problem, it is important to identify the cause of the problem and, where possible, a solution.

There are many technical reasons for the data quality problems that are typical of today's legacy systems. One reason is the lack of architecture of some of these systems. These legacy systems have been developed over a long period without a plan as to their evolution. As the systems evolved, they were patched and patched to add new functionality or modify existing functionality. This frequently leads to a situation where the data that is entered is not rigorously checked to be correct. In this case, data entry errors are not discovered and corrected early in the data life cycle.

In addition, the principles of data architecture, relational database design, and normalization had not become popular until much later. This leads to systems where the rules about the data are embedded in the legacy code rather than being part of the data. As an example, a program might use the same field to store data of different meaning, depending on the value of the data. While this conserves the amount of storage space required, it makes it very difficult to verify that the data entered is correct.

As was pointed out in Chapter 1, most legacy computer systems were designed to perform particular tasks for different operational departments. These legacy systems were designed and constructed to meet the needs of a particular operational area without concern for the needs of another area or corporate reporting. There was no general plan for sharing data from one operational data silo to another. This situation is illustrated again in Figure 7-4.

In order to enable the sharing of data from one system to another, it is necessary to design and use common unique identifiers or keys in the data elements in the different systems. This enables the unique identifier in one system to be matched with a unique identifier in another system to match records. A social security number is used in the United States in a variety of systems to uniquely

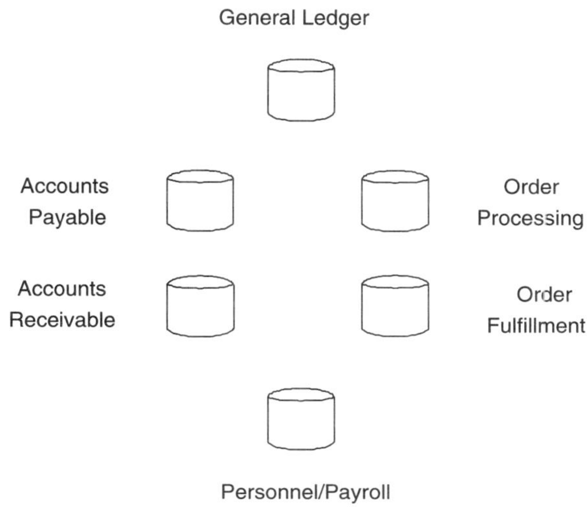

Figure 7-4 Lack of connections between data silos increases the errors in derived data.

identify the person associated with that number. Without a unique identifier to match records, some other less reliable method must be used to match records. This leads to errors in the data in other systems because of errors in matching data records that are transferred to other systems.

Process problems are frequently caused by data being entered into an operational system at the wrong point in the operational process. Process problems are also frequently caused by lack of understanding of the meaning of the data in the operational systems and how to resolve questions about the operational computer system. Both of these problems can be reduced by training and excellent on-line help features. Process problems can also be improved by raising the awareness of the importance of quality and rewarding people for quality work.

People problems are usually caused by lack of understanding or organizational emphasis on quality. Difficulties with people entering incorrect data into systems can be decreased by changing the emphasis on pure speed of processing to quality of processing where quality is composed of both speed and accuracy. Systems that track the user who entered the data are valuable because they make it possible to measure the quality of people's work.

In summary, there are many root causes for the generation of incorrect data. The important point is to identify the sources of data errors and work within the organization's culture and technical infrastructure to eliminate these causes of errors.

7.4 METHODS TO EVALUATE THE VALUE OF QUALITY DATA

There are many ways that the value of quality information in the data warehouse can be assessed. In order to place a value on the quality of the data in the warehouse, it is imperative to understand the organization and the impact of data in the organization. The cost of poor data quality can also be a measure of the value that quality data could be to the organization.

As an example of the value of quality data, it is interesting to study the concept of lifetime customer value. A customer of a grocery store may keep shopping at that store for seven to ten years. During the period of time that the customer will be shopping at the store, the average customer will generate profits that are equivalent to some lump sum paid today. The lifetime present value of the customer might be $1000. Suppose that the store mails advertisements to 4 million of the known customers and that 5 percent of the names on the mailing list are incorrect. Of the 5 percent that receive advertisements with incorrect names, 2 percent are offended enough to shop at a new store. In other words, 4000 customers changed stores because of the mailing error. If the lifetime value of the customer is $1000, the error cost roughly $4 million.

As another example of the value of quality data, it is illustrative to consider the advertisements we all receive in the mail. Suppose that a major retail organization mails 50 million advertisements. Each advertisement cost 60 cents to create and mail. If 7 percent of the addresses in the database are incorrect, the address error problem cost $2.1 million. If 30 percent of the people who did not receive an advertisement due to the address error would have purchased a product with an average profit of 75 cents, the address error cost $788,000 in unrealized profit.

The important point to evaluating the cost of data errors is to understand the business and develop a good understanding of the impact of the data errors on the business operation. The examples just given were both centered on retail operations, but the reader will be able to extrapolate these examples to new situations.

7.5 FOR WHAT QUALITY SHOULD WE STRIVE?

The selection of a data quality target by an organization should be based on fact but driven by corporate culture and philosophy. Some organizations believe that virtually all-identifiable data errors must be identified and eliminated. This is part of an organizational philosophy. The organizational mission, values, and goals will state that flawless operation is an essential component of the organization's success.

In other organizations, the approach to data quality will be an investment in profitability. In this case, marginal return on the investment is a good way to determine the level of quality that should be sought in the data warehouse. This concept is illustrated in Table 7-1.

Table 7-1 Marginal costs and returns for reducing errors in the data

Percentage Error	Marginal Cost	Marginal ROI
6	0	0
5	500	2000
4	550	1500
3	650	1100
2	800	800
1	1000	600

The basic idea of marginal cost is that if I invest a dollar, we would like to get at least a dollar returned over some period of time. In the example shown in Table 7-1, we have selected a three-year return period. We will continue investing until the amount that is returned is equal to or less than what we invested. The same principle works for investment in data quality. From a strictly financial perspective, investments in quality should be made until the marginal return is equal to the marginal investment. Using the example shown in Table 7-1, reducing the error rate from 6 percent to 2 percent will match marginal cost with marginal ROI.

7.6 METHODS TO EVALUATE THE DATA

There are many ways that the current data can be evaluated. Some of these methods are manual, and some of them are automated. One of the first things that the author does is list a portion of the data to the screen. The human mind is an amazing thing, and it is usually a simple thing to spot irregularities in the data or metadata. The author will use whatever query tool is available to select rows from an important table joined with other tables as necessary. As the values scroll by on the screen, it is easy to notice changes in the patterns, such as length or values. This is an important way to become acquainted with the data and to internalize the meaning of the data presented in the metadata browser.

Another interesting manual method to get a feel for potential errors in the data is to perform specific selects of data to look for common data errors. As an example, the author receives mail with the last name spelled 10 or 12 different ways each month. Selecting names in the customer database using wild cards or a similar statement in the SQL where clause will find a group of names that might be entered incorrectly in the database.

Another way to discover opportunities for improvement in the legacy system data is to ask users, programmers, and systems analysts if they know of any particular problems with the data. Frequently, there will be a body of knowledge in the organization about existing data problems. The author has worked on several data warehouse projects where one of the users pointed out that a certain customer was in the system several times with different names. By using the select trick described in the preceding paragraph, it was discovered that one customer was in the system 27 times.

Finally, software tools can be used to examine the data. The advantage of using software to search through the data is obviously that large amounts of data can be examined very quickly in predetermined ways. Some tools are very good at fixing particular data problems such as mailing address errors. Other tools are more generally capable and will detect, or detect and correct, a wider range of errors. These programs are discussed in greater detail in the following section.

7.7 TOOLS TO EVALUATE THE DATA

There are a very large number of software tools that are available to evaluate the quality of source system data. These software tools have a wide range of features and prices. Generally speaking, these tools fall into one of four categories: audit, cleansing, preventive, and rule discovery.

An audit program will search the data for incomplete records, duplicate records, invalid values, and lack of synchronization of data in different environments. An audit program will indicate where the problems exist and indicate the number and percentage of errors that it discovered. An audit program does not "fix" or "cleanse" the data. Once the problems in the data have been identified, a cleansing program will correct the data if possible.

A rule discovery program identifies patterns in the data. The patterns in the data that can be identified are both relationships between data fields and allowed values of data fields. As an example of a possible relationship between the data elements, we know that a state abbreviation also indicates a range of zip codes. For instance, a state code of OR for Oregon might indicate that the zip code should be in the range 97000 to 97200. A value restriction on a field would be that a U.S. postal state code should be contained in the set (AK, AL, …,WY).

A cleansing program identifies data errors and corrects them. The data errors are identified with rules that have been programmed into the tool, have been discovered by the tool, or a combination of the two. When the tool finds a violation of the rules, it uses the rules to correct the problem.

A preventive program uses a set of rules to identify problems and perform edit checks on the input of data to a program. Programs of this type improve the quality of data that is maintained in operational systems by improving the quality of data that is initially entered.

While the software products for data quality enhancement can be categorized into four rather simple categories, the capabilities and strengths of the products that are commercially available vary greatly. The match of features, price, and performance to a particular situation must be done based on the requirements of the situation and the capabilities of the project. The list of data quality programs shown in Table 7-2 is not complete and should be considered illustrative only.

In addition to commercially available software products, it is obvious that custom software can be developed to meet the needs of a particular situation. Due to the cost of developing and maintaining custom software and the relatively low price of some commercial products, commercial off-the-shelf software is usually purchased to fulfill data quality enhancement needs. In cases where there is significant expertise in the organization in writing data extract and cleansing programs or these programs already exist, it might be cost-effective to use custom software to perform the cleansing.

7.8 DATA EVALUATION OR AUDIT

We have investigated the value of quality data, the process to get quality data, and the tools to examine the data. In Section 7.1, we outlined briefly how to get an information quality program started. The problem that remains is the discovery of the nature and depth of data quality issues for a given project. A data audit or evaluation is the best way to quantify any data quality problems that exist in the organization. An initial data evaluation or audit must be done to sell a sponsor on the nature and severity of the problem. Once an information quality project has a

Table 7-2 Examples of data quality programs

Vendor	Product	Category	Operating System
Carleton	Passport	Cleansing	Win 3.1 & 95,NT, OS/2
ETI	Extract	Cleansing	Solaris, HP UX, AIX
Information Builder	EDA-SQL	Cleansing	MVS, AIX, HP UX, Solaris
Platinum Technology	InfoRefiner	Cleansing	MVS, most Unix, OS/2, Windows 3.1,95, and NT
PostalSoft	TrueName, ACE	Preventive Cleansing	UNIX, NT UNIX, NT
QDB Solutions	QDB Analyze	Audit	Windows 95, NT
SAS Institute	SAS Warehouse Administrator	Cleansing	MVS, UNIX, Windows
Vality Technology	Integrity Data Reengineering	Cleansing and rule discovery	MVS, UNIX
WizSoft	WizRule WizWhy	Rule discovery Audit	Windows 95 Windows 3.1/95

sponsor, the data audit will show where the project should focus. This points to the usual problem of finding sponsorship for a project that is not understood well enough to state the benefits without having the funding to understand the project. This is the proverbial chicken-and-egg problem.

The purpose of the initial data audit is to quantify the current data quality situation. This will help identify potential areas for improvement and start the process toward being able to state the benefits of improving the data quality. If a data quality improvement process is already in progress or has finished, a data audit will quantify the improvements that were generated.

The key to success is to start small, stay limited to the data fields that will give the best return, and stay focused. It is very important that the data audit completes in a very short period of time, say, a month or two for the first audit. The data and metadata are changing while the audit is taking place, and a long data audit process will guarantee that the data or metadata has changed enough during the audit to make the results questionable. Sponsors also want demonstrable results quickly. It is important that the data audit not become a process like the enterprise data modeling efforts that failed due to their size and inability to deliver a timely and useful result.

The areas in the data quality flow diagram of Figure 7-1 that are covered in a data audit are the determination of the quality of data definitions or metadata and the determination of the quality of the stored data. These are the boxes labeled 2 and 3 in the figure. It is impossible to determine if a word is used correctly in a sentence without a definition of the work. Similarly, it is impossible to know if an instance of data is correct or incorrect without a definition of the data field. This makes it imperative to start a data quality program with an investigation of the quality of the metadata. After the metadata has been investigated, the data that is stored can be investigated to determine correctness as defined by the metadata.

What constitutes good metadata? Data definitions must be meaningful to the business user and conform to the organization's data modeling standards. A good data definition must be understandable to business users and should be stated using language and abbreviations that are meaningful to the business. The definition must be unambiguous, complete, clear, and precise. The data definition must also contain any business rules that cover use of the data element along with any rules that govern integrity or relationships with other data fields. There must be only one definition of the data element in use in the organization.

In addition to using software to discover problems with the data, what other ways are there to discover errors in the data contents? In other words, how do we do the data content audit that is suggested by box 3 in Figure 7-1? People, things, and events can all be used to check the accuracy of stored data.

People such as customer service representatives and salespeople will have opportunities to verify data content with the customer and the rest of the outside world. A salesperson can ask a customer if she still lives at 123 Adams Drive in Denver, Colorado. H-P has used telemarketers to verify the data collected about customers. Another option is to send a survey to customers via first-class mail.

Improperly addressed mail will be returned, and this is an indicator of a problem with the mailing address.

Events such as a customer order provide an opportunity to verify that the address on the order is the same as the address that is stored in the system. Some companies will verify order details by calling the customer back immediately and confirming the order. Customers calling to complain is another opportunity to fix the data.

Another way to improve the quality of data is to verify any physical properties that are stored in the database. For instance, the data might state that a product has a certain width, height, depth, and weight. These physical dimensions can be verified simply by measuring the product. A good question to ask is: Do the physical dimensions include packaging?

Once the initial data quality audit has been performed, a data quality program can be implemented. For organizations with very clean data, the data quality program might consist simply of periodic data audits. Organizations with more extensive data challenges will need to implement a more extensive program in order to correct these data problems. These organizations will need to implement a full version of the corrective measures illustrated in Figure 7-1.

QUESTIONS

7.1 Nicknames are a problem and opportunity to the world of data quality. In addition to the problem of knowing to address someone as Robert versus Bob or Elizabeth versus Liz, there are names such as Jack and John where the legal name might be John but the person prefers to be called Jack. Develop a plan to make a customer database more accurate and more intimate.

7.2 Please identify the names of the roles and the responsibility of the roles involved in the creation and maintenance of quality information.

7.3 Describe the function of a data audit software program.

7.4 Describe the function of a data cleansing software program.

7.5 Describe the function of a data quality problem preventive software program.

7.6 Describe the function of a data rule discovery software program.

7.7 Suppose that a store mails advertisements to 50 million of its customers, 10 percent of the addresses on the mailing list are incorrect, and these advertisements are not delivered. Each piece of mail costs 79 cents to print and mail. In addition, 10 percent of the customers who did not receive a mailer would have purchased a product that on average would have generated $1 in profit. What is the cost of the data errors?

7.8 Explain the factors that would be part of a buy-versus-construct decision of data cleansing tools.

Table 7-3 Marginal costs and returns for reducing errors in the data

Percentage Error	Marginal Cost	MarginalROI
5	0	0
4	$600	$1800
3	$1200	$1200
2	$2000	$1100
1	$3000	$1050

7.9 Describe the various ways that errors in data happen and methods of correcting or preventing them.

7.10 State the qualities that a good definition of a data field must have.

7.11 Given Table 7-3, for which optimal percent error should we strive? Explain in as much detail as possible.

7.12 What are the steps to starting a data quality program?

7.13 Your organization has been working on an ongoing metadata quality program for five years. You are sure that the metadata for the organization is excellent. How would the steps illustrated in Figure 7-1 be altered for this case?

7.14 The data in Tables 7-1 and 7-3 was given without explanation. How could this data be obtained?

PROJECTS

7.15 Call behavior analysis is the analysis of the phone calls that a traditional phone or long-distance customer might make. The analysis is done to look for trends in the calls to determine if the customer could benefit from special services or pricing. Demographic information about customers is obtained from external sources. The information is gathered by the switch that routes the call. What opportunities for data quality improvements would there be in this system? Which tables and elements should be audited first? State several examples of good data definitions using the data model for this project.

7.16 The network that actually connects a telephone call is a very expensive and valuable resource. Planning for network expansion is a very important task due to lost revenue if telephone calls don't go through or the increased cost if the network is too large in the wrong location. Network information is captured by a variety of systems. What opportunities for data quality improvements would there be in this system? Which tables and elements should be audited first? State several examples of good data definitions using the data model for this project.

7.17 Buying trend analysis is performed by car manufacturers and dealers to best determine the car and options that certain demographic groups are likely to purchase. What opportunities for data quality improvements would there be in this system? Which tables and elements should be audited first? State several examples of good data definitions using the data model for this project.

7.18 Stores use buying trend analysis to best determine the products that certain demographic groups are likely to purchase. For example, an electronics store could determine which demographic groups are likely to purchase which products. A premium clothing store could track demographic groups that are likely to purchase certain products. What opportunities for data quality improvements would there be in this system? Which tables and elements should be audited first? State several examples of good data definitions using the data model for this project.

7.19 Manufacturing organizations can use a data warehouse to track the compliance of their suppliers to their agreements. The agreements normally cover at a minimum the delivery timing of products and product quality. The manufacturing organization does this to increase part quality and reduce the cost of having too much inventory. Other technologies, such as electronic data interchange (EDI), allow the manufacturing company and its suppliers to exchange information orders for parts and deliveries of parts electronically. What opportunities for data quality improvements would there be in this system? Which tables and elements should be audited first? State several examples of good data definitions using the data model for this project.

7.20 Financial organizations can use a data warehouse to analyze the risk of consumer and certain other scenarios. This data warehouse can use data such as demographic data or payment history data to determine the risk of the loan. This enables the financial institution to estimate and manage the risk. What opportunities for data quality improvements would there be in this system? Which tables and elements should be audited first? State several examples of good data definitions using the data model for this project.

7.21 Airlines can analyze the travel trends of their frequent fliers in different demographic groups. This information can be used to target market frequent fliers in the correct market groups. The demographic data is usually obtained from external sources. What opportunities for data quality improvements would there be in this system? State several examples of good data definitions using the data model for this project.

7.22 Airlines can use a data warehouse to track the seasonal variations and growth expected in travel between locations. This data could also show how much food and beverages are consumed in different flights. This will help the airline select aircraft and catering to match needs. Which tables and elements should be audited first? State several examples of good data definitions using the data model for this project.

7.23 Educational institutions can use a data warehouse to analyze trends in class enrollment, grade history, and student evaluation of professors. The data for the data warehouse will be loaded at the end of every academic period. Information about class enrollment will come from the registration system, and student evaluation data can be loaded from the academic dean's computer system. What opportunities for data quality improvements would there be in this system? Which tables and elements should be audited first? State several examples of good data definitions using the data model for this project.

7.24 Health care providers can use a data warehouse to track diagnosis codes (usually, ICD9 codes), the procedures and treatments for that diagnosis (called CPT codes), and the cost of those procedures and treatments. This can be used to analyze the success rates of procedures for a diagnosis or the cost versus the insurance reimbursement. What opportunities for data quality improvements would there be in this system? Which tables and elements should be audited first? State several examples of good data definitions using the data model for this project.

7.25 Hotels can analyze the staying trends of their frequent guests in different demographic groups. This information can be used to target-market frequent guests for vacation packages. The demographic data is usually obtained from external sources. What opportunities for data quality improvements would there be in this system? Which tables and elements should be audited first? State several examples of good data definitions using the data model for this project.

7.26 Hotels can use a data warehouse to track the total value of a frequent guest's stay. The value of the stay is the total amount the guest spends during the stay, including room, restaurant, room service, gift shop, and other incidental charges. What opportunities for data quality improvements would there be in this system? Which tables and elements should be audited first? State several examples of good data definitions using the data model for this project.

8

THE CONCEPTUAL AND LOGICAL DATA WAREHOUSE

8.1 INTRODUCTION

In the development of our outline of a methodology of building a data warehouse thus far, the business needs for information have been identified and the data required to meet those needs designed. This is a little like knowing there is going to be a fine ball in town, but still needing to purchase tickets, a tuxedo, a gown, and flowers. The successful data warehouse project will still need to create and implement a plan to create the infrastructure and implement the data warehouse. Selection and implementation of the correct data warehouse architecture is an important next step.

The correct architectural selection for a data warehouse is a very important early step in the construction of a warehouse. An incorrect architecture will lead to structures that will not scale to meet the needs of the organization and the enterprise data warehouse. It is possible to develop a data warehouse architecture that is impossible to implement. It is a constant dilemma to the data warehouse architect to choose between an elegant architecture and a simple implementation. Some architecture is both elegant and simple. In the world of physical structures, the Washington Monument is both simple and elegant. One design objective of the warehouse architecture should be the development of an architecture that is simple, elegant, and meets the needs of the organization.

Many people have studied how businesses can better use information technology to further the objectives of the business. The author has had the opportunity to work on some of these projects in addition to working with consultants and corporate IT staff who have spent their professional lives doing just that. These experiences have ranged from small organizations to some of the largest. Through this experience, best practices have been developed that will guide in the construction of an information technology architecture that will further the objectives of the business. Some best practices in data warehouse architecture will be developed here.

The increasing pace of change of business and technology demands that an organization develop methods of adapting rapidly to these changes. When these changes occur, the organization needs a way to make rapid technology and business decisions. A structure of well-defined information architecture principles will assist an organization adapt to these changes. The architectural principles will help an organization select new technology that is in tune with the existing infrastructure. The architecture principles act as guiding statements or road maps for the selection of new technology.

As the information technology industry moves toward open system and commercial off-the-shelf technology, the interest in technology architectures has greatly increased. This interest is based in part on the need to be able to select implementation components intelligently, and it is driven in part by the fact that traditional corporate standards failed. The corporate standards were very siloed and were best at guiding specific projects or classes of applications. Projects that did not fall into these particular standard silos were forced to make decisions without the help of guidance of the bigger view or corporate IT direction.

End users and line-of-business managers are the ones driving these changes. Users have more practical understanding of technological than ever before. Users are no longer intimidated by the big machines in the glass house, and they believe they have needs that can be met with technology they have seen. They also have seen resources committed to projects that did not work or were rapidly replaced. This leads to frustration and lack of trust in the way that this is done. These users want a structure that will guide future decisions to be made in a manner that is more robust than what happened before. The information systems architecture will be the chief guide in the future. This guide should reduce the number of failed projects, increase the reuse of IT technology, and leverage learned skills from one project to another.

In this chapter a set of principles is developed that will guide the development of architectures that meet the needs of an enterprise data warehouse. From the various architectures possible, recommendations will be provided that will assist in the selection of an architecture that matches the organization. Once the architecture has been selected, a plan must be developed to implement that architecture.

8.2 WHY PRINCIPLE-CENTERED?

It seems that every few months, an individual or vendor has an idea or product that is designed to save the universe of IT from the fine mess into which we have gotten ourselves. Depending upon what has been proposed and what the need is, some of these methods or products sound very interesting, but how do we evaluate these offerings? What hardware will be best over a substantial period? As an IT organization, how do we deliver what the business customer demands? Is the "forward predictive Blasserhasset software" package for which a department is asking what the organization needs?

The principles of the architecture are a statement of the organizational values as they pertain to information technology. While these principles are for the construction of the IT architecture, the principles must be founded on general business values and processes. This overarching statement of values must guide the selection of specific architectural decisions by providing a framework for the abstraction, conceptualization, design, and implementation of information architecture.

Experience is a great teacher. Many of the experiences in information technology to date have taught us that IT decisions made from the bottom up or from point-solution type corporate standards are difficult to live with. These decisions were usually very narrowly focused on a specific problem or project that did not enable them to be leveraged across the organization into new applications. This resulted in silos of narrowly defined standards and architectures that were expensive to maintain compared to a more global solution.

So, is the Blasserhasset software package what the organization needs? The way to answer this question has several steps. Although there are many considerations for each question, the general approach to this question is to ask a series of questions. These questions are:

- Does this match the corporate values?
- Does this match the principles of the architecture?
- Does this match the architecture?
- Does this match the corporate standards that were established to support the architecture?
- Does the product or method do what it is said to do?
- Is this vendor relationship a relationship that we want?

Principle-centered architecture serves an organization in the same way that the laws of physics serve a physicist. If someone brings a perpetual motion machine to a physicist, the physicist will not bother to examine the machine to see how crank A turns gear B. The physicist will simply examine the physical laws known as the laws of thermodynamics, and he or she will state that it is impossible to create a perpetual motion machine. No other examination is necessary. The laws serve as a shortcut to guide the examiner to the correct conclusion. Principle-centered architecture acts in the same way. When a new product or IT concept is introduced, we can examine the principles and the principle-centered architecture and determine if the product is within this framework. If the product fits within the framework, we then analyze its other properties. If the product or technology has other properties that are interesting, it may be selected by the organization.

In the case of this book, we are interested in developing a principle-based architecture for a data warehouse. While the approach to the development of a principle-based architecture is common to both a general information technology architecture and a data warehouse architecture, the fact that we are building a data warehouse will always be our guide and reason.

Why is an entire chapter of this book devoted to architecture? The example was given in the preface to this book that if you were getting on a commercial airline flight and the pilot told you he had no plan for how he or she was going to get you there, you would probably get off the plane. Similarly, you would not buy a house from a person who had a lot and a pile of lumber but no plan for the house. A flight plan is necessary to fly a commercial airplane, and a blueprint is necessary to build a quality house. Planning is important, and planning for the architecture that will deliver the data warehouse service is very important.

The commercial flight analogy can be expanded to illustrate the value of IT architectural planning. When planning a commercial flight, a plan must be made that will specify all of the requirements to get the plane to its destination in addition to having the necessary cabin crew and meals to meet the needs of passengers. The flight plan will specify the radio frequencies, altitude, heading, and the time the aircraft will spend on each heading. A calculation of the fuel required must be part of the flight plan and the amount of fuel that will be left in reserve. If it is necessary to stop for fuel, the location of the fuel stop and the amount of fuel that will be added will have been calculated. Alternative places to land are also specified in the flight plan. For the comfort of the passengers, the appropriate number and type of meals, drinks, water, and ice must be loaded onto the plane before takeoff.

When constructing a data warehouse, we must plan to have the appropriate technical infrastructure in place to make the project a success. Just as the aircraft flight plan will guide the pilots and ensure that the appropriate resources are available, the data warehouse data architecture will help to ensure that the resources needed are available when they are needed. If changes in the data warehouse plan are necessary, the plan will tell us how much contingency was built into the plan that can be used for the change.

There are many reasons why designing the technical architecture of the organization is beneficial. The impact of the architecture on the project plan is tremendous. A complex architecture takes much longer to implement than a simple architecture, and details of the construction of the IT infrastructure will be embedded in many parts of the project plan.

8.3 METAPRINCIPLES: PRINCIPLES ABOUT THE PRINCIPLES

How are the principles of the principle-based conceptual architecture developed? The development of the principles must have some guidelines that will help with the development of the principles. The principles that will help us develop the principles are called metaprinciples. *Metaprinciples* are principles about principles just as metadata is data about data.

Metaprinciples are simple statements about the creation of principles. Metaprinciples are developed through experience with principle-based architectures and some common sense. The basic set of metaprinciples is:

- The principles should be simple in statement and implication. They should be understandable to both information technology and business professionals. The principles must be simple enough to leave no room for ambiguity.
- The principles must be complete. Construction of the conceptual architecture should need no other fundamental reference source.
- The principles must be consistent. A conflict in the principles indicates that a change needs to be made to the principles.
- The principles should be pragmatic. The purpose of the conceptual architecture is to bring technology to bear on business problems. It is not an exercise in technology expansion. The principles should support this development
- The implications of an architectural principle must be identifiable. If the general characteristics of the system cannot be deduced from the principles, the principles must be refined.
- The principles, like religion and politics, are open to debate. People who are equally knowledgeable, skilled, and reasonable will have different opinions. The principles should be developed through consensus.

The metaprinciples seem obvious to most people, but it is worthwhile to define how the principles will be defined. The metaprinciples will be a simple guide to the data warehouse team during development of the principles.

8.4 THE PRINCIPLES

Now that a guiding framework for development of the principles has been defined, the principles of typical data warehouse architecture can be stated. The principles are usually grouped by general category. While different warehouse architects will have different taxonomy of architectural principles, the principles listed below are at least a minimal set. This basic set of principles can be expanded upon, depending on the situation. In the summary, the major groupings of principles are:

- General principles
- Data principles
- Query principles
- Working store principles
- Metadata principles
- Scalability principles
- Warehouse management principles

The data warehouse architecture itself is usually divided into three parts: the access architecture, the data architecture, and technology architecture. The *access architecture* is centered on how data from and to the warehouse is made available to the end user. The *data architecture* is a description of the structure and life cycle of warehouse data. The *technology architecture* is a description of the technology details of the warehouse and the data warehouse interactions with legacy systems and existing technologies. The actual statement of the principles of the architecture depends upon the environment in which the architecture is to be constructed. The categories listed above usually have some general statements that can be made as guidelines for the reader.

Recall that the purpose of these principles is to create an architecture that will lead to a physical implementation of the high-level data warehouse conceptual model, shown again in Figure 8-1. This architecture must be scalable enough to meet the needs of an enterprise data warehouse. Although the conceptual model shown in Figure 8-1 seems simple, there are other ways to arrange the functions that do not scale or shield the user from the details of the warehouse as well as this one.

8.4.1 General Principles

The starting point for the specification of a principles-based architecture is a statement of the general principles that will guide construction of the warehouse. As an example, a general principle is that the principles of the architecture should be consistent across the entire organization. Other general principles can usually be stated in one or two sentences. Another example of a general principle would be that the present architecture will not be in alignment with the new principles-based architecture, but the principles will be implemented over time. Other general principles would be:

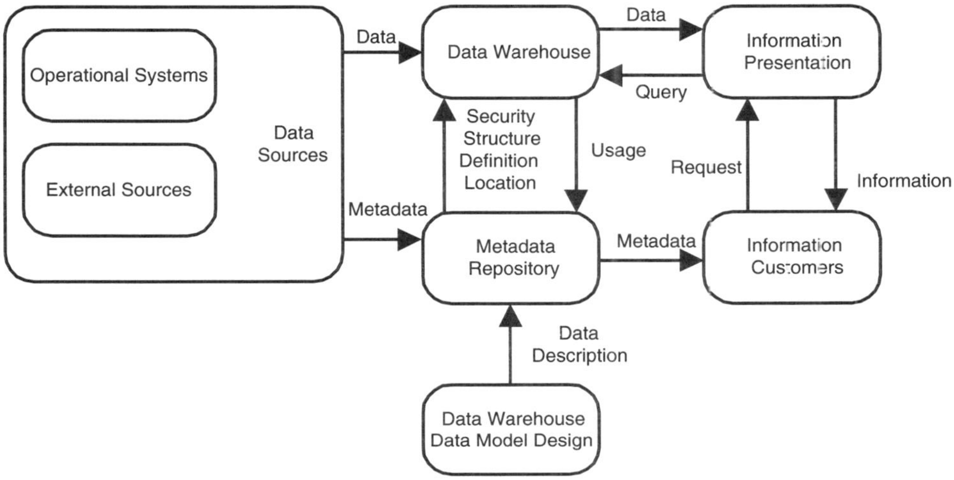

Figure 8-1 High-level conceptual view of the data warehouse.

- Data warehouse construction is an iterative process.
- Business needs drive the warehouse construction.
- The architectural framework is driven by business needs.

8.4.2 Data Principles

Clearly, data is key to a data warehouse. After the general principles of the data warehouse are stated, it is best to develop the data principles next. There are many principles about data that reflect on both the data warehouse and operational systems. As a good example of a data principle, the data for all decision support systems should be extracted once from the source system. All decision support systems should receive data from this initial extract. If multiple decision support systems are performing separate extracts, the system has regressed to the unplanned decision support architecture.

Another principle is that source systems are responsible for the quality of information supplied to the data warehouse. The data extracts that feed the data warehouse with difficulty can rationalize and cleanse the data but cannot correct incorrect data. As mentioned in Chapter 7, other principles that govern the data in the warehouse could be:

- The organization's data model must contain an integrated view of both OLTP and DSS data. The data warehouse will derive its data model from the organizational model.

- The organization's DSS data model will define the definition, format, and values of data stored in the data warehouse.
- The data warehouse is responsible for the quality of information provided.
- Since warehouse data is time variant, it must contain a time stamp or time reference.
- Data in the data warehouse must be obtained from many source systems and integrated.
- Businesses subject areas and dimensions of analysis drive the organization of information in the warehouse.

8.4.3 Query Principles

A principle that is very important to the success and usability of a data warehouse is to have the user know as little about the details of how the data is stored in the warehouse as possible. To the business user, the data in the warehouse should appear to have a very simple structure, and the structure should represent something that the business user understands. As an example for a sales analysis data warehouse, the business user will easily understand that customers purchase products from stores. The data should be presented to the business user in a form that is no more complex than that. Other details, such as the existence of summary tables, should also be hidden from the user.

Once the information user has selected the business fields and values necessary to satisfy the query, the query processor should determine the database fields, tables, and data stores needed to satisfy the query. The query processor will generate the query statements necessary to retrieve the data from the data stores, and the intermediate results are joined or aggregated to provide the required answer. The data is formatted in the manner expected by the user, and the data is returned to the user. Information needed to map a business field to a data store field and perform aggregation is stored in the metadata. The user should be given an estimate of the volume of data that will be returned and the amount of time required to process the query while the query processor is starting.

Any access security should be provided with the query mechanism. Access security should be based on user identification, and the option of value-based security is valuable as well. The user identification part of the access security is used to determine if the information worker is allowed access to a data store or table. Value-based security is used to determine if the information worker is allowed access to rows in a table. As an example of value-based security, a store manager might be given access to the data for his or her store and no other store.

The query principles should be provided by a software component. Several choices are available. These choices are discussed in Section 9.8.

8.4.4 Working Store Principles

It is a common occurrence in the world of data warehousing that a person or group will want to have a collection of data available to them. This data usually represents a particular selection, format, or summarization. The data might even have been organized for the use of a specific tool. Data warehouse information workers will frequently request that space be provided in the data warehouse for the storage of these tables. It is impossible to create data stores in the warehouse for this working store of user information.

In order to satisfy this very valid need, the architectural principle of personal working stores is necessary. The architectural principles of the personal working store are:

- The working store structure is created and maintained by the information user.
- The working store is populated by the information user.
- The working store may be populated with data from both the data warehouse and data from other sources.
- The data warehouse is unaware of all working stores. The warehouse does not contain any information in the metadata about working stores.
- The lifetime of the working store may vary from a second to years.

8.4.5 Metadata Principles

The importance of metadata was investigated at some length in Chapter 5. Metadata is data that describes data or controls its use. It should not come as a surprise to the reader that architectural principles about metadata are important to the success of the data warehouse. The metadata contains the data necessary to construct, administer, and maintain the data warehouse.

In Chapter 5, two ways to categorize metadata were introduced. One way to categorize metadata is whether it is used during run time or during construction of the warehouse. The other way to categorize metadata is by coverage of the Zachman framework. Starting with the usage model of metadata, the various uses of the metadata can be expanded upon and architectural principles derived. Information about the data required to implement and continue to implement or maintain the data warehouse must be stored in the data warehouse metadata. Data required for humans and programs to use the data warehouse must also be stored in the data warehouse metadata. As pointed out in Chapter 6, the metadata performs the following tasks:

1. *Data descriptions*. The data descriptions describe the data and data structures that are used to store the data in the information warehouse. The data stored in the data warehouse becomes information when it is organized in a business context. The context includes:
   - Descriptions of the business meaning of the data in the warehouse
   - Field and business names, including aliases, for the data in the warehouse
   - Examples of data stored in the fields, including types and valid ranges
   - The relationships between tables, including the business rules and definitions
   - Data owner
   - Calculations or transformations used to generate a field
   - Change history

2. *Policy descriptions*
   - Service-level agreements
   - Data retention policy
   - Backup and recovery procedures
   - Security policy and mechanisms

3. *Warehouse usage information*
   - Actual field usage
   - Table usage
   - Summary table usage
   - Query times by table
   - Volumes returned
   - Query and tool failures

4. *Security information*
   - User's identity
   - User roles
   - User groups
   - Access scope by identity
   - Access by group
   - Assess by role

This leads us to the following architectural principles:

- The data warehouse metadata must provide the information necessary to perform the tasks listed above.
- The data warehouse is developing, changing, and evolving continuously, and the metadata must change and evolve with the data warehouse.
- The metadata may be stored in several tools and repositories, but it must be consistent across all tools and repositories.
- Revision history and user information must be kept to support access of older versions of the information.

8.4.6 Scalability Principles

One of the most overlooked design issues is the set of issues surrounding the scalability of the warehouse. When designing a data warehouse, it is imperative to remember that the data warehouse will grow the amount of stored data and number of users and functions served over time. Design sins that might have been forgiven in less demanding environments will become deadly in the data warehouse environment. We will focus the scalability principles in three areas: data architecture, physical storage, and information processing. These are the areas where scalability issues hit the hardest.

The data architecture must be based on a set of principles that will enable scalability:

1. For a large data warehoue, the data should be partitioned, and storage (DASD) should be designed to enable it to be partitioned appropprately.
2. The processing tasks needed to create, manage, maintain, and use the data warehouse must be capable of being partitioned and distributed.

One feature of a design that aids scalability is the ability to add data in discrete units without reworking all the data that has already been placed into the warehouse. In other words, the data must be partitioned. While the star schema model implies partitioning into entities that are an improvement over flat files, it is usually possible to partition the entities. Because a data warehouse contains historical information, the detail tables must contain a time reference. One way to partition the data is by date. Another partition schema would use the location of the store that sold the item. The table could be partitioned by both data and location.

As an example of physical partitioning of a detail table, a conceptual detail table called sale_item might be composed of the logical tables sale_item1, sale_item2, ..., sale_item36. Each of the physical sale_item tables will contain one month of sales information of a three-year period. When a new set of data is available to populate the database, the oldest month of data is archived, the oldest data is purged, and the newest data is placed in the now-empty table. The metadata tracks the location of data in the logical tables as a function of time period. This is illustrated in Figure 8-2.

The creation of physical storage that will expand in size and performance as the warehouse size expands is difficult. Any given computer configuration will have a limited I/O capability. The disk storage system will also have a limited I/O capability. The usual solution to the limit of a single facility in the computer world is to use several in parallel. This can be applied to the storage problem by using multiple I/O channels from the computer attached to multiple I/O channels on the storage devices with multiple logical storage units. The mapping of logical to physical storage will change over time as table sizes change, summary tables are created and removed, and indexes are created. This concept is explained in greater depth Chapter 9.

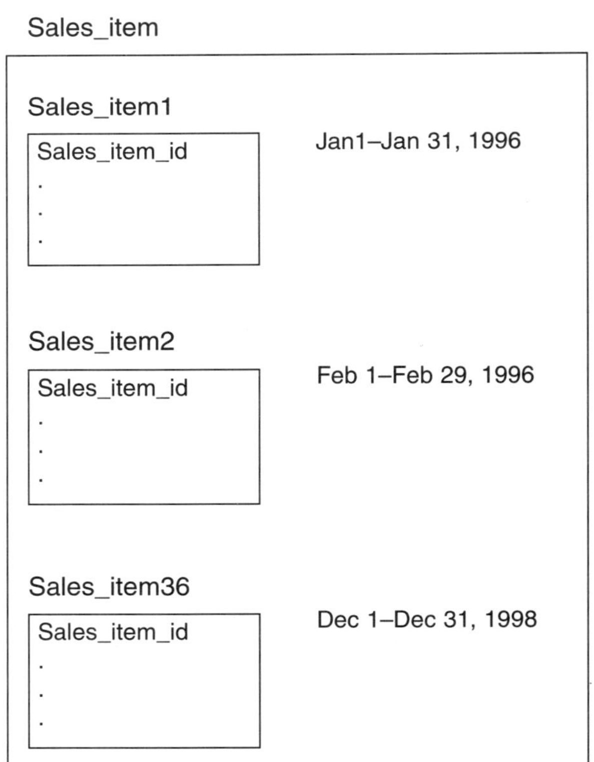

Figure 8-2 The table sale_item has been partitioned by time into multiple tables.

The processing needs of the data warehouse will change as the warehouse adds subject areas and users. The software used to create, maintain, manage, and query the data warehouse will change over time. Because it is almost impossible to eliminate tools and functionality once they have been introduced, the trend will be to add functions and new processing requirements as the warehouse grows. One of the basic and important concepts of client-server processing is the ability to partition and distribute the processing tasks over several different computer engines in a potentially heterogeneous environment. This implies that the processing tasks necessary to create, manage, maintain, and use the data warehouse should be capable of being partitioned and distributed.

8.4.7 Warehouse Management Principles

The warehouse must be administered over the entire life cycle of the warehouse. Thus, the activities that are part of the warehouse management will start with the design, continue with the implementation phase, and develop with the maturation of the warehouse. The tasks required by the warehouse at the different phases are many. Some of the tasks are listed below.

1. Design the data model.
    - Identify data organization and partitioning.
    - Design data audits.
    - Design data in naming standards.
    - Determine data volumes.
    - Define meaning.

2. Manage storage.
    - Manage capacity.
    - Design and implement backup and recovery routines.
    - Modify schema.
    - Modify indices.

3. Establish and maintain data population.
    - Determine capacity needed.
    - Implement data audits.
    - Implement data architecture changes.
    - Create indices.

- Archive, purge, and load data.
- Create and modify cleaning and transformation routines.

4. Provide for disaster recovery and backup.
   - Design backup procedures.
   - Design recovery procedures.
   - Implement backup and recovery procedures.
   - Test procedures.
   - Revise procedures.

5. Provide for configuration control, version control, and release management.
   - Design configuration control procedures.
   - Design version control procedures.
   - Implement configuration control.
   - Implement version control.
   - Test procedures.
   - Revise procedures.

6. Design and maintain security.
   - Identify security restrictions.
   - Determine access methods.
   - Determine access approval methods.
   - Design security scheme.
   - Define and store user names and passwords.
   - Determine and store user groups.
   - Determine information access.

This leads us to the following architectural principles:

- The data warehouse metadata must provide the information necessary to perform the tasks listed above.
- The data warehouse is continuously developing, changing, and evolving. The warehouse must change and evolve with the users' needs for information.
- Ownership of the many tasks must be clear and documented

The reader should be advised that the list of activities given that metadata must support is only a partial list. An unabridged list must be developed for each data warehouse project based on the unique environment of that project.

8.4.8 Architectural Principles and the Zachman Framework

The data warehouse principles should completely cover the aspects of who, what, when, where, why, and how that are specified in the Zachman framework. Of course, the complete set of principles does cover the rows and columns of the Zachman framework. As an example, the general architectural principles have aspects that cover the activities, location, entities, people, motivation, and time dimensions of the Zachman framework. The mapping of the architectural principals to the Zachman framework is illustrated in Table 8-1. In some cases, every dimension of the Zachman framework will be covered by one of the groupings of architectural principles. In most cases, the entire set of architectural principles will cover the categories of the Zachman framework.

8.4.9 Architectural Principles Summary

The architectural principle groups and specific principles listed in the table below are typical examples for a generic project. They are not a complete set of principles for every project. It is difficult to stress enough that the particular principles must be matched to the particular project, development methodology, and organizational culture. This is no different than other aspects of data warehouse construction, where selections of such things as methodology or team composition are driven by a large number of considerations, including organizational environment, organizational size, and project type. The principles should be developed initially with the architecture team, which should be a subset of the entire JAD team or with the help of an internal or external consultant who has experience in this area.

Table 8-1 Architectural principles in the Zachman framework

	Activities	Location	Entities	People	Motivation	Time
General	✓	✓	✓	✓	✓	✓
Data			✓			✓
Query	✓		✓	✓		
Working store		✓	✓			
Metadata	✓		✓	✓		✓
Scalability			✓		✓	✓
Management				✓		✓

8.5 CONCEPTUAL MODELS

The data warehouse principle-based architecture provides the rules and framework for the construction of conceptual and logical models and their physical implementation. The very high level model of Figure 8-1 that has been used as our reference model hides many of the important details of the operation of the data warehouse. Although a high-level conceptual model should hide most of the details, implementation of the principle-based architecture in a more detailed manner requires some exposure of these details. There are many different ways to implement the basic functions of the high-level conceptual model. The various implementations usually meet the architectural principles in different degrees. A method for the selection of the conceptual model is presented in Section 8.6.

The high-level conceptual model shown in Figure 8-1 hides many of the details of the actual construction, implementation, data flow, processing, and use of a data warehouse. An excellent way to design services in the warehouse is through the use of rigorous IT service management methodologies as introduced in Chapter 2. This will provide formalism and design standardization to all the IT processes in the data warehouse.

One example of hidden detail in Figure 8-1 is the movement of data from data sources to the data warehouse. This typically happens in several steps. The data is first extracted from the operational system and placed into a file for export. In the mainframe world, the easiest file to generate is a flat file, and this is the form the export usually takes. Data from one flat file record must be matched with the data from other flat file records and the records cleansed of improper data. After all this has occurred, the data can be loaded into the data warehouse. Data extraction and cleansing are discussed in detail in Chapter 10. The remainder of this chapter is devoted to the distribution of processing and data for the data warehouse.

The middle part of the conceptual warehouse model—the metadata, model design, and the warehouse itself—was described in detail earlier in the book. The right side of the conceptual diagram, the query processing and information presentation pieces, is discussed in Chapters 11 and 12.

8.5.1 UNPLANNED DECISION SUPPORT

One way to construct a data warehouse is by repeating the unarchitected or unplanned environment of the past. Since this approach was the approach that caused so much trouble in the past, one might think that this approach would not be repeated. This is not the case. Unplanned decision support systems are still being constructed every day. The advantage to the unplanned approach is that it is cheap in the short run, easy to implement, and needs no central planning. The statement that it needs no central planning means that there is no planning between data marts, but each data mart might be carefully planned.

The disadvantages are the same as those stated in Chapter 1. An unplanned environment will cause duplication in extract and report programming. The data will not have been defined by a central group, and different reporting will result from the same data. Different reports will use different source systems and fields for what should be the same information. This lack of agreement as to the source system of record also causes reports to disagree.

8.5.2 Virtual Data Warehouse

An architecture that is occasionally proposed is the virtual data warehouse shown in Figure 8-3. In this architecture, the data is not extracted from legacy systems and reorganized into a new system. The query management tool has metadata that describes the location and extraction algorithms of the data in the operational systems. When the user starts a query, the query management tool uses the metadata to create the queries necessary to extract the data from the operational systems. The query processor then joins the data received from the transactional systems as necessary and presents the result to the user. This architecture clearly violates our architectural data principle that data should be extracted once and only once.

There are several advantages to this architecture. One advantage is that the system uses mostly existing hardware to produce the virtual data warehouse. The query management system may require a new computer on which to operate, but most of the system uses existing infrastructure. The legacy systems are doing the bulk of the query work, and the query management tool simply manages the result and presents it.

There are several disadvantages to the virtual data warehouse. The queries that are placed on the legacy system can have a significant performance impact on

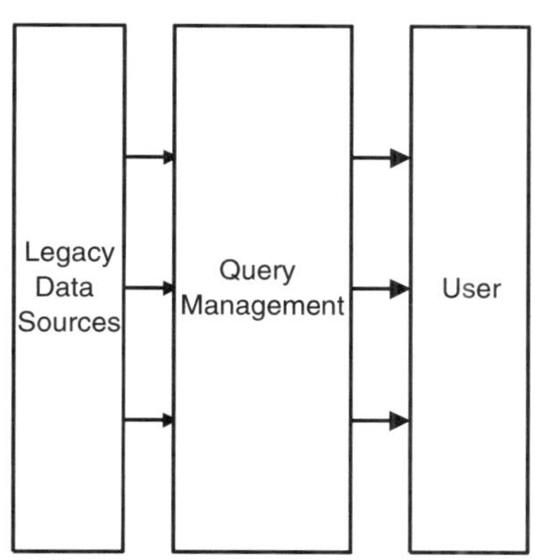

Figure 8-3 Virtual data warehouse

those systems. If 50 users perform the same query every day, the legacy systems will perform the same 50 queries. The data will be joined the same way 50 times to produce the result presented to the user.

The other problem is that the operational systems usually don't have the same field structure, codes, or primary keys. This returns us to the discussion of Chapter 1 about unplanned decision support. This lack of common field structure, codes, and primary keys is one of the hardest things about building a true data warehouse. The problem with building a virtual data warehouse is the need to join the results of queries from multiple systems every time the query is executed as opposed to once when the query is created. Because of different maintenance procedures in the various legacy systems, it is possible for a virtual warehouse query to produce different results at different times depending on the data archive schedule of the legacy systems.

8.5.3 Semantic Integration of Subject Areas

The next architecture is a data warehouse that is conceived and organized by subject area like Inmon's definition, and it is physically partitioned by subject area. In other words, subject area 1 and subject area 2 are stored in different data schemas. While all of the subject areas must be designed using the same high-level enterprise data model that was introduced in Chapter 5, the data can be stored in physically distinct databases. Using the enterprise data model to guarantee that the subject areas have the same field structure, codes, or primary keys will guarantee that the subject area information can easily be joined with information from other subject areas to provide information of greater scope.

Another advantage to this architecture is that the subject areas can be constructed independent of each other. This allows multiple design and construction teams to work in parallel to construct a data warehouse. Once the data extract routines and subject area linkages have been established, the subject area construction teams can work independently. This approach speeds implementation of the enterprise data warehouse.

At first glance at Figure 8-4, one might expect that each subject area requires its own extract. This would violate our principle that the data extracts should happen only once per system. The extract programs should be written in a way that eliminates redundant extracts. The extract process performs the semantic integration that is necessary to construct the data warehouse subject areas. The extract data for all the subject areas is stored in a data staging area that is not shown explicitly in the drawing. The extract data is stored only as long as needed to populate the subject areas; then it is archived and purged.

The architecture shown in Figure 8-4 has the admirable advantage that the necessary infrastructure is easy to develop. Since the subject area infrastructure can be developed independently, it is possible to construct the subject areas as funding and other resources are available. Each subject area that is made operational and

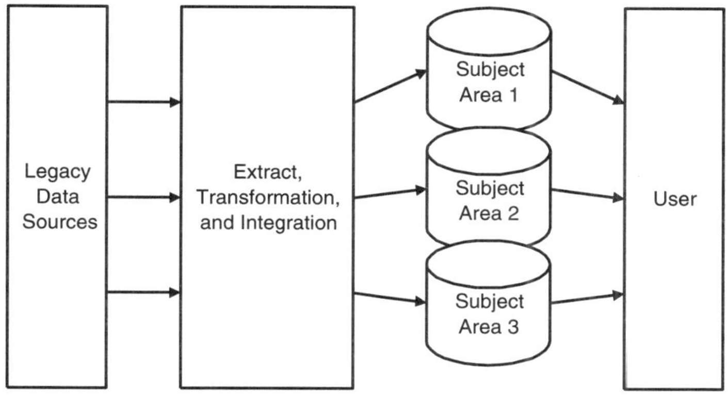

Figure 8-4 Data warehouse organized by subject area.

moved into production will provide value to the business and prove the value of data warehousing to the skeptics.

The disadvantage of this architecture is the requirement that the user understand the data structure in two subject areas if the user wishes to join data between subject areas. This architecture does not have a query-processing layer to abstract the data from the query. In other words, this architecture could violate one of our architectural principles if users perform queries that join data across subject areas. The user will also be required to know about the existence of summary tables and be knowledgeable about their use.

8.5.4 Query-Managed Subject Areas

The architecture shown in Figure 8-5 remedies the inadequacies of the previous architecture by providing a query management layer. The query management function removes the necessity of the user knowing details about the structure of the data stored in each subject area. The information user is presented with a simple description of the data that is available in terms the business user understands.

The difficulty with the architecture shown in Figure 8-5 is a difficulty of scope. If the information required to provide the information to a business problem is stored in more than one subject area, the database management software or query management tool must perform a join of data from two or more subject areas in order to satisfy the request. Although this doesn't sound like a problem, joining three tables with 100 million rows will take a long time. If the two subject areas are in the same database and a relationship between the necessary entities has been established, the necessary columns will have indexes. The difficulty of having all the information in one table is that the ability to browse the database quickly diminishes as the number of joined entities grows.

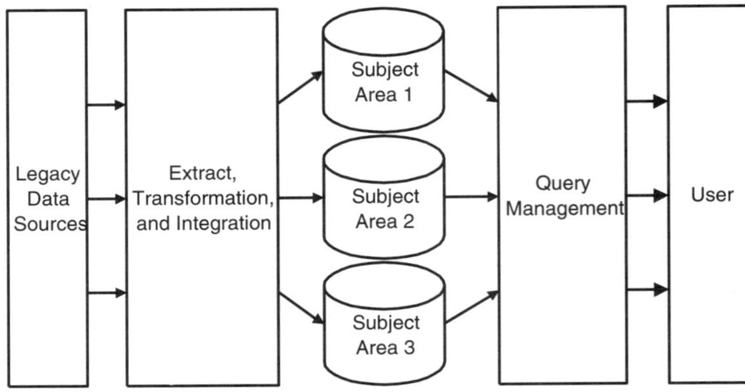

Figure 8-5 Data warehouse with physically distinct subject areas and query management.

8.5.5 MONOLITHIC WAREHOUSE

An architecture that integrates all the subject areas into one very large database is shown in Figure 8-6. This "giant database in the sky" is the type of data warehouse that many people think of when they hear the term *data warehouse* but are not really familiar with the concept. The monolithic warehouse is called many different things by many different authors and consultants. One of the many things this architecture is called is the *business data warehouse.* This monolithic warehouse

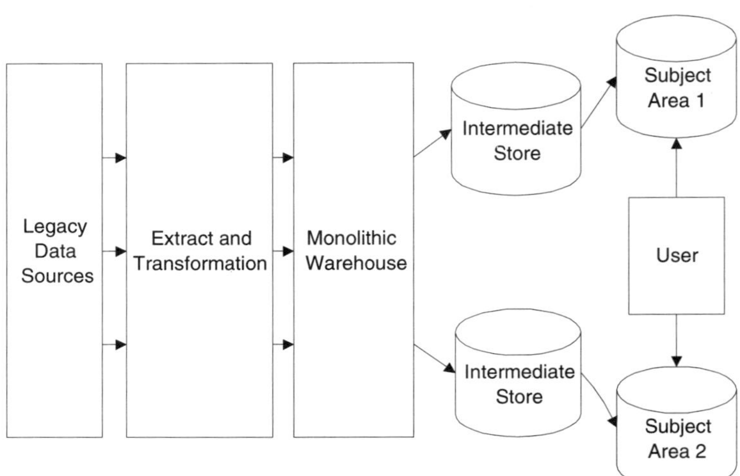

Figure 8-6 Monolithic data warehouse.

is really nothing more than a repository of all of the currently available operational data. Although the data might have undergone some transformation on the way to the monolithic data store or warehouse, it is still in the lowest level of granularity and is normalized.

No end-user queries run against the monolithic warehouse. The data is extracted and staged in several potential intermediate server layers before reaching a subject area data store that is used by a knowledge worker. These layers are sometimes called the *staging business information warehouse,* and the subject area data warehouses and data marts are called *business information warehouses.* This architecture has the potential advantage of having increased flexibility for the IT department at the expense of extra complexity, cost, and lack of flexibility for the end user. This type of architecture fits the culture of a centrally managed organization.

The disadvantage to the business data warehouse or monolithic warehouse is the huge amount of redundancy that is designed into the architecture. This redundancy requires a large number of IT staff to maintain. It is also very expensive and time-consuming to design and implement. While the redundancy might add flexibility for the IT staff, it is inflexible from the standpoint of the end user.

8.5.6 Standard Data Archive

The next architecture to be investigated is the standard data archive architecture. In this architecture, shown in Figure 8-7, the semantic integration process and data staging area have been replaced with the standard data archive. The standard data archive is a persistent store of semantically integrated data that will be used to populate the subject area data warehouses and data marts.

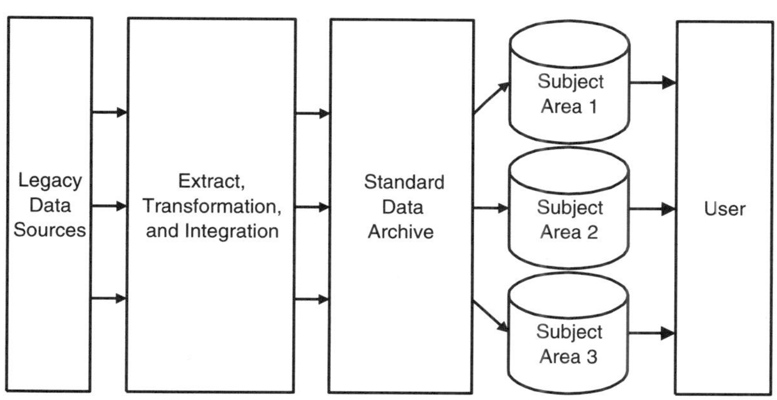

Figure 8-7 Standard data archive architecture.

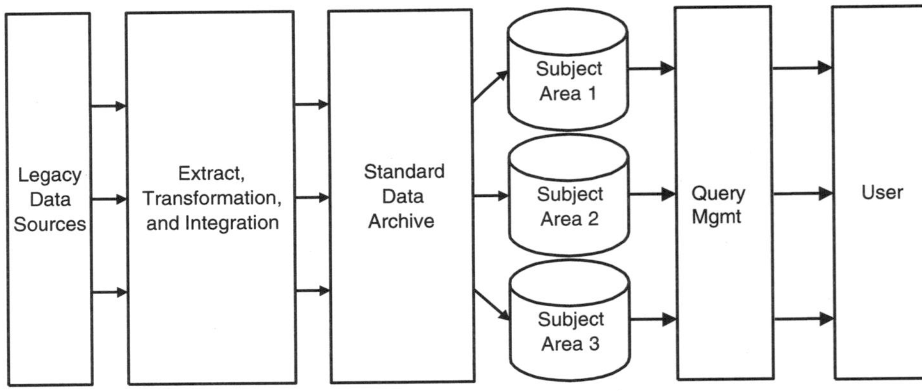

Figure 8-8 Standard data archive with a query management interface.

The strengths of this architecture are the coordination of data from source to population in the data marts and warehouses. The standard data archive is an integrated source of all DSS data. After the first few subject areas have been constructed, the infrastructure is in place for the easy construction of new data marts. This architecture will grow to become an enterprise architecture.

The disadvantage of this architecture is the cost of storage associated with the standard data archive. The data in the standard data is maintained for operational or "drill-down" queries from the data warehouse. This cost of storage can be quite high. The standard data architecture also has a higher maintenance requirement than the same architecture without the standard data archive. The last disadvantage to this architecture is the lack of integration of the individual subject areas. A query processing stage such as the one shown in Figure 8-8 will improve the usability of the data warehouse by logically integrating the subject areas.

8.6 ARCHITECTURE SELECTION

Seven different architectures were listed in Section 8.5. The question now before us is: What architecture fits a particular situation and organizational constraints? The deciding factors typically are:

- The size of the budget
- The number of IT professionals allocated to the project
- The amount of time to complete the project

- The structure of the organization
- Organizational decision support system and data warehouse experience

These factors come together in a complex fashion to determine the best approach to the problem for a given organization and project. These trade-offs are discussed as a function of warehouse architecture in the following subsections.

8.6.1 Unplanned Decision Support

This architecture was the most widely deployed decision support architecture prior to 1993. The reason why this architecture has been so widely accepted and deployed has been mentioned before. At the risk of being redundant, these reasons are:

- It is cheap in the near term.
- It is simple.
- Data warehouse ideas were not well developed prior to 1993.
- Users demand solutions and will not wait for an organization-wide plan.

This architecture has frequently already been implemented in parts of the organization, and the organization wants to deploy an enterprise architecture. Although the unplanned decision support architecture is not an enterprise architecture, a tremendous amount of good information about the needs, requirements, source data, and business processes are documented during the construction of the unplanned decision support environment. This information will be a vital starting point to the construction of a new data warehouse environment.

An unplanned decision support environment can be successful in instances. An example of this is a very autonomous organization where different departments have very limited interactions. Each department should have a relatively small budget and a need for only one data mart or data warehouse now or in the near future. In this case, the data warehouse or data mart will be deployed in a short time frame, and the problems of data inconsistencies between departments should not surface.

8.6.2 Virtual Data Warehouse

Like the unplanned decision support structure, the virtual data warehouse can provide a number of difficulties in implementation. The potential problems that were mentioned before are:

- Inconsistent keys make joins impossible.

- Queries swamp source systems.
- Fields in the source systems are inconsistent.
- There are replicating source system data errors in the warehouse.

The virtual data warehouse can be successful in certain circumstances. The source systems must be able to limit the amount of resources that can be consumed by a query from the virtual data warehouse. The source systems must have common identifying fields, and these fields must have common codes and keys across all the systems. The source data must be of unusual quality. One example of a scenario where a virtual data warehouse would work is a retail chain that has UPC codes as a common identifier in all the systems that are involved with the movement of goods. These systems must also have excess processing capacity that can be allocated to the virtual data warehouse. In most cases, either source systems do not have excess capacity or they do not have common key fields. Many of the legacy systems that are in operation use proprietary technology that might not be cost competitive with open systems technology. In this case, the necessity of purchasing new equipment and reworking the data model will push the design toward some other architecture.

8.6.3 Semantic Integration of Subject Areas

Organizations that are planning to deploy more than one data warehouse in the near future should select an architecture other than the unplanned decision support architecture. The integrated subject areas will take longer to construct than the unplanned decision support environment, but this architecture requires less time to implement than other architectures that will migrate to an enterprise scope. This architecture would be a good candidate for an organization that needs quick results but has a limited budget. The organization should have plans for multiple subject area data warehouses or multiple data marts and a desire to integrate the information from the different subject areas. This architecture fits well in a corporate culture that is decentralized but has a central IT administration.

8.6.4 Query-Managed Subject Areas

Semantically integrated subject areas with query management are an improvement over previous architecture. This type of architecture is appropriate for organizations that wish to develop several data marts for specific work groups and the ability to perform joins across the data marts on an infrequent basis. This is another architecture that fits well into a decentralized organization with central IT administration.

8.6.5 Monolithic Warehouse

Although this type of architecture is recommended by several data warehouse vendors and consultants, it is this author's opinion that this type of monolithic warehouse has far too many tiers and redundant layers of data and process to be successful. This type of architecture could be successful if:

- The organization has a huge budget.
- The organization will devote a very large staff to this project for a long time.
- The organization is very centralized with a command and control management style.
- The organization does not wish to see the benefits of the data warehouse for a year or two.

8.6.6 Standard Data Archive

This architecture is the most logically consistent and scalable architecture presented. This architecture is simple and elegant, yet it will scale to any size required by the organization. All data warehouse and data mart population will occur from the standard data archive. The standard data archive will coordinate all extract, transformation, and cleansing of the data.

The standard data archive matches a project that has several distinguishing characteristics. One characteristic is that the decision support environment should have a large number of data sources. The processing cost associated with extracting, transforming, and cleansing the data should be significant for this type of architecture to pay for itself. The project should be centrally managed, and a large budget has been established for the project.

Organizations that find the monolithic warehouse attractive like the standard data archive architecture if a "mega" data warehouse is added between the standard data store and the data marts and user data warehouses. This type of architecture is attractive if frequent cross-subject-area joins are done. This type of architecture still has fewer layers, less redundancy, less maintenance, and lower cost than the monolithic warehouse architecture.

8.7 LOGICAL MODELS

The construction of the logical model is the start of the process of moving the architecture from the abstract world of the conceptual model to the physical world of hardware, scalability, response time, and throughput considerations. The purpose of this layer of abstraction to the design is the mapping of conceptual model to a model where the functionality is defined before the hardware is defined. The selection of a data warehouse conceptual architecture is based on a series of trade-offs driven by organization size, requirements, and funding limitations. The selection of a logical model will also be based on organizational IT architecture master plans and standards. The data warehouse must conform and interoperate with all of the other systems in the enterprise.

As an example of one implementation, an organization may wish to implement a relatively simple data warehouse as a first step away from an unplanned decision support environment (Figure 8-9). For the purpose of this section, all of the examples will be based on this starting point. As is typical of many organizations today, this organization has a tremendous amount of experience with unplanned decision support. All of the experience with data extraction and cleansing can be used in the construction of the new data warehouse. The experience of gathering the user requirements for the unplanned decision support system and the successes and failures of that system will become part of the starting point of the design for the data warehouse.

The organization that is building this warehouse has a large library of data extract code for the legacy system. This code will be reused to perform data extracts for the new data warehouse project. The organization also has selected BrioQuery as the information presentation engine for the data warehouse. The organization has experience with ERwin as a data architecture tool, and this tool will be used to extract metadata from the legacy systems. The metadata from ERwin will also be used to populate the metadata for BrioQuery. Because both Erwin and Brio publish the metadata format, this is particularly easy.

As an example of a data warehouse solution that is founded on a single vendor's tools, the architecture shown in Figure 8-10 is shown. By selecting a single vendor, we reduce the number of choices for the components, but the result is increased interoperability of the components. A similar logical model could be

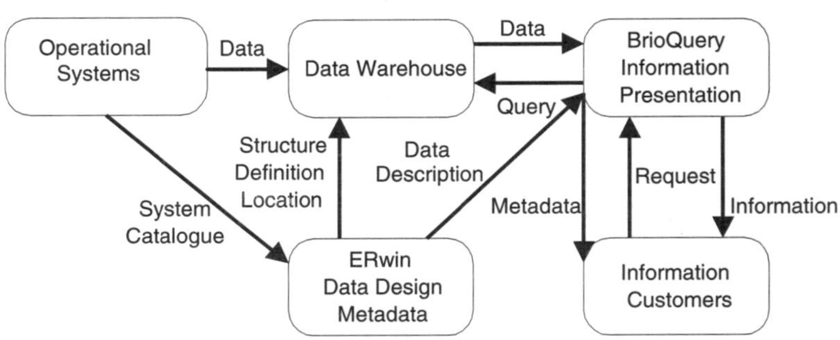

Figure 8-9 Logical model of a warehouse with a simple but elegant implementation.

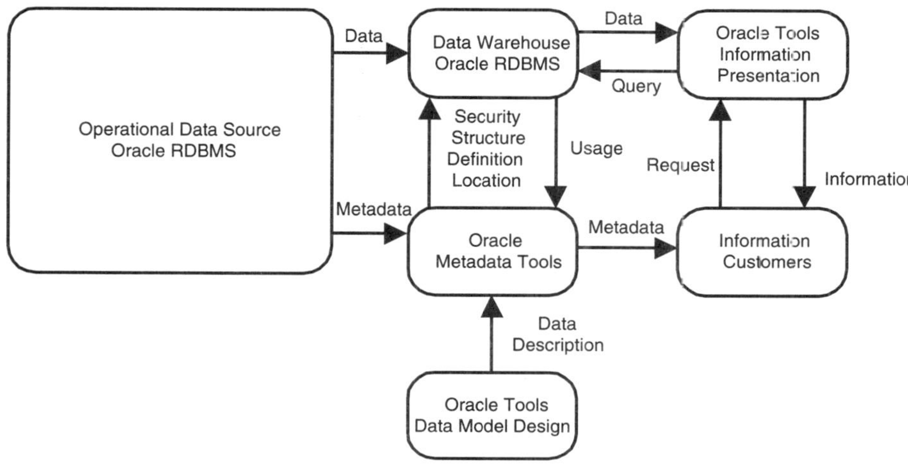

Figure 8-10 Logical model using tools from a single vendor.

developed using tools from the other merchant database vendors. The data source could be an enterprise software package such as PeopleSoft, Oracle, or Baan. All of these packages can use Oracle as the underlying database.

The data will be extracted for the Oracle source system with the use of SQL statements. Since the ERP applications are new applications, they usually have fewer problems with data quality than some legacy systems that evolved without a development plan. This eliminates some of the problems with data quality. Oracle metadata and data model tools will be used for the creation of the decision support data models and capture of the metadata. This metadata can be browsed by the information customer in addition to being used by the Oracle tools that are presenting the information. This is an example of the interoperability of tools and the importance of shared metadata.

While the interoperability and common design of the single-vendor tools do make the construction of the infrastructure easier, greatly limit the selection of vendors and tools. Practically, the single-vendor approach is taken because of organizational standards in addition to interoperability. An approach that is more common is to select tools from a variety of vendors based on the functional needs of the project. This could be called a smorgasbord approach.

As an example of a situation that is more typical of an enterprise data warehouse, the warehouse shown in Figure 8-11 uses software from many vendors to obtain the functionality needed to implement the data warehouse. The source data is in DB2, and ETI's Extract has been selected to cleanse and rationalize the data. Redbrick has been selected as the data warehouse database, and a database must have metadata. Intelligent Warehouse will provide query processing in addition to having metadata. The ERwin product from Platinum is being used to model the

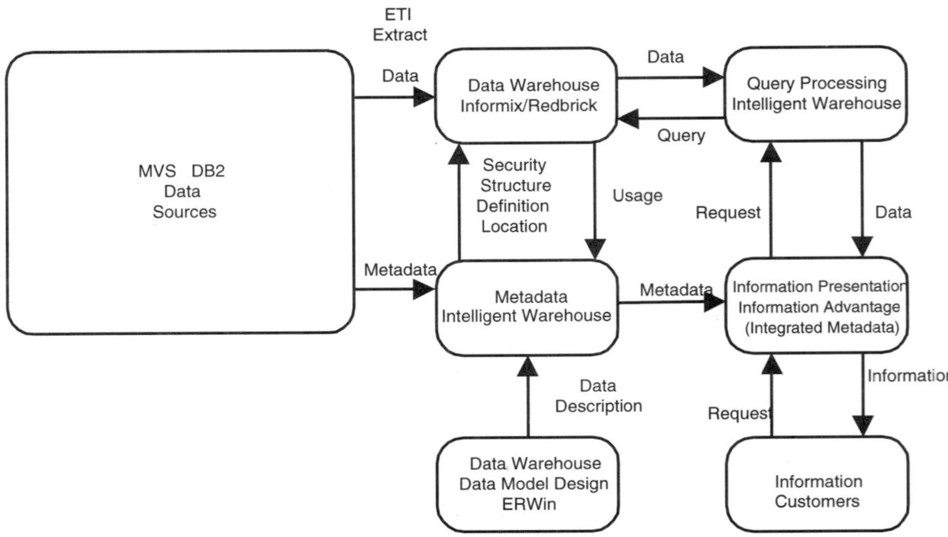

Figure 8-11 Heterogeneous environment typical of an enterprise data warehouse.

data, and ERwin will have its own metadata. Information Advantage tools are being used to present the data, and Information Advantage has metadata. The important point to note here is that some very good tools have been selected, but they all have separate metadata repositories, and it is important to keep the metadata synchronized between the various repositories. This can be true even with tools from a single vendor.

In summary of the logical model, the conceptual model can be mapped to several different logical models. A "short list" of tools and different procedures can be developed that will implement the conceptual model, and all the different permutations are different logical models. These logical models will have trade-offs in functionality, maintainability, scalability, and usability. These trade-offs must be assessed before the physical implementation is performed. Factors that must be understood when deciding on a physical architecture are explained in Chapter 9.

QUESTIONS

8.1 What is the reason for the development of metaprinciples?

8.2 What is the reason for the development of a principle-based architecture?

8.3 Six different types of conceptual architecture were discussed. Create a table of the pros and cons for each of the six types of conceptual architecture.

8.4 The Zachmann framework decomposition shown in Table 8-1 is arguable. In other words, bright people with different backgrounds would argue about the placement of the principles in the framework. How could the arrangement be changed?

PROJECTS

8.5 Recall that call behavior analysis is the analysis of the telephone calls that a traditional telephone or long-distance customer might make. The information is gathered by the switch that routes the call. This information will include the number of the telephone originating the call, the telephone number of the receiver of the call, and how long the call lasted. The newer switches, called SS7 switches, can capture other information, such as calls that are not completed because of a busy signal. Create the principles for the principle-based architecture for a call behavior analysis data warehouse. Explain the principles in as much detail as possible.

8.6 Design the conceptual architecture for the call behavior analysis data warehouse. Explain your decisions in as much detail as possible including how the architecture meets the architectural principles.

8.7 Design the logical architecture for the call behavior analysis data warehouse. Explain your decisions in as much detail as possible, including how the architecture meets the architectural principles.

8.8 The network that actually connects a telephone call is a very expensive and valuable resource. Planning for network expansion is a very important task, due to lost revenue if telephone calls don't go through or the increased cost if the network is too large in the wrong location. Create the principles for the principle-based architecture for a network usage data warehouse. Explain the principles in as much detail as possible.

8.9 Design the conceptual architecture for the network usage analysis data warehouse. Explain your decisions in as much detail as possible, including how the architecture meets the architectural principles.

8.10 Design the logical architecture for the network usage analysis data warehouse. Explain your decisions in as much detail as possible, including how the architecture meets the architectural principles.

8.11 Buying trend analysis is performed by car manufacturers and dealers to best determine the car and options certain demographic groups are likely to purchase. Create the principles for the principle-based architecture for an automobile buying trend data warehouse. Explain the principles in as much detail as possible.

8.12 Design the conceptual architecture for the automobile buying trend data warehouse. Explain your decisions in as much detail as possible, including how the architecture meets the architectural principles.

8.13 Design the logical architecture for the automobile buying trend data warehouse. Explain your decisions in as much detail as possible, including how the architecture meets the architectural principles.

8.14 Stores can use buying trend analysis to best determine the products certain demographic groups are likely to purchase. For example, an electronics store could determine which demographic groups are likely to purchase which products. A premium clothing store could track demographic groups that are likely to purchase certain products. Create the principles for the principle-based architecture for an electronics store sales analysis data warehouse. Explain the principles in as much detail as possible.

8.15 Design the conceptual architecture for the electronics store sales data warehouse. Explain your decisions in as much detail as possible, including how the architecture meets the architectural principles.

8.16 Design the logical architecture for the electronics store sales data warehouse. Explain your decisions in as much detail as possible, including how the architecture meets the architectural principles.

8.17 Manufacturing organizations can use a data warehouse to track the compliance of their suppliers to their agreements. The agreements normally cover at a minimum the delivery timing of products and product quality. Manufacturing organizations do this to increase part quality and reduce the cost of having too much inventory. Other technologies, such as electronic data interchange (EDI), allow the manufacturing company and its suppliers to exchange information orders for parts and deliveries of parts electronically. Create the principles for the principle-based architecture for a vendor compliance data warehouse. Explain the principles in as much detail as possible.

8.18 Design the conceptual architecture for the vendor compliance data warehouse. Explain your decisions in as much detail as possible, including how the architecture meets the architectural principles.

8.19 Design the logical architecture for the vendor compliance data warehouse. Explain your decisions in as much detail as possible, including how the architecture meets the architectural principles.

8.20 Financial organizations can use a data warehouse to analyze the risk of consumer and certain other scenarios. This data warehouse can use data such as demographic data or payment history data to determine the risk of the loan. This enables the financial institution to estimate and manage the risk. Create the principles for the principle-based architecture for a risk analysis data warehouse. Explain the principles in as much detail as possible.

8.21 Design the conceptual architecture for the risk analysis data warehouse. Explain your decisions in as much detail as possible, including how the architecture meets the architectural principles.

8.22 Design the logical architecture for the risk analysis data warehouse. Explain your decisions in as much detail as possible, including how the architecture meets the architectural principles.

8.23 Recall that airlines can analyze the travel trends of their frequent fliers in different demographic groups. This information can be used to target-market frequent fliers in the correct market groups. The demographic data is usually obtained from external sources. Create the principles for the principle-based architecture for a frequent flier data warehouse. Explain the principles in as much detail as possible.

8.24 Design the conceptual architecture for the frequent flier data warehouse. Explain your decisions in as much detail as possible, including how the architecture meets the architectural principles.

8.25 Design the logical architecture for the frequent flier data warehouse. Explain your decisions in as much detail as possible, including how the architecture meets the architectural principles.

8.26 Airlines can use a data warehouse to track the seasonal variations and growth expected in travel between locations. This data could also show how much food and beverages are consumed in different flights. This will help the airline select aircraft and catering to match needs. Create the principles for the principle-based architecture for an airline flight segment data warehouse. Explain the principles in as much detail as possible.

8.27 Design the conceptual architecture for the airline flight segment data warehouse. Explain your decisions in as much detail as possible, including how the architecture meets the architectural principles.

8.28 Design the logical architecture for the airline flight segment data warehouse. Explain your decisions in as much detail as possible, including how the architecture meets the architectural principles.

8.29 Recall that educational institutions can use a data warehouse to analyze trends in class enrollment, grade history, and student evaluation of professors. The data for the data warehouse will be loaded at the end of every academic period. Information about class enrollment will come from the registration system, and student evaluation data can be loaded from the academic dean's computer system. Create the principles for the principle-based architecture for an educational institution's data warehouse. Explain the principles in as much detail as possible.

8.30 Design the conceptual architecture for the educational institution's data warehouse. Explain your decisions in as much detail as possible, including how the architecture meets the architectural principles.

8.31 Design the logical architecture for the educational institution's data warehouse. Explain your decisions in as much detail as possible, including how the architecture meets the architectural principles.

8.32 Health care providers can use a data warehouse to track diagnosis codes (usually ICD9 codes), the procedures and treatments for that diagnosis (called CPT codes), and the cost of those procedures and treatments. This can be used to analyze the success rates of procedures for a diagnosis or the cost versus the insurance reimbursement. Create the principles for the principle-based architecture for a health care diagnosis data warehouse. Explain the principles in as much detail as possible.

8.33 Design the conceptual architecture for the health care diagnosis data warehouse. Explain your decisions in as much detail as possible, including how the architecture meets the architectural principles.

8.34 Design the logical architecture for the health care diagnosis data warehouse. Explain your decisions in as much detail as possible, including how the architecture meets the architectural principles.

8.35 Hotels can analyze the staying trends of their frequent guests in different demographic groups. This information can be used to target-market frequent guests for vacation packages. The demographic data is usually obtained from external sources. Create the principles for the principle-based architecture for a hotel frequent-guest data warehouse. Explain the principles in as much detail as possible.

8.36 Design the conceptual architecture for the hotel frequent-guest data warehouse. Explain your decisions in as much detail as possible, including how the architecture meets the architectural principles.

8.37 Design the logical architecture for the hotel frequent-guest data warehouse. Explain your decisions in as much detail as possible, including how the architecture meets the architectural principles.

8.38 Hotels can use a data warehouse to track the total value of a frequent guest's stay. The value of the stay is the total amount the guest spends during the stay including room, restaurant, room service, gift shop, and other incidental charges. Create the principles for the principle based architecture for a hotel spending analysis data warehouse. Explain the principles in as much detail as possible.

8.39 Design the conceptual architecture for the hotel spending analysis data warehouse. Explain your decisions in as much detail as possible, including how the architecture meets the architectural principles.

8.40 Design the logical architecture for the hotel spending analysis data warehouse. Explain your decisions in as much detail as possible, including how the architecture meets the architectural principles.

9

THE PHYSICAL DATA WAREHOUSE

9.1 INTRODUCTION

The conceptual data warehouse architecture is a statement of wish about the way we would like the data warehouse to function. Like most wishes, the conceptual architecture does not come true. The logical architecture was a mapping of the conceptual architecture onto technologically available tools and processes based on organizational standards. The physical architecture will map the structure of the logical model onto hardware.

During design of the conceptual model, it is important to design flexibility and scalability into the architecture. The design of flexibility into the conceptual architecture is done in many ways, but the selection of software and processes that will work on several operating systems and platforms is a good design procedure. Flexibility within the organization is also important.

Conceptual, logical, and physical architecture is only in part a design exercise in technology. It is also an exercise in understanding the organization, its needs, and the political situation. The introduction of a data warehouse is usually interesting from an organizational point of view because it means data will be shared. Depending on the type of data and how it is shared, this can change the landscape of organization substantially.

Other considerations that affect the selection and design of the architecture are organizational experience with the technologies proposed. As an example, an excellent software tool might be available that requires a Microsoft NT server, and the organization has limited experience with an NT server in a production environment. This would normally indicate that another selection should be made. Once the organization has experience with an NT server in a production environment, it might wish to add the tool to the architecture.

Another essential component of the development of the architecture is the delivery of a service to the business information customer. The data warehouse sponsor must understand that a specified service will be provided for a specified cost. The type of service specified and the requirement of that service change the way the service is implemented. As an example, a data warehouse that must be available for user queries 24 hours a day every day will have a different physical design than that of a warehouse that must be available for queries only during normal business hours. The team, including the sponsor, must understand these requirements and the impact on the design and cost of the solution.

The difficulty of matching business needs to the technology solution returns us to the concept of IT service management. The goal of IT service management is to provide the information service the business demands in a cost-effective, reliable, and user-friendly fashion. The delivery of this service should expand as the business expands without gaps in service or huge price increases. This type of service delivery is the goal of IT service management. The IT service management components and their interrelationships are shown in Figure 9-1.

While on a geographic or intellectual journey, it is always helpful to understand your location on the route. The first few chapters of this book focused on pieces of the top-left quadrant of the IT service management circle. We are now in the middle of the architecture discussion that investigates parts of the bottom left of the IT service management circle. In Volume 2, the right side of the circle will be explained.

9.2 PHYSICAL STORAGE

The data to be stored in the warehouse and converted to information must be stored on some type of physical medium is usually a physical disk. We will assume that the reader understands the basic physical properties of hard disks and will not explain that technology. Readers interested in further information about hard disk technology can obtain it from one of the disk manufacturers' Web sites.

The advent of client–server computing caused interest in two- and three-tier architectures. A two-tier architecture would be composed of a client and a server, and a three-tier architecture would be composed of a database server, an application server, and a client, as illustrated in Figures 9-2 and 9-3. Storage devices were always thought of as part of the computer.

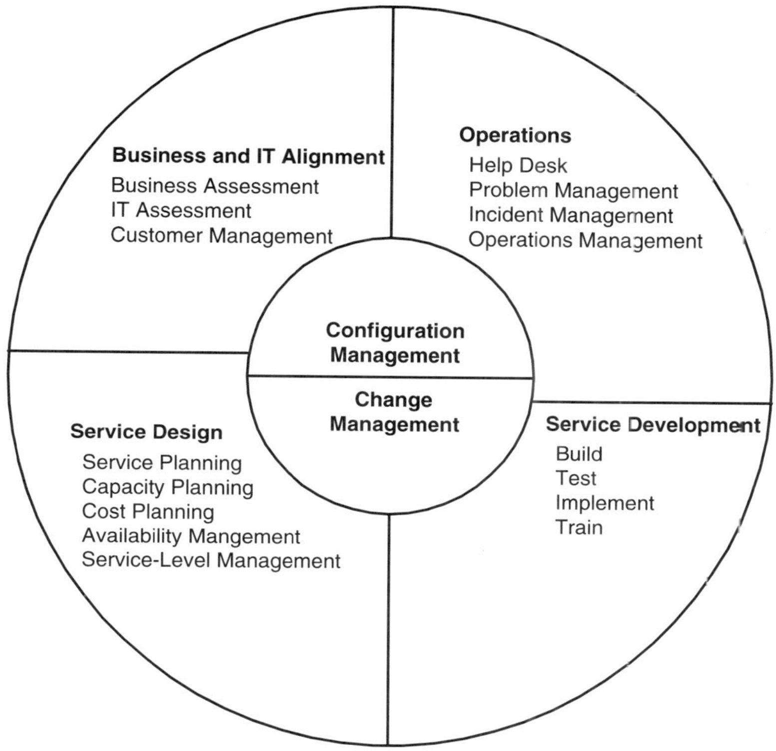

Figure 9-1 IT service management framework.

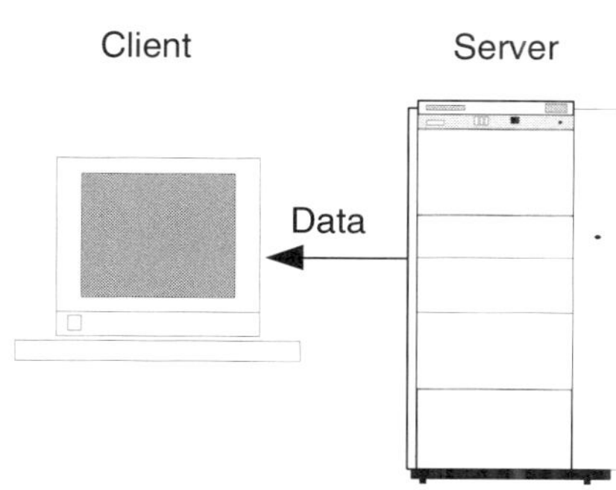

Figure 9-2 Two-tier architecture.

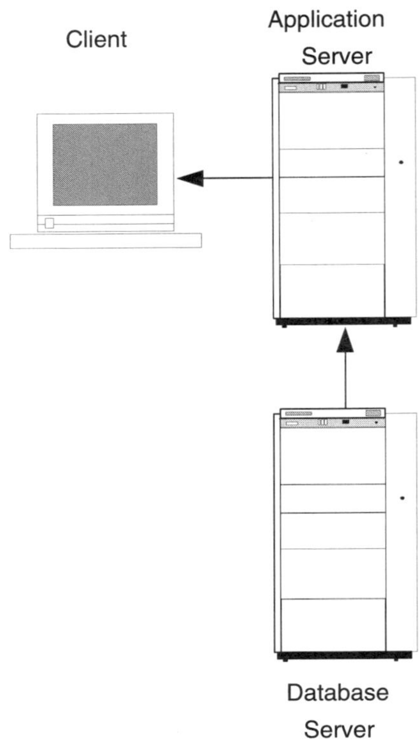

Figure 9-3 Three-tier architecture.

Large data warehouses and transactional systems use tremendous amounts of disk storage. The disk storage units might have as much random access memory as the computer to which it is attached. Managing this huge storage area can be a challenge. This has lead to an architecture where the enterprise storage systems form another tier in the architecture. This storage tier is frequently called the storage area network. The query management system that is part of a data warehouse architecture forms the fifth tier. This is illustrated in Figure 9-4.

The storage area network consists of one or more disk storage systems with fiber channel connections between storage enclosures and between the servers and the storage enclosures. An alternative to the fiber channel connections is SCSI connections. Inside the storage enclosure will be the hard disk mechanisms, disk controllers, cache memory, software, and processors. The storage systems' integrated cache, processors, and firmware allow the storage system management activities to happen without interaction with the other computers.

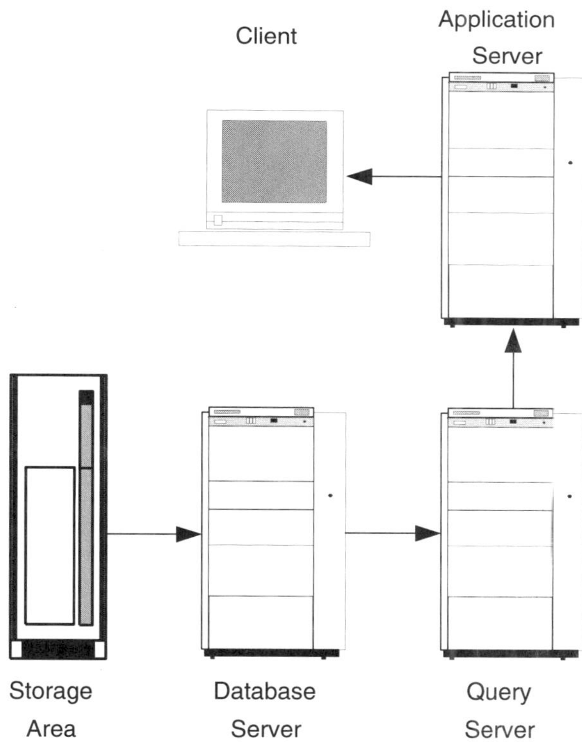

Figure 9-4 Five-tier architecture with a storage area network.

One of the management activities that can occur is changing the RAID [redundant array of inexpensive (or independent) disks] arrangement of the disks. A RAID array is an assembly of disk drives that act as a single storage system. The main purpose of this assembly of disks is to tolerate the failure of a drive without losing data. A group of researchers at University of California at Berkeley developed the RAID concept, and they defined six different types of RAID arrangements. These different RAID systems arrange the data on the disk drive mechanism in a different manner to achieve a trade-off between price and performance.

- RAID level 0 provides no redundancy, and it does not truly fit the RAID acronym. With level 0, data is spread across drives, resulting in higher data throughput. Since no redundant information is stored, the performance of the array is very good, but the failure of any hard disk drive in the array results in data loss. This is commonly called *striping.*
- RAID level 1 provides data redundancy by duplicating the data from one drive on another drive. The data throughput performance of a level 1 array

is about the same as a single drive, but if either drive fails, no information is lost. Since only two drives are required, this is a good starting point for a RAID system, but since one drive is used to store a duplicate of the data, the cost of storage per megabyte is very high. This level is commonly called *mirroring.* An interesting point to note about mirrored disks is that the computer system cannot address the mirrors separately.

- RAID level 2 uses Hamming error correction codes. This level is designed for use with drives that do not have built-in error detection. All SCSI drives have built-in error detection, so this level is not used with SCSI drives.
- RAID level 3 stripes data a byte at a time across several drives, and parity is stored on one drive. It is otherwise similar to level 4. Byte-level striping must be implemented through hardware.
- RAID level 4 stripes data a block at a time across several drives, with parity stored on one drive. The parity information allows recovery from the failure of any single drive, but the use of a single drive for parity introduces a throughput bottleneck. The performance of a level 4 array is the same for reads as RAID level 0. Writes require that the parity data on the single parity disk be updated each time. This slows small writes, but sequential writes or large writes are still fast. Because only one drive in the array stores redundant data, a level 4 RAID array can be very cost-effective.
- RAID level 5 stripes data at a block level like RAID level 4, but this scheme distributes parity among the drives. Since the parity disk does not become a bottleneck, this can increase the throughput of small writes in multiprocessing systems. Because during reads the parity data must be skipped on each drive, the performance for reads is less than a level 4 array. The cost per megabyte of storage is the same for level 5 as for level 4.

The protection of data with RAID configured disks does not eliminate the need for routine backups. It is still possible for someone to delete the data. The existence of a mirrored disk does not protect the data from be destroyed from software rather than a hardware failure. One of the many features of an intelligent storage system is the ability to create a second mirror of the disk and make the second mirror addressable independently. EMC is a company that is a leader in the field of intelligent storage systems, and EMC's term for an additional mirror that can be independently addressed is a *business continuity volume* (BCV). The mirrored RAID level 1 disks and the BCV are shown connected to two computers in Figure 9-5.

An interesting use for the BCV is as a separate storage volume for reporting or as the data source for backup. The BCV can be split from the RAID system and addressed separately. While the normal data warehouse activity occurs on the system that is still attached to the RAID disk, standard reports or backup can be performed on the BCV. This allows operations that do not need to occur in a timely manner to take place in a way that does not affect information access. Once the

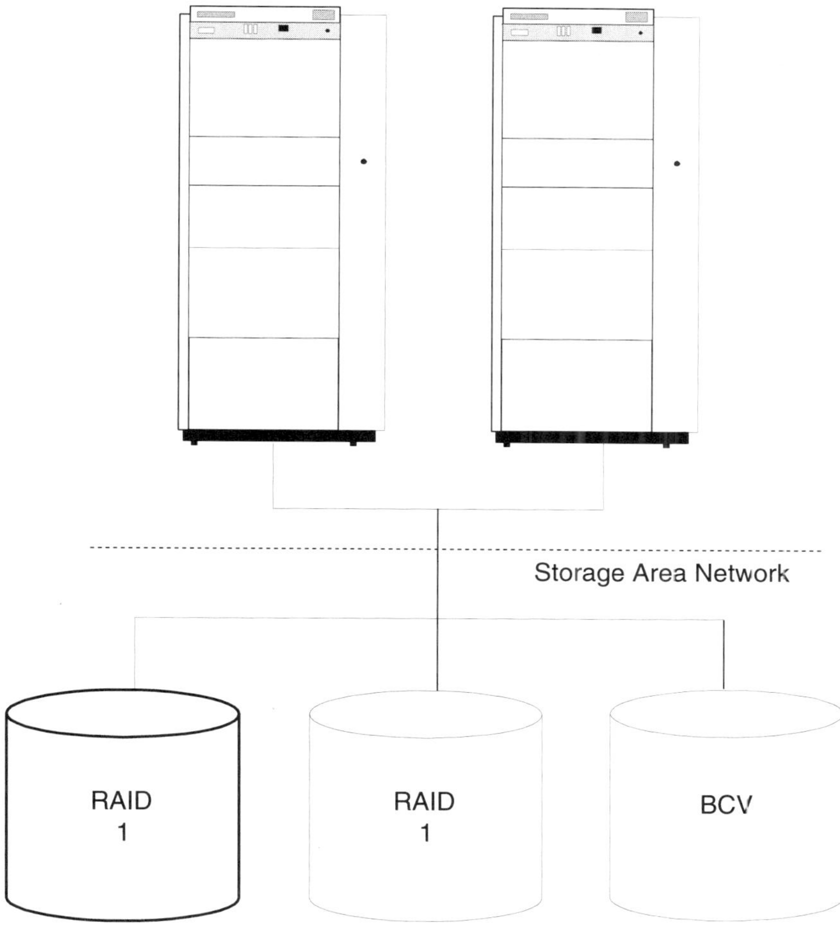

Figure 9-5 Arrangement of a BCV and RAID level 1 disks.

reporting or backup has taken place, the BCV is connected to the RAID group and synchronized with that data. This is illustrated in Figure 9-6. Another use for the BCV is to keep the data warehouse operational while the data is being loaded. Normal data warehouse queries can occur from the BCV while the data is being loaded into the RAID-protected storage area. In general, this arrangement keeps the data warehouse available while maintenance occurs on the data warehouse.

The large internal cache and disk arrangement that the intelligent storage system contains improve the performance of both reads and writes. If the write occurs to memory cache, the write operation will happen much faster than a write to a hard disk. The intelligent storage system also will have a read-ahead algorithm that

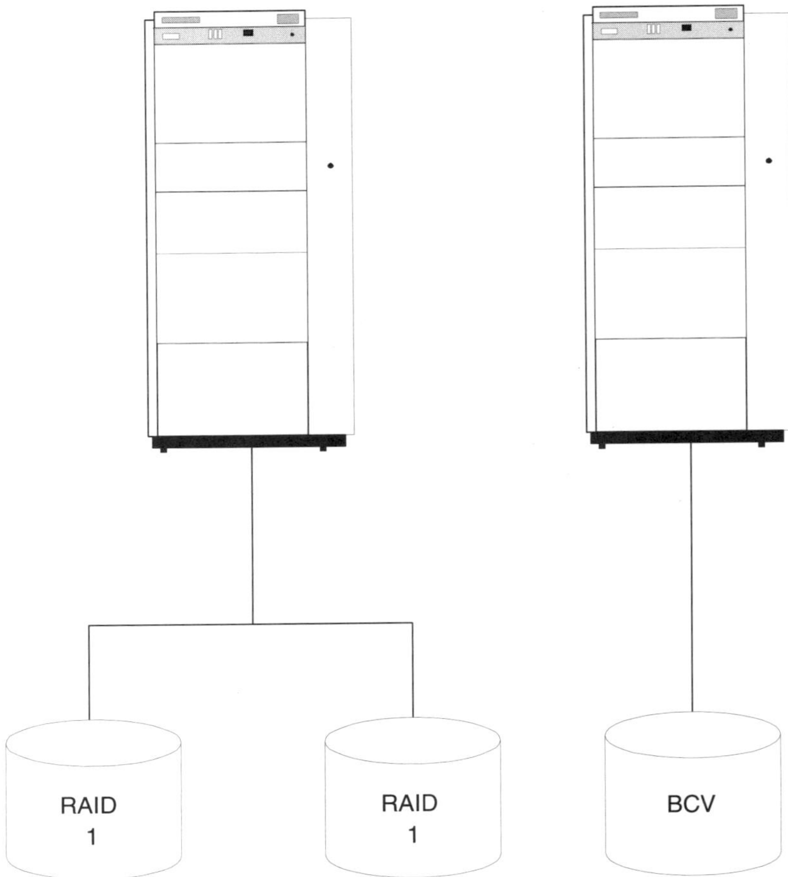

Figure 9-6 BCV being addressed separately from the raid array.

attempts to anticipate the need for data and move that data from disk to cache, where it will be available for fast access.

The inclusion of intelligent storage options in the architecture has operational, financial, and business implications, all of which are positive. The availability of technology like the BCV eases the operational constraints of the data warehouse. It makes it possible to perform maintenance while keeping the system operational. This implies a positive business advantage because the business information flow and decision making can continue while technical issues are resolved. Because the business remains operational, the activities that generate profit are still occurring while the technical activities are occurring. This is the positive financial impact. These three impacts are the reason that intelligent storage systems have become very popular.

9.3 DATABASE CONSIDERATIONS

Most of the interesting database features that are of interest to the data warehouse architect but not the OLTP architect are the ability to perform certain operations in parallel. The typical operations that take the most amount of time in the maintenance of the data warehouse are the loading of data, the indexing of data, the query of data, and backup of data. Some databases can use multiple CPUs, I/O channels, disk controllers, and hard disk assemblies at the same time. This will greatly reduce the time it takes to complete common database tasks on the very large amount of information that is used in a data warehouse.

The features mentioned above will be implemented in a different way by different databases based on the architecture of the database. These different architectures will have different performance characteristics for different database tasks based on the trade-offs of the architecture. As an example, some database software is designed so it can take full advantage of the parallel features of the operating hardware by sharing no parts of the hardware between processes. Other database software is designed to have shared access to disk. The architectural differences between shared nothing and shared disk will have an impact on the performance of the database for different tasks. The important point to remember is to match the characteristics of the database with the characteristics of the data warehouse project.

The ability of the database to perform parallel loads of data is dependant on both the design of the database and the structure of the database that is being loaded. Most general-purpose databases, such as DB2, Informix, Sybase, and Oracle, have parallel load features. While the capabilities of each database are different, they are all affected by the way the data is laid out on the disk, and the way the disks are connected to the computer or computers. In other words, it is very important to have good software and hardware with which to work, but the software and hardware battle is always a leapfrogging of technology. The data warehouse architect has no control over this. The way the data is physically laid out in the system is something the data warehouse architect can control. The appropriate way to layout data is something that should be assigned to a skilled DBA or consultant.

A bulk load utility is built into every one of the merchant databases. The bulk loader is designed to get the data into the database as quickly as possible. Because the bulk loader is usually the fastest way to get data into the database, it is important to become familiar with its abilities and features. In addition, it is usually possible to take advantage of other database options, such as turning logging off while the load occurs. It is important to understand the features of the database load options and exercise them judiciously.

Indexing is to a database as a card catalogue is to a library. Rather than searching through the entire library for a book, the book location can be looked up in the catalogue and then found in the library. Rather than search through an entire database for a value, the location of the value can be determined by an index and the record in the database accessed directly. There are many types of indexes. The more common types of indexes are the B-tree index, hash index, and bit-mapped index.

One of the first types of data structures that computer science students learn about is the B-tree. A B-tree index is very good index for columns that have a large number of values. Another way to say this would be to say that the column has high cardinality or a large domain. When a column has a B-tree index, a data structure is established that has all the values stored in the column and a list of the row id's that have the value. This data structure consists of a set of nodes that are connected with memory pointers. This is illustrated in Figure 9-7. In order to find the list of row id's that have a data value, we start at the root node. If the value at the node is not the value that is desired, we will look to the left if the value we are looking for is less than the value stored in the node. Similarly, we will look to the right if the value we are looking for is greater than the value in the node. This procedure is repeated until the node with the desired value and associated list of row id's is found.

Another way to index a column in the database for rapid access is with a hashed index. A hashed index uses an algorithm to convert the information from the column to a smaller number of bits and convert it to a row id. Because a hashed index uses an algorithm to find a value rather than a data structure search, it can be a very fast method of accessing the information.

Some database management software can use something called a bit-mapped index. Bit-mapped indexes are particularly good with columns of low cardinality. A bit-mapped index is a string of bits that represent all possible values that a column can have and a bit set to indicate if a row in the database contains

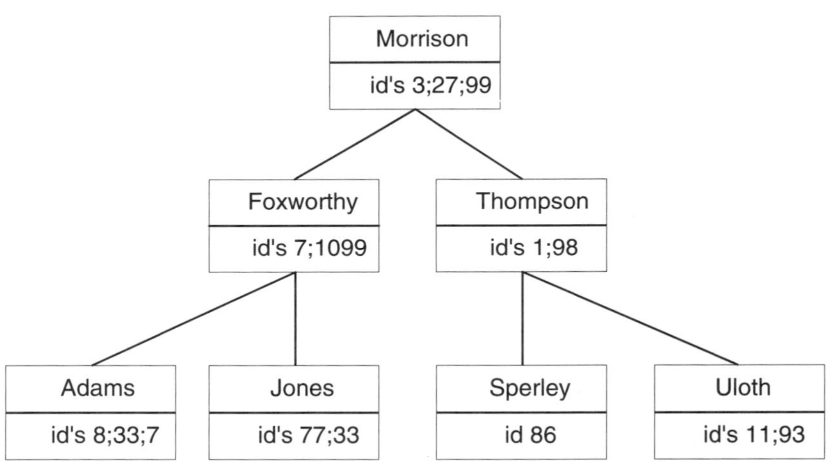

Figure 9-7 B-tree index.

that value. Computer processors can perform the types of operations needed to manipulate a bit map very quickly. Thus, bit-map indexes can be very efficient.

A key to good database performance is proper selection of the index method for a table. A general rule of thumb is to use a B-tree index on the primary key of the largest fact tables. Hashed indexes may be appropriate for smaller fact tables or nonprimary keys. Bit-mapped indexes are usually very good as primary key indexes for dimension tables.

Another type of database software that is very useful for data warehouse construction is the multidimensional database (MDB). Most major RDBMS database vendors supply MDB software as well. An MDB stores summary information about the dimensions of business analysis in a multidimensional matrix. A three-dimensional matrix for the analysis of sales by region, product, and time is shown in Figure 9-8. If we were to examine the cells on the face of the cube, the region would change as we move across a row on the face of the cube, but the product and time period would stay the same. As we move into the cube along the product dimension, the region and time period stay the same, but the product is changing. Similarly, as we move along a column in the MDB, time changes but the product and region stay the same. For "cubes" with more than three dimensions, it is much harder to draw the "cube," but the mathematical concept is the same.

The MDB is a very rapid way to access summary information. Because many of the cells in the "cube" will be zero, part of the key to success with an MDB is the efficient handling of sparse arrays. Because the MDB provides only summary information, it is great for trend analysis but not appropriate for things like data mining. The current trend is to provide integration between the MDB and a relational database. This makes it possible for a knowledge engineer to use the cube to monitor trends, then access the detailed information that was used to calculate the cube to analyze the reason for the trend. Middleware products such as Intelligent Warehouse can also provide the necessary integration.

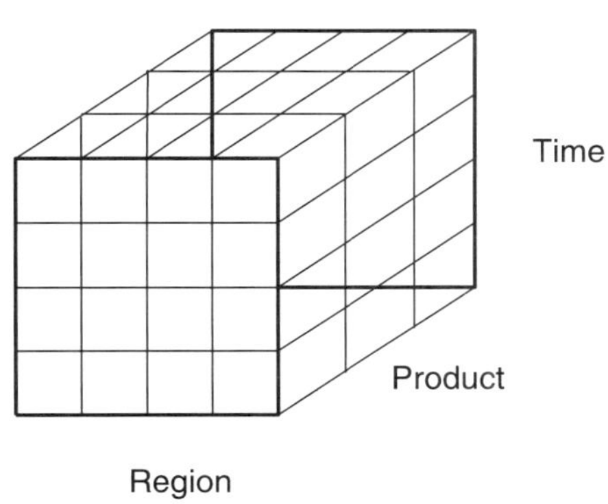

Figure 9-8 Multidimensional database.

9.4 THE DATABASE SERVER HARDWARE

The question that most data warehouse architects must answer is what type of hardware is best for running the types of software that we will encounter in the construction of a data warehouse. Similarly, the best architecture to run large general-purpose programs is also interesting to discuss and hotly debated. The components that make up good computer performance are:

- Fast processor
- Large memory and cache with good utilization
- Efficient operating system
- Advanced compiler that generates efficient code
- Fast I/O system
- Fast storage system

We have already explained the speed and operational benefits of intelligent storage subsystems. These storage subsystems can be attached to MVS and most open system vendors' computers. Most I/O systems are based on standards such as the SCSI, HIPPI, or FDDI and the standard brings a level of performance expectation that most vendors meet. Most of the time, the variance in computer performance of systems with similarly configured storage systems can be traced to the first four factors. These are discussed briefly below.

Professor Mike Flynn at Stanford University developed a way to classify processors by the number of instructions and data operations that the processor is operating on during a clock cycle. The first microprocessors operated with a single instruction and a single data operation. As an example, the microprocessor instruction would be to multiply two data elements. This would be a single instruction, single data (SISD) computer.

Engineering and scientific calculations frequently require arithmetic operations on vectors of values. A vector is an ordered list of numbers. If two vectors are multiplied, we must multiply each value in one vector by another value in the second vector. "Supercomputer" and vector processors have the ability to multiply two vectors with one instruction. Since multiple data elements are being operated on with a single instruction, this is a single instruction, multiple data (SIMD) processor or we could have multiple instructions operating on a single data element or pair. This would be called a multiple instruction, single data (MISD) processor. This does not make much sense.

The fourth option for processor design is to include enough hardware in the processor to have multiple instructions operating on multiple data elements at the same time. This would be called a multiple instruction, multiple data (MIMD) process. This has a lot of potential benefit. To understand the reason for the benefit of MIMD microprocessors, we must make a brief aside to explain how a processor branch instruction affects processor performance. Instructions are operated on in a microprocessor like an assembly line. This microprocessor assembly line is called a *pipeline*. At different stages in the pipeline, different things happen to the instruction. The usual steps are that instruction is decoded, the operands are fetched, the instruction is operated on, the result is stored, and so on.

Most programs will take branches or different paths through a code based on certain conditions. If a condition is met, the program will do one thing, but if the condition is not met, it will do something else. An example of this type of code is:

```
Instruction8
Instruction9
If (a=b) then
   Instruction10
   Instruction11
   Instruction12
   Instruction13
Else
   Instruction100
   Instruction101
   Instruction102
Endif
```

When the microprocessor comes to the branch instruction, it will generally keep filling the pipeline with the instructions following the branch. In other words, the microprocessor will keep filling the pipeline with instruction10 and instruction11 until it determines if the branch should have happened or not. If the branch should have occurred, the microprocessor must throw away everything it has in the pipeline and start working on instruction100. This is a little like a car manufacturer changing the model it is manufacturing in the middle of the process. All the minivans must be taken off the assembly line and thrown away while the sedans start to filter down the assembly line.

Suppose for a moment that the microprocessor had two complete instruction pipelines and all the other necessary hardware. The microprocessor could be working on both possibilities of the branch until it knew the outcome of the a=b operation. Because the microprocessor is working on two sets of instructions and data at the same time, it is an MIMD processor. When the processor determines the appropriate side of the branch to take, it would simply discard the unneeded instruction results. This is an improvement, but a second branch frequently follows the first. For example:

```
Instruction8
Instruction9
If (a=b) then
   If (c=d)
         Instruction10
         Instruction11
```

```
            Instruction12
            Instruction13
      Else
            Instruction20
            Instruction21
            Instruction22
            Instruction23
      endif
   Else
      Instruction100
      Instruction101
      Instruction102
   endif
```

The processor would need four complete instruction pipelines and associated hardware to follow all of the possible instruction paths. Hewlett-Packard has teamed with Intel to develop a microprocessor that is able to work efficiently with branches. This new family of microprocessors has many interesting features, and the ability to deal effectively with the branch problem is just one of the features.

Now that we have looked into some details of how processors and microprocessors are designed, we can investigate some ways the processors can be combined to generate enough horsepower to serve as a data warehouse database server. The different options that have been investigated over time are the symmetric multiprocessor (SMP) computer, the massively parallel processor (MPP) computer, and the parallel server architecture.

In the symmetric multiprocessor arrangement, several processors are connected via a bus to each other and to common resources such as memory and disk. This arrangement is illustrated in Figure 9-9. The advantage this architecture is that it is easy to build, easy to program, and easy to administer. The problem is that it is easy to saturate the bus that allows communication between the CPUs, memory, and I/O.

A different way to organize the communication between components is to isolate the CPU to memory traffic and to have the I/O communications travel on a different bus. The major bottleneck in the computer communications is between the CPU and memory. One way to overcome this is to use a concept from telecommunications called a crossbar switch. In typical SMP architecture, all CPUs communicate with all of the memory over the same bus. This is a little like having a party-line telephone that is shared between several people. Everyone must take a turn talking. This greatly limits the scalability of SMP architectures.

If we had a way to connect pairs of talkers with each other directly, they would not have to wait for other communication to finish before communicating. One device that directly connects two things that need to communicate is a *crossbar switch.* Such a switch is used in some Hewlett-Packard computers, such as the Exemplar series, to increase the scalability and performance of the architecture. This architecture is illustrated in Figure 9-10. Building enough hardware into the

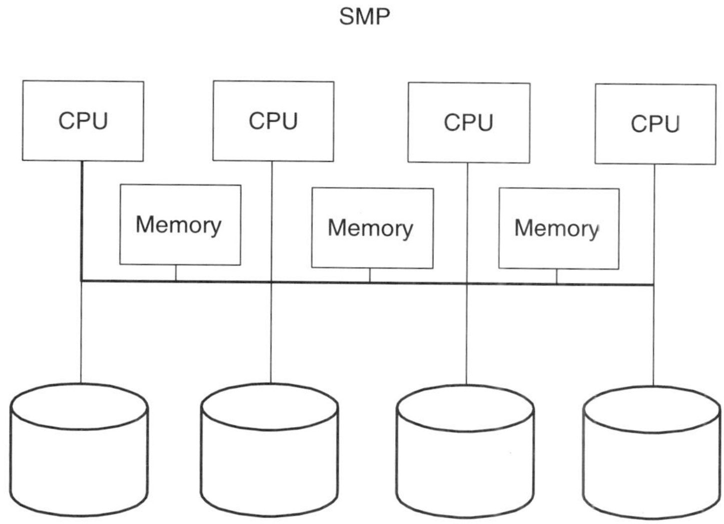

Figure 9-9 Symmetric multiprocessor computer.

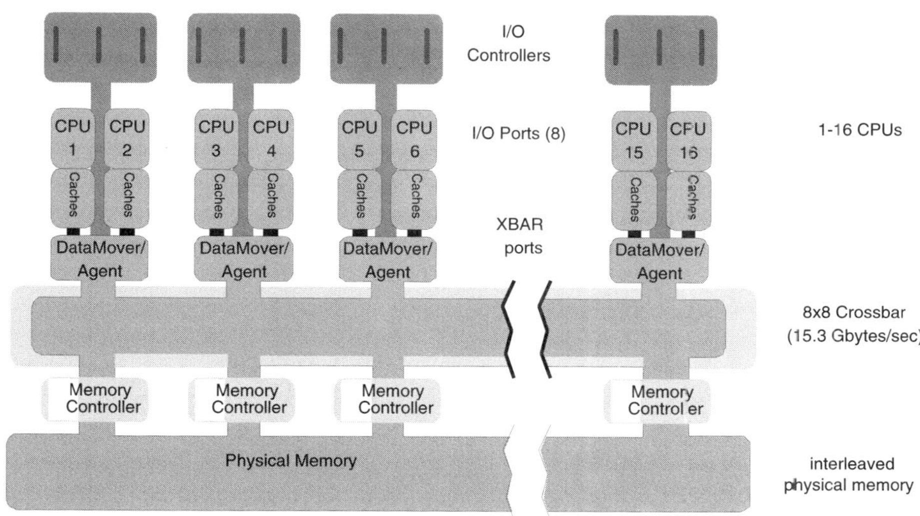

Figure 9-10 SMP architecture with a crossbar switch.

crossbar to expand indefinitely is expensive, so the crossbar is usually limited to connections on the order of eight CPU connections to eight memory connections.

In the massively parallel processing (MPP) computer, no component of one computer is shared with the CPU of another. This architecture is also called a *clustered architecture.* This architecture is easily configured and programmed. If data from one CPUs disk is needed by another CPU, the data must be transferred over the bus. The communication bus between the CPUs can become saturated with traffic. With the exception of the bus that connects the CPUs, this architecture scales well. Adding processors increases the problem of network saturation. Managing the environment can also be difficult. The MPP configuration is shown in Figure 9-11.

An architecture that is a compromise between the advantages of an SMP system and an MPP system would potentially be ideal. This system should have the scaling advantages of an MPP system with the ease of programming features of an SMP system. Ideally, the system would have a crossbar to eliminate CPU to memory contention but the ability to add processors for scalability. The architecture that seems to be becoming a de facto standard in the industry is a parallel combination of servers. In this configuration, SMP computers are added in parallel with a high-speed interconnect between the SMP computers. This architecture is shown in Figure 9-12. Each computer in a parallel server combination is called a node, and each node will have a number of processors.

We have spoken of *n*-tier architectures as if every computer in the architecture were a "separate" computer. The parallel server structure is a natural architecture match for *n*-tier architecture. Each node in the parallel server could represent a tier in the architecture, or nodes can be combined to operate as a single tier in the architecture. The advantage of the parallel server architecture is that it allows the entire system to be managed as if it were a single computer system.

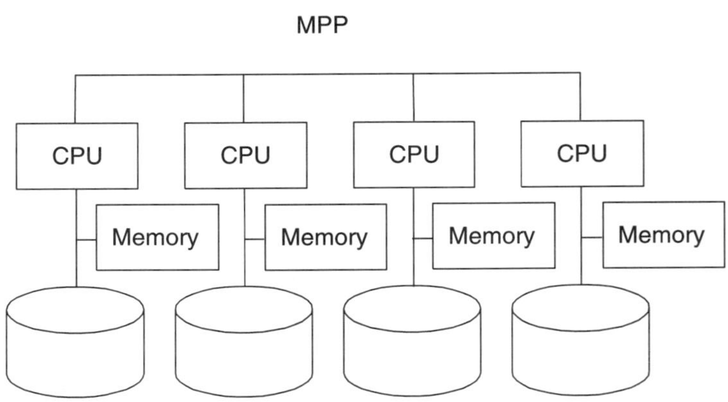

Figure 9-11 Massively parallel computer.

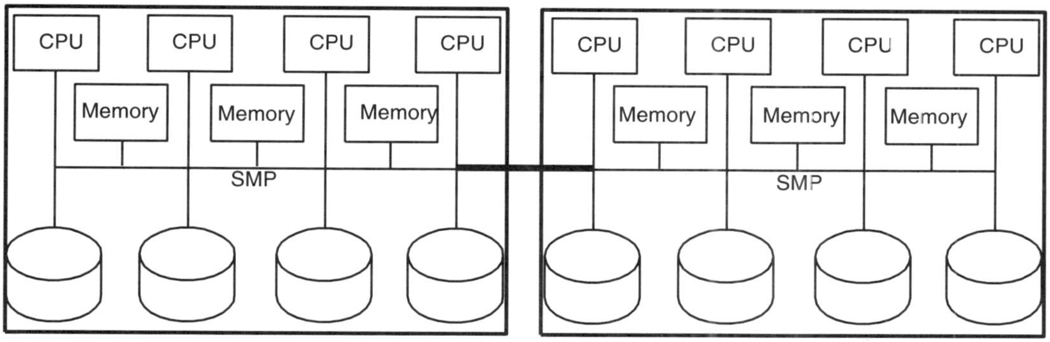

Figure 9-12 Parallel server computer.

One important driving factor for client server is application partitioning, and correct application partitioning is the reason for the conceptual, logical, and physical layers of the architecture. The idea behind application partitioning is similar to the reason convention centers have movable partitions. The movable partitions allow the flexibility to change the amount of room that is allocated to different functions. The location of the room can be changed as well. This is similar to resizing the computer or changing the location of the processing based on the changing needs of the data warehouse. There is nothing magical about the three layers of abstraction of the architecture. It is simply a useful thought process to delay the specification of components that are less dependent on the business needs and are more flexible.

9.5 OPERATING SYSTEMS

The ideal operating system will have a wide range of characteristics to suit of wide range of applications in an environment typical to that of a data warehouse. The operating system must be particularly well suited to the process-hungry applications that data warehouses employ. A 64-bit operating system is the current state-of-the-art for a data warehouse. This provides the ability to address more files, larger files, a larger process data space, more shared library segments, a large process data space, and more random access memory for higher performance and reduced swapping.

Hewlett-Packard has a framework called PRISM (performance and scalability, resilience, integration, security, and management). These are simply the characteristics of a good operating system. Extensions to the PRISM framework include standards adoption, application development, and breadth of applications. We discuss each of these characteristics below.

9.5.1 Performance

The operating system should have the ability to support platforms that range from a single-user computer to the parallel SMP systems described earlier. Unless an organization wants to support several different operating systems, the operating system could also support a wide range of applications. This includes everything from large NFS servers to very large database servers. The operating system should support:

- Kernel threads
- A very large memory model of up to 4 terabytes
- Very large file systems of up 1 terabyte either networked or local
- Variable page sizing by applications to optimize performance
- Parallel processing

9.5.2 Resilience

Because the business will be making critical decisions based on the data warehouse, the data warehouse environment must provide the highest possible uptime. The following items combine with standard operating system features to provide high availability:

- Journaled file system to guarantee file system integrity and fast recovery process in case of a system failure
- Memory page allocation to detect failed memory pages automatically without disrupting running applications
- Dynamic loadable kernel modules to support on-line modification and addition of input/output drivers

9.5.3 Integration

The operating system vendor must work closely with other software vendors to enhance the ability of the system to support a wide range of software and integrate mixed environments. It is imperative that the operating system support open systems standards for interoperability. This enables an IT architecture with a variety of operating systems and network environments, such as:

- NT
- NetWare
- Oracle Database

- Informix Database
- Sybase Database
- Netscape FastTrack
- Oracle Web Application Server
- Java Virtual Machine

9.5.4 Security

A business must feel comfortable that its data warehouse is secure. The operating system must protect the warehouse from internal and external tampering. Other people should not be reading the chief financial officer's financial reports before the chief financial officer does. Necessary features include:

- Compliance with Department of Defense C2 or better security requirements
- System auditing

9.5.5 Manageability

The system management facilities in the operating system should make it easy to manage even a complex set of networked systems. The management tools should reduce the cost of ownership and increase the productivity of the information management staff. The management features should include:

- A graphical or browser-based management tool
- A standards-based software and application update and distribution tool
- Performance monitoring
- Distributed print spooling

The PRISM feature list should serve as a guide or shopping list to the features desired in an operating system. Most organizations have based their operating systems selection on an internal standards list, and that is the list to use for that organization. The list above can be used to supplement the standards list.

9.6 THE QUERY SERVER AND THE APPLICATION SERVER

As with many other aspects of the data warehouse, the selection of a query server or application server depends on the role it will perform in the data warehouse physical architecture. In some cases, a particular software package has been selected for use in the warehouse architecture. The manufacturer of the software package will have specific recommendations as to the configuration of the computer to run the query or application software. The following commonsense guidelines are offered as a starting point in the physical architecture design and selection of these servers.

If there is a query server in the architecture, the query server will be configured differently from the database server. The database server will have much more hard disk available for long-term storage than the query server will. The other configuration parameters for the query server depend on the types of queries that are being made.

One of the major differentiating activities for sizing the query server is the size and type of joins the query server will make. If the query server is not performing joins, the query server will just pass the database query to the appropriate database server. The load will be light in this case, and any query processing software might be left on the same computer as the database. The query processing software could be placed on a separate computer for scalability reasons. In still other cases, the query processing software will be performing large joins of results from different tables on different database servers. In this case, the query server needs to have enough disk and memory to handle this task. The problem of database joins can swamp not only the query processor, but also the network that joins the database server to the query processor.

If there is a separate computer that is an application server, the server will be sized and selected based on user load and the type of application software that is running. With the increasing popularity of Microsoft NT, this has become a popular application server and client environment. Other software is based firmly on the abilities of UNIX, and this will drive the hardware selection to UNIX.

9.7 NETWORKS AND CONNECTIVITY

Networking and connectivity are the glue that holds the architecture together and links the different elements of the data warehouse physical architecture. Connectivity is a conceptually straightforward technical detail that is the foundation of any client–server system. As such, it is usually in place long before the data warehouse construction takes place. Most organizations have a networking and connectivity group that is charged with establishing and maintaining the network. If an organization is considering building a data warehouse but does not have a networking group, now would be a good time to establish one.

The biggest battle in networking is bandwidth. *Bandwidth* is a statement of the amount of data that can be moved over the network in a given period. The overall bandwidth of the system can be increased by partitioning the users and the system data to different networks. The system traffic can be placed on a

100Base-TX Ethernet, FDDI, ATM, Gigabit, or HIPPI interface. The users are typically placed on a different 10/100Base-TX Ethernet LAN than the system traffic.

The merchant database vendors all provide gateway software to link the databases to software from other vendors. Third parties have also written middleware tools that will connect to many different databases and even query and join data from heterogeneous sources. While the products from the database vendors usually function in a native mode and are much faster than the third-party products, the third-party products provide features that are sometimes missing from the database vendors.

In addition to the proprietary access mechanisms built into the databases, standards provide open system access to the database. Examples of this are the Open Database Connectivity (ODBC) standard from Microsoft and the Java Database Connectivity (JDBC) standard from JavaSoft. Because both ODBC and JDBC must be general enough to work with any database, it must do more work than a native database gateway. It is not tuned to a specific database, so it is less efficient than the database-specific gateways.

Another piece of the networking puzzle is the ability to map host names to IP addresses. The simplest way to do this is to provide an Internet Domain Name Service, or DNS, that will perform the translation from host name to IP address. As long as users specify a host name and not an IP address, we can change the physical machine they connect to by changing the mapping of hostname to IP address. Other directory services standards such as X.500 or LDAP, are gaining followers, but they are not as prolific as DNS.

To estimate the response time from a network and database server, a benchmark can be developed that loads all components of the architecture to a certain level and measures the performance. These types of tests can be extremely expense and it may take a long time to get the hardware in place to do the test. An alternative approach is to use analytical modeling and simulation to estimate the performance of a given network and server environment. The reader interested in this approach will find John Blommer's networking book in the Hewlett-Packard Prentice-Hall series very valuable.

9.8 MIDDLEWARE

"All right," declared General "Chesty" Puller during the Korean War, "they're on our left, they're on our right, they're in front of us, they're behind us. They can't get away this time." The opportunity for middleware is similar to the opportunity for General Puller. Middleware is surrounded by other data warehouse components with which the middleware must interact. The middleware must be written to work with the capabilities of all the other tools. Middleware frequently must make up for difficulties in the surrounding products. We will look at a couple of middleware packages and the types of functions they perform.

9.8.1 Usage Tracker

Usage Tracker Software by Pine Cone Systems monitors the TCP/IP packets between the database and the query manager and reports on the use of the data warehouse. The software provides information about the data warehouse user, data being accessed, and when it was accessed. The software generates a number of reports including table join report, dormant table report, dormant column report, and query duration report. With this information, the warehouse structure can be tuned to improve performance. This is done by identifying dormant data, data hot spots, and performance bottlenecks. The data architecture is then tuned to alleviate these problems.

9.8.2 Intelligent Warehouse

Intelligent Warehouse is a middleware product that makes the data warehouse easy to use and understand for both end users and IT professionals. Intelligent Warehouse sits between the end user and the data warehouse, creating an abstraction layer that hides its complexity and presents information in easy-to-understand fashion. IW has extensive query usage reports for the IT professional including adaptive tuning, database partitioning, query blocking, and security control. The query usage reports provide information about who is using the warehouse, what data is being accessed, and when it is being accessed. With this information, you can also improve warehouse structure, scheduling, and SQL performance significantly by identifying dormant data, hot spots, and performance bottlenecks. Intelligent Warehouse generates a number of reports and graphs. Custom graphs and reports can easily be created. IW provides end users with business models, automatic summary table selection, multidimensional database integration, and multitool support.

9.8.3 Transaction Processing Monitors

Transaction processing (TP) monitors such as Tuxedo were designed for use with on-line transaction processing systems. These systems are designed to be able to use whatever resource is available to complete a database transaction. In other words, if two or more computer systems are available to complete a database transaction, the transaction processing monitor will select the proper computer to complete the database transaction based on load. If one of the computers becomes unavailable, the transaction processing monitor will send all transactions to the operational computer. Transaction processing monitors have the ability to produce reports that show the performance of the DSS system. The transaction processing monitor will produce a variety of usage reports, including information about who is using the warehouse, what data is being accessed, and when it is being accessed. This can be used to tune the data warehouse database. Since a transaction processing monitor is designed to perform database writes in addition to reads, its capabilities are usually much greater than a data warehouse really needs. Summary-level seeking is not a concept that is used in the OLTP world, so this is not a feature of transaction processing monitors.

9.8.4 Middleware Selection

One of the difficulties with the selection of middleware is the simple fact that some of the functionality of the middleware is being added to the leading general-purpose databases. Before making a middleware selection, it is important to discover if the features you need are available in the database.

Some organizations select a transaction processing monitor because it fits into the organizational architecture standards. The organization has experience in the transaction processing world, and the experience is transferred to the data warehouse. The downside to that approach is the fact that the transaction processing monitor is tuned to perform reads and writes, and the monitor will not have some features (e.g., summary-level seeking) that a tool like Intelligent Warehouse has.

If the only feature in the tool that is desired is usage data, Usage Tracker from Pine Cone Systems is an excellent choice. If the list of desired features include summary-level seeking, heterogeneous joins, or value-based security, Intelligent Warehouse is a better selection.

If it seems like the author is belaboring the summary-level-seeking issue, it is because it is incredibly important to rapid query response and the success of the data warehouse. Without summary-level seeking, either users must know about the names and details of the summary levels, or they will force the warehouse to perform summary calculations on the fly. Performing summary calculations when a summary table exists is a waste of resources and kills performance for both the users causing the calculation and all other users on the system. With summary-level seeking, all users will see an increase in performance.

9.9 KNOWLEDGE ENGINEERING WORKSTATIONS

The client computers that the knowledge workers use are called either *clients* or *knowledge engineering workstations*. The features of these workstations vary widely, and the features that are needed depend on the purpose to which they are put. For example, some organizations use the data warehouse to produce canned queries that are placed on an internal Web server. In this case, the knowledge engineering workstations can be thin clients. At the other extreme, other organizations will use the or knowledge engineering workstation to create a personal data store of tens of gigabytes of information from the data warehouse and do data mining or visualization on the personal data store. In this case, the knowledge engineering workstation must be powerful enough to manipulate this large amount of information. We will divide the knowledge engineering workstations into four types—thin clients, low-end PCs, midrange workstations, high-end workstations—and discuss each in turn. Most organizations will have different groups of users for which class of workstation is appropriate, and at most organizations all the classes will be represented at some point in the architecture.

The *thin client* can be any device capable of running a Web browser. This spans a lot of space, and the capabilities of a thin client vary widely. Technically speaking, "thin" implies that the client does not have much disk storage or a large operating system because most applications and abilities will be downloaded through the Web. Most of the computing action is happening on the Web server. The thin client has a limited graphics and multimedia interface, but it will typically have a good networking system. These devices are very cost-effective and are becoming the standard desktop computer for many organizations. These will be used by the worker who will be viewing standard warehouse reports from a Web server.

A step up from the thin client is the entry-level PC, which will have a standard operating system like Microsoft Windows and enough disk and memory to store and execute necessary programs. Many of the compute cycles are happening on the PC client. The entry-level PC will usually not store much of the data that the knowledge worker will be manipulating and like the thin client, has a limited graphics and multimedia interface. The entry-level PC will be used by the knowledge worker who will be creating basic DSS reports that might involve creating a small personal data store.

A step up from the entry-level PC is the *midrange workstation,* which will have better graphics, processing, and storage capabilities than those of an entry-level PC. The midrange workstation will be used to do advanced analysis such as data mining of small local data sets or visualization of data.

The top rung on the knowledge engineering workstation ladder is the *high-end workstation,* which can have multiple processors in addition to a fast video and I/O processing system. This type of workstation, which will have more RAM than a midrange workstation, can be used to perform advanced analysis of warehouse data or act as a workgroup server.

9.10 DEPLOYING THE ARCHITECTURE

Many organizations that are building a large data warehouse are faced with the challenge of building a data warehouse infrastructure over a period of a few months to a couple of years. The challenge is to grow the physical architecture in a cost-efficient and scalable manner. The demand for the data warehouse is frequently greatly underestimated, but the growth of the architecture should enable recovery from miscalculation of required server size. The plan for deploying the physical architecture should include a plan for expansion and reuse of the hardware. This maximizes the benefit the organization sees from the warehouse for the investment. There are some clever and seemingly obvious ways to approach this deployment, but they are missed by the architecture team and will be pointed out in this section. We are assuming that nontrivial enterprise architecture is being developed. Simpler architectures will be more forgiving, but the principles will be the same.

The architecture will be deployed using the same principles as the other parts in the data warehouse architecture. The physical architecture will be developed through a program of iterative development that carries the components forward. As the architecture is developed, features will be discovered that no amount of planning would have uncovered. Only by deploying the architecture will the precise performance of the architecture be determined. Analytic modeling and simulation help in this regard, but there is nothing like the real thing to test the architecture.

The first deployment of the data warehouse will be with a limited but meaningful amount of data and will be used by a similarly limited but important and carefully selected audience. A typical scenario is as follows. The production data warehouse will be just under 1 terabyte in size when fully deployed and have around 100 users, 20 of them concurrently. The final architecture will have up to five tiers, but one of the end-user query tools does not require an application server. For the pilot, the query server can be forgone, and this leaves us with a three-tier architecture. The pilot phase of this warehouse would typically have 10 to 20 users total and an initial data size of 20 to 50 gigabytes. The database server for this configuration of the pilot does not have to be extremely powerful. For the purpose of illustration, we will call the computer that acts as the initial database server, "Mars."

There are several ways to select the components to maximize reuse and minimize the cost of deployment. If a single storage system cabinet has enough capacity to store the production warehouse, a cabinet like this is purchased with enough disk drives and cache to deploy the pilot. The storage system will be upgraded with additional disks and cache for the production system. If multiple storage cabinets are required, cabinets are added for production. The initial server that we are calling Mars can be purchased with room to grow into the database server. It can also be selected and purchased in a configuration that will enable it to become the query server or application server. Budget considerations frequently drive this decision. For the purpose of illustration, we will say that we have more room left in next year's budget, so purchase of the very large database server will be deferred until then. This decision process guides us to the pilot deployment shown in Figure 9-13.

For the first production version of the data warehouse, query and application server tiers will be added to the data warehouse. The computer that was part of Mars will move into the query server role. A very large computer that we will call Jupiter will move into the database server role, and a new computer we will call Pluto will be the application server. The configuration for the first data warehouse physical architecture deployment is shown in Figure 9-14. This physical architec-

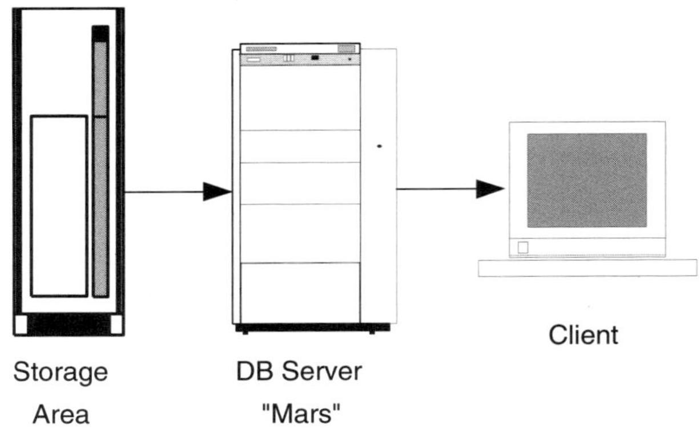

Figure 9-13 Data warehouse pilot deployment.

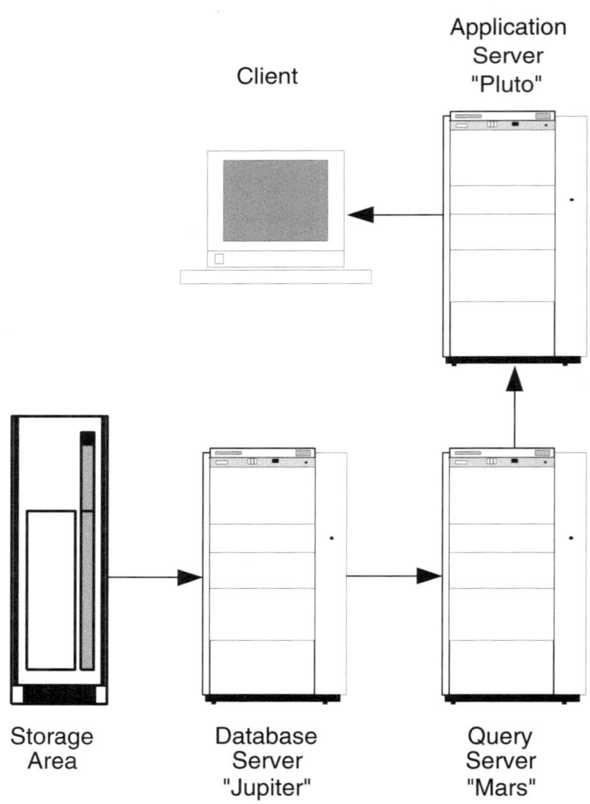

Figure 9-14 First data warehouse production deployment.

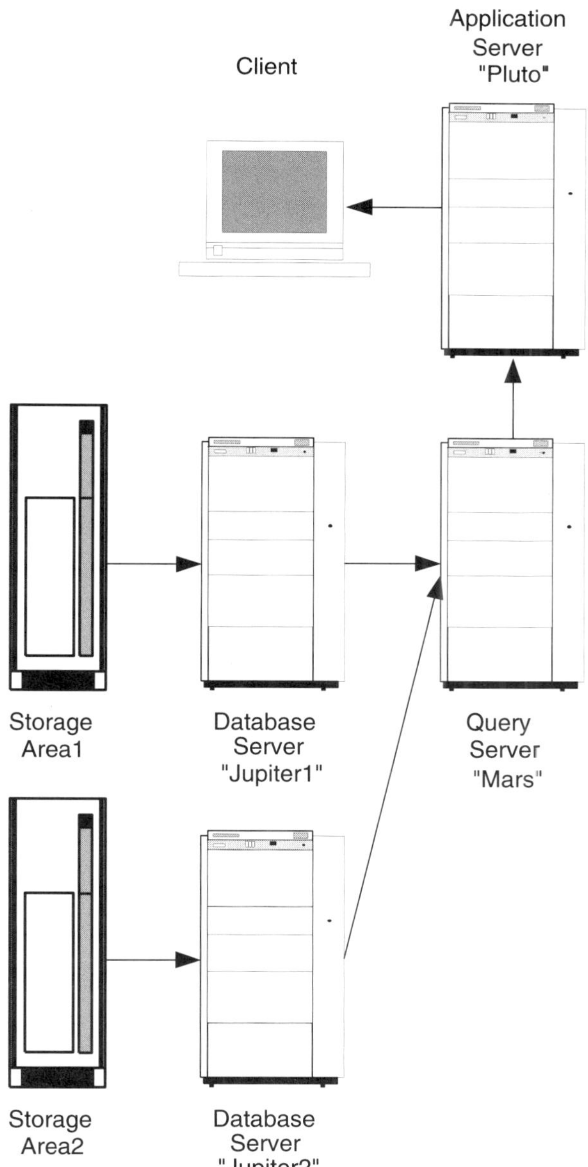

Figure 9-15 Second data warehouse production deployment.

ture is extremely scalable. Parallel servers can be added at every tier to meet user demand, and access to the warehouse can be used to segment the data warehouse users onto different application and query servers. This can help increase the manageability and scalability of the user access and security mechanisms.

When the second data warehouse subject area is added to the enterprise data warehouse, it can be added through a second logical database server and storage area. This adds computing power without adding a bottleneck in the database processing regime where most of the computing horsepower is needed. Figure 9-15 is the physical implementation of the query-managed subject area architecture shown in Figure 8-5.

It is worth reiterating that the physical partitioning indicated in Figures 9-14 and 9-15 is only one way to approach the scalability and application partitioning issue. Another way to approach this problem is to select only very large computing platforms and use software to logically partition the hardware. A software product called *process resource manager* will act as a governor to make sure that processes do not take more than an allotted amount of the system resources. This consolidated approach is usually less expensive than multiple smaller servers, but the consolidated approach frequently has less redundancy to provide for software failure in the event of hardware malfunction.

QUESTIONS

9.1 Explain the operation and features of RAID level 0.

9.2 Explain the operation and features of RAID level 1.

9.1 Explain the operation and features of RAID level 2.

9.4 Explain the operation and features of RAID level 3.

9.5 Explain the operation and features of RAID level 4.

9.6 Explain the operation and features of RAID level 5.

9.7 Is it necessary to do backups of RAID-protected disks?

9.8 Explain the value of a business continuity volume of BCV. Since it contains the same data as the RAID array, how is it different from a mirror?

9.9 Why is it recommended that an iterative approach be used in the development of the warehouse physical architecture?

9.10 Explain a multidimensional database.

9.11 Explain the differences among knowledge workstations.

9.12 Explain how the various database indexes should be selected for use with different types of data warehouse data tables.

9.13 In your own words, explain the difficulties that branches impose on a processor.

9.14 In your own words, explain the differences between SISD, SIMD, and MIMD processors.

9.15 In your own words, explain why a native mode database driver is faster than a third-party driver.

PROJECTS

9.16 Call behavior analysis is the analysis of the telephone calls that a traditional telephone or long-distance customer might make. The information is gathered by the switch that routes the call. This information will include the number of the telephone originating the call, the telephone number of the receiver of the call, and how long the call lasted. The newer switches, called SS7 switches, can capture other information, such as calls that are not completed because of a busy signal. Suppose that 1 kilobyte of data is captured for a million calls each day. Create the physical architecture for a call behavior analysis data warehouse. Explain your assumptions and the physical architecture in as much detail as possible. Explain how this architecture will be deployed.

9.17 The network that actually connects a telephone call is a very expensive and valuable resource. Planning for network expansion is a very important task due to lost revenue if telephone calls don't go through or the increased cost if the network is too large in the wrong location. Suppose that 1 kilobyte of data is captured for a million calls each day. Create physical architecture for a network usage data warehouse. Explain the architecture in as much detail as possible. Explain how this architecture will be deployed.

9.18 Buying trend analysis is performed by car manufacturers and dealers to best determine the car and options that certain demographic groups are likely to purchase. Suppose that the manufacturer sells 2 million cars each year and there is three years of history. Create the physical architecture for an automobile buying trend data warehouse. Explain the architecture in as much detail as possible. How would the architecture be different for a car dealership with 10,000 cars sold each year? Explain how this architecture will be deployed.

9.19 Stores can use buying trend analysis to best determine the products that certain demographic groups are likely to purchase. For example, an electronics store could determine which demographic groups are likely to purchase which products. The store sells 2000 products every month. Create the physical architecture for an electronics store sales analysis data warehouse. Explain the architecture in as much detail as possible. Explain how this architecture will be deployed.

9.20 Manufacturing organizations can use a data warehouse to track the compliance of their suppliers to their agreements. The agreements normally cover at a minimum the delivery timing of products and product quality. The manufacturing organization does this to increase part quality and reduce the cost of having too much inventory. Other technologies, such as electronic data interchange (EDI), allow the manufacturing company and its suppliers to exchange information orders for parts and deliveries of parts electronically. The manufacturing organization purchases a billion parts each month in lots of 10 from 10,000 suppliers. Create the physical architecture for a vendor compliance data warehouse. Explain the architecture in as much detail as possible. Explain how this architecture will be deployed.

9.21 Financial organizations can use a data warehouse to analyze the risk of consumer and certain other scenarios. This data warehouse can use data such as demographic data or payment history data to determine the risk of the loan. This enables the financial institution to estimate and manage the risk. Create the physical architecture for a risk analysis data warehouse. Explain the architecture in as much detail as possible. Explain how this architecture will be deployed.

9.22 Recall that airlines can analyze the travel trends of their frequent fliers in different demographic groups. This information can be used to target-market frequent fliers in the correct market groups. The demographic data is usually obtained from external sources. Create the physical architecture for a frequent flier data warehouse. Explain the architecture in as much detail as possible. Explain how this architecture will be deployed.

9.23 Airlines can use a data warehouse to track the seasonal variations and growth expected in travel between locations. This data could also show how much food and beverages are consumed in different flights. This will help the airline select aircraft and catering to match needs. Create the physical architecture for an airline flight segment data warehouse. Explain the architecture in as much detail as possible. Explain how this architecture will be deployed.

9.24 Educational institutions can use a data warehouse to analyze trends in class enrollment, grade history, and student evaluation of professors. The data for the data warehouse will be loaded at the end of every academic period. Information about class enrollment will come from the registration system, and student evaluation data can be loaded from the academic dean's computer system. Create physical architecture for an educational institution data warehouse. Explain the architecture in as much detail as possible. Explain how this architecture will be deployed.

9.25 Health care providers can use a data warehouse to track diagnosis codes (usually ICD9 codes), the procedures and treatments for that diagnosis (called CPT codes), and the cost of those procedures and treatments. This can be used to analyze the success rates of procedures for a diagnosis or the cost versus insurance reimbursement. Create the physical architecture for a health care diagnosis data warehouse. Explain the architecture in as much detail as possible. Explain how this architecture will be deployed.

9.26 Hotels can analyze the staying trends of their frequent guests in different demographic groups. This information can be used to target-market frequent guests for vacation packages. The demographic data is usually obtained from external sources. Create the physical architecture for a hotel frequent-guest data warehouse. Explain the architecture in as much detail as possible. Explain how this architecture will be deployed.

9.27 Hotels can use a data warehouse to track the total value of a frequent guest's stay. The value of the stay is the total amount the guest spends during the stay, including room, restaurant, room service, gift shop, and other incidental charges. Create the physical architecture for a hotel spending data warehouse. Explain the architecture in as much detail as possible. Explain how this architecture will be deployed.

10

DATA TRANSFORMATION

10.1 INTRODUCTION

The data transformation process is the nemesis of data warehouse construction. In the movie *Jaws*, we could not tell how big the shark was until we were looking into its mouth. This is similar to the problem of data transformation while building a data warehouse. A big part of the issue is data quality, and this is why we recommended that a data quality program be started prior to building a data warehouse. The data quality program will produce some very beneficial effects in addition to helping the data transformation effort.

In this chapter we point out the steps in the data extract, transformation, and loading process. Because of the large number of pieces that must come together to make a data warehouse work, it is important to plan for this carefully. The appropriate documentation and metadata must be in place to ensure that the data transformation process happens as smoothly as possible. The data extract process will impact other systems' performances, and it is important that this be considered in the change and configuration management of data source systems.

10.2 PLANNING

High-level planning of the data transformation process underlies a critical area for success in a data warehousing project. It is necessary to display what source systems are available for the data extraction as well as the planned target areas of the data. It is common for the target data sources to have been predefined during requirement definition sessions with end users, but unfortunately, the source of this data is not usually as easily unveiled. Often, the sources for data warehouse information are quite diverse, which can immensely compound the difficulty of a project (i.e., RDBMS, flat files, network databases, etc.). The high-level design highlights for upper management, in a manner that is not too technical or time-consuming, the complexity and importance of this stage of the project. It also provides for developers who are new to a project or those who have been involved and who have forgotten some of the fundamentals to obtain an initial understanding of the system that is being created, as well as the current areas used for data extraction. By doing the above, it can facilitate the shared comprehension of technical intricacies between management and developer. This joint knowledge can smooth the path to successful data warehouse development.

After high-level planning usually starts during the initial JAD process. A DSS star schema such as that shown in Figure 10-1 will have been developed. After the star schema model has been developed, the source table for each DSS table must be identified. It is helpful to draw a picture like the one shown in Figure 10-2, where the source tables are shown with arrows to the target tables. Comments can be added beside the arrow to remind the team to investigate relational integrity checks or other specifics that can be associated with each table.

After high-level planning has taken place, detailed planning must occur. There may be multiple possible source systems for a singe piece of data, but we must decide on a single source system or develop a way to determine the correct record. Since this is the start of the data transformation process, any differences in data definitions and coding schemes that are discovered can be noted at this time as well.

10.3 DATA EXTRACTION AND MOVEMENT METHODS

Tools used to extract data from a transactional system were at first "home-grown" because of the feasibility and economy of using source systems already in place and configured for particular business functions. Effectively, these tools were preliminary versions of what we now refer to as CASE tools. Often, these extract tools were used to update databases that were, in essence, rudimentary data warehouses before the terms *data warehouse* and *CASE tools* became common nomenclature. As data warehousing and decision support systems have evolved, more data transformation tools have been developed to facilitate this endeavor. The second

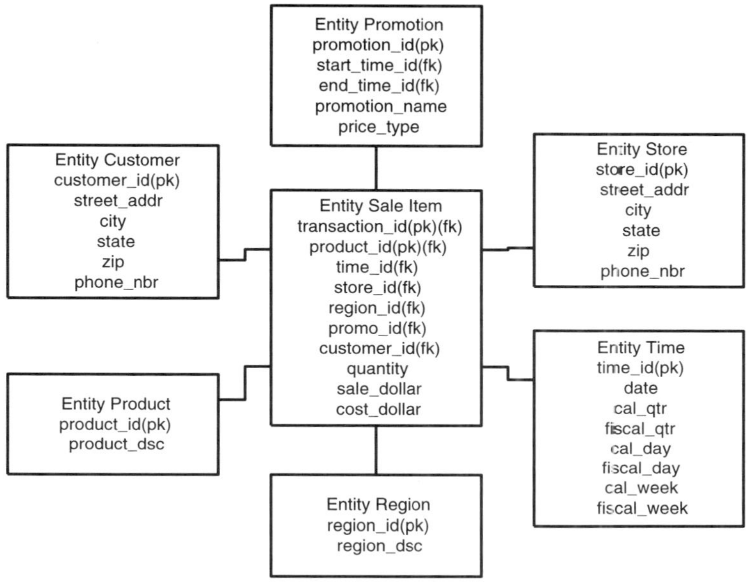

Figure 10-1 Decision support data model.

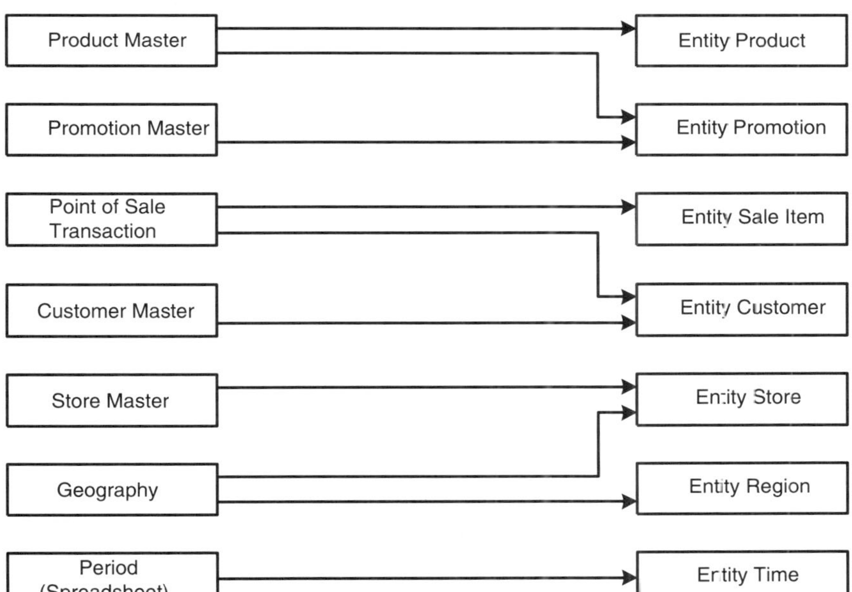

Figure 10-2 Planning the source systems.

generation of data transformation tools was assisted by an ongoing progression in technology. As the information industry continued to develop, it produced tools that were graphically more simplistic for developers to use. Many of these tools evolved to generate the metadata repository that is used in the data warehouse extraction process. Through these tools the time and energy needed to create the data warehouse became less cumbersome for the organization and more feasible. When and how to decide on a data transformation tool is not an easy decision for any organization. Ideally, a company can afford the "best-of the-best," but unfortunately, this isn't usually the case. It becomes even more problematic when the system to be transformed has been customized through years of toil, and often on many different platforms.

If an antiquated extraction process is already in place, it is essential to understand the needs met by this legacy system. Often though, this system can make it hard to refine what data is needed during the extraction process, thus complicating tool selection. Many times, the old data is not readily transferable to a new schema. In the scenario above, both the transformation process and extraction tool selection become much more difficult.

When possible, the most productive way to select a tool is to do it at the beginning of a project. Although the cost of creating a home-grown extraction process can be less expensive in dollars and time, the long-term benefit of choosing an efficient tool can completely offset the initial expense over time. After the learning curve has been passed, the benefits become apparent. Many of the newer tools utilize objects that can have the business rules built in. When these rules change, the changes are propagated to all instances in the schema that are related to that object. This saves many hours of labor. A facet of the choice in extraction tool selection is ensuring that whether it's a home-grown or market tool it has the ability to make external function calls. If proprietary information is needed to assist in data transformation, this capability can become critical. A rule as to when an organization should purchase a transformation tool can depend on the stage of the project. If management has not yet approved a project, it is safer to stay with current system development techniques.

Many source systems are heavily loaded. Any extract scheme will affect the already burdened source system. The design of the extract process must take this into account. If bulk extract is selected, there is usually a window in the batch-processing schedule when it must occur. It is imperative that the extract process be designed to fit into all of the other tasks that must occur in the glass house and be implemented in a way that will fit into a production environment. Once the data has been extracted, it usually needs to be moved from the source system to the destination. Although this is not rocket science, there are a many little obstacles that can make it difficult to automate this in a production environment. One of the advantages of data replication with a database is that it takes care of the data movement problem automatically. For those less fortunate, it is easy to write a script to perform a transfer from the source to the destination. If the source system is an MVS system, the manager of that system will usually want to control this process. In other cases the transfer can be started by the destination system. In general terms, the difficulty with this process is being able to schedule processes across platforms in a heterogeneous environment. The load process cannot start until the data movement ends, and the data movement cannot start until the extract ends. There are vendor tools that enable this process, and these can be very valuable in a heterogeneous environment.

Storage system manufacturers have some products that aid in the data movement problem. Companies such as EMC manufacture enterprise storage systems that will attach to both MVS and open-system computers. If the source systems and data warehouse systems are located in the same data center, they can share an enterprise storage system. The movement of data from source to data warehouse can happen inside the storage system without affecting the network. MVS-to-open system data transfer uses cycles on the open-system processor.

When the source and data warehouse systems are not co-located, the data must be moved over the WAN from the source to the warehouse. This usually occurs over leased lines, and this usually causes the computer security people some nightmares. One way to protect data is to encrypt the data. For the bulk transfer of files, this is a fairly satisfactory solution. If data replication is being used, all the data packets must be encrypted. Because there is very little information in any particular network packet, data thieves would probably wait a long time before getting anything interesting. If they managed to break into the source or recipient system, life would not be fun.

An alternative data trickle movement method is to use one of the disaster recovery features from a storage or software vendor to create a data trickle to the data warehouse facility. As an example, EMC has a product called Symmetrix Remote Data Facility that will replicate the data from the source server storage to the warehouse storage (Figure 10-3). It should be very difficult for a hacker to attempt to break into the server side because the SRDF connection is configured to send data only. If the hacker records the traffic on the WAN, it is difficult to convert the storage I/O packets into meaningful information. If a hacker attempts to inject traffic to the warehouse server, the transaction will not appear correct to the recipient and will be rejected.

10.4 DATA TRANSFORMATION

After analyzing and completing a high-level plan, it is necessary to create detailed transformation plans for the tables involved. A prioritization needs to be done on what tables to start with while considering their far-reaching complexity. Often, the source data tables and/or files are better resources for this section of the data transformation process, utilizing graphics to depict the connection to the target tables. All of the detail tables must be processed before the master table. The detail tables are usually fairly independent of each other and are linked together via a fact table.

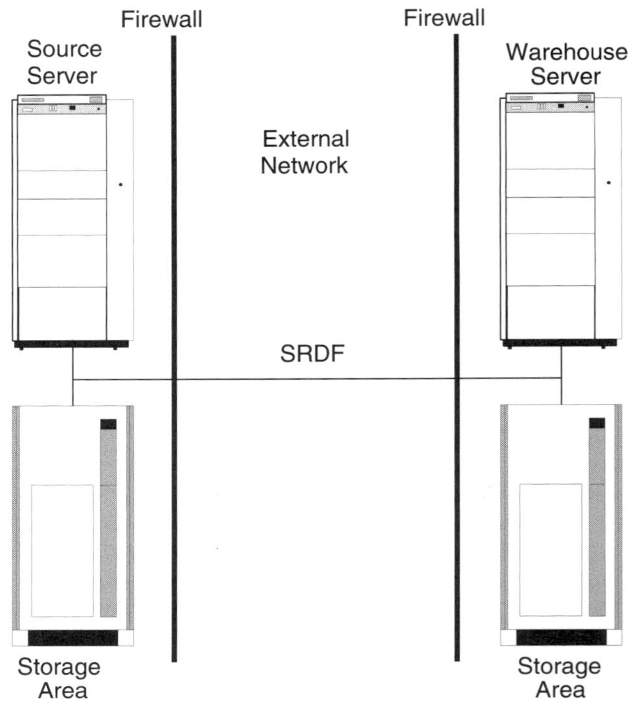

Figure 10-3 Data is moved across an SRDF connection outside the firewall.

The data transformation area is where a huge part of the task of creating a data warehouse occurs. The data comes in where it is cleaned, aggregated, stored, and sent to one or more server platforms. The ultimate purpose of the data transformation process is to prepare the data for transmission to a server platform, usually a relational DBMS or an OLAP engine. If there is system compatibility in the source data and target system (an example of which would be that both are relational databases and transfer time does not affect the system critically), it behooves the development team to do all within the relational system. Unfortunately, this is not normally the reality, due to multiple platforms, proprietary systems, and so on. It can often be easier to create a flat file developed from diverse areas to load the data into the transformation area. This can be done by sorting on a few different tables and files at a time, and using the new file in loading the data to the target.

The easiest way to start the transformation process is to utilize tables that are static in their transactional sources. They are much easier to populate, as the source is normally more simplex. When there is no static data set with which to begin, choosing the most simplistic data set is the best option. Also, it is always wise to keep the organization team that has knowledge in this business function involved in the loop. They can provide you with information concerning the creation, update process, accessibility, and maintenance of the source data. This knowledge can save hours trying to play detective on the I/O hunt as well as keeping everyone involved in the project on the same page.

To retrieve the data that must be transformed, there are two primary options. One is using a direct database extract. This is not a constant update (i.e., "trickle") to the transformation database but a process that extracts the data from the source system. It reassembles it through the transformation tool and then updates the transformation database in one continuous, but finite by instance process. The other option is to develop a tool that creates a flat file to be loaded into the transformation area. This at first seems more onerous than simple database extraction, but has benefits of its own. The down side is that there are more steps required to create the flat file. The up side is that after it has been created, the ability to reuse and recover if system failure occurs during the extraction or transfer process to the target system is often much easier. Also, the flat file can be encrypted and compressed for aiding in reducing strain on system resources during these transmissions of the data. Since the communication link where large amounts of data often need to be transmitted rapidly can be the bottleneck in success. Flat files can also prove beneficial when trying to combine different types of data sources by rolling the information into one source for transformation. While not as quick to produce results as direct database extracts, these features of flat files can be profitable to all over time.

Another important part of the data transformation process is converting the data types of individual fields from one type to another. EBCDIC to ASCII is usually an easy exchange, due to the many tools that have been created on almost every major production system. It is usually not the most brain-cell-engaging activity, and one can usually wade through it fairly painlessly.

Simple transformation effects can also help the user to appreciate the effort being made to create a data warehouse for them. An example of this is utilizing tools that make the data more pleasing to the eye. For instance, the tool may take field names and capitalize those that we mere mortals would normally capitalize. For many users already lost in a technical Babylon, these little efforts reap huge benefits for the development team.

Assigning surrogate keys is the next part of transforming the data. After designing tables in which you have complete confidence as to their accuracy to integrate with other newly designed tables and that will provide for the needed business functions, surrogate keys need to be assigned in the schema. Especially important at this point is preserving the link between the source system and the target system. Sometimes there are intermediate tables that are used in the transformation process but which aren't needed in the final design. To preserve a relationship between tables A and B, a table that maps A to B provides a connection between the source and the target system. An example of such a table is shown in Table 10-1.

Table 10-1 Tracking the mapping of surrogate keys

Data Warehouse Key	A key	B key
Patient_id	Pat_no	Pat_id
54997	28772	3819
51579	21871	3165
3678	315	4872

The use of a table to track the matches of data between source and destination systems is not limited to primary keys. Other code table values are tracked in a table along with the matching information. As an example, the data warehouse may have a field for eye color called Eye_clr that uses Blue and Green as possible values. Source system A has a similar field, called Eye, that uses a value of 1 to represent Blue. Source system B also has a similar field, called Color_of_eye, and that uses a value of Bl to represent Blue. To track all of these conversions, a table is created like the one shown in Table 10-2.

A backup is critical before the intermediate tables have been deleted, and preserving the intermediate tables in some form of data storage is highly recommended. These crucial backups allow an organization to backtrack in case some redesign engineering or recovery needs to be performed. As important, the main source to target data table is used extensively during the transformation process, and if lost, can cause huge difficulties for all involved in the data warehouse project.

The way that surrogate keys are assigned varies with the source, and target systems. If your transformation platform is in a relational database management system, the assigning surrogate keys can be a graceful process. Basically, the surrogate key is incremented by one for each instance in the table. For a file-based transformation system, the process is a little different. Normally, the increment value (current or next) needs to be maintained in a simple repository in order to have the value readily available and to decrease system load use during the transformation process. In other words, to cycle and sort through the file during each transformation process can burn system resources best used elsewhere.

Table 10-2 Tracking the mapping of code values from sources to the data warehouse

DW Key	Value	A Key	Value	B Key	Value
Eye_clr	Blue	Eye	1	Color_of eye	Bl
Eye_clr	Green	Eye	2	Color_of eye	Gr
Hair_clr	Brown	Hair	1	Color_of_hair	Br
Hair_clr	Gray	Hair	3	Color_of_hair	Gy

As a general rule of thumb, all of the primary keys in the data warehouse should be surrogate keys because it makes it much easier to maintain the warehouse. Some DBAs call surrogate keys *technical keys*. The surrogate keys give the data warehouse maintenance team the flexibility they need to respond to changing descriptions and features that are discovered in the raw data. Changes in dimension tables are the primary reason for the introduction of surrogate keys. It is also possible that production keys will be changed over time.

The complexity of this particular stage in the data warehousing creation process increases when there are multiple platforms from which data must be extracted, integrated, and linked. Often it is difficult to find a common ground that matches the properties for these systems. They can come close, but they're not quite the same. In human brains, close but not the same is readily transformable. A person just clarifies what he or she means during a verbal interaction. Unfortunately, that is not the case with data processing systems. The systems' connectivity abilities are restricted by the boundaries set through database layout, coding, and platforms.

Tools have been created to help facilitate this process. They do the talking between the various tables and platforms. Although these tools expedite the transformation process, they cannot do it all. Despite all the sorting and matching mechanisms in place, human intervention almost invariably occurs to put the final touches to the joining of multiple systems. Once in place, however, this joining can be propagated when changes do occur. Another important part of the data transformation process is validating the relational integrity of the tables sourced and created. Sorting and comparing between two newly created tables and then reversing the process can verify the integrity of the transformational schema.

10.5 DATA LOADING

It's time to load the data! The data transformation process is complete, and the database needs to be populated. There are several steps involved in this process, but it is straightforward. The first step usually taken is utilizing the bulk loader on the system that has been chosen. Almost all standardized databases have this utility available. Its primary purpose is to load data into the database in the most efficient and timely manner possible. An important note is that when a transformation tool has been utilized, it is crucial to ensure compatibility between the transformation tool and the bulk loader.

Significant features of a bulk loader often include the following:

- The ability to turn off logging
- Presorting of files by index
- Data type conversions and manipulations
- Data aggregations

By turning off logging, the system resources are freed up tremendously, allowing a much faster transfer of the data from the transformation area to the data warehouse system. If the bulk loader has a data set that has been presorted on a primary index field, it can speed up the data loading immensely, and utilizing it will help this stage. Features in a bulk loader sometimes also include the ability to aggregate the data. When available, it is definitely worth using.

Before loading a warehouse table, it is frequently necessary to remove the data that is already in the table. This is particularly true for partitioned tables, where the data is removed from an "old" partition and the new data added. The fastest way to remove the data from the table is through the use of the truncate table command. The truncate command does not log the transactions or restructure the table as it works. Since the transactions are not logged, it is not possible to recover the data removed without resorting to backup tapes. It is a good idea to double check the table names before pressing the enter key. Another trick that helps the load speed is to presort the data in the order of the primary key. This can be done with a home-grown program or with a program like Syncsort. The bulk loader or index system on the database may also have a feature to presort the data.

Indexes are the boon and bane of the life of a DBA. Because of all the ad hoc queries that the warehouse receives, the database will have a larger number of indexes than the average OLTP database. The indexes are important to the performance of the database and provide an acceptable response time to users. When loading the database, the indexes can take a long time to generate. Each row that is added to the database will cause the generation of all the indexes for that row. After many rows have been added, the index structure may be out of balance, and the query performance will be degraded.

The two options available with regard to indexes while loading are to keep the indexes and let the load process populate both the database and indexes at the same time. This will greatly slow down the load, but it is not necessary to index the tables after the load. The problem with this approach is that it can take a very long time to load and index a data warehouse fact table. Also, it is usually advisable to rebuild indexes periodically. If the indexes are going to be rebuilt anyway, we might as well build them after the table has been populated. The other option is to drop the indexes, load the data, and recreate the indexes. This approach works particularly well with partitioned tables. The entire partition can be truncated, loaded, and indexed in sequence. This keeps all the indexes balanced and reduces the need to get the index fill factors correct.

The best way to find out if it is better to load with or without indexes is to try it both ways and measure the CPU and elapsed time to do it. Details like this that depend on system configuration and data design are why the iterative approach is so beneficial. It is impossible to estimate all the factors the first time around, but it is possible to try it both ways and find the trade-off point. The general approach the author takes is to load the dimension tables first since these are small tables. Next, the smaller fact tables are added. Finally, the large fact tables are loaded. This load sequence give the data warehouse team time to build up to the really difficult tables, which are the large tables.

One challenge to the data warehouse is that dimension tables will attain additional attributes during construction of the data warehouse that are not needed in the OLTP systems. These attributes mean something to the business analyst but mean nothing to the OLTP system. Most of these attributes are added during the transformation and cleansing steps. Examples of such attributes would be scoring and householding attributes. Some dimension tables, such as the entire time period table, never existed in the OLTP world. The difficulty now is to maintain these dimension tables.

The ideal solution to the dimension table problem is to create a closed-loop system and send the updated dimension tables back to the source systems. Since source systems are generally responsible for the creation and maintenance of dimension tables, source systems are usually better equipped to maintain analytical attributes with other attributes. If all else fails, the data warehouse can maintain the source of record for dimension tables. The warehouse team can give the team responsible for the maintenance of dimension tables access to warehouse dimension tables and make them responsible for maintenance. This data also needs to be replicated into the data and metadata for the extract and transformation process.

In Chapter 5 we introduced the concept of a slowly changing dimension table. As an example, a customer table could be considered a potentially very large but slowly changing dimension table. People move, and as they move the organization may want to keep track of their history with the organization. It is the goal of the warehouse to track such changes. Another example of a slowly changing dimension would be changes in geographic sales districts over time. The difficulty is that we may want to ask questions about historical facts in addition to current trends. If a customer lived in a different house, do we include them in the report for the new store they shop at or the old store? How can we compare the sales of computers in sales district 5 when the definition of the district has changed?

As the reader may recall, there are three methods of handling slowly changing dimensions. One way is to have a value that is part of the primary key that identifies the dimensional attribute as the old attribute or new attribute. This enables the warehouse to keep both values available for comparisons of the before and after type. The second way to handle a slowly changing dimension is to erase the old value and replace it with the new value. This might be perfectly acceptable for things such as customer address or phone number. The most robust way to handle the change in dimensions is to keep a history of all the dimensions by changing the surrogate key with each new occurrence of the dimension. This is the best thing to do when the changes are true changes and not just error corrections or minor updates. Once again, the important point is to match the mechanism to the business need. The last step is to create the summary table values or multidimensional table values that match the new entries in the data warehouse. Some bulk-load mechanisms allow the creation of summary table information as a side effect of the load process.

Once all of the data has been loaded, it is important to have an audit process to make sure that the data loaded in the manner that was designed. This can be done by using the data extract and cleaning techniques that were developed for the operational systems only now used on the data warehouse. As an example of an audit procedure, the total number of rows in the load file should equal the total number of new rows in the warehouse. As another example, the total dollar value of sales in the month just loaded into the data warehouse must equal the total dollar amount of sales in the operational system. Once the data has been verified, the metadata is updated and the information worker community is notified of the availability.

QUESTIONS

10.1 Why is it important to perform high-level planning of data movement?

10.2 What is the difference between bulk and trickle data extraction?

10.3 What is the impact of object-oriented technology on the data transformation process?

10.4 Why is it important for a transformation tool to be able to call an external function in order to transform data?

10.5 Why should all the primary keys in a data warehouse be surrogate or technical keys?

PROJECTS

For each of the following project scenarios, you will need to select the extract and transformation tool or tools that are needed for the scenario. To do that, explain the data sources, types of data sources, and targets that the tools will use. This can be done by making some assumptions as to the way the source system functions by using information given to you by the instructor or by using your personal experience.

10.6 Determine the extract and transformation tool types needed for a call behavior analysis data warehouse. Explain your assumptions in as much detail as possible.

10.7 Determine the extract and transformation tool types needed for a network usage data warehouse. Explain your assumptions in as much detail as possible

10.8 Determine the extract and transformation tool types needed for an automobile buying trend data warehouse. Explain your assumptions in as much detail as possible. How would your assumptions be different for a car dealership with 10,000 cars sold each year?

10.9 Determine the extract and transformation tool types needed for an electronics store sales analysis data warehouse. Explain your assumptions in as much detail as possible. Explain how this architecture will be deployed.

10.10 Determine the extract and transformation tool types needed for a vendor compliance data warehouse. Explain your assumptions in as much detail as possible.

10.11 Determine the extract and transformation tool types needed for a risk analysis data warehouse. Explain your assumptions in as much detail as possible.

10.12 Determine the extract and transformation tool types needed for a frequent flier data warehouse. Explain your assumptions in as much detail as possible. Explain how this architecture will be deployed.

10.13 Determine the extract and transformation tool types needed for an airline flight segment data warehouse. Explain your assumptions in as much detail as possible.

10.14 Determine the extract and transformation tool types needed for an educational institution data warehouse. Explain your assumptions in as much detail as possible.

10.15 Determine the extract and transformation tool types needed for a health care diagnosis data warehouse. Explain your assumptions in as much detail as possible.

10.16 Determine the extract and transformation tool types needed for a hotel frequent-guest data warehouse. Explain your assumptions in as much detail as possible.

10.17 Determine the extract and transformation tool types needed for a hotel spending data warehouse. Explain your assumptions in as much detail as possible.

11

DATA ACCESS

11.1 INTRODUCTION

At this point in our development of the data warehouse, the warehouse has been populated with data. A metadata repository has been created that describes the data for both business and technical users. A method for the user to get the data must be developed. Depending on what is meant by "get the data," it seems that there are a million ways to provide this feature. By presenting data in an organized, meaningful, and business-centric manner, information is created from data.

Most organizations will have different groups that have different needs for information presentation. A mistake that many data warehouse projects make is to attempt to select one tool as the standard for all users. In an attempt to find one tool that will fit the needs of all users, a long list of requirements is generated. The tool must be easy to use but feature rich. The tool should have a great graphical user interface and a programmatic interface to define an information query. The tool should run on a wide range of desktop computers, but it must look great on all of them. Many of the requirements will conflict. As an example, usually a tool that is feature rich is not easy to use. If a tool is found that meets all the needs of all the information customers, it probably is mediocre at most of them because trade-offs were made in many categories. It is usually better to select two or three tools for different users of the data warehouse. These tools cost a small amount compared to the cost of analysts' time, and it is very hard to tell what the information workers will want until they have experience with different tools.

One way to hedge your bets is to make sure that the architecture will support any query tool that can connect to the data warehouse with a standard connection such as ODBC or JDBC. If the warehouse architect makes two or three of the best tools in the world available, there will still be groups or individuals with specific requirements for other tools. If the warehouse supports common access methods, it will be easy to let these users or groups use their own tools.

11.2 TOOL SELECTION

The data access tools for the data warehouse fall into a few categories. The first category is the general-purpose data manipulation tool of a spreadsheet. Another user access tool type is the query tool. The decision support and executive information system tools are a step up the complexity ladder from the query tool category. Data mining tools look for patterns in the data. Visualization tools present the data in a way that is designed to help the human mind find patterns in the data.

The best way to select a user tool starts with the development of a product requirement matrix. The requirement matrix will be used to compare the different access tools against the requirements of the organization. The requirements matrix should have the user and technical requirements listed, and each requirement should be weighted as to how necessary the requirement is. Each tool will be evaluated as to how well it meets the requirements. Each tool will receive a score that measures how well it meets the requirement. The score is multiplied by the weight to obtain the tools' total score for that requirement. The weighted scores for all the requirements are added up to give the total score for each tool.

An tool requirement matrix is shown in Table 11-1. The purpose of this example matrix is solely to illustrate the technique. It is impossible to place into a book a sample tool requirement matrix that could capture the user needs of all data warehouse projects. Remember that the first step in all of the data warehouse activities is to discover the needs of the business information workers.

11.2.1 INFORMATION CONSUMER TYPES

One way to understand the needs of information consumers is to examine the current reports that are in use in the organization. This will help give some insight into the types of business problems that are being addressed, the types of information that are required, and the way the information is presented. Next, the data warehouse architect should consider the types of information consumers and their information analysis style. The author categorizes information consumers into four types, and the data presentation tool needed by each of these groups

Table 11-1 Tool requirement matrix

Category	Weight	Tool 1 Points	Tool 1 Total	Tool 2 Points	Tool 2 Total
Ease of use	9				
Windows platform	2				
Web enables	8				
Printed reports	7				
Vendor quality	8				
Standard vendor	5				
Graphics ability	7				
MDB support	6				
Documentation	9				
Web support	8				

may be different. The number of users that may exist in each of the groups does not indicate the importance of the group to the data warehouse or the business.

Report readers like to look for answers to questions on the same familiar report. They usually do not have a large amount of variance in approach or information requirements from day to day. These people dislike using even the most easy-to-use system. They usually require personalized help for their initial foray into the data warehouse report world. This group is given information through canned reports, DSS, or executive information systems.

Information browsers need a little extra training to understand the data warehouse tools, but they are very happy to build simple reports if they are given an appropriate tool. Information browsers do not need a powerful tool, but they do need a tool that is easy to use. They are best addressed with a system that hides the complexity of the data warehouse, such as a query management system that makes the access tool easier to use. Information browsers will also use some canned reports.

Advanced users will want to build their own queries and reports, but they will find some of the complexities of the data warehouse annoying. Advanced users will like such features as automatic aggregate seeking, because they can rapidly develop reports without worrying about data model details.

Power users are the ones who constantly challenge the data warehouse. Power users want access to up-to-date information at a moment's notice. They want the fastest route to the data, and the semantic integration work that you did for the other users can get in the way of the power user. Power users will stress all aspects of the data warehouse and will want to know what aggregate-level information is available. In the user community, this group will use the metadata repository the most and be most interested in data mining.

11.2.2 All That FLAP

The trade press is full of articles and advertisements espousing the virtue of various approaches, which have such acronyms as OLAP, MOLAP, and ROLAP. The applications that use data from the warehouse and present information to users are usually called *on-line analytic processing* (OLAP) applications. OLAP tools enable the information worker to navigate through the data and ask complex, what-if questions. Tools that use data from a relational database are usually called *relational on-line analytic processing* (ROLAP) tools. Access tools that use multidimensional databases are called *multidimensional on-line analytic processing* (MOLAP) tools. Now that this technology is common, it is not displayed as prominently in the advertisements as it once was.

The important point is to ignore the technical terminology and investigate the features of each tool. Report readers will view OLAP-generated reports but will not use the power of an OLAP tool. With some training, Information Browsers will use the OLAP tools to "slice and dice" the data in different ways. They will generally start with reports that others have developed and explore them further. Advanced users and power users will get the full benefit from OLAP tools.

11.2.3 Vendor Selection Criterion

In many situations, tools from several vendors will satisfy the needs for one of the tool categories. In this case, the decision is based on the vendor. In general, it is important to make vendor factors part of the decision process for a tool. There are a number of important considerations in the selection of a vendor. If your organization already purchases products from a vendor, it may be more convenient to expand the relationship and acquire new products from the same vendor. One the other hand, your organization may have discovered that a vendor with which you are currently working is not desired as a partner. When selecting a new vendor, it is important to consider if this is a vendor your organization wants as a partner. In addition to the value of a vendor as a partner, some other things to consider are references, documentation, training, and technical support.

When selecting a new vendor, it is usually a good idea to ask for reference sites. If it is going to be a major purchase, it is a good idea to try to contact people at the reference locations and discuss their experience with the product. You can ask the salespeople for a reference site and contact or use your professional network to find out how your peers have fared with a vendor and product.

Documentation is another important consideration in the selection of a product. The documentation must be well written and complete. It should be available in a variety of formats. In addition to paper form, it should be available in electronic form, such as HTML or XML. If documentation updates are available from the vendor via the Web, this can be a real advantage.

The ability to obtain training for business and technical users can be an important decision point. The location of the training process can make a big difference in the ability to get the organization's people to cooperate in the training. Some vendors have very limited training abilities. Some vendors will have training available only at their corporate office or regional training centers. Other vendors will train anywhere, including your office. The quality of training varies widely from vendor to vendor. Some vendors have full-time professional instructors, and other companies have technical professionals who also train. Because either of these approaches can work well, it is wise to ask for references for the training.

Technical support can be another essential differentiator of software vendors. The deciding factors for technical support are the amounts and types of availability. Some vendors can provide technical support via a trained support staff 24 hours a day, every day. Other vendors will only provide access to a live person during normal business hours for their location. In addition to being able to contact a human being who does support, it is very convenient to be able to go to a Web page or bulletin board to obtain product updates or patch information.

The cost and availability of both technical support and product updates are another vendor differentiator. It is easy to focus on the initial purchase price of a tool rather than the total cost of ownership of the tool over the life of the tool. It is usually necessary to purchase updates of the tool after the initial warranty period ends. The cost of this maintenance support can be high, and it should be calculated into the total cost of owning the product.

11.3 INFORMATION DISTRIBUTION

In the "good old days," people in an organization were on the distribution list for certain reports. The creation and maintenance of the distribution lists could become a major organizational challenge. As people join, leave, and change positions in the organization, the number of copies of a report that need to be generated and distributed change. Information consumers need different information at different times in the business cycle. This is why there were mountains of unused paper reports around an organization.

There are at least two ways to solve this problem electronically. One way is to publish the information and let those who need the information get it. In this scheme, the users must know where and when to get the data. The information consumer is responsible for getting the latest copy of all the reports when they are available. In other words, users must pull the information to their desktops. The knowledge worker must also find any new sources of information. Users should also be able to publish their data and reports for use by others in the organization.

An alternative approach is to publish the information and have the information consumer subscribe to the published information. The information is then pushed to all those who have subscribed. This approach eliminates the problem of forcing users to remember the update schedule and to retrieve the data. The information consumers should be able to subscribe to information by category such as sales, in addition to specific data or reports, such as sales of a particular product.

The information that users receive can vary greatly. The information could be the data used to create specific reports. It could be links to Web pages that contain the reports. It could be the reports in electronic form. It could be the server name and data access methods for obtaining data. The important consideration is that the information is something the information consumer needs and it is presented in the best possible way for that user group.

As another example of a publish/subscribe system, keeping the software that is used by the information consumers up to date is a challenge for the data warehouse IM team. One way to do this is through the use of a desktop management system, one component of which is a method whereby desktop computers can subscribe to data warehouse and other application updates. When the new applications are available and the desktop checks in on the network, the application is automatically downloaded to the desktop.

11.4 WEB ACCESS

Web-oriented tools have many advantages for both the end user and the IM community. Web access tools are available for any platform, require little maintenance, and are low in cost. This has caused many end users and IT groups to demand Web access to data warehouses. The problem is that most user-tool vendors designed an integrated product with special data access methods built into the tool. This has made it hard to adapt the full features of the product to the Web. The data warehouse market is huge, and it attracts new vendors. Some of the new Web-based products are developed by companies that do not have the experience with the warehouse environment that the more established vendors do. The result of this is an opportunity for the IT group to deploy a new version of a warehouse user access tool or an entirely new tool every six months to a year. Changing Web-based tools is usually less traumatic than changing a client-server application and tool.

The first uses of the Web to deliver warehouse information employed the simple conversion of paper-based reports to Hypertext Markup Language (HTML). Many companies are still using Web sites simply to publish existing reports on the Web. Changing paper-based reports into HTML is simple and easy. This enables companies to deliver information rapidly electronically rather than shipping paper-based reports to remote locations.

The next Web sites that were developed enabled interactive warehouse queries. The information consumer would supply data with a Web browser via a HTML form. The Web server sends the information request to a Web enabled database gateway. These gateways use common gateway interface scripts or proprietary APIs such as the Netscape Server API (NSAPI). The gateway then submits the query to the database. Next, the gateway receives the results, translates the data into HTML pages or CGI scripts, and sends the data over the Web to the user. Transforming large amounts of data into HTML or CGI can be very CPU intensive.

The latest trend in Web-enabled data warehouse technology is the use of Web-based application servers that use JDBC or applets written in Java to execute functions on the desktop. The use of Java or ActiveX applets will bring true interactivity to Web-based warehouse access tools. The Web applets make it possible for the user to have all the functionality of the warehouse without installing an application on the client.

Vendor strategies have closely followed the development of the Web. The first strategy of the tool supplier is to provide the ability to convert reports to HTML scripts. This does not provide an interactive interface, but it does allow users access to canned reports. The information can be sent from the Web server to the user almost instantaneously. The ubiquitous 80–20 rule applies to data warehouse queries. A good estimate is that 80 percent of all warehouse users have simple requests that can be satisfied with HTML-based reports or CGI-based interfaces. Most warehouse users do not need the interactivity that Java applets provide.

The next step in the development of Web-enabled user access tools was the configuration of the tool as a helper application for the Web browser. The Web browser acts as a type of data access mechanism, and the user tool still performs actual manipulation of the data. The disadvantage of this approach is the simple fact that the software on the desktop must still be managed. The advantage of this approach is that data can be fully analyzed on the desktop once it has been downloaded.

Browser plug-ins are "helper" applications that are downloadable over the Web before their first use. As the name implies, browser plug-ins add specific features to the browser. The features that are added to the browser are the ability to interact with data in a variety of ways. The disadvantage to plug-ins is the fact that they are designed to work with a particular browser on a particular operating system. This eliminates the open system and portable nature of the Web.

Another route to a Web data warehouse server is to port a portion of the desktop access tool to a server. A server centric Web tool lets users interact with the warehouse database and view the dynamically generated HTML Web pages. This approach does not require the installation of any special helper applications or plug-ins on the desktop. Since no special software is maintained on the client, this supports the thin client approach that is rapidly gaining popularity. A development to watch is the use of XML as a Web access mechanism for OLAP tools.

The last approach option for a tool vendor is to redevelop the tool using a development environment tuned for the Web, such as ActiveX or Java. The problem with this approach is the amount of effort required to redevelop an application and the emerging nature of Web technology. While ActiveX is more mature than Java, both environments are relatively new compared to most of the other technology, that the IM department moves into a production.

ActiveX components have the disadvantage of running only on Windows platforms and are larger than Java scripts because they contain dynamically linked libraries that are needed to execute. This makes it difficult to download these rather large components over the Web. The advantage of ActiveX is the fact that it is based on the COM object architecture and OLE. These components have been around for a while and are relatively mature.

Java is new as programming languages are concerned, and some of the bugs are still being worked out at the time this book is being written. Since Java is interpreted, it can be slow, but it does work on a tremendous variety of machines. Java programs can execute on the client, the server, or a mixture of both. Also, Java-services APIs are still being defined, and it is hard to write code to an API that is under definition.

The rather complete approach that some vendors have selected is to provide standard HTML access and a tool proprietary access with the aid of a plug-in or helper application. Information consumers with a standard Web browser will have access to the data but have limited functionality. Knowledge workers with helper or plug-in applications have the full set of OLAP tool features to which they are accustomed. The difference is that the information is delivered to the desktop by the Web server as the result of a query by the Web server, as opposed to the desktop performing the query itself.

11.5 SPREADSHEETS

The spreadsheet that comes with the office productivity package has a tremendous amount of functionality that can be used as a warehouse analysis tool. The usual reasons for using this tool are:

- The organization has already purchased it.
- It is cheap.
- It has tremendous analytical capability.
- Some users have a lot of experience analyzing data with spreadsheets.
- It is highly integrated with other Windows tools.

As an example of the use of a spreadsheet to analyze data, we will use Microsoft Excel. Like most spreadsheet products, Excel does not have the built-in ability to query a database, so this is provided with the aid of a query tool called Microsoft Query. The query tool is invoked by selecting "Get external data, create new query" from the data menu, as shown in Figure 11-1.

To create a new query, we must attach to a database. An ODBC connection called Brio has already been established, and this will be used for the query connection. This is illustrated in Figure 11-2.

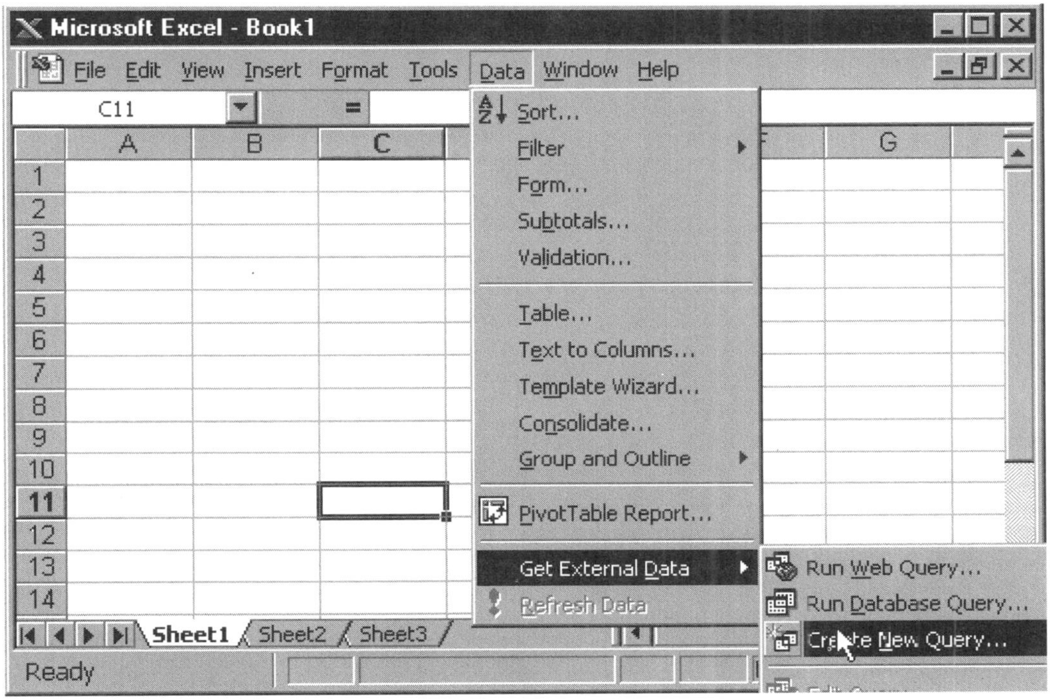

Figure 11-1 The user creates a new query to obtain new data for the spreadsheet.

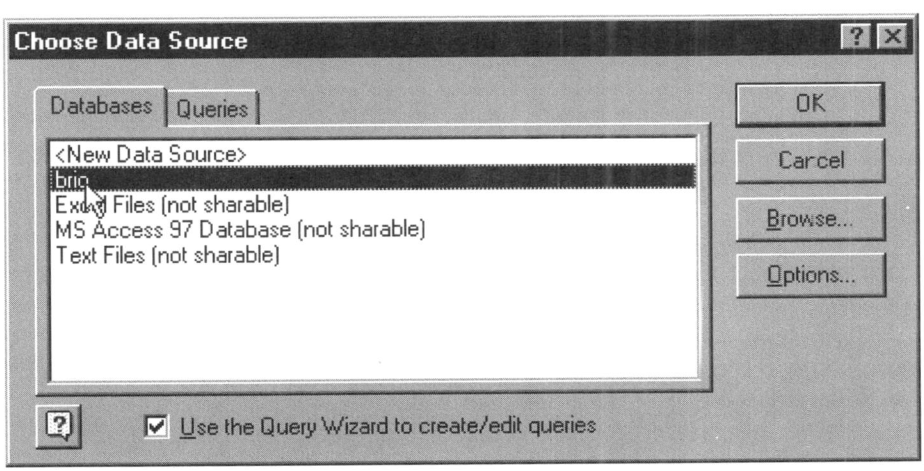

Figure 11-2 The user selects a data source.

Once the data source has been selected, the tables or columns in the database that are needed for the report that is being created are selected. This is illustrated in Figure 11-3. The information worker selects the tables or columns, then clicks on the right arrow button to include the column or table in the query.

When all of the tables and columns have been selected, Microsoft Query will display the screen shown in Figure 11-4. The user will indicate how the tables are joined by dragging the column name from one table on top of the joining column in the second table. Stated in a different way, the user indicates the joins by dragging the foreign key from one table on top of the primary key in the second table. The results, shown in the field at the bottom of Figure 11-4, are then ready to be returned to the spreadsheet. This is done simply by selecting the return data to Microsoft Excel option from the file menu as illustrated in Figure11-5.

Once the data is in the spreadsheet, all of the power of the spreadsheet can be used to analyze the data. Spreadsheets are typically very well integrated into the platform on which they operate, so it is easy for the user to mover graphs and tables from the spreadsheet to a word processor or to a tool that is generating a Web page.

The point of this example is that the spreadsheet may be a great analysis tool, but it is somewhat troublesome getting data into the spreadsheet. Users who have a great deal of experience with the spreadsheet are more than willing to learn the extra steps of the query process. Users who are new to this environment would find a tool that is designed as a query tool for the warehouse environment easier and faster to use.

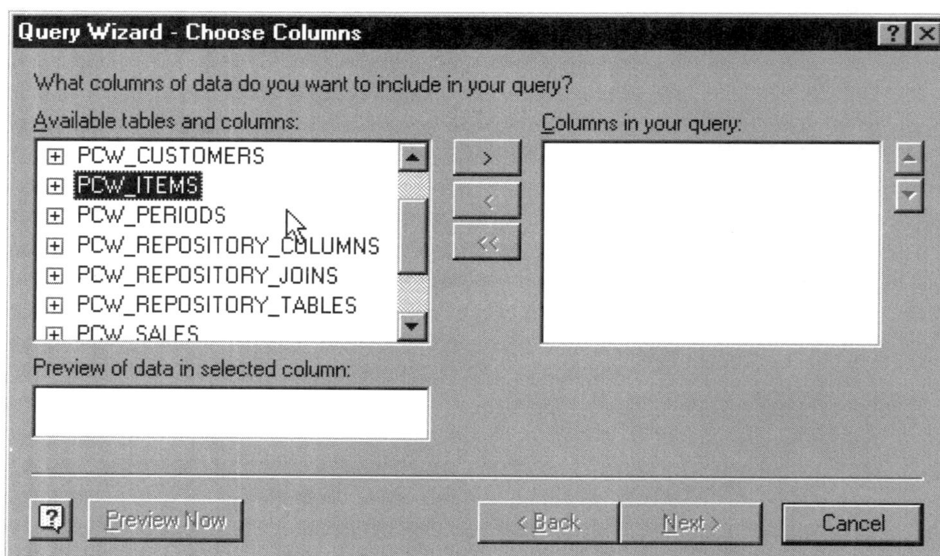

Figure 11-3 The user selects the tables and fields for the query.

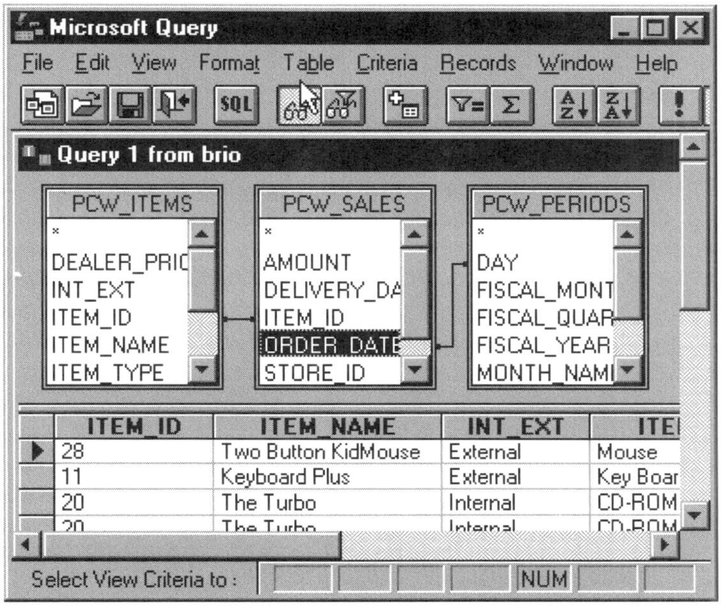

Figure 11-4 The user joins the tables not joined automatically.

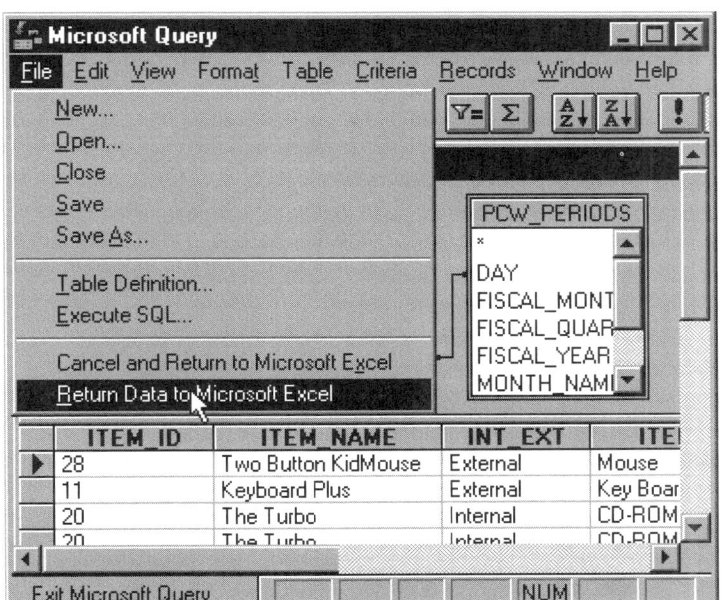

Figure 11-5 The user returns the data to Microsoft Excel.

11.6 VISUALIZATION TOOLS

Visualization tools suffer some of the same problems as spreadsheets. To get data into a visualization tool, the user must create a query using a different tool. After the query has been created, the data must be converted into a form the visualization tool can use. Once the data has been made available to the visualization tool, it can prepare graphs and perform data analysis in ways that can be very enlightening. Examples of tools in this category are:

- CrossGraphs by Belmont Research
- DataVista by Visualize
- Diamond by SPSS
- Graph-FX by GP-FX
- Generic Visualization Architecture by United Information Systems
- IMAGIX 4D by Imagix
- Techplot by Amtec Engineering

To illustrate the use of a visualization tool, CrossGraphs will be used. Many fine visualization products are available, of which CrossGraphs is an excellent example. The types of graphs that a visualization product should be able to produce include:

- Waterfall
- Contingency table
- Counts
- Histogram
- Picket fence
- Scatter
- Spatial
- Survival
- Time line
- Trend

The first step in using a visualization program is to prepare the data and attach the visualization program to the data file. This is done in a manner similar to the way the data was selected for Microsoft Query. The data fields selected become the variables that are available to plot as shown in Figure 11-6. The variable that will determine the *x*-axis, "treatment" in this case, is dragged and dropped on the x-axis box. The variable that determines the y-axis is dragged and dropped on the y-axis box. The graph type box is dragged and dropped on the graph type field in the lower right-hand corner, as illustrated in Figure 11-6.

The user then requests generation of the report, as illustrated in Figure 11-7, and the very nice set of graphs shown in Figure 11-8 is generated. The graphs produced by the program look better on the computer screen than they do here.

Visualization tools are capable of performing a huge variety of analysis and presentation. The difficulty with the tool is the same as with a spreadsheet. Since the tool does not have an integral query generation facility, the user must switch between a data preparation and query tool and the visualization tool. This slows the process and interferes with the speed of the thought process the graphs are enabling.

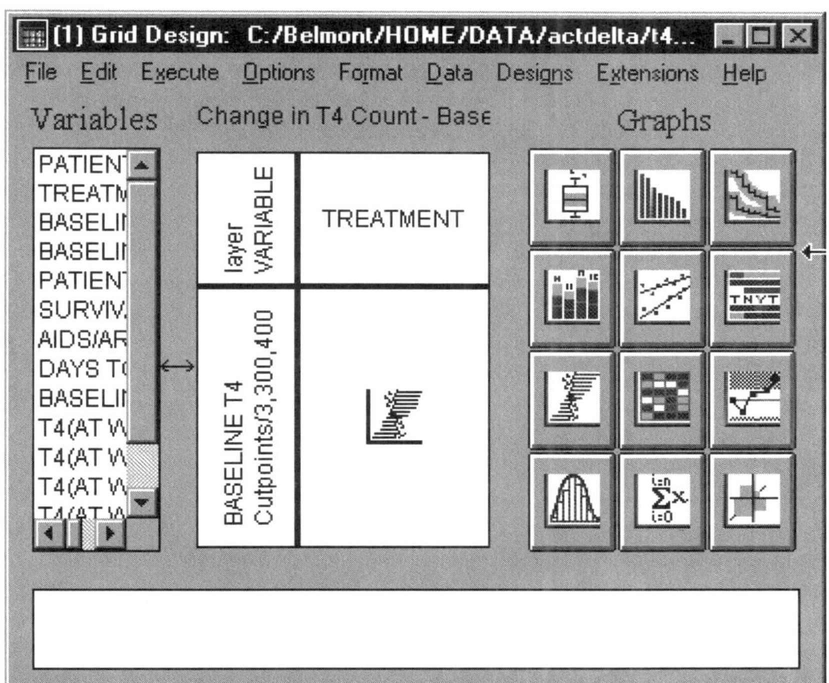

Figure 11-6 The user selects the graph variables and the plot type.

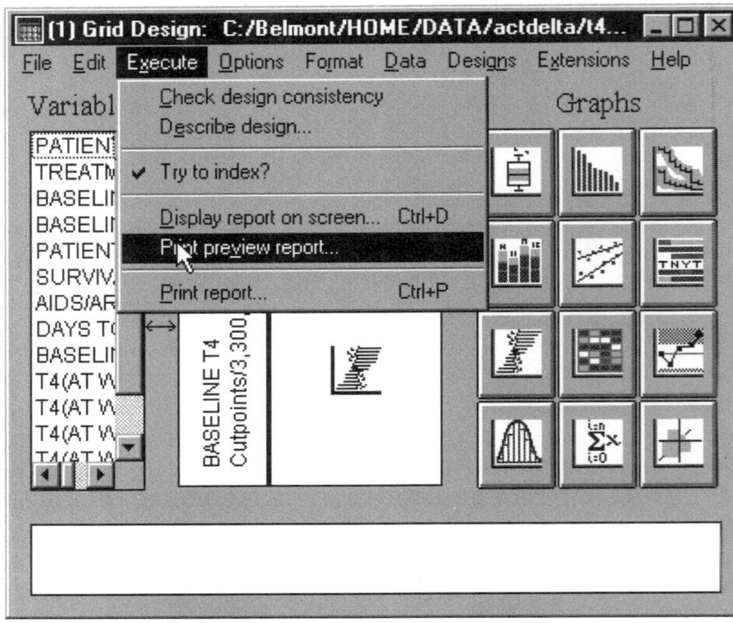

Figure 11-7 The user requests generation of a graph.

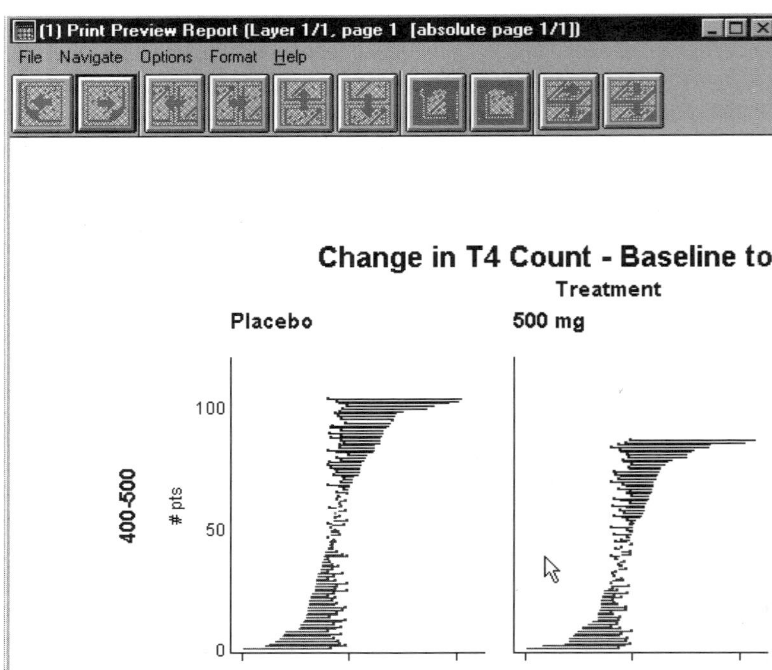

Figure 11-8 The program generates the graphs requested.

11.7 QUERY TOOLS

Tools that enable the information consumer to create a query and manipulate the result cover a broad range of tools. These tools meet the needs of at least 80 percent of data warehouse users. These tools must enable nontechnical data warehouse users to access the information in the warehouse easily and intuitively. These ad hoc queries must be unconstrained by parameters or previous formulation. There are four important areas of functionality that the ad hoc query tool must provide: technical functionality, query functionality, presentation functionality, and interface functionality. We explore each of these functional areas next.

11.7.1 TECHNICAL FUNCTIONALITY

Technical functionality provides the nuts and bolts that users expect but often do not anticipate. As an example, a user will launch a huge query that will return millions of rows and take many hours of processor time. The user should be able to cancel their query when they detect that it will not return the expected results. Some tools cancel the query from the tool's perspective, but the cancel does not propagate to the database. The user tool should be able to cancel the query at the database level.

Other technical functionality would include multitasking. The user tool must use the multitasking features of the operating system for which it was designed. There are few things more annoying than using a query tool that holds the user's workstation captive while the query is running. The user tools also typically have a scripting language that enables the queries to run with a group of input parameters. For long reporting procedures that have been scripted, it is best from the user's point of to have them run at a time when it will not interfere with other work the user is doing. This requires that the tool have a report scheduling capability.

Some technical abilities in the tool enable the user to do advanced queries or have advanced query features. One such feature would be the ability of the tool to add successive constraints to the query. Frequently, a query will return more information than the knowledge worker expected. In this case, the user should be able to add a constraint to the first query and execute the query with the new constraint. The user should be able to do this repeatedly until the desired result is achieved.

11.7.2 QUERY FUNCTIONALITY

If a data warehouse has two or more data sources and does not have a query management system, the user query tool must be able to select data from one database and join the result with data that was selected from a different database. Since several steps of SQL are performed to achieve the result, this is called multistep or multipass SQL. Multistep SQL is frequently a desired feature in an enterprise data warehouse tool, but data mart users will usually not require this feature.

Executives and managers want to know if something has changed in the business. If an opportunity presents itself to the business, the business will want to act on the opportunity as soon as possible. Similarly, early problem identification leads to early problem solution. Alerts are a tool feature that indicates values that have fallen outside defined ranges. As an example, the business might want to set an alert to generate a report if a sales region is below 80 percent of its sales quota.

11.7.3 Presentation Functionality

From the user's point of view, the tool must be intuitive and easy to use. To formulate queries, the user must have access to metadata. If the metadata is an integral part of the query portion of the tool, it is much easier for the user than having metadata supplied through an add-on application. The user will need to specify values as conditions of the query, and the query tool must enable the user to find sample values and pick lists in order to specify query conditions. Sample values are an integral part of the metadata.

Another important feature is integration into Microsoft Windows or other operating system's information exchange mechanism. In the Windows world, this implies that the application should work with OLE or DDE to exchange data with other Windows applications. An example of this integration would be the ability of the application to exchange data with a Web page creation tool for the generation of HTML.

Most user access tools have a report generation feature. This should include a user-friendly development environment that assists the user in the creation of reports without the assistance of the IM department. The tool must enable the creation of attractive reports with tables and graphs in the same report. Some tools allow the creation of active reports where the data is embedded in the report and the user can view the data in other manners than what was presented originally. This will enable the recipient of the report to drill into the report. Another way to do this is through linked reports. With linked reports, detailed reports are linked to summary reports. Users can obtain detailed information through automatic access to the detailed reports. Iterative reporting where numerous reports are generated by changing a parameter such as store id is also an important feature of a query tool. The user should be able to generate these reports based on time periods, alerts, or events.

11.7.4 Interface Functionality

Once all of this very valuable business information has been created, there must be a flexible delivery system that will get the information to the people in the organization who require it. One way to do this is through a publish and subscribe method, as described earlier. Information consumers can subscribe to particular reports or classes of reports. The reports are sent to them when they are available.

Another way to get the information to the information consumer is through the Web. With the subscribe and publish system just discussed, the user will receive a document with links to the Web sites that have the reports. The Web reports will usually contain linking between reports for drill-down analysis. The Web pages can also contain mechanisms for downloading the data and scripts that generate the reports to the user.

Now that we have created all of this information and have an easy interface to the data, we must provide security to protect the data. One way to protect the data is through a standard logon to the reporting system. This is a not an entirely satisfactory solution because we may want an information consumer to have some of the data in the data warehouse but not all of the data. In this case, row-level security is needed. With row-level security, the user is granted access to particular rows of data based on some characteristic of the row. As an example of row-level security, a store manager would be given access to the sales performance figures for the store they are responsible for and no other store.

As an example of an end-user query tool, we will use BrioQuery Enterprise. Information browsers and power users should both be happy with a tool in the BrioQuery class of tools. This should not be considered an endorsement by the author of a particular product over another. There are many excellent products in this product space. The appropriate selection of a user query product must be made with an understanding of the environment in which the tool will be used. This cannot be done in a general way.

Once BrioQuery has been started, the BrioQuery Advisor will guide the user through the steps needed to create a data warehouse query. This is illustrated in Figure 11-9. The connect cable icon in the bottom right corner of the screen with a cross through it and the message in the Advisor window indicate that BrioQuery has not been connected to a database. Figure 11-10 illustrates the start of the connection process to the data. There is a check next to auto-join, and this indicates that BrioQuery will infer from identical field names in different tables that the tables are to be joined by that field. The first step is to connect the tool to the data and open the table catalog.

Once the table catalogue has been selected, the BrioQuery user starts the design of a query simply by dragging table names from the catalogue to the query screen. The table and the fields in the table then appear. If the auto-join feature is turned on, the tables will be joined automatically as they are dragged from the table catalogue to the query design screen. Tables that do not join automatically can be joined by dragging the field name from one table on top of the field in the second table to which it is joined. Figure 11-11 shows three tables that have been placed on the query screen. The field item_id was joined automatically from pcw_items to pcs_sales. The field order_date was manually joined to the field day.

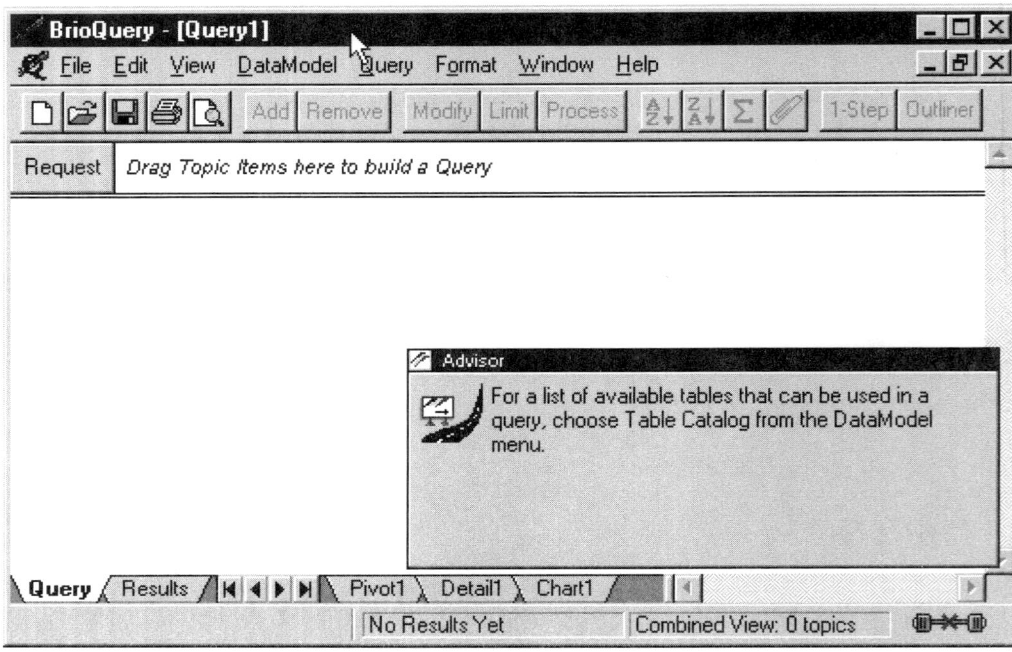

Figure 11-9 A user starts a query.

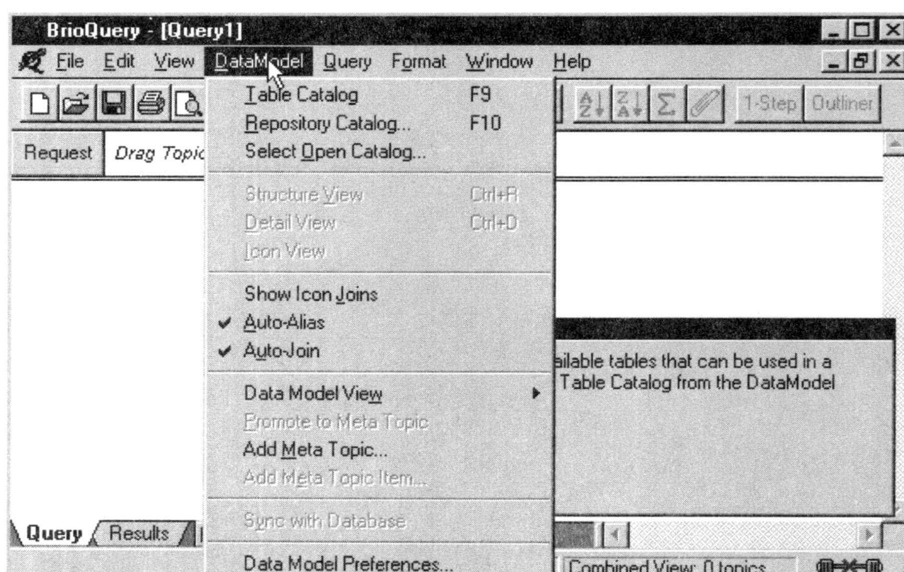

Figure 11-10 A table catalog is selected to connect to the data.

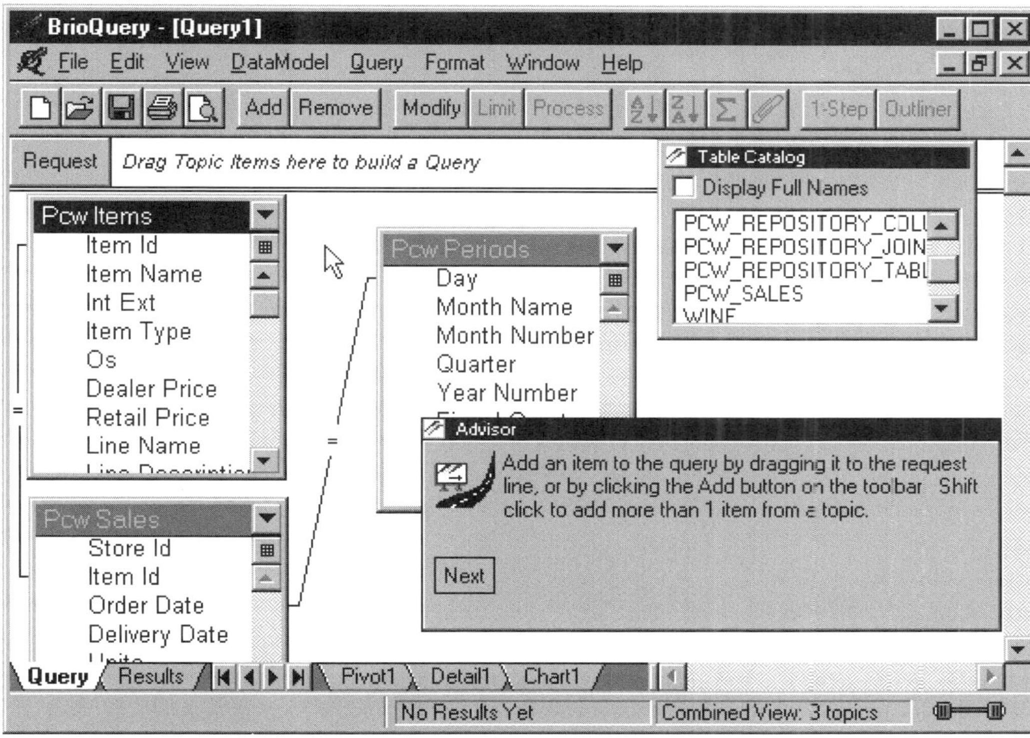

Figure 11-11 Tables are joined automatically when dragged to the query screen.

To specify the fields that are needed from the query, the user simply drags the fields from the tables and drops them on the request line. Qualifiers of the data are also specified at this time. As an example of a qualifier, the user could set the store_id equal to a value to obtain a report just for that store. This is illustrated in Figure 11-12.

Once the query has been developed, the user can run the query by pressing the process button. The data that is returned is then shown under the results tab. An example of data returned to the result window is shown in Figure 11-13. This data will be the foundation of the other reports that are created.

As an example of a report that can be generated from the result data, Figure 11-14 illustrates the generation of a pivot chart. To select the variable for the left side of the pivot, the user drags item_id from the request line to the left side of the BrioQuery Outliner box. Store_id and quarter are dragged and dropped on the horizontal access. The value to be displayed as a function of the other variables, amount, is dragged and dropped onto the value part of the Outliner box. The pivot chart is created as soon as all parts report are specified.

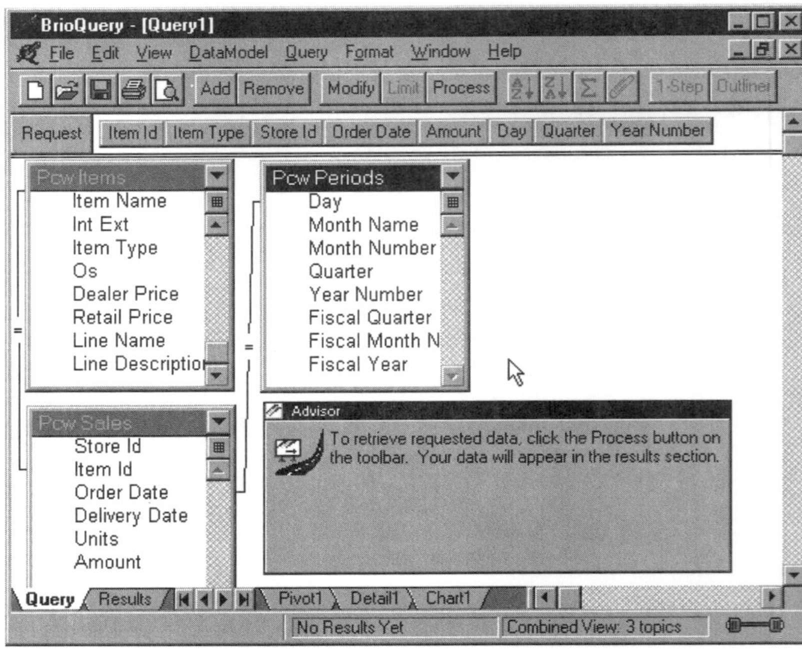

Figure 11-12 The field names for the query are specified.

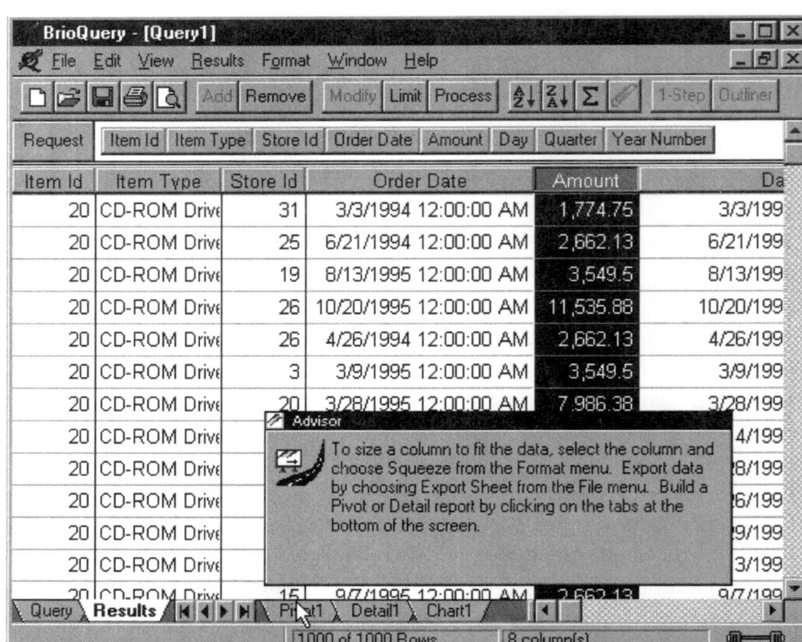

Figure 11-13 The results of a query are shown.

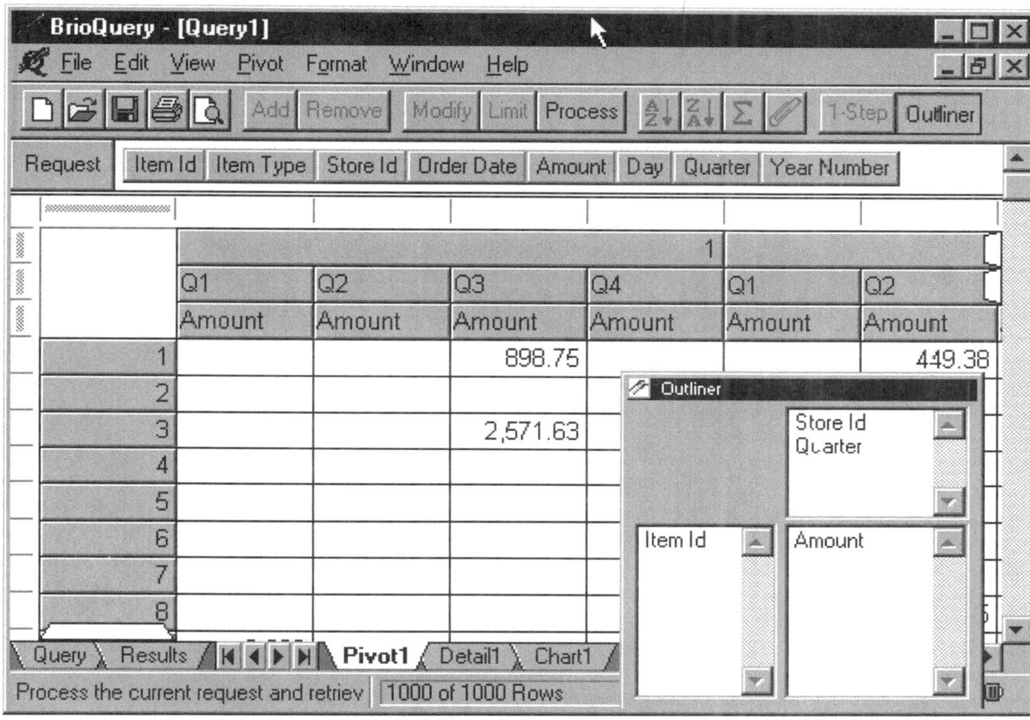

Figure 11-14 A pivot table is created by dragging column names to the Outliner design screen.

Figure 11-15 illustrates that it is very easy to change the way a table or graph looks and the information is presented. This is very important for OLAP-type tools. By dragging the tab on the quarter header label down and to the left, the quarter variable was reorganized by item_id, and the graph was regenerated automatically.

The integration of the query generator and the reporting tools into one tool such as BrioQuery makes it very easy to iterate between the query and the result. The difficulty of rapidly iterating between query and report with a spreadsheet or visualization tool is what makes a tool in that category hard to use for most data warehouse information consumers. The ability to iterate between query and report at the speed of thought is what makes a tool in the BrioQuery class so valuable.

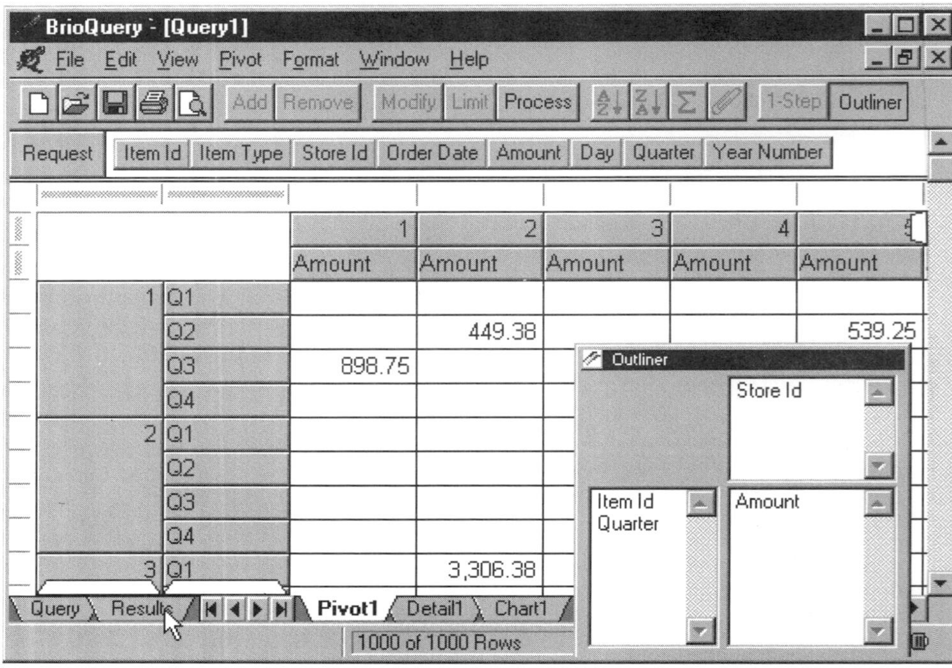

Figure 11-15 The fiscal quarter variable is pivoted to the left side simply by dragging and dropping.

11.8 EIS AND DSS TOOL TYPES

The report reader user group will be most satisfied with an executive information or decision support system type of tool. These tools have all the features of a query tool in addition to query management features. DSS tools, which usually have better coverage of features than the simpler and less costly query tools, must be extremely simple to navigate. They must have a very well designed graphical user interface, which is usually programmed by the IT department to provide the reporting system that the organization requires. The features that one should expect in a DSS tool are:

- Easy creation of powerful user screens
- Intuitive user interface controls
- Easy navigation
- Alerts to indicate values that fall out of a user-definable range

The general feature of EIS and DSS tools that makes them easy to use is query process management. The question for the data warehouse architect is where in the architecture the query management process should be located. If a middleware tool such as Intelligent Warehouse or a TP tool is used, all the access tools in the environment can take advantage of the query management facilities. If an EIS or DSS tool is selected for the warehouse, the tool will have a proprietary query process management facility. This proprietary query management facility will not be available to other tools. The third possibility is for the query management to reside in the database. The query management tools that are becoming part of the database engine have the advantage of being available to all of the user tools. The problem with the database-level query management process is that it is usually not able to perform query management of data on other databases.

Even the tool vendors have had some challenges deciding where to put query management. Some DSS tools have the query management in the front-end tool, and others have a separate application server layer that performs the query management. In either case, the query management process is not available for use by other tools. If a DSS tool is selected and some other query management tool is selected as well, there will be some redundancy in both query management and metadata.

11.8.1 Query Management

The qualities of a good query management or query processing system have been stated before, but it is an important topic worth repeating. The query processor will accept the knowledge worker's format of the query and generate a different query for the database. The query management system should present a user view of the database that hides all the details of the joins and aggregate availability. The query processor should be aware of important business periods and dates. For example, there should be a table of dates that can be used to translate automatically between fiscal quarters and calendar dates. This would be used to calculate the summary information for a fiscal quarter by selecting all the days in the quarter. When the user submits a query, the query is reformatted to join the necessary tables, use aggregates if available, or perform summary calculation if the aggregate is not available. The query processor should be able to do multipass queries if necessary to join information from different databases or partitioned tables.

Some DSSs and EISs require modification of the database design to accommodate the tool. For example, some of the tools put summary information in the same table as the detail information. A column is added to the database to indicate that a particular instance of a row is a summary row and the level of summarization. The difficulty with this approach is that other tools do not know how to use this information. A user could easily combine summary information with fact information to create a report that is very wrong.

If the query processing exists in a layer outside the user tool, it is possible to build a very satisfactory executive DSS system with a simpler tool, such as an OLAP tool, Microsoft Access, or Microsoft Visual Basic. The advantage to this approach is that it is easier to replace access components as the marketplace changes.

11.9 DATA MINING INTRODUCTION

Human beings have long been interested in extrapolating what they know to new situations. We also seem very interested in attempting to predict the future. Modeling is an endeavor to use mathematics to describe the world around us in a way that lets us extrapolate what we know to new situations or attempt to predict aspects of the future. The mathematical models that are used to predict the weather are excellent examples of this. Data mining is the broad definition of this field of study. An introduction to data mining is presented here because it is another method of accessing the data. A more detailed examination of data mining is presented in Chapter 12.

The origin of data mining is the statistical analysis and neural network investigation that have been going on since the 1960s. Statistical analysis is the common statistical methods of regression, correlation, and chi-square. The SAS and SPSS companies have had these routines available since the 1960s, and they are still supplied today. Bernard Widrow, a Stanford University professor, was performing research on an adaptive linear element or *adaline*, a type of neural network, since the 1960s as well. The point is that these techniques are not new; they are just packaged and more developed than they were in the 1960s. Now that we have enough computing power and data to tackle a large problem, the techniques are more interesting.

Data mining is a topic that has been written about by many authors and fills many books. Thus, we can not adequately describe it in a section of a chapter of a book. Chapter 12 is dedicated to data mining. This section serves as an introduction to the major approaches and ideas in data mining. Data mining algorithms can be broken into four major classifications: clustering, classifying, modeling, and affinity analysis.

Clustering algorithms attempt to group the data into the best set of partitions or clusters. The clustering algorithm will generate information about the centroid of the clusters into which the data has been divided. As an example, companies frequently have information about their customers. A clustering algorithm could be used to determine different customer purchasing groups. The centroid would give some indication of the characteristics of the customers in that group. The only input the clustering algorithm needs is the number of groups into which the data is to be clustered.

As an example of clustering, a financial institution might want to cluster their credit card customers into a profitable group, a normal group, and a risk group. The clustering algorithm would be used to develop three groups and the group characteristics. A classification algorithm is an algorithm that associates a data point with a cluster or classification that was already determined. As an example, the financial institution created a clustering scheme for credit card customers. If a new credit card customer requests a card, the classifying algorithm would be used to determine if the new customer is a credit risk.

Models are generated to provide numerical estimates of outcomes or activities. Returning to the financial institution studies, a model could be generated that would indicate the profitability of good credit card customers as a function of income and interest rate. This profitability model could be used to tune the interest rates to attract new customers through a direct mailing campaign.

Affinity grouping is an extension of clustering to determine events that occur together. In the medical field, affinity grouping could be used to determine that being jabbed with a rusty nail frequently leads to tetanus. The famous affinity grouping example is from the retail grocery world. A grocery store chain was analyzing cash register transactions to determine items that sell together. As the story goes, dads sometime pick up some extra time with the kids on the weekend, so beer and diapers sell well together on Fridays. In other words, beer and diapers have an affinity.

QUESTIONS

11.1 How should a data access product be selected?

11.2 What process should be used when selecting a tool vendor?

11.3 How are spreadsheets and visualization tools different from query and DSS tools?

11.4 Explain the difference between DSS and ad hoc user query tools.

11.5 What characteristics of a spreadsheet or visualization tool make it hard to iterate between query and reporting?

11.6 What is the purpose of a query management tool?

11.7 State in your own words the purpose of data mining.

11.8 What is clustering? Supply your own example.

11.9 What is classification? Supply your own example.

11.10 What is modeling? Supply your own example.

11.11 What is affinity grouping? Supply your own example.

PROJECTS

For each of the following project scenarios, you will need to select the access tool or tools that are needed for the scenario. To do that, explain the information groups and types of information workers that will use the tools. This can be done by making some assumptions as to the way the organization functions, by using information given to you by the instructor, or by using your personal experience.

11.12 Determine the access tool types needed for a call behavior analysis data warehouse. Explain your assumptions in as much detail as possible.

11.13 Determine the access tool types needed for a network usage data warehouse. Explain your assumptions in as much detail as possible

11.14 Determine the access tool types needed for an automobile buying trend data warehouse. Explain your assumptions in as much detail as possible. How would your assumptions be different for a car dealership with 10,000 cars sold each year?

11.15 Determine the access tool types needed for an electronics store sales analysis data warehouse. Explain your assumptions in as much detail as possible. Explain how this architecture will be deployed.

11.16 Determine the access tool types needed for a vendor compliance data warehouse. Explain your assumptions in as much detail as possible.

11.17 Determine the access tool types needed for a risk analysis data warehouse. Explain your assumptions in as much detail as possible.

11.18 Determine the access tool types needed for a frequent flier data warehouse. Explain your assumptions in as much detail as possible. Explain how this architecture will be deployed.

11.19 Determine the access tool types needed for an airline flight segment data warehouse. Explain your assumptions in as much detail as possible.

11.20 Determine the access tool types needed for an educational institutions data warehouse. Explain your assumptions in as much detail as possible.

11.21 Determine the access tool types needed for a health care diagnosis data warehouse. Explain your assumptions in as much detail as possible.

11.22 Determine the access tool types needed for a hotel frequent-guest data warehouse. Explain your assumptions in as much detail as possible.

11.23 Determine the access tool types needed for a hotel spending data warehouse. Explain your assumptions in as much detail as possible.

12

DATA MINING

12.1 INTRODUCTION

When driving a car, there exists a clear relationship between the inputs to the car and the way the car responds. If the driver steps on the gas, the car usually accelerates, and the increase in speed is indicated on the speedometer. If the driver steps on the brake while moving, the car will slow down, and the decrease in speed will indicate on the speedometer. The relationships between the variables in business situations are usually not as clear, and the indicators are frequently less clear. It is the goal of data mining to find the relationships between variables. This is a restatement of our theme that data is a strategic asset, and companies that use data well will have a strategic advantage. Data mining is another way to use data to a strategic advantage.

As an example, you could have a hypothesis that homeowners between the ages of 25 and 55 are the most likely purchasers of digital satellite TV systems. Testing this hypothesis and developing a model with an OLAP or EIS tool would be very difficult. The advantage of a data mining tool is its ability to develop a mathematical model. The mathematical model can verify a hypothesis and establish an indicator of the reliability of the model.

A data mining tool is important because of the amount of data in the data warehouse. The data warehouse combines information from many different sources to create a single instance of data with more columns or attributes than were in any single source system. Although this increases the accuracy of the data mining tools, it makes it difficult for the human observer to sort through the massive amounts of information and find the trends. The data warehouse is also too valuable not to take every advantage of the information. All of the factors encourage the use of data mining in conjunction with a data warehouse. The result of data mining can be improved revenue, decreased costs, or a combination of both.

There are numerous specific uses of data mining. In customer relations, data mining can be used to find factors that determine profitable customers or customers that are likely to move to a competitor. In the field of medicine, data mining can be used to determine which procedures are the most effective or which patients are the best candidates for surgery. In the field of marketing, data mining can be used to determine which customers are interested in certain products or methods of increasing the effectiveness of a sale. In the field of manufacturing, data modeling can be used to determine which process parameters most affect the quality of the product.

There are many methods of data mining. A statistician would argue that all forms of data mining are just different forms of regression. Statistical methods are certainly an important set of data mining tools, and the available packages for the leading vendors are usually very good. The data mining methods that will be discussed in this chapter are neural networks, genetic algorithms, clustering, and decision trees. Each of these methods has strengths and weaknesses with different types of problems. The strengths and weaknesses of the method are also discussed in the following sections.

All data mining methods use a mathematical model that will capture certain features but not others. The mathematical model can be thought of as a caricature of the real world. In much the same way that a caricature drawn by an artist at the circus or street corner captures some of the major characteristics of the subject but not others, the mathematical model will capture some but not all of the characteristics of the physical world. The mathematical model will predict some of the response and features of the physical world, but it is not the physical instance and will not act exactly like the physical instance.

Not one of the data mining methods will produce high-quality results if the data is not understood or the data is of poor quality. A data mining effort will not produce a result that is better than the data or the hypothesis. This is a simple restatement of the usual computer science acronyms GIGO and NINO. GIGO stands for garbage in, garbage out, and NINO stands for nothing in, nothing out. Humans may be very good at recognizing "noise" or bad data, but automated methods are not. Although it is frequently possible to fit a meaningless data mining model to random noise, to obtain meaningful results the data must be very clean. In addition, it is very difficult to generate a correct hypothesis if the data columns are not understood or poorly defined and used. The importance of quality data for data mining reminds us of all of the previous explanations of the importance of data quality in the data warehouse.

Poor-quality data causes the introduction of noise in the true data. *Noise* is anything that the data mining model does not explain. Noise can also be introduced by unnecessary rows or columns. The important point is that the data mining algorithm should be well behaved and degrade smoothly as the noise in the data increases.

There are several steps in the process of data mining. The first step is knowing the data. This is done through the use or creation of metadata. This should have been one of the first steps in the creation of the data warehouse and the data quality improvement program. The next step is any cleaning of the data that must be done. Data cleaning is also one of the steps of the data quality improvement program. The next step is data preparation. Some data mining experts will claim with good reason that data preparation is the most important part of data mining. Model development is the next step. Once the model has been developed, it is used to mine the data. Once the model parameters have been determined, they are interpreted in business context and extrapolated to new cases. Finally, the model must be tuned over time as events change parameters that affect the model. In summary, the steps are:

- Data definition and understanding
- Data quality improvement
- Data preparation
- Data mining model development
- Data mining
- Interpretation and extrapolation
- Model tuning

Because metadata development and data quality improvement have been explained in depth in previous chapters, we begin in the next section with the third step in the process, data preparation. The other steps in the data mining process depend on the data mining method. The specifics of model development, data mining, interpretation, and model tuning are developed in the sections on the specific data mining methods.

12.2 DATA PREPARATION

There are two steps in the data preparation process. The first step is data cleansing. Since we are assuming that a data warehouse has been constructed with cleansed data, the cleansing step will be skipped. The next step consists of data preprocessing. The data preprocessing steps include:

- Data selection
- Computation

- Coding
- Grouping

Each of these topics is discussed in the following paragraphs.

The compute time required when performing a data mining experiment depends on the number of columns or variables and the number of rows or cases. Performing a data mining effort on a large data warehouse would be an extremely time consuming operation. Every data mining experiment could take several days and yield no useful result. One way to speed the data mining operation is to perform the data mining experiments on a statistically significant subset of the data. In Chapter 5, the concept of placing a random number into the database design for selecting a statistically significant subset of the data was introduced. This random number could be used to sample the data for data mining.

In addition to the cost saving of performing at least the initial data mining on a sample of the data, there are other reasons to argue for sampling the data. The database is usually a sample of a large population. Large databases will have a huge amount of missing data. Very good data mining can still be done with a sample of the data. Classic examples of the fruitful use of sampled data are auditing financials and forecasting elections. In either case, a small fraction of the data is used to validate or predict the entire data.

Other reasons for sampling the data will include the ability to capture the data. As an example, corporations file quarterly tax statements, and the tax information will not be available more often. Another reason for sampling the data would be that the data is available faster than the model can be trained. In this case, the data mining model must be trained on a portion of the data.

There are many different types of sampling, including simple, clustered, stratified, and systematic. To use sampling successfully, the user must understand the data and the type of sampling in order to treat the data appropriately. There are situations when it is not a good idea to sample the database. In these cases, the loss of data is too great. A small database should not be sampled. If we are looking for small effects such as fraud in a large database, the database should not be sampled because the small effects can be lost in the sampling.

Computation is done to create derived data from the base fact data. As an example, debt divided by income produces a ratio that might be interesting to a loan risk analysis data mining operation. Net worth might be an interesting value that could be computed from assets and liabilities. Another interesting ratio might be the ratio of age to income. Individuals with rapid increases in pay for their age probably have different spending patterns than the population in general.

Grouping is the art of segmenting continuously valued data into groups. This discretization action introduces noise into the data. As a typical example, people are frequently grouped by age range and income range. The important part of selecting ranges is to select the appropriate number of ranges with the best size. Once the ranges have been selected, the members of the population are placed in the range that represents the member.

As an example of grouping, we will consider grouping by income. The income groups that we might select are:

- Under $10,000
- $10,000 to $19,999
- $20,000 to $29,999
- $30,000 to $39,999
- $40,000 to $49,999
- Over $50,000

If a member of the population earns $20,100, he or she is placed in the $20,000 to $29,999 range. The interesting practical question is does the person act more like the population in the $20,000 to $29,999 range, or does he or she "act" more like the $10,000 to $19,999 range? Some organizations that the author has worked with have developed fuzzy logic programs to place the data in the most appropriate range bins.

As mentioned earlier, the grouping operation adds noise to the data. This can be thought of in the following fashion. We can think of the grouping operation as an operation that places all of the data in the range at the same value in the range. This value might be the midpoint of the range. As an example, all of the rows of data with income within the $10,000 to $19,999 range are given a representative income of $15,000. In other words, the effect of placing all the incoming values within the $10,000 to $19,999 range in that range and representing the range by a single coded value is to add noise to the data that makes the income $15,000. If a person has an income of $19,000, we add noise of -$4,000 to the income to obtain the $15,000 value.

Coding is the art of representing the data in a way that best enables the data mining technique to discover the trends in the data. The correct coding depends on the data. As an example, consider the income ranges that were grouped in the previous example. One way to code the income ranges is to use a binary scheme with a variable for each range. This coding scheme is illustrated in Table 12-1.

Table 12-1 Representing the income ranges

Income Range	X1	X2	X3	X4	X5	X6
Under $10,000	1	0	0	0	0	0
$10,000 to $19,999	0	1	0	0	0	0
$20,000 to $29,999	0	0	1	0	0	0
$30,000 to $39,999	0	0	0	1	0	0
$40,000 to $49,999	0	0	0	0	1	0
Over $49,999	0	0	0	0	0	1

Table 12-2 Representation of values for the determination of odd or even

Value	Odd/Even	X1	X2	X3	X4	X5	X6
1	Odd	0	0	0	0	0	1
2	Even	0	0	0	0	1	0
3	Odd	0	0	0	0	1	1
4	Even	0	0	0	1	0	0
5	Odd	0	0	0	1	0	1
6	Even	0	0	0	1	1	0

In other situations, the coding scheme used in Table 12-1 would be a dismal failure. As an example, suppose that a neural net is being trained to distinguish odd numbers from even numbers. We clearly could not use a different input to represent every possible number that could be encountered. If we selected a binary representation of some range of number, it should be easy to train the neural net to identify an odd number by the one that appears in the least significant digit. Similarly, a zero in the least significant digit indicates an even number. This is illustrated in Table 12-2. This coding scheme makes it trivial to determine from the data if a value is even or odd and to distinguish this feature in the data.

All of the important considerations in data preparation are the reason why many organizations are willing to talk about what they are doing with data mining, but they are not willing to talk about how they prepare the data. It can be very difficult to repeat a result with incorrect data preparation. The data preparation is the essential step in the data mining process.

12.3 NEURAL NETWORKS

A data mining neural network or neural net is designed to replicate the neural net found in nature. A biological neural network consists of neurons with wires called dendrites that connect neurons to other neurons or other biological elements, such as muscles. Inside the neural network of the brain, neurons are usually connected to several other neurons. When a neuron receives enough input stimulation, it will "fire" and send a signal along the dendrite to whatever it is connected to. Through the arrangement of the connections and the weighting of the connections, the biological neural network can recognize sites, sounds, and names, and do all of the other amazing things that the human mind does every day.

The history of artificial neural networks is very interesting. The original work on an artificial neuron that is modeled after a biological neuron was done in a 1943 paper by McCulloch and Pitts. Their paper discussed something they called a threshold logic unit (TLU). In his 1959 paper, Rosenblatt introduced the concept

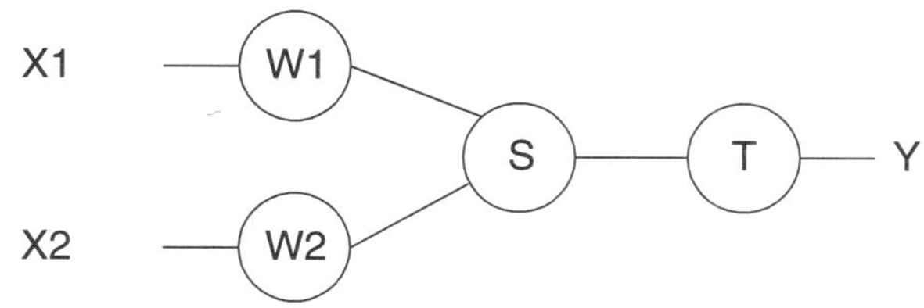

Figure 12-1 Single-layer neural net model.

of an artificial neuron called a Perceptron. Minsky and Papert published a paper in 1969 that showed that a Perceptron could not solve a simple exclusive OR problem, and neural networks lost the interest of the academic community. Neural networks gained the attention of the research community again when it was discovered that the combination of Perceptrons with TLUs arranged in multiple layers could solve complex problems.

A computer model of a neuron network is shown in Figure 12-1. The computer model of the neuron operates in the following manner. The input X1 is weighted or multiplied by W1. Similarly, the input X2 is multiplied or weighted by W2. The outputs of W1 and W2 are summed at S. The output of S is sent to the threshold function T. The output of T, called Y, will be 1 if the input is greater than zero. The output of T will be zero if the input is zero or less than zero.

As a simple example, suppose we are constructing a neural network that will perform the equivalent of the logical OR operation. In other words, if I1 or I2 or both are equal to 1, the output will be 1. If both weight W1 and weight W2 are set at some small positive number, then if either I1 or I2 are greater than zero, the output will be 1. This is illustrated in Table 12-3.

For the sake of ease of notation and drawing, all of the components of the neuron will be combined in a single symbol. An ellipse will be used to denote the neuron components. With the new symbology, Figure 12-1 appears much simpler, as shown in Figure 12-2.

The ability of the neural net to respond to complex inputs can be greatly increased by inserting a second layer of "neurons" between the input and the output.

Table 12-3 Response of a neural net with W1 = W2 = 0.1

X1	X2	I1 = X1W1	I2 = X2W2	S = I1+I2	T
0	0	0	0	0	0
0	1	0	0.1	0.1	1
1	0	0.1	0	0.1	1
1	1	0.1	0.1	0.2	1

Figure 12-2 Simpler neural net drawing with the weights, summation, and threshold hidden.

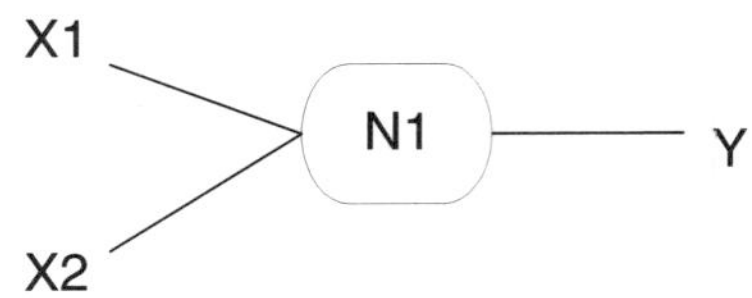

While the first layer of neurons always has a number of weights equal to the number of inputs, the second layer of neurons can have as many or as few neurons as needed to model the data. The selection of too many neurons in the second layer will cause the model to overfit the data. Too few neurons in the second layer will cause the model not to have enough degrees of freedom to model the data. Selection of the proper number of neurons in a neural network for an arbitrary problem can be problematic and is usually done by trial and error. A two-layer neural net is illustrated in Figure 12.3.

The following notation will be used for the neural nets. The output from node i will be denoted Yi. The weighted and summed input at node j is called Ij. The notation for the weight for the connection from node i to node j is Wji. Thus, Ij equals the sum from I = 1 to the number of nodes of WjiYi.

Another key to the success of a neural network model is the selection of the weights. This process is called *training* the network. For a single neuron, training starts with setting the weights to some value. The initial value for the weights could be random values or the weights that were obtained with a previous training session. Another standard technique is to set a limit to the range of the weights. A set of training data that consists of rows of inputs X1, X2, ..., Xn and correct output Y is then applied to the neuron. The weights of the neuron are adjusted after each row according to the formula

Wi(new) = Wi(old) + BXiY

where B is 1 if the neuron had the correct output and -1 if the output was incorrect. One complete pass through the training data is called an *epoch*. The neuron can be trained on the data with the data presented in a fixed order or in a random order.

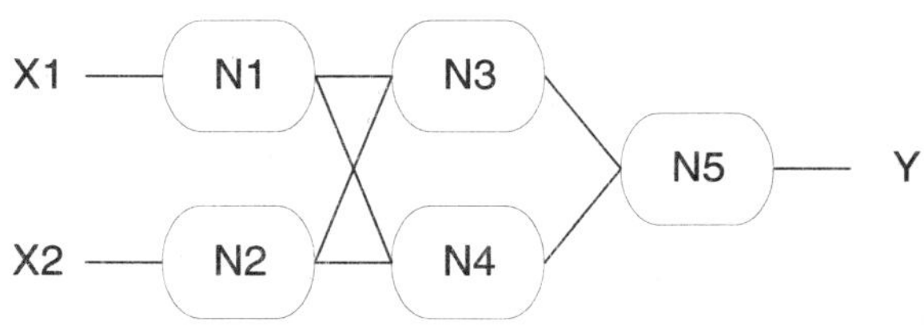

Figure 12-3 Two-layer neural network.

One key to the training procedure is the procedure that stops the training. A simple method to determine the stopping point is by limiting the number of training epochs, elapsed computer time, or CPU time used. Another method of indicating an appropriate stopping point in the training occurs when the RMS error reaches a predetermined value. Finally, the training may be stopped when the change in the RMS error is less than some predetermined value.

If the training does not lead to a convergence on a set of weights with an acceptable error rate, some things can be done to lead to better convergence. One approach is to start with different initial values of the weights. Another approach is to slow the learning rate by not changing the weights by the full amount indicated with each input. The input order can be changed to random rather than sequential. The threshold can be adjusted to some value other than zero. If it is a single neuron that is being trained, hidden nodes or layers can be added. If a multilayer neural net is being trained, the number of hidden layers or the number of nodes in the hidden layer can be changed. Finally, it is possible that the weights do not converge because the data does not support a relationship, and you have a case of nothing in, nothing out.

Once the neuron or neural network has been trained, it should be tested. It can be tested either by running a different sample from the same data set through the network or by running one epoch of the test data through the network with learning turned off. In either case, the root-mean-sequence (RMS) error should be close to the training set RMS error. If the neuron or neural network fails with the test set, hidden nodes or layers can be added or removed. It is also possible that the network is overfitted to the training data. If this is the case, noise can be added to the training data to relax the fit.

One of the interesting things about training neural nets is that the error does not decrease monotonically as the network is trained (Figure 12-4). In plain English, the error rate can decrease to an acceptable level but increase for periods of the training. This can be caused by adjustments in the neural net during training that move the net away from a local minimum toward a global minimum. During the transition away from the local minimum, the errors will increase briefly. After a brief increase, they generally will decrease.

As one might intuitively expect, training neural networks with hidden layers is usually much more complex than training a single neuron. When training a neural network, the input and correct output are known, but the weights in the hidden layer must be adjusted based on information that is one layer removed. One common procedure is called *back propagation.* The basic notion of back propagation is to use the error at the output and the algorithm for training a single neuron to train the net by propagating the error from the output back through the network to the input. The first step in the process is to compute the error in the output as is illustrated in Figure 12-5.

Once the error in the output has been computed, we can compute a new set of weights that will reduce the error in the output. This is illustrated in Figure 12-6. The new set of weights in the output layer should in general reduce the error in the

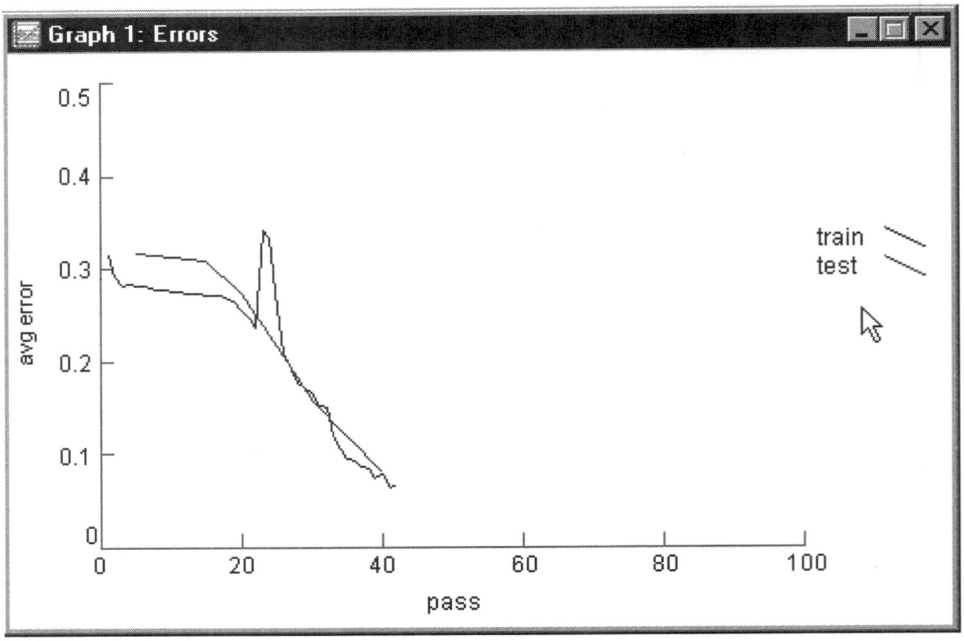

Figure 12-4 The errors can decrease in a nonmonotonic manner.

output, but the hidden layer remains to be adjusted. To adjust the hidden layer, we start by calculating the error in the output from the hidden layer. This is illustrated in Figure 12-7. Once error in the output from the hidden layer has been determined, the weights in the hidden layer are adjusted as illustrated in Figure 12-8. Finally, this procedure is repeated for the input layer.

It is not uncommon to find neural network models in use in businesses with tens to hundreds of input variables and three or four layers of neurons. These models are used for fraud detection, customer relations, and many other business applications. One of the difficulties of using a neural network is determining the business meaning of a neural network model. If a neural network has been developed with a particular arrangement of weights and neurons, it is difficult to relate the weights back to the business case. Stated in other terms, it is difficult to develop a conceptual meaning or business importance of having a model like the one shown in Figure 12-8 with W31 being much larger than W41. For simple networks, we might be able to interpret a meaning such as income as more important than time with an employer when evaluating credit risk because income is weighted heavier. With more complex models with many layers of neurons, it is usually much more difficult to determine the business meaning of the model.

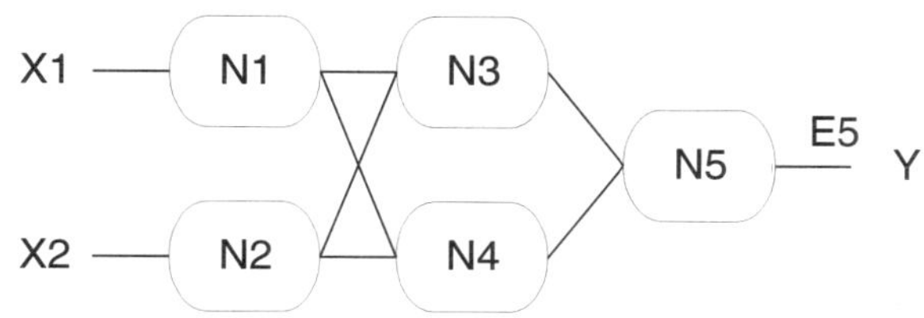

Figure 12-5 The first step in back propagation is computation of the error at the output.

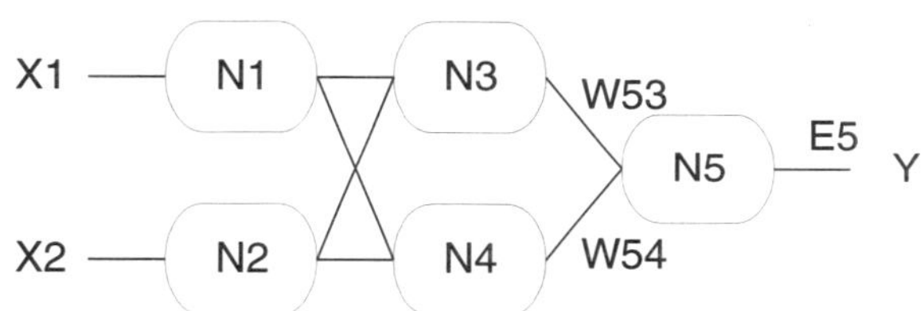

Figure 12-6 The weights in the output layer are computed.

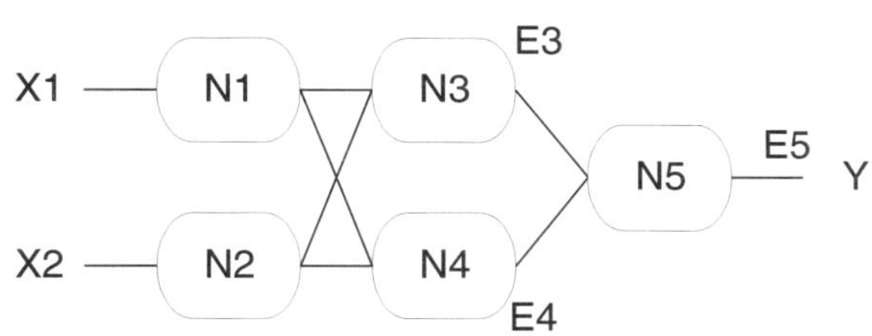

Figure 12-7 The error in the hidden layer is computed.

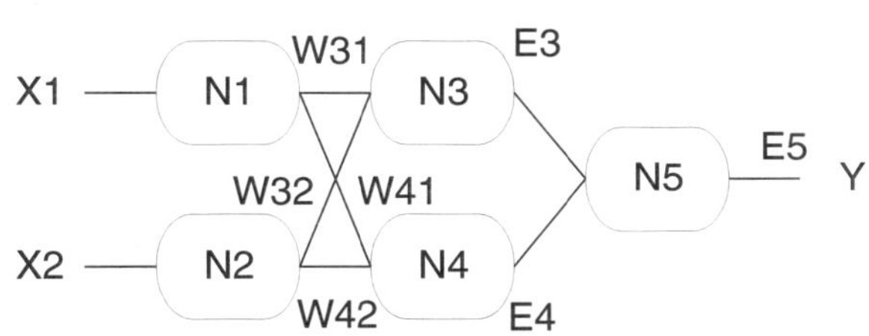

Figure 12-8 The weights in the hidden layer are adjusted.

12.4 THE GENETIC ALGORITHM

A genetic algorithm is a search technique that has the goal of finding the best solution or population of solutions. The search technique is a type of combinatorial optimization based on processes that mimic biological evolution. The genetic algorithm is based on the idea that evolution has selected the fittest of the species. Genetic algorithms are applied to data mining to obtain the "fittest" population or solution.

Of all of the data mining methods, the genetic algorithm is currently the least understood and a method that is experiencing a tremendous amount of basic research. In many respects, the father of the genetic algorithm is Charles Darwin, and the idea for the genetic algorithm dates to his 1859 book *On the Origin of Species*. In 1957, Box's paper entitled "Evolutionary Operation: A Method of Increasing Industrial Productivity" related evolution to industry. Probably the most influential fundamental paper is Bremermann's 1962 work entitled "Optimization Through Evolution and Recombination."

The genetic algorithms are excellent at determining groups of data that should be clustered together because they are the fittest members. The genetic algorithm is essentially a two-step algorithm. After the data has been preprocessed into an encoded representation that can be considered the "chromosome" of the individual, a fitness function is applied. The genetic representation or chromosome is usually a binary representation of the data. In the second step, an operator is applied that can change the chromosome.

In the first step, the fitness function identifies the individuals who are the "fittest." If the genetic algorithm is used to classify data, the fitness function identifies the individuals who are best classified into a group. The fitness function is any function that identifies some data elements as a better fit than others. As the data sets are processed, the fitness function is applied to each data point or "individual" to determine the "fitness" to match a given function. If the genetic algorithm is being used to cluster data, the fitness function measures the level of match of the data in the set. The fittest members of the population are selected to undergo an operation that represents mating in biological terms to create the next iteration or "generation."

In the second step, an operator is applied that creates the chromosomes of the next generation. Typical options for operations that select the chromosomes of the next generation are crossover and mutation. These are both events analogous to events that happen in the biological world. As an example, the features of a population are encoded in binary format, and there are two members of the population with features or "chromosomes" of (11010001) and (01011011). Usually, the fittest members of the population have operators applied to produce the child chromosomes. With the crossover operation, genes from one of the two "parent" chromosomes move to the other parent chromosome when creating a child's chromosome. Applying crossover to the two parent chromosomes might give the two child chromosomes (01010001) and (11011011). A random change or mutation in a child's chromosome could also occur via a mutation operation. As an example, the first child's chromosome could become (01010101). The operators produce the child chromosomes for the next generation.

The "mating" or application of the operators to the parent chromosomes continues in order of fitness until a new generation is created. An algorithm is used to replace the old population with the new population until some objective is met. Unless a stopping criterion has been met, the process then repeats with the selection of the fittest chromosomes for mating to create the next generation through crossover and mutation.

12.5 CLUSTERING AND CLASSIFICATION

Clustering is the technique of finding groups of related items. The groups are usually determined by grouping data points that minimize a criterion such as the distance between the points. The groups can be determined by the system in advance. This is called *supervised clustering.* If the groups are determined by the system, it is called *unsupervised clustering.* While most clustering algorithms use a distance such as a Euclidean or Manhattan distance, it is possible to use a neural net to determine the cluster.

Once the clusters have been defined using the existing data, new points can be classified as to the cluster to which they belong. As an example, all credit card customers could be classified into good and bad risk. When a new customer applies for a credit card, the classification algorithm can be used to determine if the customer is a good or bad credit risk.

One possible algorithm to classify data is the K nearest-neighbor algorithm. In this algorithm, a distance measure is used to determine the K points that are nearest to the new point. The new point n and the K nearest points indicated by X's are shown in Figure 12-9. The n-dimensional circle shown drawn around the

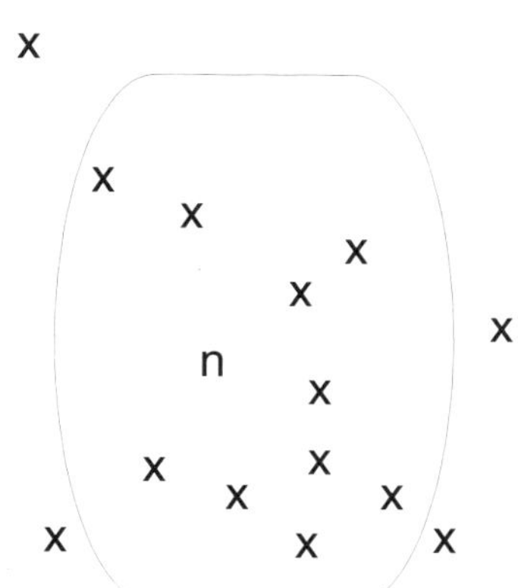

Figure 12-9 A new point n is classified according to its probability of being in the same class as one of its K nearest neighbors.

new point encompasses the K nearest points. The number of points in each of the different classes that are inside the circle are counted, say, k1, k2, …, kq for one class and k1, k2, …, kj for a second class. We then estimate the probability of the new point being in class m as km/K. The new point is classified as being in the class with the highest probability.

The advantages of the method is that it is easy to understand, it can always be used, and it works well. The disadvantages are all of the computations must be made every time, all of the data must be stored, and the result can depend on the distance measurement.

12.6 DECISION TREES

Experts in a field have developed a decision process for their domain of expertise. Through experience, people develop a method of solving problems that appears to be the most effective. The decision process can be drawn as something that resembles a tree. Treelike structures have been used in computer science to organize and describe data for many years. It is a natural extension to use trees to describe decision processes. The CART algorithm for decision tree development was described in the 1984 book *Classification and Regression Trees* by Breiman, Friedman, Olshen, and Stone. Many new algorithms have been developed since then. In 1986, Quinlan wrote a paper for *Machine Learning* entitled "Induction of Decision Trees" that described the ID3 algorithm.

An example of a decision tree for the determination of good and bad credit risk is shown in Figure 12-10. A good feature of a decision tree is that it is easily understood. This is in sharp contrast to a multilayer neural net that is difficult to understand. One interesting feature of a machine-generated decision tree is that the decision process is probably not the same as an expert in the field.

All decision tree algorithms have a similar method of building the tree, but they use different mathematical approaches to deciding the optimal use of the available variables to build the decision tree. The decision tree creation process usually starts with the user selecting the dependent and independent variables. The algorithm works by finding an unsplit node or grouping of data that can be split and splitting it. As an example, suppose that there are 20,000 data points representing the dependent variable of credit risk and the independent variables of income, time in job, and current debt. Of the entire training set, 14,000 represent a good credit risk, and 6000 represent a bad credit risk. The algorithm determines that the first split should be based on income, and the decision point is $40,000. This splits the data into two sets, as shown in Figure 12-11.

The algorithm continues the procedure by finding the two unsplit nodes and finding a variable that splits the nodes. The left node is split based on years in an employment situation. The right node is split based on the debt load of the customer. When the right node is split, it produces two "pure" nodes. This means that

Figure 12-10 Example of a decision tree.

these nodes cannot be split further. It is possible to split the second of the two "leaf" or end nodes on the left. The resulting tree is shown in Figure 12-12.

Once the tree has been created, new data can be applied to the tree and classified according to the results. The data is classified according to the node at which the data arrives. For nodes that are not pure, the data is assigned to the largest or modal class in the leaf. As an example, data that arrives at the leaf node with 5000 good credit risks and 1000 bad credit risks will be assigned a good credit risk classification. This decision tree model also illustrates the need to tune the model over time. As general population income levels increase over time, the $40,000 decision point will probably change. In addition, social factors that change over time will change the ability of people to maintain debt.

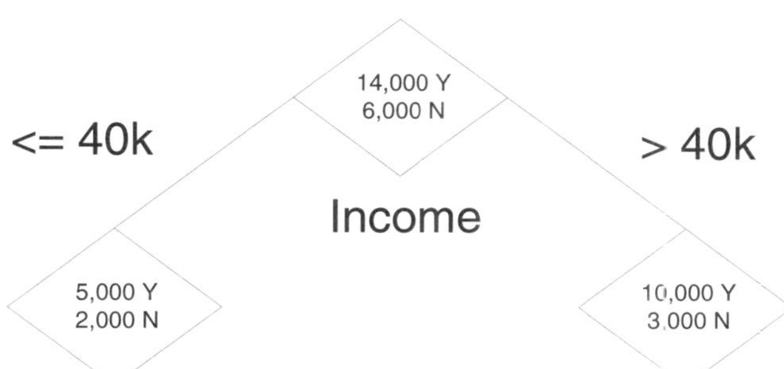

Figure 12-11 First split based on income.

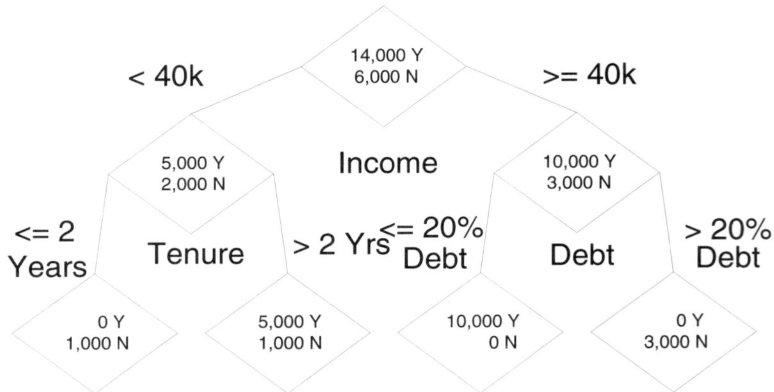

Figure 12-12 Example of a decision tree.

12.7 STATISTICS

Statistics have long been used to investigate the world around us. Fermat and Pascal started the study of statistics through a series of letters that were written discussing possible ways of studying gambling problems mathematically. Regression analysis was developed by Francis Galton as a method of quantifying genetics. Galton developed the concept of regression toward a mean during his study of the heights of children.

It was mentioned earlier that many mathematicians would argue that all data mining methods are actually statistical methods that are well disguised. Statistical methods include methods such as statistical inference that are used to create models of sets of data. This could explain why some of the leading data mining software vendors are the software vendors that were already well established in the area of statistical analysis.

12.7.1 Regression Modeling

An equation that estimates a dependent variable using constants and a number of independent variables is called a *regression equation*. As an example of a regression equation, consider the equation

$$Y = AX1 + BX2 + CX3$$

where Y is the dependent variable and X1 through X3 are independent variables. While the example equation is a linear equation, many other techniques have been applied to generate regression equations. Although linear regression models are not typically used for many of the things for which data mining is used, regression can be combined with conditional probability to perform prediction. A linear regression model that is used to predict outcomes is called a *linear probability model* (LPM). Situations that are not being solved with linear models can be approached with nonlinear regression or multiple nonlinear regression models. Many other statistical methods can be used, including coefficients of multiple or partial correlation.

12.7.2 Discriminant Analysis

The process of finding a set of weights W1 to Wk to the linear classification function

LCF = W1V1 + W2V2 + … + WkVk

that maximally separates the group of variables V1 through Vk is called *discriminant analysis.* The weights are called *discriminant coefficients.* A threshold is determined that classifies a variable into a group. If the LCF evaluated at the variable is greater than or equal to the threshold, it belongs to one group. If the LCF is less than the threshold, it belongs to a different group. Discriminant analysis can be used to cluster data or determine the grouping of data. Many commercially available statistical software products have the ability to perform discriminant analysis. The difficulty with discriminant analysis is that the model does not provide great insight into the nature of the groups.

12.8. SOFTWARE PRODUCTS

A simple search using the World Wide Web will produce a long list of vendors supplying data mining products. Some of the leaders in the field include:

- Angoss
- Business Objects
- Cognos Software
- DataMind
- IBM
- NeoVista
- Red Brick
- SAS Institute
- SPSS

As a standard example, we will consider the NeoVista Decision Series. The Decision Series consists of four data mining engines that sit on top of the DecisionAccess data transformation engine. The architecture is characterized in Figure 12-13. The four data mining engines are:

- DecisionNet
- DecisionAR
- DecisionCL
- DecisionGA

DecisionNet uses an extended back propagation neural network algorithm. DecisionNet is a possible selection as a neural network product for use at predicting a future outcome based on past experience. Like many of the neural network products on the market, DecisionNet contains proprietary technology not contained in the generic algorithm as discussed in textbooks. The DecisionNet technology helps the network to train faster and avoid settling into a local minimum.

DecisionAR is a rules-based association algorithm that determines the likelihood of events occurring together at either the same instant in time or sequentially. The patterns are expressed as rules with a confidence level. As an example, a typical dependency rule might be that event A occurred 90 percent of the time that event B occurred; then event C occurred 37 percent of the time within five days.

DecisionCL is a distance-based clustering algorithm. The groups can be fixed in advance through supervised clustering or determined by DecisionCL. DecisionCL will use not only simple distance measures such as Euclidean or Manhattan distance, but the more complex functions such as DecisionNet are used to decide if two items belong to the same group.

DecisionGA is a user-extensible genetic algorithm that finds the best mating selections based on a variety of fitness measures. DecisionGA can be used to construct representative populations and groups based on a number of specific cases. The cases will converge on the best solution based on the fitness measure.

The interesting thing to the user about the Decision Series and other typical commercial software is the ability to use different data mining techniques on the same data set. This enables the knowledge worker relatively easily to explore different

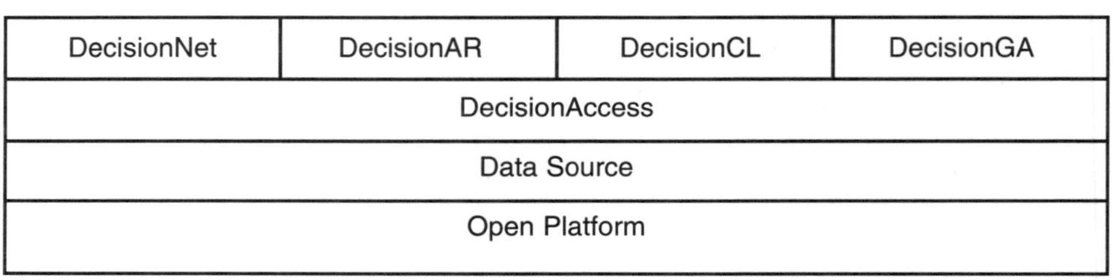

Figure 12-13 NeoVista Decision Series architecture.

solutions to a data mining problem. The DecisionAccess software is the piece of the architecture that enables this. Once the data access has been determined, different mining methods are easily performed.

12.9 SOFTWARE EXAMPLE

As an example of the look, feel, and functionality of data mining software, we will use Simulnet developed by Edward Rzempoluck at Simon Fraser University in Canada. Once Simulnet has been started, the user selects the type of data mining that is desired. This is illustrated in Figure 12-14. The software is also capable of several other operations in which data mining users will be interested. As an example, the software will graph data, perform data transformations, and perform several data analysis functions, including discrete Fourier transforms.

Once a type of data mining technique has been selected, the user must input the location of the data file and other necessary parameters for the data mining method (Figure 12-15). Once the parameters have been entered, the user clicks on the train button, and the software performs the data mining operation requested.

Once the training has finished, the software produces both data files and graphs showing the results of the operation. A representative graph of the reduction in errors as a function of training is shown in Figure 12-16. The resulting neural network and the weights connecting the neurons are shown in Figure 12-17. Once the neural network has been developed, the network can be saved for use later. Other data sets can be applied to the network, and the response measured.

If the knowledge worker decides that the results of the neural network are not what were desired, the data can be preprocessed in a different manner for a different

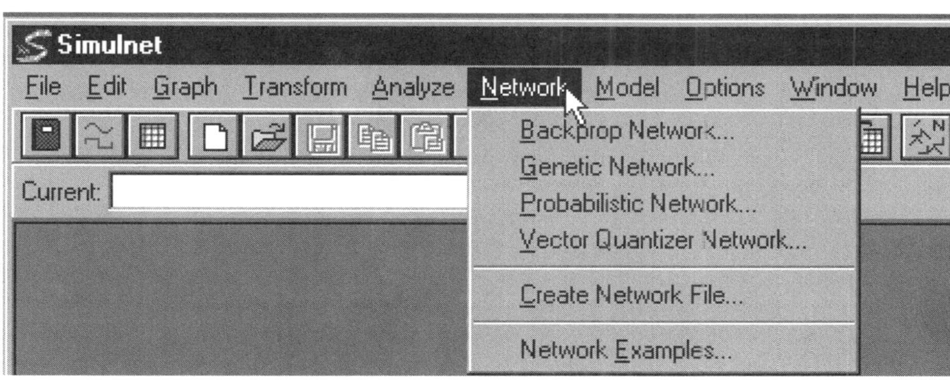

Figure 12-14 The user selects the type of data mining to be performed on the data.

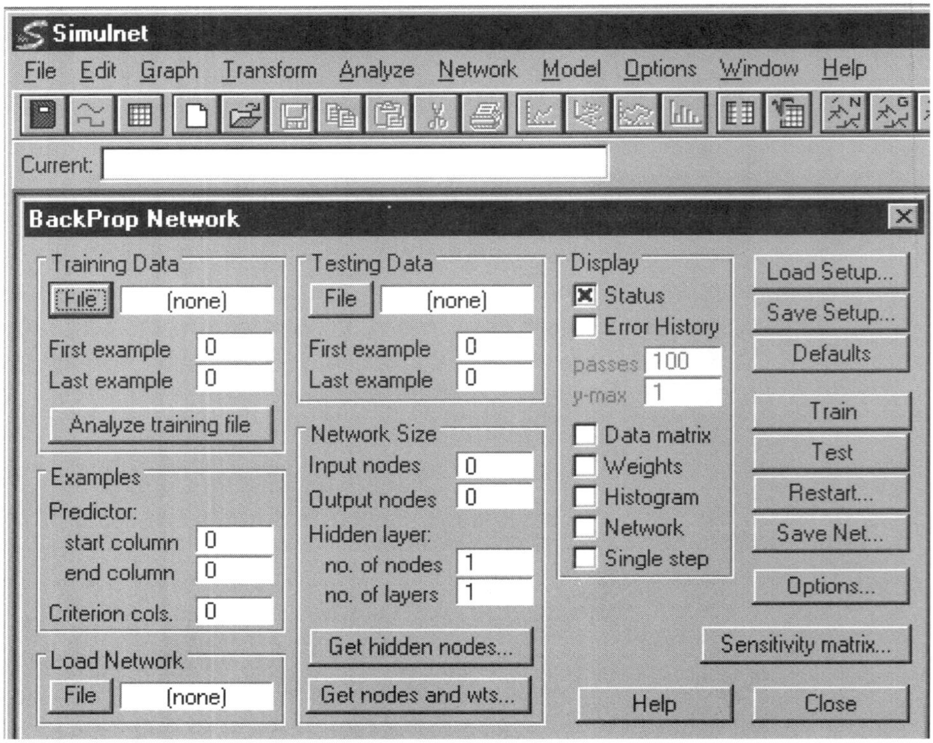

Figure 12-15 The user provides the software with the input file and parameters necessary to develop the data mining mode.

data mining algorithm. The different data mining algorithm can then be applied to the data. All of these can occur from the data mining applications interface.

The most important function of the data mining operation is the operator. The knowledge worker who is using the data mining tool must have sufficient understanding of the business to know where to look for the data nuggets. As an example, the sale of electric fans is usually brisk for home and hardware stores in early summer. An astute user of a data mining system would know to look for trends in electric fan sales in early summer. If the knowledge worker was mining the data for electric fan sales and profits, he or she might find a correlation between the number of fans ordered and in stock and the number of fans sold. There is frequently an anomaly that can be found for some stores that have fans but have not sold any. It takes an experienced knowledge worker to look for these anomalies, and it takes even more experience to figure out what happened. The usual cause for a situation like this is that the fans are in stock but not on the shelf. Items that are not on the shelf do not sell. It takes a knowledge worker with an understanding of retail operations to look for such trends.

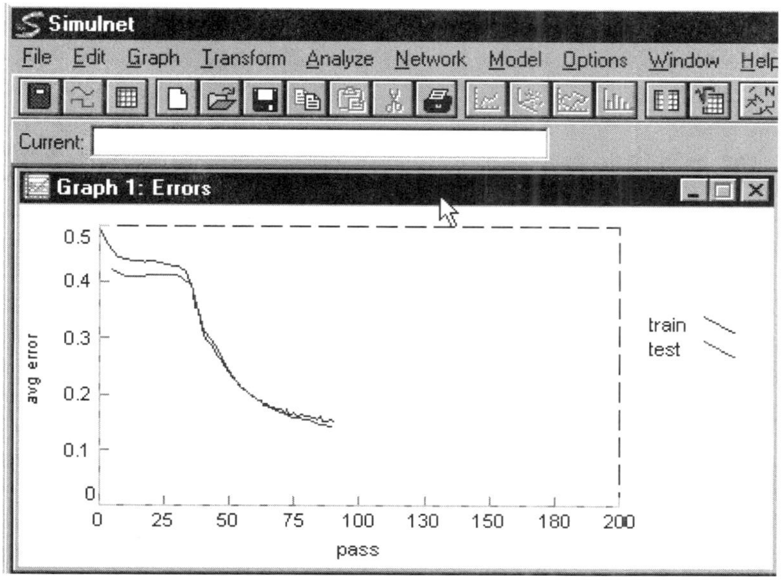

Figure 12-16 Reduction in errors as a function of training.

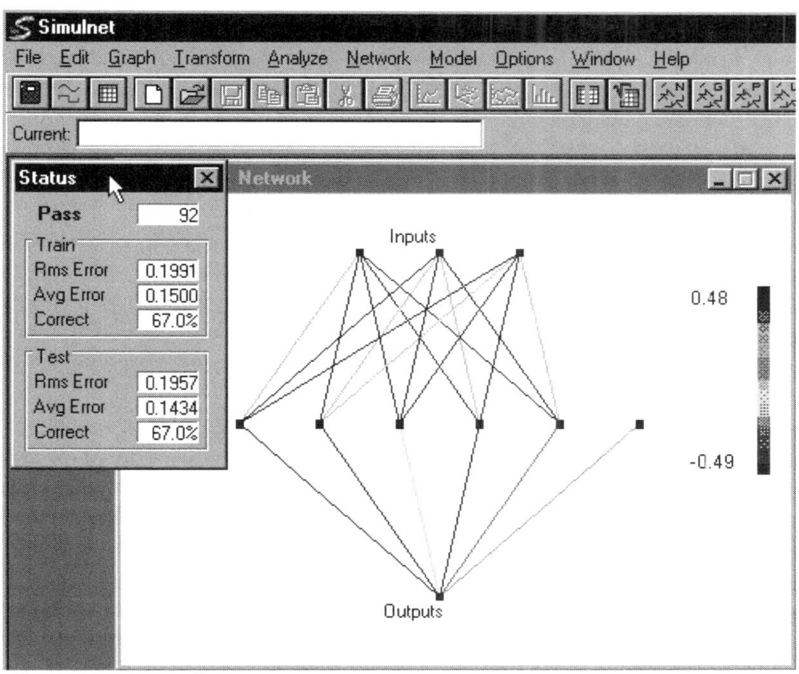

Figure 12-17 Derived neural network.

QUESTIONS

12.1 Explain the purpose of and activities in the data selection step of data preparation.

12.2 Explain the purpose of and activities in the computation step of data preparation.

12.3 Explain the purpose of and activities in the coding step of data preparation.

12.4 Explain the purpose of and activities in the grouping step of data preparation.

12.5 What is a fitness function?

12.6 What is crossover?

12.7 Explain mutation in terms of the genetic algorithm.

12.8 What is a pure node?

12.9 What is regression modeling?

12.10 What is discriminant analysis?

12.11 What is the most important piece in a data mining operation? Why?

12.12 Of the 20 neighbors nearest a new point, 8 belong to class n, 11 to class m, and 1 to class k. What is the likelihood of the point belonging to each class?

PROJECTS

12.13 Write the software necessary to implement the genetic algorithm. This can be a very limited case. The purpose of your software and this project will be to experiment with different fitness, mating, and population selection algorithms.

For each of the following project scenarios, you will need to select the data mining method or tools that are needed for the scenario. To do that, explain the objectives that the user who will use the tools will have and how the data mining method meets that objective. This can be done by making an assumption as to the way the organization functions, by using information given to you by the instructor, or by using your personal experience.

12.14 Determine the data mining tool types needed for a call behavior analysis data warehouse. Explain your assumptions in as much detail as possible.

12.15 Determine the data mining tool types needed for a network usage data warehouse. Explain your assumptions in as much detail as possible

12.16 Determine the data mining tool types needed for an automobile buying trend data warehouse. Explain your assumptions in as much detail as possible. How would your assumptions be different for a car dealership with 10,000 cars sold each year?

12.17 Determine the data mining tool types needed for an electronics store sales analysis data warehouse. Explain your assumptions in as much detail as possible.

12.18 Determine the data mining tool types needed for a vendor compliance data warehouse. Explain your assumptions in as much detail as possible.

12.19 Determine the data mining tool types needed for a risk analysis data warehouse. Explain your assumptions in as much detail as possible.

12.20 Determine the data mining tool types needed for a frequent flier data warehouse. Explain your assumptions in as much detail as possible. Explain how this architecture will be deployed.

12.21 Determine the data mining tool types needed for an airline flight segment data warehouse. Explain your assumptions in as much detail as possible.

12.22 Determine the data mining tool types needed for an educational institution data warehouse. Explain your assumptions in as much detail as possible.

12.23 Determine the data mining tool types needed for the health care diagnosis data warehouse. Explain your assumptions in as much detail as possible.

12.24 Determine the data mining tool types needed for a hotel frequent-guest data warehouse. Explain your assumptions in as much detail as possible.

12.25 Determine the data mining tool types needed for a hotel spending data warehouse. Explain your assumptions in as much detail as possible.

GLOSSARY

ANSI (American National Standards Institute) Creates standards levels in all walks of life, including relational database management systems (RDBMSs).

CASE (computer aided software engineering) Software that documents and maintains integrity and consistency with respect to a system's development cycle. Typically supports development methodologies based on the information engineering approach to the development of systems. May also generate database schemas and/or program code.

Data dictionary A repository of data about data (i.e., structure, definition, and meaning).

Data warehouse An inventory of subject-oriented, integrated, and time-variant informational data.

Database management Layer of software that controls, manages, and protects the underlying data while allowing multiple accessors.

4GL (fourth generation language) Programming language one generation removed from COBOL, FORTRAN, Pascal, etc.

GUI (graphical user interface) End-user presentation services.

Information engineering A methodology conceived by, most notably, James Martin for a structured top-down approach in developing systems.

Metadata Data about data; typically held within a data dictionary/repository.

Motif interface Graphical user interface endorsed by the Open Software Foundation. It has become the standard user interface in the UNIX world.

Object oriented An alternative methodological approach, gaining popularity and credibility, for analyzing and designing systems, based on the concept of objects (i.e., an object of interest encapsulated in methods).

OLQP (on-line query processing) Data extraction in decision support systems.

OLTP (on-line transaction processing) Transaction-based operational applications used in commercial environments.

OS/2 IBM's PC operating system.

Relational database Structured design of data, based on Ted Codd's 12 rules for a relational model.

Repository *See* Data dictionary.

SNA (systems network architecture) IBM's proprietary networking protocol announced in 1974.

SQL (structured query language) Originally conceived by IBM and adopted by ANSI as a standard database language for relational databases; current standard level is ANSI SQL/2 (intermediate level).

SQL optimisor Low-level RDBMS software layer that compiles an SQL statement into what it considers to be most efficient manner of execution.

Subject-oriented A stable image of business processes capturing the basic nature of the business environment.

TCP/IP (transmission control protocol/internetworking protocol) Networking protocol using the ISO (International Standards Organization) seven-layer model from the application layer through to the physical hardware connection.

Time-variant The warehouse is time-variant because of the distinction between operational data and informational data. Each data point is associated with a point in time, and data points can be compared along that axis.

Bibliography

Barquin, Ramon. *Data Warehousing Step by Step*. Prentice-Hall, 1998.

Barquin, Ramon and Herb Edelstein, eds. *Building, Using, and Managing the Warehouse.* Prentice-Hall, 1997.

Barquin, Ramon and Herb Edelstein, eds. *Planning and Designing the Data Warehouse*. Prentice-Hall, 1996.

Brackett, Michael H. *The Data Warehouse Challenge*. John Wiley & Sons, 1996.

Brodie, Michael L. and Michael Stonebreaker. *Migrating Legacy Systems: Gateways, Interfaces, and the Incremental Approach*. Morgan Kaufmann, 1995.

Cabena, Perter. *Discovering Data Mining: From Concept to Implementation*. Prentice-Hall, 1997

Corey, Michael and Michael Abbey. *Oracle Data Warehousing*. McGraw-Hill, 1996.

Corey, Michael, Michael Abbey, Ian Abramson, and Ben Taub. *Oracle8 Data Warehousing*. McGraw-Hill, 1998.

Devlin, Barry. *Data Warehouse: From Architecture to Implementation*. Addison-Wesley, 1997.

Dodge, Gary and Tim Gorman. *Oracle8 Data Warehousing*. John Wiley & Sons, 1998.

Gill, Harjinder and Prakash Rao. *The Official Client/Server Computing Guide to Data Warehousing*. Que, 1996.

Groth, Robert. *Data Mining: A Hands On Approach for Business Professionals.* Prentice-Hall, 1997.

Gupta, Vivek R. *Data Warehousing with MS SQL Server Unleashed.* SAMS, 1997.

Inmon, W.H. *Building the Data Warehouse, second edition.* QED Publishing Group, 1996.

Inmon, W.H. and Richard D. Hackathorn. *Using the Data Warehouse.* John Wiley & Sons, Inc., 1994.

Inmon, W.H., Claudia Imhoff, and Greg Battas. *Building the Operational Data Store.* John Wiley & Sons, 1996.

Inmon, W.H., J.D. Welch, and Katherine Glassey. *Discusses Maintaining Data Warehouses.* John Wiley & Sons, 1997.

Inmon, W.H., John Zachman, and Jonathon Geiger. *Data Stores, Data Warehousing, and the Zachman Framework.* McGraw-Hill, 1997.

Kelly, Sean. *Data Warehousing: The Route to Mass Customization.* John Wiley & Sons, 1994.

Kimball, Ralph. *The Data Warehouse Toolkit.* John Wiley & Sons, 1996.

Kimball, Ralph, Laura Reeves, Margy Ross, and Warren Thornwaite. *The Data Warehouse Lifecycle Toolkit: Tools and Techniques for Designing, Developing, and Deploying Data Marts and Data Warehouses.* John Wiley & Sons, 1998.

Mattison, Rob. *Data Warehousing: Strategies, Tools and Techniques.* McGraw-Hill, 1996.

Meyer, Don and Casey Cannon. *Building a Better Data Warehouse.* Prentice-Hall, 1998.

Poe, Vidette. *Building a Data Warehouse for Decision Support.* Prentice-Hall. 1997.

Sanchez, Angela. *Data Warehousing with Informix: Best Practices.* Prentice-Hall, 1998.

Silverston, Len, William H. Inmon, and Kent Graziano. *The Data Model Resource Book: A Library of Logical Data Models and Data Warehouse Designs.* John Wiley & Sons, 1997.

Simon, Alan R. *90 Days to the Data Mart.* John Wiley & Sons, 1998.

Simon, Alan R. *Data Warehousing for Dummies.* IDG Books, 1997.

Singh, Harry S. *Data Warehousing: Concepts, Technology, and Applications.* Prentice Hall, 1997.

Watson, Hugh and Paul Gray. *Decision Support in the Data Warehouse.* Prentice-Hall, 1997.

Welbrock, Peter R. *Strategic Data Warehousing Principles Using SAS Software.* SAS Institute, 1998.

Yazdani, Sima and Shirley Wong. *Data Warehousing with Oracle: An Administrator's Handbook.* Prentice-Hall, 1997.

REFERENCES

Blommers Blommers, John. 1996. *Practical Planning for Network Growth.* New York: Prentice-Hall.

Boar Boar, Bernard. 1993. *The Art of Strategic Planning for Information Technology.* New York: John Wiley and Sons.

Carey Carey, Jean. 1991. *Quality Management and Performance Measurement in Information Services.* Ardmore, PA: Carey Project Organization, p. 25.

Devlin Devlin, Barry. 1996. *Data Warehouse: From Architecture to Implementation.* New York: Addison-Wesley.

Grove Grove, Andy. 1996. *Only the Paranoid Survive: How to Exploit the Crisis Points That Challenge Every Company and Career.* New York: Currency/Doubleday.

Hammer Hammer, Michael, and James Champy. 1993. *Reengineering the Corporation.* New York: HarperCollins.

Hosier Hosier, Jeffrey. 1992. "Rapid Application Development." *User Survey-Development Methods and the Application Backlog.* England: Xephon, p. 91.

Inmon Inmon, William. 1992. *Building the Data Warehouse.* New York: Wiley.

Inmon 97 Inmon, William, John Zachman, and Jonathan Geiger. 1997. *Data Stores, Data Warehousing, and the Zachman Framework.* New York: McGraw-Hill.

Kimball Kimball, Ralph. 1996. "The Data Warehouse Toolkit." *Practical Techniques for Building Dimensional Data Warehouses.* New York: Wiley.

Moore Moore, Geoffrey. 1995. *Crossing the Chasm: Marketing and Selling High-Tech Products to Mainstream Customers.* San Francisco, CA: Harper Business.

Porter 83 Porter, Michael. 1983. *Cases in Competitive Strategy.* Cambridge, MA: Free Press.

Porter 98a Porter, Michael. 1998. *Competitive Advantage: Creating and Sustaining Superior Performance.* Cambridge, MA: Free Press.

Porter 98b Porter, Michael. 1998. *Competitive Strategy: Techniques for Analyzing Industries and Competitors.* Cambridge, MA: Free Press.

Peppers Peppers, Don and Martha Rogers. 1997. *Enterprise One to One: Tools for Competing in the Interactive Age.* New York: Currency/Doubleday.

Tzu Tzu, Sun and James Clavell, eds. 1989. *The Art of War.* New York: Delacorte Press.

Wetherbe Wetherbe, James C. 1991. "Executive Information Requirements: Getting It Right." *CASE Strategies, vol. 1, no. 7*

Zachman Zachman, John. 1987. "A Framework for Information Systems Architectures." *IBM Systems Journal, vol. 26, no. 3.*

INDEX